The Early History of Heaven

THE EARLY HISTORY

OF HEAVEN

J. Edward Wright

New York   Oxford

Oxford University Press

2000

Oxford University Press

Oxford   New York

Athens   Auckland   Bangkok   Bogotá   Buenos Aires   Calcutta
Cape Town   Chennai   Dar as Salaam   Delhi   Florence   Hong Kong   Istanbul
Karachi   Kuala Lumpur   Madrid   Melbourne   Mexico City   Mumbai
Nairobi   Paris   São Paulo   Singapore   Taipei   Tokyo   Toronto   Warsaw

and associated companies in
Berlin   Ibadan

Published by Oxford University Press, Inc.
198 Madison Avenue, New York, New York 10016

Oxford is a registered trademark of Oxford University Press

Library of Congress Cataloging-in-Publication Data
Wright, J. Edward.
The early history of heaven / J. Edward Wright.
p. cm.
Includes bibliographical references and indexes.
ISBN 0-19-513009-X
1. Heaven—Judaism—History of doctrines.   2. Heaven—
Christianity—History of doctrines—Early church, ca. 30–600.
3. Heaven—Comparative studies.   4. Literature, Ancient—History and
criticism.   5. Apocalyptic literature—History and criticism.
I. Title.
BM645.H43W75   1999
291.2'3—dc21   98-49461

1   3   5   7   9   8   6   4   2

Printed in the United States of America
on acid-free paper

for
Keeley and Angela

PREFACE

Heaven is large and affords space for all modes of love and fortitude.

Ralph Waldo Emerson, *Essays* (1841)

When we think of heaven, we generally conjure up positive, blissful images. Heaven, after all, is where God is and where good people go after death to receive their reward for having lived noble lives. But how and why did Western cultures come to imagine the heavenly realm in such terms? Why is heaven generally thought to be "up there" far beyond the visible sky? We humans have always been fascinated by the sky, and it has been a part of every human neighborhood since the dawn of history. Nonetheless, the sky has also been the most mysterious part of our world, and even today we continue to be awed by its vastness and complexity. The sky has also inspired the religious imagination of all human civilizations. People from almost every generation and location have imagined that the gods reside somewhere "up there" in the great beyond. Moreover, the gods have been associated with the celestial bodies because they seem to influence life on earth: the sun provides heat, the moon regulates the tides, the north star guides travelers, and the predictable movements of various celestial bodies enable us to track the passing of time. Diviners and astrologers of all sorts believe that the celestial bodies also provide portents of things to come, and since these portents come from the sky where gods are thought to dwell, they are taken as indicators of the gods' existence and interest in human affairs. It was essential, therefore, to know something about the realm "up there."

The structure of the universe has been an object of human study since the dawn of human history.[1] The great popularity of Carl Sagan's book and television series *Cosmos* and Steven Hawking's book *A Brief History of Time* attest to our continuing fascination with the secrets of the cosmos. We now know that our planet is just a small planet orbiting a medium-sized star in a remote corner of our rather common spiral galaxy. There are vast galaxies teeming with activity that are just now becoming visible through our increasingly more powerful telescopes. As we approach the beginning of a new millennium, there will no doubt be a resurgence of interest in speculations about these other realms among scientists and charlatans. But when many people look to skies, they see more than stars, planets, and galaxies: they see the Divine lurking just behind the mystical veil of the cosmos. Moreover, many religions have imagined that the post mortem abode of the righteous is in this heavenly realm with God. How, why, when, and where did such a belief begin? That humans, whose lives are best summed up in the biblically inspired phrase "from dust to dust," should even presume to have a place with the gods seems to be the height of egotism. Yet this is a central belief in many Western religions. How did this come to be and how did human images of the heavenly realm evolve? This volume traces the origin and early history of human speculations about "heaven," the realm of the divine, the realm "up there."

I am assuredly not the first to be interested in this issue. At the beginning of this century Wilhelm Bousset suggested that the Jews learned about the heavenly realms from Babylonian or Persian astronomical speculations.[2] Hans Bietenhard's research dealt rather insightfully with many of the inhabitants and objects found in the heavenly realm, but he did not discuss the vast variety apparent in the several cosmographical models popular during the Greco-Roman period.[3] Colleen McDannell and Bernhard Lang have provided an outstanding survey of two-thousand years of Christian beliefs about heaven, yet due to the survey nature of their work, they pass over the ancient period in just a few pages.[4] Martha Himmelfarb examined the many early Jewish and Christian apocalypses and traced the development of the theme of ascent to heaven in early Judaism and Christianity.[5] Jeffrey Burton Russell has provided a history of later Christian beliefs about heaven with a more theological focus.[6] Most recently, Marc Lachièze-Rey and Jean-Pierre Luminet, two astrophysicists, have written a lavishly illustrated volume in conjunction with an exhibit at the Bibliothèque nationale in Paris that traces the evolution of how the heavenly realm has been represented in western art, philosophy, and religion and how those representations accord with the evolution of scientific images of the sky.[7] My focus differs from all these fine works in that I will try to trace the backgrounds, origin, and development of early Jewish and Christian speculations on what the heavenly realm actually looks like and whether or not humans can go there. It will become apparent that early Jewish and Christian speculation on the heavenly realms built on biblical, ancient Near Eastern, and Greco-Roman models and was characterized by great variety. I will show that within the broad contours of early Jewish and Christian cosmic speculation, the details of any one schema reflect only the particular author's knowledge or beliefs. There was no monolithic "ouranography" (image of the heavenly realm) in either early Judaism or Christianity to which all subscribed, a diversity matched in other cultures as well.[8]

To understand how early Jews and Christians imagined the heavenly realm, one must begin with an appreciation of the images of the heavenly realm found in the religiously authoritative texts that formed the religious, intellectual, and cultural foundation of these two religious communities—the Hebrew Bible (Old Testament). But even these biblical traditions stem from a broader cultural context that also needs to be understood. I will begin this study, therefore, with an examination of the beliefs of ancient Israel's neighbors about the heavenly realm. The cultures of Egypt, Mesopotamia, and Greece antedate ancient Israel by nearly two millennia in some cases. I will analyze many ancient textual and artifactual sources that provide insight into how these cultures imagined the heavenly realm. This presentation of major themes or beliefs about heaven among ancient Israel's neighbors will provide a sketch of the intellectual context in which the biblical traditions emerged and evolved.

Early Judaism inherited more from its ancient ancestors than what is found in the pages of the Hebrew Bible alone. Archaeologists have made many important inscriptional, artifactual, and textual discoveries that now allow us to draw a much more complete picture of how ancient Israelites lived and what they believed. As any good editor would do, the final editors of the Hebrew Bible did not include material that conflicted with their literary or theological goals. By combining biblical texts and archaeological artifacts, I hope to give a voice to the people whose beliefs about the gods and their realm were merely bypassed or purposefully suppressed by the biblical editors, beliefs that certainly were very common in the popular religious imaginations of many ancient Israelites.

Although the ancient biblical traditions were influential in the development of early Jewish cosmic speculations, these Jews lived in the cosmopolitan Greco-Roman world and had access to at least popular notions of Greco-Roman astronomy. I will trace how these Greco-Roman models may have influenced early Jewish portrayals of the cosmos. These Jews inherited biblical traditions but articulated them within a Greco-Roman context, and as a result they transformed these ancient traditions under the influence of Greco-Roman culture. While some Jews appear to have adopted Greek models with little or no alteration, others continued to promote a model of the heavenly realms based on their ancient religious traditions. Why they continued to maintain an "obsolete" view of the universe will say a great deal about how they adapted to changes in the culture around them.

While it has been fashionable to state that Jewish religious ideas developed significantly during the so-called Babylonian Exile (ca. 586–539 BCE), it is more accurate to say that Judaism changed most in the wake of Alexander the Great's conquests (333–323 BCE) as Hellenistic culture increasingly began to transform Israelite and other ancient Near Eastern cultures. This is no more clearly evident than in their cosmic speculations. The ancient Near Eastern three-tiered universe (heaven–earth–netherworld) was largely displaced by models of the cosmos in which the earth is surround by several heavenly spheres. Some Jews transformed the biblical depictions of the universe to fit these newer models; consequently, they shaped how people would depict the universe for well over a millennium. This is an important aspect of Western cultural history, and it is hoped that this volume will provide further insight into the origins and early development of Western views of the heavenly realms.

The ancient Israelites inherited views of the universe from their Canaanite ancestors and then transformed these views to accord with their particular theologies. The tradents of the Hebrew Bible took theses traditions and further refined them to fit a strictly monotheistic theology. The Jews of the Greco-Roman period faced a dilemma: the model of the heavenly realm they inherited from the biblical materials was becoming obsolete as they learned the newer Greek models of the cosmos. Jewish texts and artifacts of the Greco-Roman period indicate that while some were content with the traditional view of the heavens inherited from the Bible, others had abandoned the biblical traditions in favor of the Greek models of the universe. Even the later rabbis, traditionalists to be sure, adopted a model of the universe that was more Hellenistic than biblical. The earliest Christians also depicted the universe in Hellenistic fashion. When Christianity became the religion of the empire, the state became the enforcer of theological and scientific orthodoxy. Variety in the depictions of the universe began to disappear. There remained, both in the religious as well as in the 'scientific' community, those voices proposing alternate models. This study traces how the many early Jewish and Christian depictions of heaven and the structure of the universe evolved and how this evolution reflects the religious and social tensions within the early Jewish and Christian communities regarding tradition and modernization.

I have tried to make this volume valuable for both the general audience and the specialist. The general reader will want to read the text and ignore the endnotes, while the specialist will find all the standard documentation and extended discussions of more technical matters in the endnotes. My hope is that I have created a volume that will benefit both communities of readers.

I have benefited from the insights of not only the scholars cited in the notes, but also from critiques offered by the following colleagues and friends who have kindly read earlier versions of at least portions of this material: Tzvi Abusch, Theodore Burgh, Randy Chesnutt, William Dever, Devorah Dimant, Michael Fishbane, Isaiah Gafni, Adel Gamal, Michael Hepler, Joel Hunt, Anitra Bingham Kolenkow, Gary Marcus, Beth Alpert Nakhai, Peter Pettit, William Schniedewind, Lou Silberman, Michael Stone, Raymond White, Richard Wilkinson, and David Wright. I also owe great debts of thanks to Holly Smith, Dean of the College of Social and Behavioral Sciences at the University of Arizona, for a Junior Sabbatical that allowed me to finish the final version of this material; to Moshe Berlin and the Yad Hanadiv Foundation for a Fellowship in Jewish Studies that supported my research in Jerusalem in 1995–96; and to Sy Gitin and the board of the W. F. Albright Institute for Archaeological Research for a Post-Doctoral Fellowship in 1995–96. I should also like to thank the department chairs at the University of Arizona who have supported my work these past six years: Daniel Swetschinski, Rohn Eloul and Leonard Dinnerstein of the Committee on Judaic Studies; William Dever, Michael Bonine, and Charles Smith of the Near Eastern Studies Department; Jerrold Green and Amy Newhall of the Center for Middle Eastern Studies; and Robert Burns of the Committee on Religious Studies. I also thank my faculty colleagues at Western Seminary in Portland, OR (1989–90) and at the University of Arizona (1990–) for the vibrant intellectual collegiality I have enjoyed this past decade. All of these people have supported and encouraged my research and teaching in many helpful ways. This work would not have been possible without the resources of many libraries and the help of the librarians at the following institutions: the University of Arizona (especially Ruth Dickstein and Midhat Abraham), the Hebrew University and National Libraries in Jerusalem, the W. F. Albright Institute of Archaeological Research, the École Biblique et Archéologique Française, Western Seminary, Andover-Harvard Library, Brandeis University, and the Boston Public Library. All these people have proven to me that saints reside not only in heaven but right here on earth.

Finally and most importantly, I want to thank Keeley and Angela Wright. Keeley, you are the best life partner a person could imagine, and I thank you for making my life complete. Angela, you are the joy of your parents' lives, and I thank you for teaching me about what must be the joys of heaven.

Tucson, Arizona
June 1998

CONTENTS

ABBREVIATIONS

AB	Anchor Bible
ABD	D. N. Freedman (ed.), *Anchor Bible Dictionary*
ABRL	Anchor Bible Reference Library
AfO	*Archiv für Orientforschung*
AHW	W. von Soden, *Akkadisches Handwörterbuch*
AJSRev	*Association for Jewish Studies Review*
ALD	Aramaic Levi Document
AnBib	Analecta biblica
ANEP	J. B. Pritchard (ed.), *Ancient Near East in Pictures*
ANET	J. B. Pritchard (ed.), *Ancient Near Eastern Texts*
AnOr	Analecta orientalia
ANRW	*Aufstieg und Niedergang der römischen Welt*
AO	Der Alter Orient
AOAT	Alter Orient und Altes Testament
AOT	H. F. D. Sparks (ed.), *The Apocryphal Old Testament*
APAT	E. Kautzsch (ed.), *Die Apokryphen und Pseudepigraphen des Alten Testaments*
APOT	R. H. Charles (ed.), *The Apocrypha and Pseudepigrapha of the Old Testament*
BA	*Biblical Archaeologist*
BARev	*Biblical Archaeology Review*
BASOR	*Bulletin of the American Schools of Oriental Research*

BBR	*Bulletin for Biblical Research*
BETL	Bibliotheca ephemeridum theologicarum lovaniensium
BHM	A. Jellinek, *Bet ha-Midrasch*
Bib	*Biblica*
BibRev	*Bible Review*
BIFAO	*Bulletin de l'institut français d'archéologie orientale*
BJS	Brown Judaic Studies
BKAT	Biblischer Kommentar: Altes Testament
BM	A. Wertheimer, *Batei Midrashot*
BO	*Bibliotheca orientalis*
BZAW	Beihefte zur *Zeitschrift für die alttestamentliche Wissenschaft*
BZNW	Beihefte zur *Zeitschrift für die neutestamentliche Wissenschaft*
CAD	*The Assyrian Dictionary of the Oriental Institute of the University of Chicago*
CBQ	*Catholic Biblical Quarterly*
CBQMS	Catholic Biblical Quarterly Monograph Series
CD	Damascus Document (Cairo)
CII	*Corpus inscriptionum iudaicarum*
ConBOT	Coniectanea biblica, Old Testament
CPJ	*Corpus Papyrorum Judaicarum*
CRIANT	Compendia rerum iudaicarum ad novum testamentum
CT	*Cuneiform Texts from Babylonian Tablets in the British Museum*
CTA	A. Herdner (ed.), *Corpus des tablettes en cunéiformes alphabétiques decouvertes à Ras Shamra—Ugarit*
DJD	Discoveries in the Judean Desert
ExpTim	*Expository Times*
GKC	Gesenius' Hebrew Grammar, ed. E. Kautzsch, trans. A. E. Cowley
HALAT	W. Baumgartner, et al., *Hebräisches und aramäisches Lexikon zum Alten Testament*
HALOT	W. Baumgartner, et al., *Hebrew and Aramaic Lexicon of the Old Testament*
HR	*History of Religions*
HSM	Harvard Semitic Monographs
HTR	*Harvard Theological Review*
HTS	Harvard Theological Studies
HUCA	*Hebrew Union College Annual*
IEJ	*Israel Exploration Journal*
JANES	*Journal of the Ancient Near Eastern Society*
JAOS	*Journal of the American Oriental Society*
JBL	*Journal of Biblical Literature*
JCS	*Journal of Cuneiform Studies*
JJS	*Journal of Jewish Studies*
JNES	*Journal of Near Eastern Studies*
JNWSL	*Journal of Northwest Semitic Languages*
JQR	*Jewish Quarterly Review*
JRAS	*Journal of the Royal Asiatic Society*

JSHRZ	Jüdische Schriften aus hellenistisch-römischer Zeit
JSJ	*Journal for the Study of Judaism in the Persian, Hellenistic and Roman Period*
JSNT	*Journal for the Study of the New Testament*
JSOT	*Journal for the Study of the Old Testament*
JSOTSup	Journal for the Study of the Old Testament—Supplement Series
JSP	*Journal for the Study of the Pseudepigrapha*
JSPSup	Journal for the Study of the Pseudepigrapha—Supplement Series
JTS	*Journal of Theological Studies*
KAI	H. Donner and W. Rollig, *Kanaanäische und aramäische Inschriften*
KAR	E. Ebeling, *Keilschrifttexte aus Assur religiösen Inhalts*
KTU	M. Dietrich, O. Loretz, and J. Sanmartin, *Die keilalphabetischen Texte aus Ugarit einschiesslich der keilalphabetischen Texte ausserhalb Ugarits 1: Transkription*
LCL	Loeb Classical Library
MRS	Mission de Ras Shamra
NIDNTT	C. Brown (ed.), *The New International Dictionary of New Testament Theology*
NTS	*New Testament Studies*
OBO	Orbis biblicus et orientalis
Or	*Orientalia*
OTP	J. H. Charlesworth (ed.), *The Old Testament Pseudepigrapha*
PGM	K. Preisendanz (ed.), *Papyri graecae magicae*
PMR	J. H. Charlesworth, *The Pseudepigrapha and Modern Research with a Supplement*
PVTG	Pseudepigrapha Veteris Testamenti graece
RA	*Revue d'assyriologie et d'archéologie orientale*
RB	*Revue biblique*
RevQ	*Revue de Qumran*
RSR	*Recherches de science religieuse*
SANT	Studien zum Alten und Neuen Testament
SBL	Society of Biblical Literature
SBLDS	SBL Dissertation Series
SBLMS	SBL Monograph Series
SBLSCS	SBL Septuagint and Cognate Studies
SBLTT	SBL Texts and Translations
SBLWAW	SBL Writings of the Ancient World
SBT	Studies in Biblical Theology
SC	Sources chrétiennes
SNTSMS	Society for New Testament Studies Monograph Series
SVTP	Studia in Veteris Testamenti pseudepigrapha
TAPS	Transactions of the American Philosophical Society
TDNT	G. Kittel and G. Friedrich (eds.), *Theological Dictionary of the New Testament*
TDOT	G. Botterweck and H. Ringgren (eds.), *Theological Dictionary of the Old Testament*

TU	Texte und Untersuchungen
UBL	Ugaritisch-Biblische Literatur
UF	*Ugarit-Forschungen*
VT	*Vetus Testamentum*
VTSup	Vetus Testamentum, Supplements
WMANT	Wissenschaftliche Monographien zum Alten und Neuen Testament
WUNT	Wissenschaftliche Untersuchungen zum Neuen Testament
WVDOG	Wissenschaftliche Veröffentlichung der deutschen orientgesellschaft
ZA	*Zeitschrift für Assyriologie*
ZAW	*Zeitschrift für die alttestamentliche Wissenschaft*
ZNW	*Zeitschrift für die neutestamentliche Wissenschaft*

The Early History of Heaven

ANCIENT EGYPTIAN TRADITIONS

The doors of the sky are opened for you, the doors of the starry sky are
thrown open for you . . . for you belong to the stars who surround Re.

Ancient Egyptian Pyramid Texts

In order to understand how early Jewish and Christian authors depicted the
heavenly realm, one first needs to investigate the religious, cultural, and "scientific" perspectives they inherited from the Hebrew Bible, the religiously
authoritative text for both Jews and Christians. We must seek to understand,
therefore, how this authoritative document depicted the heavenly realm because it influenced how later Jews and Christians thought about this subject.
In turn, how the editors and authors of the many texts in the Hebrew Bible
depicted the heavenly realm was influenced by the world in which they lived.

Recent scholarship in the inter-related fields of Hebrew Bible, Syro-
Palestinian archaeology, and ancient Near Eastern languages and cultures indicates that ancient Israel participated fully in the cultural milieu of the ancient
Near East.[1] The phrase "ancient Israel" as used here includes the people of
both the northern kingdom of Israel and the southern kingdom of Judah during the Iron Age (ca. 1200–586 BCE). Although these people possessed their
own unique culture, this culture was no more advanced than their neighbors,
as previous generations of biblical scholars have thought.[2] Ancient Israel's culture, language, and religions have clear affinities and continuities with those of
its neighbors and predecessors. Israel emerged from amidst the ancient Canaanite
peoples and brought with it vestiges of the rich culture of Canaan. Moreover,
ancient Israel was situated along the major crossroads of the Near East, and its
history was closely intertwined with the histories of the great powers surrounding it and intermittently dominating it. In its origin and geopolitical relations,

3

then, Israel was intimately involved with the surrounding cultures of the ancient Near East. As it relates to this study, therefore, one must realize that one
cannot understand the biblical depictions of the cosmic realm without first
gaining some appreciation of how ancient Israel's neighbors imagined that realm.
The ancient Israelites did not invent the notion of heaven as a realm of the
gods above the earth; they inherited it from the ancient Near Eastern cultures
preceding them and neighboring them. Images of this heavenly realm varied
among Israel's neighbors to the north, south, and east, neighbors with whom
Israel had long interacted. The neighbor to the south, Egypt, dominated the
eastern Mediterranean intermittently during the biblical period and during these
times surely had a cultural impact on the peoples of this region.

Most of Egyptian history takes place within a few miles of either side of the
Nile river. The river's annual ebb and flow regulated ancient Egyptian life. In
fact, it structured many aspects of agricultural life in Egypt until the completion of the Aswan High Dam in 1972. The weather along the Nile is fairly
consistent; the clear skies and temperate climate allowed the ancient Egyptians
to watch the sun, moon, and stars rise in the east and make their daily journeys to the west. The Egyptians learned to use the stars to predict when the
Nile would flood its banks, leaving its nutrient rich soil when it receded. Life
along the Nile was largely consistent and predictable. Likewise the Egyptian
gods were generally stable and predictable, unlike the raucous gods of the
Mesopotamian and Canaanite pantheons, as we shall discuss in the following
chapters.

Before the conquest of Egypt by the Persians in the fifth century BCE, the
people of the Nile enjoyed a long and glorious history.[3] Not surprisingly, there
was no single dominating view of the cosmos among the Egyptians during its
long history. Instead, there were many views that evolved through time. Radical
changes in the Egyptian conceptions of the cosmos did not, however, come
about until its conquest by the Persians, and later by the Greeks and Romans,
who introduced entirely new elements into Egyptian culture and religion.[4]
Reading the texts and artifacts from Ancient Egypt with an eye to discovering
their views of the cosmos leaves one with the impression that Egyptian ideas
on this subject were at best a confused mix of beliefs and images. To us, their
views seem contradictory and at times nearly incomprehensible. The problem, however, is not with the ancient Egyptians but with our expectations of
logical consistency. These seemingly contradictory views of the cosmos actually made sense to the ancient Egyptians, who lived happily with these diverse,
even conflicting, beliefs. These people did not feel compelled to create one
logically consistent, all-encompassing, and all-explaining theory—precisely the
kind of theory we westerners should like to find.[5]

> The way of the Egyptian was to accept innovations and to incorporate them
> into his thought, without discarding the old and outmoded. This means that
> it is impossible to find in ancient Egypt a system in our sense, orderly and
> consistent. Old and new lie blandly together like some surrealist picture of
> youth and age on a single face.[6]

The Sources

Belief in a realm far above the earthly plane appears in some of the earliest Egyptian documents. It seems that a hope to join the celestial bodies and become part of the great cosmic circuit after death was common in Egypt from earliest times. Apart from isolated comments in historical and other texts, there are several collections that provide glimpses into how the ancient Egyptians imagined the otherworldly realms.[7] One of our earliest textual sources, the Pyramid Texts, is a collection of inscriptions from the walls of the Old Kingdom (2686–2160 BCE) pyramids. The Pyramid Texts consist of omens, prayers, and rituals that describe the postmortem journey through the netherworld and that were intended to help the deceased Pharaoh ascend to take his place among the gods.[8] These texts recount the wishes of the deceased pharaoh to be aided and protected during his postmortem journey from the tomb, through the netherworld, and up to the celestial realm were he would join the cosmic circuit.[9]

> Nu has commended the King to Atum, the Open-armed has commended the King to Shu, that he may cause yonder doors of the sky to be opened for the King, barring (ordinary) folk who have no name. Grasp the King by his hand and take the King to the sky, that he may not die on earth among men.[10]
> . . . stand at the door which keeps out the plebs. . . . comes out to you and grasps your hand, he takes you to the sky, to your father Geb. . . . he sets you at the head of the spirits, the Imperishable Stars.[11]
> The doors of the sky are opened for you, the doors of the starry sky are thrown open for you . . . for you belong to the stars who surround Re', who are before the Morning Star, you are born in your months as the moon, Re' leans upon you in the horizon, the Imperishable Stars follow you. Make yourself ready until Re' comes, that you may be pure when you ascend to Re', and the sky will not be devoid of you for ever.[12]

Or, in the words of the sky-goddess Nut to the Pharaoh: "Open up your place in the sky among the stars of the sky, for you are the Lone Star, the companion of Hu."[13] Apparently, in the early periods common Egyptians did not hope to join the stars or the sun after death. Instead, as we will discuss below, their beliefs centered around a hope to continue in a reflection of their earthly lives in the netherworld or in a mythical Field of Reeds. The act of a human ascending to heaven is the first step in personifying the heavenly realms. To be sure, the Pharaoh was a god, but this god had a human form while on earth.[14] In the earliest Egyptian texts, therefore, the heavenly realm was a place for gods, and only the divine pharaoh could hope to join the vast cosmic circuit after death. The early Egyptian heaven was a most exclusive place indeed!

A later and related body of literature, the Middle Kingdom (2040–1633 BCE) Coffin Texts, was patterned after the Pyramid Texts and was likewise intended to guide the deceased through the dangers on his way to the stars, but instead of being written inside the pyramids and funerary halls, these were inscribed inside coffins. While the Pyramid Texts were for royalty, the Coffin Texts were an adaptation of the mortuary themes from the Pyramid Texts intended to serve commoners. Thus, there was a transition in the views of who could ascend into heaven, the democratization of heaven, as it were, following the tumultuous times of the First Intermediate Period in Egyptian history.[15] The Coffin Texts continue the themes of the Pyramid Texts on the hope of an afterlife, and serve as a compendium of information that the deceased would need in the afterlife.

The omens, prayers, and rituals of the Pyramid and Coffin Texts were further revised and expanded during the New Kingdom (1558–1085 BCE) in a funerary collection that was known as the Book of the Coming Forth by Day, but now more popularly known as the Book of the Dead.[16] In the following I will try to describe the ancient Egyptian conceptions of the celestial realm by relying on the narratives in these religious texts and the iconographic depictions that accompany many of them. One must recognize at the outset, however, that this is a reconstruction that covers the basic themes and not a detailed account of the origin and development of ancient Egyptian theology. Again, my goal in discussing the Egyptian ideas is to create the context in which the ancient Israelite ideas about the heavenly realm emerged and evolved.

Egyptian Models of the Celestial Realm

The overall picture of the cosmos that can be reconstructed from the ancient Egyptian religious and historical texts is rather complex and even contradictory. Nevertheless, the realm above the earth was depicted in four basic forms: a bird, a cow, a woman, and a flat plane. The Egyptians were not as conscious as we might be in clearly distinguishing these metaphors. Some texts show that they combined the elements from these and other different metaphors without hesitation, creating depictions that seem like a confused jumble to us. Nonetheless, these seem to have been the four basic depictions of the celestial realm.[17] As far as astronomy itself is concerned, it seems that the Egyptians did not develop much beyond a basic observational astronomy.[18] Nonetheless, the ancient Egyptians were fascinated by the sky and can be considered the first astronomers in many ways.

The Celestial Bird

Probably the earliest Egyptian image of the heavenly realms is that of a giant bird.[19] When many ancient Egyptians gazed skyward they imagined that they were looking at the underside of an enormous falcon flying above the earth. According to this model of the heavens, the falcon's eyes were the sun and the moon, and the stars were represented by the whitish speckles on its breast feathers. The flapping of the falcon's wings as it flew caused the winds.[20] In figure 1.7 the wings that stretch between the two staves on which the wings rest represent this celestial bird. That a bird was early identified with the vast overhead expanse is really quite natural, for birds are the beings who alone inhabit this space. Moreover, Horus, the ancient god of the heavenly realm, was identified as one of the mightiest of birds, the falcon (cf. figure 1.13). The connections between the real world and other Egyptian images of the heavenly realm are not as readily apparent.

The Celestial Cow

One account of the origin and structure of the celestial realm is found in the Book of the Divine Cow, and it conceives of the cosmos as a giant celestial cow.[21] Although the celestial cow is a manifestation of the sky goddess Nut,[22] this cow is also typically identified as the goddess Hathor.[23] According to the Book of the Divine Cow, the sun god Re in his old age had become angry with humans and decided to destroy them. Fortunately, he relented and instead sought to distance himself from them. He mounted the back of the celestial cow and had her carry him into the sky. The cow stood over the earth facing west, and on its belly appear the sun and stars, shining down to earth where humans could see them (figure 1.1).[24] The sun god Ra (or Re, here depicted as the figure standing in the boat with the sun disk on his head) makes his journey across the cow's belly in his celestial barge. No matter which of the four basic depictions of the cosmos is used, the sun typically travels across

Figure 1.1: The Celestial Cow; reprinted with permission from James H. Breasted, *A History of Egypt: From Earliest Times to the Persian Conquest,* 2d ed. (New York: Charles Scribner's Sons, 1924), 55, figure 30.

the sky in this barge. Ra has one barge for rising in the morning and travers-
ing the sky and another one for setting in the evening and making his nightly
journey to return to the east, as two royal inscriptions attest: "as Re sets in the
evening-barque, as he rises in the morning barque . . ."[25] Upon his throne in
the Morning-Barque, Great in brilliance in the Evening-Barque."[26]

Apparently the cow consumed the sun in the evening and gave birth to it
the following morning. One omen from the Coffin Texts mentions that the
deceased person whom the omen was designed to help "saw Re being born
yesterday from the buttocks of the Celestial Cow."[27] Thus, the sun returned
to the eastern horizon through the body of the cow. More commonly, the
Egyptians imagined that the sun traveled the sky in the "Day Barge" and then
descended into the Netherworld in the "Evening Barge." During the night
the sun god returned to the east by sailing in this Evening Barge through a
series of caverns in the Netherworld.[28]

A HYMN OF PRAISE TO RA WHEN HE RISETH UPON THE HORIZON, AND WHEN HE
SETTITH IN THE LAND OF LIFE. Osiris, the scribe Ani, saith:—Homage to thee,
O Ra', when thou risest [as] Tem-Heru-khuti. . . . Thou goest forth to thy
setting in the *Sektet* boat with [fair] winds, and thy heart is glad; the heart of
the *Matet* boat rejoiceth. Thou stridest over the heavens in peace, and all thy
foes are cast down; the never resting stars sing hymns of praise unto thee, and
the stars which rest, and the stars which never fail glorify thee as thou sinkest
to rest in the horizon of Manu. . . .[29]

  This great god addresseth words to the gods who dwell in this city, that is
to say, to the gods who are the sailors of the boat of Ra and to those who will
transport [him] through the horizon so that he may take up his position in
the eastern hall of heaven.[30]

The celestial cow model, therefore, mixes seemingly contradictory themes:
the sun god travels in a boat that should sail on water, not on the underside of
a cow. Since the sky goddess was thought to be a cow, and since the sun god
travels in a boat during his daily travels across the skies and his nightly return
through the underworld, the Egyptians simply combined these two incompatible motifs in their celestial cow model of the celestial realm as figure 1.1
indicates. The cow was a sacred animal, and when some ancient Egyptians
looked to the skies, they fittingly imagined it as a vast cosmic cow.

The Celestial Woman

When the heavenly realm is depicted as the celestial woman, she is the goddess Nut who faces west and arches over the earth, balancing on her feet and
hands (figure 1.2):[31] "I am Nut the Great, the Mighty, the Brilliant One, . . .
I have filled all places with my beauty, the earth is under me to its limit."[32]
The sun and stars traveled from east to west on the goddess's belly. The air-
god Shu supports her midriff, while the earth god Geb (Keb) lies at the feet of
Shu stretched out between the arms and feet of Nut: "I am the soul of Shu, for

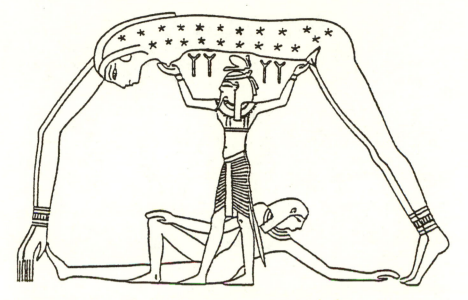

Figure 1.2: The goddess Nut supported by Shu and arched over Geb; reprinted with permission from Breasted, *History of Egypt*, 55, figure 31.

whom Nut was placed above and Geb under his feet, and I am between them."[33] Thus the Egyptians can refer to the entire surface of the earth as that area "which the sun encompasses, that which Geb and Nut enclose."[34] A Pyramid Text succinctly describes Shu's role: "the arms of Shu are under the sky [Nut] when he raises it."[35] As was the case with the celestial cow image, the sun god crosses the sky (i.e., the goddess's body) in a barge, as can be seen clearly in figure 1.3 where the sun god Ra' rises in the morning on the legs of Nut in the east and descends in the evening on her arms in the west.[36]

The most detailed depiction of the goddess Nut comes from the cenotaph of Seti I (ca. 1318–1304) at Abydos.[37] This elaborate drawing appears on the ceiling of Seti's tomb and is accompanied by an inscription that sheds considerable light on some of the details. As the accompanying text and other depictions indicate (see figures 1.4–1.5),[38] Nut consumes the celestial bodies in the west and gives birth to them on the eastern horizon in the morning. "These stars sail to the end of the sky on her outside at night whilst they show themselves and are seen. They sail in her inside in the day-time whilst they do not show themselves and are not seen. . . . They enter her mouth in the place of the head in the West. Then she ate them."[39]

Stars are inscribed in thirty-six columns across the long belly of Nut, and these represent a "star clock" that the Egyptians used to determine the hours of the night and the helical rising of stars.[40] The deceased wish to join these stars in their celestial journeys and so identify themselves with a star or constellation in funerary texts: "I am Sah (Orion) who travelleth over his domain and who journeyeth along before the stars of heaven, [which is] the belly of

Figure 1.3: The goddess Nut and the Sun's Barge; reprinted from Othmar Keel, *The Symbolism of the Biblical World: Ancient Near Eastern Iconography and the Book of Psalms*, trans. Timothy J. Hallett (New York: Seabury Press, 1978; reprint Winona Lake, Ind: Eisenbrauns, 1997), 36, figure 32; used with permission of the author.

my mother Nut."[41] The bottom of the sarcophagus of Seti I wonderfully illustrates the deceased's wish to be joined to the body of Nut. Here a full figure of Nut is painted with her arms open and ready to receive the body of the king.[42]

A depiction of the goddess Nut from the Ptolemaic period (323–30 BCE) presents the goddess twice as she bends over the earth (figure 1.6).[43] As we shall discover in chapter 4, it may be that the Greeks who dominated Egypt during the Ptolemaic period, as part of their attempt to blend Egyptian and Greek myths, here have taken the idea of multiple heavens common to the Greeks and fused it with the image common to the Egyptians. Thus, in figure 1.6 the goddess Nut appears twice, once as the celestial sphere of the moon, that is, the lower Nut, and once as the celestial sphere of the sun, that is, the upper Nut. Although the ancient Egyptians did not conceive of multiple levels in the celestial realm, the Hellenistic Greeks did and so adapted the much older Egyptian motif to their astronomy.

The Celestial Plane

The third common depiction of the heavenly realm is as a flat (at times convex) surface, a great plane.[44] In fact, the Egyptian hieroglyph for the terms *heaven* and *sky* is ⌐⌐⌐, and it appears in several depictions of the sky, "the great celestial plain on which the gods rest."[45] The celestial realm is often thought to have a river or other vast body of water running across it. It is precisely such a

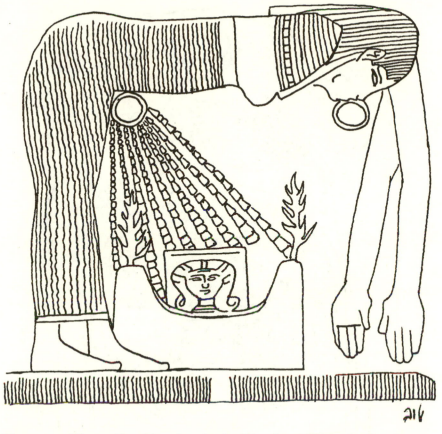

Figure 1.4: The goddess Nut; drawing by Theodore W. Burgh after photo in Hermann Kees, *Der Götterglaube im altern Ägypten*, 3d ed. (Berlin: Akademie Verlag, 1977), tafel IIIb; used with permission of the author.

body of water that fits well with the idea of the sun god sailing across the sky. This body of water is mentioned frequently:

> Thou makest a Nile in the underworld,
> Thou bringest it forth as thou desirest
> To maintain the people (of Egypt) . . .
> All distant foreign countries, thou makest their life (also),
> For thou hast set a Nile in heaven,
> That it may descend for them and make waves upon the mountains,
> Like the great green sea,
> To water their fields in their towns. . . .
> The Nile in heaven, it is for the foreign peoples
> And for the beasts of every desert that go upon (their) feet;
> (While the true) Nile comes from the underworld for Egypt.[46]

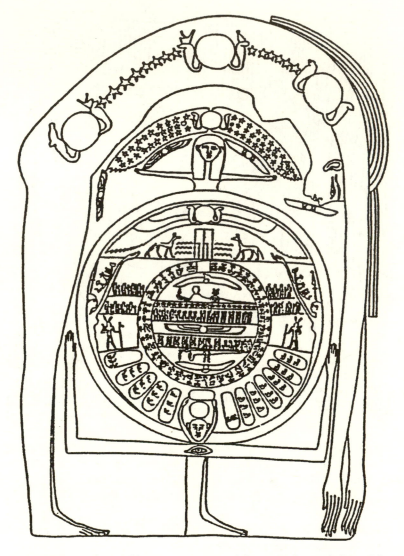

Figure 1.5: The goddess Nut; reprinted from Keel, *Symbolism of the Biblical World*, 38, figure 33; used with permission of the author.

Thou didst create the earth, thou didst fashion man, thou didst make the watery abyss of the sky, thou didst form Hapi, thou didst create the watery abyss, and thou dost give life to unto all that therein is.[47]

. . . you are happy now that you have arisen today as Horus of the Netherworld; now that you have arisen today and have ascended into the Celestial waters.[48]

Figure 1.6: Depiction of the goddess Nut from the Hellenistic era; reprinted from Keel, *Symbolism of the Biblical World*, 34, figure 30; used with permission of the author.

. . . may you bathe in the celestial expanses, may you bathe in the pool of the firmament ... may you not die.[49]

The celestial plane itself is either supported by pillars, staves, or scepters, or is set on top of the mountains at the extreme ends of the earth (see figures 1.7 and 1.8).[50] Although these supports appear typically in pairs in Egyptian iconography, the pair in fact represents four supports, thus the "four corners of the earth."[51] The tombs of pharaohs Tutankamon, Seti I, and Ramses II in addition to the figures of the celestial cow or woman have alternate depictions of the sky being supported by pillars or by people holding staves of some kind. These images also appear in many texts.[52]

I set the glory of thee and the fear of thee in all lands, the terror of thee as far as the four supports of heaven. . . . That which the Ocean encircles is enclosed within thy grasp.[53]

Figure 1.7: Staves supporting the sky; reprinted with permission from Henri Frankfort, *Kingship and the Gods: A Study of Ancient Near Eastern Religion as the Integration of Society and Nature* (Chicago: University of Chicago Press, 1948), figure 17.

O thou . . . who shinest from thy Disk and risest in thy horizon, and dost shine like gold above the sky, like unto whom there is none among the gods, who sailest over the pillars of Shu . . .[54]

Great Circle, the sea, the southern countries of the land of the Negro as far as the marsh lands, as far as the limits of darkness, even to the four pillars of heaven.[55]

Figure 1.8: Staves supporting the sky; reprinted from Keel, *Symbolism of the Biblical World*, 27, figure 20; used with permission of the author.

Figure 1.9: Flat sky resting on mountains; reprinted from Keel, *Symbolism of the Biblical World*, 24, figure 15; used with permission of the author.

The idea that these pillars kept the earth in place inspired the scribe of Thutmose III to state in his inscription describing Thutmose's renovations of the Karnak Temple in Luxor that these improvements were done "in order that this temple might be established like the heavens, abiding upon their four pillars."[56] In fact, it may be that the pillared halls of temples such as the Karnak Temple were meant to remind one of the pillars that support the sky. Amenhotep III, regarding the many pillars in the Karnak Temple, states: "Its pylons reach heaven like the four pillars of heaven."[57] Otherwise, the sky rests on the tops of the mountains: "I know that mountain of Bakhu upon which the sky rests; it is of crystal, 300 rods long and 120 rods wide."[58] Depictions of the sky resting on the mountains appear in two forms: flat (figures 1.9–1.10) or vaulted (figures 1.11–1.12).[59] Figure 1.9 represents the flat sky resting on the mountain tops, while figure 1.10 depicts the sky resting on the heads of two lions whose images are often associated with the sunrise and sunset. Figure 1.11 is nearly identical to figure 1.10, with the exception that the sky is slightly vaulted in 1.11.

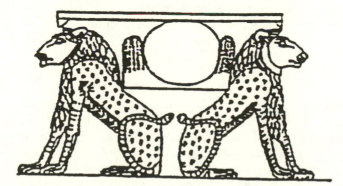

Figure 1.10: Flat sky resting on lions; reprinted from Keel, *Symbolism of the Biblical World*, 26, figure 17; used with permission of the author.

Figure 1.11: Vaulted sky resting on lions; reprinted from Keel, *Symbolism of the Biblical World*, 26, figure 18; used with permission of the author.

Figure 1.12 shows the vaulted sky resting on mountain tops as the sun rises in the east. Figure 1.13 also depicts the sunrise with the sun represented by the image of Horus with a solar disk, but in this case there are no mountains; instead, the apes who are associated with the mountains of the sunrise in figure 1.12 appear on either side of the vaulted sky.[60] These images, and the hieroglyphic term for sky or heaven, ⬜, (*pet*) indicate that the ancient Egyptians thought the celestial realm was a vast expanse that was either flat or slightly convex. Both models are easy to understand given the basic observations of the Egyptians. The sun, moon, planets, and stars rise on the eastern horizon, ascend to a level high overhead, proceed across the sky, and then descend into the western horizon. If such is the case, the shape of the celestial vault must be flat. On the other hand, as any school child can observe, when the moon or sun is on the horizon, it seems much bigger than when it is over head, and as it rises it appears to become smaller. If such is the case, the celestial bodies must travel on a convex surface and reach their apex in mid-sky.

Egyptian Images of the Afterlife

Egyptians imagined the afterlife as a journey punctuated by several threatening dangers. After death and burial one's *ka* (soul or life spirit) descended into the netherworld in a boat and sailed through a series of gates and chambers where one faced all manner of dangers and trials intended to test one's character.[61] In the end, the just person was aided by the gods to ascend to the earthly or celestial plain where he or she would enjoy a good life that shared many features with life on earth. Otherwise, one would either remain in the netherworld for brutal punishment or return to the region of his or her tomb only to wander back and forth between the netherworld and the earthly plane.[62]

Figure 1.12: Vaulted sky resting on mountains; drawing by Theodore W. Burgh after photo of the papyrus in Evelyn Rossiter, *Le Livre des Morts: Papyrus égyptiens (1420–1100 av.J.C.)* (Geneva: Productions Liber SA, 1984), 26; used with permission of the author.

The person who escaped the dangers of the netherworld and was admitted into the realms of the blessed—be these realms on earth or in the sky—could go about freely from the skies to the earth and netherworld to visit friends and relatives.

Let me have the power to manage my own fields in Tattu (Mendes), and my own crops in Annu (Heliopolis). Let me live upon bread made from white grain, and let my beer be made from red grain, and may my ancestors, and

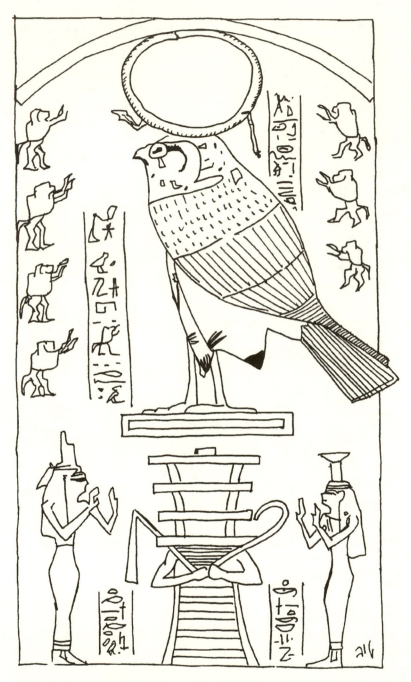

Figure 1.13: Vaulted Sky over the god Horus; drawing by Theodore W. Burgh after photo of the papyrus in Rossiter, *Le Livre des Morts*, 80–81; used with permission of the author.

my father and my mother be given unto me as guardians of my door and for the ordering of my territory.[63]

Hail, Ra'! Hail, Tem! Hail, Seb! Hail, Nut! Grant ye to Sepa that he may traverse the heavens (or sky), that he may traverse the earth, that he may traverse the waters, that he may meet his ancestors, may meet his father, may meet his mother, may meet his grown up sons and daughters, and his brethren, and his sisters, may meet his friends, both male and female, may meet those who have been as parents to him, and his kinfolk (cousins?), and those who have worked for him upon earth, both male and female, and may meet the concubine whom he loved and knew.[64]

There seems to be no doubt that the Egyptians believed in a life after death and in the possibility of ascending into the celestial realms.[65] While the following is said of the Pharaoh in the early texts, the theme applies potentially to all Egyptians in later times: "O King, you have not departed dead, you have departed alive."[66] As befits a god, Pharaoh joined the company of celestial gods. The rituals performed for the deceased Pharaoh and recounted in the Pyramid Texts are so detailed that one can visualize the activities as one reads them.[67] The ancient Egyptians believed that there were doors or gates in the eastern and western horizons through which the celestial bodies would pass on their daily journeys.[68] As the ancients would have passed through gates to enter a city, or doors to enter their homes, so, they imagined, the sun and other celestial bodies must pass through gates as they enter the observable sky.

I know that middle gate from which Re' issues in the east; its south is in the Lake of Waterfowl, its north is in the Waters of Geese, in the place in which Re' navigates by rowing or by wind. . . . I know those two sycamores which are of turquoise between which Re' goes forth, which go strewing shade at every eastern gate from which Re' shines forth.[69]

Figure 1.14 provides three depictions of the gates through which the sun god passes in the morning.[70] As will become evident in the following chapters, this image of gates for the celestial bodies to enter or exit the visible sky will appear elsewhere in texts from across the ancient Near East. This is part of the intellectual and religious world that influenced Israelite depictions of the celestial realm. Beyond being the doors for the celestial bodies or winds, these doors or gates likely provide the model for the idea that the righteous ascend into the heavenly realm (or descend from there) via doors or gates. In other words, the Egyptians believed that there were passageways between the earthly and cosmic realms, and these passageways were blocked by gates that could prevent the deceased from ascending.[71] The funerary texts we have been discussing contain many prayers enlisting the help of the gods to enable the deceased to ascend safely into the celestial realm.

Figure 1.14: Door or Gates for the sun; reprinted from Keel, *Symbolism of the Biblical World*, 24, figures 10–12; used with permission of the author.

> The doors of the sky are opened, The doors of the firmament are thrown open at dawn for me myself. I go up into the Field of Rushes, I bathe in the Field of Rushes.[72]
>
> May the doors of heaven be opened unto me. . . . May the goddess Sekhet make me to rise so that I may ascend unto heaven. . . .[73]
>
> The doors of the sky are opened because of your goodness; may you ascend and see Hathor. . . .[74]
>
> O my soul, my spirit, my magic and my shade, open the doors of the sky, throw open the gates of heaven, may your ornaments be secured on yourself so that you may enter to the great god who is in his shrine and see Re' in his true shape.[75]

At death the *ka* (soul or life-spirit) of a person is released from the body. Often the *ka* takes on the form of a human-headed bird, the *ba*, a creature that can fly through the skies or walk on the earth: "he (Osiris) opens for you the doors of the sky, he throws open for you the doors of the firmament, he makes a road for you that you may ascend by means of it into the company of the gods, you being alive in your bird-shape."[76] Figure 1.15, an illustration from the Ani Papyrus of the Book of the Dead, shows how the deceased takes on the form of the *ba*-bird and leaves the corpse. The same papyrus shows this bird escaping from the doorway of the tomb and rejoining the land of the living (figure 1.16): "The tomb is opened for you, the doors of the tomb-chamber are thrown open for you."[77] In the Book of the Dead the deceased, having successfully navigated through the dangers and trials of the netherworld, flies to heaven as a spiritual being, sometimes expressed as taking the form of the hawk, the symbol of the god Horus.

> May I journey on, may I come into the uttermost parts of heaven. . . . [I am] a spiritual body and possess my soul, and will speak unto thee the things which concern me. . . . I have risen up like the divine hawk, and Horus hath made for me a spiritual body through his own soul, to take possession of that which belongeth to Osiris in the Tuat.[78]

Figure 1.15: *(top)* Deceased takes the form of a "soul-bird" and leaves the body; drawing by Theodore W. Burgh after photo of the papyrus in Rossiter, *Le Livre des Morts*, 11, 49; used with permission of the author. Figure 1.16: *(bottom)* Soul-bird exiting the tomb; reprinted with permission from E. A. Wallis Budge, *The Book of the Dead: An English Translation of the Chapters, Hymns, Etc., of the Theban Recension, with an Introduction, Notes, Etc.* (3 vols. in one, 2d ed., Routledge & Kegan Paul Ltd., 1960), 2.295.

Those who ascend to the celestial realm may also arrive there by ascending a celestial ladder fashioned by the gods.[79]

> Now let the ladder of the god be given to me, let the ladder of Seth be given to me, that I may ascend on it to the sky and escort Re' as a divine guardian of those who have gone to their doubles.[80]
>
> Hail to you, daughter of Anubis, who is at the windows of the sky, the companion of Thoth, who is at the uprights of the ladder! Open my way that I may pass.[81]

But ascending to join the stars in the great celestial circuit is only one of the ways ancient Egyptians conceived of the afterlife. Exactly where the deceased expected to go after successfully navigating through the dangers and trials of the netherworld and being found just before Osiris, god of the netherworld, is not quite clear. As I mentioned at the outset, Egyptian theology is not as logically consistent as we might hope. Instead, their religious beliefs are generally a complex mix of ideas that seem contradictory, and this is no less true about their ideas regarding the ultimate destiny of the just. The Egyptians did have an idea of a blessed place where the righteous would reside after death besides that of becoming a god in the celestial realm. What is not clear is whether this land of the blessed was on the terrestrial or the celestial plane.

Some ancient Egyptian texts seem to locate this land of the blessed on earth, at some mystical place far removed from the everyday world of humans. This place is commonly called the Field of Rushes, or Field of Offerings. This is a place of Edenic peace and abundance where the deceased expected to do everything that they did on earth: "may I eat therein, may I drink therein, may I plough therein, may I reap therein, may I fight therein, may I make love therein, may my words be mighty therein, may I never be in a state of servitude therein, but may I be in authority therein."[82] There they would live like royalty, sating themselves on the abundance of the land.

> I know that Field of Rushes which belongs to Re', the wall of whose enceinte is of iron; the height of its barley is four cubits, its ear is one cubit, its stalk is three cubits; its emmer is seven cubits, its ear is two cubits, its stalk is five cubits. It is the horizon-dwellers who reap it, nine cubits long in the presence of the Souls of the Easterners. . . .[83]
>
> I will cross over to the sky, I will live on what they [i.e., the gods] live on, I will eat what they eat of, my booth is in plenty, my abundance is in the Field of Offerings, and I am well-supplied in company with the gods, for I am one of them. . . .[84]
>
> I will live on the white emmer which is in the eastern corner of the sky. I have gone up as a swallow, I have cackled as a goose, I have alighted on this great plateau; as for anyone who alights on it, he will never die, and he whose hands are hidden will be seen as a god.[85]

In the religious imagination, this is more than simply a place, it is an ideal. Thus, the ancient Egyptians could hold the two ideas of a celestial paradise

and an earthly one in a delicate balance. The point for the religious imagination is that there is a place where the just have a continued blessed existence
beyond the grave. The idea of this as a fecund place surely comes from an
Egyptian agricultural setting. What likely started as an image based on the best
possible environment an agricultural society could imagine was transferred
analogically to the heavenly realms once it had been fused to the idea of an
astral afterlife. Thus, the earthly paradise was relocated to the heavenly realm.[86]
Pyramid Text §517 seems to locate the Field of Rushes in the celestial realm.
"O you who ferry over the righteous boatless as the ferryman of the Field of
Rushes, I am deemed righteous in the sky and on earth, I am deemed righteous in this Island of Earth to which I have swum and arrived, which is between the thighs of Nut."[87] This tradition assumes that the righteous king swims
to some remote island where he can then be ferried over (up?) to the Field of
Rushes. Not all ancient Egyptians hoped to live in the Field of Rushes. While
some hoped to join the celestial bodies in their unending journeys, others hoped
for a life in the Fields of the Rushes where life went on as usual, but better.
Still others spoke of both—to join the stars and yet live in the Field of Rushes
in the heavenly realm, and for this group the two ideas were not mutually
exclusive. Either way, after death they expected that they would become eternal,
forever blessed, unchanging beings.

The image of living in the land of the blessed is only part of the picture as
we have seen above. The righteous also hoped to join the stars: "I have ascended among the stars, I have bathed in the celestial waters."[88] One hymn
expresses the hope for being joined with the stars of the sky. "May the soul of
Osiris Ani (i.e., the deceased), the triumphant one, come forth from with thee
(Ra) into heaven, may he go forth in the *Matet* boat. May he come into port
in the *Sektet* boat, and may he cleave his path among the never resting stars in
the heavens."[89] The god's response to this request was: "Thou shalt come forth
into heaven, thou shalt pass over the sky, thou shalt be joined unto the starry
deities."[90] Perhaps these two images of living in the Field of Rushes and becoming a god in the form of a star were blended into a complex of ideas about
the afterlife and the other realm and were not two separate ideas. Thus, the
Field of Rushes could be transferred to the celestial realm: "Cross the sky to
the Field of Rushes, make your abode in the Field of Offerings among the
Imperishable Stars, the followers of Osiris."[91] Chapters 110–11 and 149 of the
Book of the Dead describe the regions of the blessed. Budge, in his English
translation of this text, has even given chapters 110–11 the heading "Elysian
Fields." This is a vast, verdant place of abundance and peace with many divisions and many gods. Although this place seems to be on earth, since the deceased had already become a bird, it appears that given the immediate context
in the Book of the Dead this place is in the celestial realm and not at some
distant, mythical place on earth, although that is surely where the image began.

After the deceased join the gods in the celestial realm, they participate fully
in the cosmic activity—they become gods. While it was customary to believe
that the pharaoh ". . . went forth to heaven, having mingled with the gods,"[92]
this eventually came to be the hope of all. Just as the celestial goddess Nut

gives birth to the sun, so she gives birth to the deceased once they have as-cended and joined the gods. "I am exalted like the holy god who dwelleth in the Great Temple, and the gods rejoice when they see me in my beautiful coming forth from the body of Nut, when my mother Nut giveth birth unto me."[93] They hoped to become a god in every respect.

> My booth is plaited with rushes, my drink-supply is in the field of Offerings, my food-offerings are among you, you gods, my water is wine like that of Re', and I go round the sky like Re', I traverse the sky like Thoth.[94]
>
> The Osiris Nu (deceased's name) saileth round about in heaven, he travelleth therein unto Nut, he journeyeth along with Ra. . . . Behold, grant thou that the Osiris Nu may be great in heaven even as thou are great among the gods.[95]
>
> And there, in the celestial mansions of heaven which my divine father Tem hath established, let my hands lay hold upon the wheat and the barley which shall be given unto me therein in abundant measure, and may the son of mine own body make [ready] for me my food therein. And grant ye unto me therein sepulchral meals, and incense, and wax, and all the beautiful and pure things whereon the god liveth. . . .[96]

In fact, in the omens and prayers of the funerary literature the deceased iden-tifies himself explicitly with the god: "I indeed am Osiris, I indeed am the Lord of All, I am the Radiant One, the brother of the Radiant Lady; I am Osiris, the brother of Isis."[97]

Summary and Conclusion

What is clear is that the Egyptian depictions of the cosmic realms lack what appears as a complete celestial kingdom with all its officers and royal activities (i.e., grades of superior and inferior divine beings), such as in Mesopotamia, Syria-Palestine, and Greece. On occasion, however, one encounters statements that the deceased Pharaoh kept his royal accouterments[98] or that the celestial realm was inhabited by gods who lived in mansions,[99] but the interactions between these beings does not receive much attention. The early Egyptian ideas evolved from imagining that only Pharaoh could obtain a place in the cosmic realms (third millennium) to believing that all might attain such a post-mortem existence (first millennium). The pharaoh, as god's son, was equipped by his nature as a god for life in the realm of the gods. For the commoner, however, the ka (soul or life-spirit) of the dead either lingered around the tombs, went to the Field of Rushes, or ascended into the celestial realm to become one of the stars. These ideas seem contradictory to us, but apparently were not to the Egyptians. The transition from the pharaoh as the only one qualifying for postmortem ascent into the heavenly realms to all people potentially able to do this seems to have begun after the First Intermediate Period (ca. 2100 BCE) when people saw their pharaohs overthrown as if they were but mere mortals. The Egyptians then looked to the dying and rising god Osiris as the model of what happens to all people after death.

Although their astronomical expertise was not as advanced as that of the peoples of Greece and Mesopotamia, the Egyptians can be credited with having one of the earliest, if not the earliest concept of humans having a blessed afterlife in the heavenly realms. But did they "invent" heaven? It seems, as we shall see in the following chapters, that the peoples of Mesopotamia and elsewhere also imagined that there was a realm "up there" populated by divine beings. Since such a theme appears so widespread in early human history, it is impossible to credit one culture with having invented it. Nonetheless, the ancient Egyptians were certainly the ones who eventually made access to the heavenly realm available to the masses.

ANCIENT MESOPOTAMIAN TRADITIONS

O great Lord who sits on an awesome throne in the pure heavens,
golden crown of the heavens, fittest for kingship; O Shamash, shepherd
of the people, noble god who examines the land, leader of the people
who guides the fugitive to the right path; O Shamash, judge of heaven
and earth who directs the Igigi gods, who grants incense offerings
to the great gods, I Ashurbanipal, a son of his god, call on you in the
pure heavens. I seek you out in your splendid dwelling.

Hymn to Shamash (KAR 55)

As we turn to consider the views of Mesopotamian peoples about the heavenly realms, we must be cautious. The sources at our disposal are abundant,
but how they fit within the contexts of official religion on the one hand or
popular religion on the other is not clear. In fact, one noted Assyriologist
maintained that "a systematic presentation of Mesopotamian religion cannot
and should not be written."[1] In the following, therefore, I will try to sketch
the salient features of Mesopotamian beliefs about the heavenly realms. Once
again, given the nature of the sources, we must steer a course between the
Scylla of complete nihilism and the Charybdis of excessive optimism when it
comes to reconstructing the beliefs of these ancient peoples. It must be remembered that most of this literature predates the biblical materials—the
Sumerian literature by more than a millennium! Because of the continuities in
many aspects of Mesopotamian religion from the late third millennium to the
middle of the first millennium BCE, this material will enable us to understand
more fully the intellectual context in which the biblical materials evolved.[2]

Sumer

According to one scholar, "History Begins at Sumer."[3] The Sumerians were
one of the first cultures to develop writing and many other features of organized society. Sumerian literature had an enormous cultural influence on the

later Babylonians and Assyrians. Sumerian writing began—or better, the earliest extant evidence of Sumerian writing begins—with economic records shortly before 3000 BCE.[4] Although precious little of Sumerian literature has been preserved in Sumerian itself, we know this literature from copies made into Akkadian by later Babylonian and Assyrian scribes. The Sumerians were a non-Semitic people who appeared in Mesopotamia in the fourth millennium BCE, and they dominated the region until the rise of the great Semitic king, Sargon of Akkad (ca. 2334–2279). Sargon expanded Semitic control of Mesopotamia and limited the Sumerians to the south. When the great Sumerian city of Ur was destroyed around 2050 BCE, the Sumerians ceased as a people. From then on Mesopotamia was dominated by one of two Semitic powers, both of which spoke dialects of the Akkadian language—the Assyrians and Babylonians.

The Sumerian Cosmos

The general outlines of the Sumerian ideas about the nature of the universe can be drawn from their myths.[5] In the beginning there was water, the goddess Nammu. Nammu gave birth to An (the sky-god) and Ki (the earth-goddess); these two in turn begot the air-god Enlil. Sky and earth were at first united, and the Sumerian term for universe is An-Ki, "sky-earth." The universe was conceived as a giant mountain with its base on the earth and its summit reaching into the sky. In Sumerian it is called "the mountain of heaven and earth."[6] Eventually the air god Enlil separated heaven and earth.[7] The gods were superhuman, immortal beings, and they ruled their respective areas of the universe just as any human rulers would oversee their realms. The sky gods dwelt in heaven, various gods and demons on earth, and the mortuary gods in the netherworld. Humans were created from a lump of clay for the sole purpose of serving the gods. There was rank among the gods in a manner that parallels the hierarchical structure of urban societies.[8] Since the greatest human institution was the kingdom, the pantheon of the gods was imagined by analogy as a kingdom, and the gods administered their subjects on earth through their earthly palace, the temple. Moreover, the gods were arranged in heaven on the model of an earthly kingdom with a king at the head of the pantheon and a group of royal functionaries assisting him. In every way, whether for good or bad, in strength or weakness, the gods were like humans.

The Sumerians typically built their temples on the summits of artificial hills called "ziggurats." These elevated temples dominated the flat landscape of Mesopotamia and could be seen from a great distance. A synonym for ziggurat (*ziqqurratu*), is *hur-sag-galam-ma*, "storied tower."[9] It may be that these temples were models of the celestial realm. They were surely the places where heaven and earth intersected according to the religious beliefs of the people. One approached this elevated temple via steps and then passed through a gate or door in order to enter the shrine itself. A well-known example is the Ziggurat of Ur that dates to roughly 2000 BCE (figure 2.1).[10] Tellingly, the ziggurat in Babylon was called *E-temen-an-ki*, "the temple of the foundation of heaven and earth."

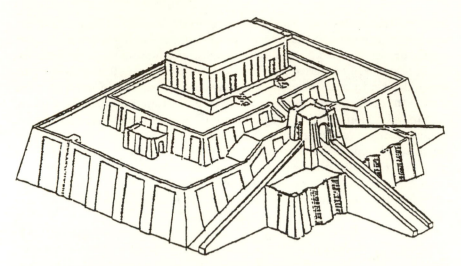

Figure 2.1: Ziggurat of Ur; reproduced with permission from P. R. S. Moorey, *Ur "of the Chaldees": A Revised and Updated Edition of Sir Leonard Wooley's Excavations at Ur* (Ithaca: Cornell University Press, 1982), 48.

In the minds of the Mesopotamians, the high gods controlled all aspects of earthly life from their abode in heaven. Even human kingship was not initiated by humans but was "lowered from heaven" by the gods.[11] The Sumerians were the first to connect the idea of the gods residing in heavenly palaces with the shrines and temples built for them on earth. The chief god of the Sumerian pantheon was Enlil, and his principle earthly residence was the Ekur temple in Nippur. Regarding this temple, a hymn in praise of Enlil states:

> Nippur—the shrine where dwells the father, the "great mountain,"
> The dias of plenty, the Ekur which rises . . . ,
> The high mountain, the pure place . . . ,
> Its prince, the "great mountain," Father Enlil.
> Has established his seat on the dias of the Ekur, lofty shrine; . . .
> The Ekur, the lapis-lazuli house, the lofty dwelling place, awe-inspiring,
> Its awe and dread are next to heaven,
> Its shadow is spread over all the lands,
> Its loftiness reaches heaven's heart.[12]

A Sumerian hymn praising the temple of the god Enki in Eridu calls that structure the "Foundation of heaven and earth, 'Holy of Holies,' Eridu."[13] A hymn praising the temple of Inanna in Uruk states that the great goddess of heaven and earth sits as queen in this temple: "The great queen of heaven and earth, Inanna, has, O Eanna, placed the house upon your . . . , has taken her place on your dais."[14]

For the Sumerians the universe was a tripartite structure—heaven (the place of the high gods), earth (the realm of humans), and the netherworld (the realm of deceased humans and the mortuary gods). According to S. N. Kramer, since the Sumerian word for tin is "metal of heaven," it may be that the Sumerians thought that the floor of heaven was made of tin or some comparable metal.[15] It also appears that the Sumerians considered the sky to be a vault or dome because we read of heaven having a zenith.[16] Although our information on Sumerian images of the cosmos is admittedly meager, it is nonetheless apparent that the general features of their images agree with the more complete descriptions we have from later Mesopotamian peoples.

Sumerian Images of the Afterlife

It is not clear exactly what the Sumerians believed happened to people after death, but it does not appear that a beatific life in "paradise" was in store for many. Their burials suggest that the quality of life one enjoyed in the netherworld after death depended more on one's social or economic position than on one's virtue.[17] There was an idea of paradise, but this was not the destiny of most people. In fact, to draw a line from the Gilgamesh Epic, a tale whose roots go back to Sumerian times,[18] we learn that ancient Mesopotamians viewed the grave as the final destiny of all humanity: "O Gilgamesh, where are you headed? You will not find the immortality you seek. When the gods created humanity, they appointed death for humanity, and kept life in their own hands" (Old Babylonian version, x.iii.1–5). Or, as this appears in a later version of the Gilgamesh Epic: "The Anunnaku, the great gods, were assembled, . . . They established life and death. Death they fixed to have no ending."[19] It seems, therefore, that the Sumerians had no idea of humans being united with the gods in heaven after death. Instead, ". . . the Sumerians were dominated by the conviction that in death the emasculated spirit descended to a dark and dreary beyond were 'life' at best was but a dismal, wretched reflection of life in earth."[20] Punishment for evil deeds typically came in this life, but suffering was not always inflicted fittingly on the unjust. The struggle of theodicy, that is, of understanding why the just suffer, a theme known commonly from the biblical *Book of Job*, appears in Sumerian literature, thus antedating the biblical story by approximately two millennia.[21] Humans toiled from birth to death and the grave was their end. Punishment came from the gods in life. If afflicted, the Sumerian could turn to a god for help through prayer and ritual. In the end, however, all had the same inescapable fate—the grave. Ur-Nammu (ca. 2112–2095), one of the great Sumerian kings, was lamented touchingly in death for in the netherworld he could no longer enjoy the company of his family: "The shepherd who no longer cared for his home, His wife whom he no longer fondled on his lap, His son whom he no longer raised on his knee."[22]

There was a Sumerian paradise of sorts, and according to some myths this was located on earth in the land of Dilmun:

> The land Dilmun is pure, the land Dilmun is clean. The land Dilmun is clean, Dilmun is bright. . . . In Dilmun the crow screams not . . . , the lion kills not, the wolf snatches not the lamb, the dog knows not to subdue the kid, . . . the eye-sick one says not "I am eye-sick," the one suffering from headache says not "I am headache-sick," its old woman says not "I am an old woman," its old man says not "I am an old man."[23]

Dilmun was a land of abundant water and fruitfulness—altogether, a paradise.[24] But in the Sumerian myths, this paradise was for gods or superhumans alone. The Sumerian myth of the Flood recounts that its hero Ziusudra, the Sumerian counterpart to the biblical Noah, was transferred to "the land of Dilmun, the place where the sun rises," by the gods as a reward for his behavior. From the story it seems that this place was east of Sumer near where the sun rises, and where there were exceptionally aromatic cedar trees. While some scholars locate Dilmun in southwestern Iran,[25] the evidence suggests that Dilmun was the ancient name of the island of Bahrain in the Persian Gulf.[26] The Sumerians called their paradise the Land of the Living,[27] and this is where the super-mortals like Ziusudra and Utnaphishtim lived, the Noah-like heroes of the Sumerian and Babylonian versions of the Flood myth.[28] The noted Sumerologist S. N. Kramer thinks that the idea of paradise originated with the Sumerians,[29] but as we have already seen, the Egyptian Field of Rushes indicates that a similar idea appeared in Egyptian thought at least as early as in Mesopotamia, if not earlier. One of Sumer's well-known myths, Gilgamesh and the Land of the Living, recounts how king Gilgamesh intended to go to this place: "The lord, Gilgamesh, toward the Land of the Living set his mind" (*ANET*, 48, line 2). As the later versions of the Gilgamesh Epic recount, Gilgamesh journeyed here to visit Utnaphishtim and obtain the secret to immortality.

According to the Sumerian myth, The Descent of Inanna to the Netherworld, the goddess Inanna was the queen of heaven but for some reason decided to visit the netherworld.[30] Before embarking on her dangerous journey, Inanna asked her attendant to plead with the gods of heaven if she did not return in three days: "When I shall have come to the nether world, Fill heaven with complaints for me, In the assembly shrine cry out for me, In the house of the gods rush about for me, . . . To the Ekur, the house of Enlil, all alone direct thy step. Upon entering the Ekur, the house of Enlil, Weep before Enlil."[31] This passage shows that in Sumer the people imagined the skies as the abode of the gods, and that the place to communicate with them was from the appropriate temple on earth. It also indicates a tripartite universe: heaven, earth, netherworld. The text continues with Inanna leaving heaven and proceeding to the gateway that led down into the netherworld. She then proceeded through seven gates, removing an article of clothing at each (*ANET*, 55, lines 126–60). The goddess would have remained in the netherworld had it not been for the intervention of the great god Enki who sent two beings to take the "water of life" and the "food of life" into the netherworld to revive Inanna (*ANET*, 56, lines 218–72). It seems, therefore, that the Sumerians thought that death was the ultimate fate of all. Perhaps the superhumans or gods could go to the land of Dilmun, paradise if you will, but for everyone else except for Inanna, the netherworld was every one's inescapable destiny.[32] Moreover, after having received the assistance of the gods, Inanna ascended from the netherworld to the earth and eventually to heaven. Thus, with the assistance of other divinities a god or goddess can ascend to heaven, but this is meant only for the gods, for everyone knew from painful personal experience that no human ever returned from the grave.

Sumerian Astronomy

The ancient Sumerians had a text that they apparently identified as the "Tablet of the Stars of Heaven."[33] Since this tablet was made of the bluish lapis-lazuli stone, "the Sumerians may have thought of the sky as giant cosmic lapis lazuli tablet inscribed with stars. . . ."[34] Otherwise, the lack of astronomical and astrological texts and traditions in Mesopotamian until the late second millennium indicates that astronomical speculation was not common in Sumer. Von Soden boldly claims that "the divergent view of the Pan-Babylonians . . . , that astronomy is to be traced back to the Sumerians in the fourth millennium, can no longer be reconciled with the known sources, although this view is still sporadically represented."[35] But the Sumerians at least made a start with astronomy as they had calendrical calculations based on the movements of the celestial bodies.[36] Moreover, although the extant astronomical texts date from the second millennium, there must have been a vast collection of naked-eye observations to provide the database for these later texts, and these observations would have had to have been collected for some considerable time. An Akkadian text from Ur that lists earlier Sumerian texts includes a title that seems to refer to the astronomical series Enûma Anu Enlil, the series that later became the canonical astronomical series of Mesopotamia, as will be discussed presently.[37]

The Sumerians had no idea of an afterlife in heaven where humans would be reunited with the gods. Heaven was for the gods, earth for humans. Heaven is beyond all humans: "Man, the tallest, cannot reach to heaven."[38] All humans shared the same, inescapable fate—the grave. After death humans entered into life in the netherworld. Here they continued as they had lived on earth, but their surroundings were only a gloomy reflection of their former life: "Bitter is the food of the Netherworld, brackish is the water of the Netherworld."[39] Already, however, humans had come to view the world as a tripartite structure, as Gilgamesh shows when he makes a solemn oath: "Gilgamesh swore by the life of heaven, life of earth, life of the nether world."[40]

Assyria and Babylonia

The Babylonian and Assyrian empires dominated the Near East for most of the second and first millennia BCE. These empires were geographically centered at the major crossroads of the ancient Near East in modern Iraq, Syria, and western Iran. Peoples, traders, and armies traveling from north, south, east, and west used the Tigris and Euphrates rivers to pass through this region. As a result, history in this region is much more volatile than in Egypt. Whereas Egyptian history is to some extent characterized by stasis, Mesopotamian history is dynamic.[41]

The Assyrians and Babylonians were deeply indebted to their Sumerian ancestors for many aspects of their culture. Although these later Mesopotamians made significant cultural and scientific advances of their own, their literature does not dwell self-consciously on their contributions or on their theoretical innovations. Instead, their literature reflects an emphasis on how their ideas have continuity with older ones: in ancient Mesopotamia, tradition and continuity were prized over innovation.[42] The Mesopotamian pantheon has its local varieties and examples of fusion of different gods and goddesses, but in general we can identify three basic groupings of gods: the celestial gods (mostly identified with celestial bodies), the mortuary gods (gods of the netherworld), and personal gods. It is not clear how involved the common person was with the official state cults except to observe the major public festivals. The personal gods, however, were of crucial importance for they were the ones to whom the individual turned to ward off a host of malevolent deities and demons that might threaten one's well-being. The many omens and magical texts that intend to prevent such harm attest to this.[43]

The Assyrian and Babylonian Cosmos

The basic Mesopotamian beliefs about the structure of the cosmos appear in the creation myth, the Enûma Elish. This text, whose chief purpose is to recount how the god Marduk became the head of the Babylonian pantheon, also describes how Marduk created the universe. After defeating his mighty opponent the goddess Tiamat, Marduk created the universe from her corpse.[44]

Then the lord paused to view her dead body,
That he might divide the monster and do artful works.
He split her like a shellfish into two parts:
Half of her he set up and ceiled it as sky,
Pulled down the bar and posted guards.
He bade them not to allow her waters to escape.[45]
He crossed the heavens and surveyed the regions.
He squared Apsu's quarter, the abode of Nidimmud,
As the lord measured the dimensions of Apsu.
The Great Abode, its likeness, he fixed as Esharra,
The Great Abode, Esharra, which he made as the firmament.
Anu, Enlil, and Ea he made occupy their places.[46]
He constructed stations for the great gods,
Fixing their astral likenesses as constellations.
He determined the year by designating the zones:
He set up three constellations for each of the twelve months.

After defining the days of the year [by means] of (heavenly) figures,
He founded the station of Nebiru to determine their (heavenly) bands,
That none might transgress or fall short.
Alongside it he set up the stations of Enlil and Ea.
Having opened up the gates on both sides,
He strengthened the locks to the left and the right.
In her belly he established the zenith.
The Moon he caused to shine, the night (to Him) entrusting.
He appointed him a creature of the night to signify the days:
"Monthly, without cease, form designs with a crown.
At the month's very start, rising over the land,
Thou shalt have luminous horns to signify six days.
On the seventh day be thou a [half]-crown.
At full moon stand in opposition in mid-month.
When the sun [overtakes] thee at the base of heaven,
Diminish [thy crown] and retrogress in light.
[At the time of disappearance] approach thou the course of the sun,
And [on the twenty-ninth] thou shalt again stand in opposition to the sun."[47]

Marduk split the salt water goddess Tiamat into two: the upper portion became the sky and the lower portion became the earth. The narrative then focuses on how Marduk created the celestial bodies, their positions and regular movements. This text provides the basic components of the Mesopotamian image of the universe: sky, atmosphere, earth, and the watery realm beneath the earth. The great gods reside in the sky as celestial bodies. The overall schema is once again tripartite: heaven, earth, and netherworld.[48]

The Akkadian terms most often used for heaven or sky are *šamû* and *burūmû*.[49] While *burūmû* is a term used principally for the night sky, the realm of the stars,[50] *šamû* is the term used for both the visible sky and for heaven, the place where gods dwell.[51] The phrase *elât šamê*, "height of the sky," regularly occurs in the phrase *ištu išid šamê ana elat šamê*, "from the base of the sky (i.e., the horizon) to the height of the sky."[52] This phrase suggests that the sky rests on the earthly horizons and raises up to its zenith in mid-sky.

Some ancient Mesopotamians thought that the sun returned to the eastern horizon by passing through the netherworld, bringing light to the dead who reside there.[53] Beliefs about the sun's nighttime activities, however, are inconsistent or even contradictory. The sun exited the visible sky at dusk via a door in the west. The sun then either traveled through the netherworld where it shed its light and judged the dead, or it retired to its chamber in "heaven's interior" whence it emerged at dawn to pass through the eastern door of heaven and begin its daily journey across the sky. It seems, therefore, that at least some Mesopotamians thought that the sun remained in the heavenly realms throughout the day and night and did not descend into the netherworld. The divine celestial bodies (sun, moon, and stars) pass through doors or gates as they become visible in the sky.[54] Descriptions of the celestial bodies entering the visible sky via gates are augmented by cylinder seals depicting the sun god rising between mountains[55] that are oftentimes surmounted by open gates (figures 2.2–2.3).[56] This image is verbalized in prayers to the sun god Utu:

> Utu, when you emerge from the great mountain, when you emerge from the great mountain, the mountain of springs, when you emerge from Holy Hill, the place where destinies are decided, when you emerge from where heaven and earth embrace, from heaven's base.[57]

> O Shamash on the foundation of heaven thou hast flamed forth,
> Thou hast unbarred the bright heavens,
> Thou hast opened the portals of the sky.[58]

The ancient Mesopotamians had other images of the heavenly realms that differed somewhat from the structure presented in the Enûma Elish. According to the Akkadian text *KAR* 307, the cosmos is composed of six levels: three celestial and three terrestrial.[59]

> The upper heavens are *luludānītu* stone.
>   They belong to Anu.
>   He settled the 300 Igigi therein.[60]
> The middle heavens are *saggilmut* stone.
>   They belong to the Igigi.
>   Bel sat there in a chamber on a lapis-lazuli throne.
>   He lit a lamp made of *elmešu* stone.
> The lower heavens are jasper.
>   They belong to the stars.
>   He drew the constellations of the gods on it.[61]
> On the level of the upper earth he set down the spirits of human beings.

Figure 2.2: Sun god rising between mountains and gates; reproduced with permission from Henri Frankfort, *Cylinder Seals: A Documentary Essay on the Art and Religion of the Ancient Near East* (London: Macmillan, 1939), plate XVIIIa.

Figure 2.3: Sun god rising between mountains; reproduced with permission from Urs Winter, *Frau und Göttin: Exegetische und ikonographische Studien zum weiblichen Gottesbild im alten Testament und dessen Umwelt*, OBO 53 (Göttingen/Freiburg: Vandenhoeck & Ruprecht/Universitätsverlag Freiburg, 1983), 183.

On the level of the middle earth he settled Ea his father.
. . . he did not let rebellion be forgotten. . . .[62]
On the level of the lower earth he shut in the 600 Anunnaki.[63]

The most striking feature in this text is the fact that the floor of each heaven is made of stone. The lowest heaven has a floor of jasper, a greenish stone,[64] while the other levels are blue and red. Why the ancient Mesopotamians who composed this text came up with this color scheme is not completely clear. Reiner and Pingree note, however, that "one of the results of the refraction of the light of a star or planet when the body is close to the horizon is the separation of that light into three rays—blue-violet above, green in the middle, and red below. . . . The star or planet as it sets, therefore, may appear as one of these three colors or as variegated."[65] The starry host is drawn directly on the underside of the first heaven's floor.[66] According to the Mesopotamian astronomers, as we shall presently see, the stars move across the visible sky in one of three bands or paths; from north to south these were the path of Enlil, the path of Anu, and the path of Ea.[67] *KAR* 307 notes that the stars are inscribed on the underside of the lowest heaven, but it does not mention these three paths.

The second heaven's stone floor is made of the bluish saggilmut stone. Since the daytime sky is predominately blue, this statement may indicate that the authors of this text thought that the stone floor of the lowest heaven was clear or transparent so that humans could see through it to see the blue tone of the second heaven. Otherwise, they may have thought that the greenish lower heaven is one of the lighter hues of the daytime sky when it appears as a vague light blue. The floor of the third and highest heaven is made of the *luludanitu* stone, apparently a reddish stone.[68] Why they considered this heaven to be made of red stone is not readily apparent. This heaven is where the god Anu resides and is known in other texts as a place where the other gods occasionally congregated, thus assuming that they normally resided elsewhere.[69] *KAR* 307, therefore, understands the celestial realm to consist of three layers.[70] Since divinities are settled in two of the heavens, it appears that between the "floors" of the various heavens there is an airy expanse, just as there is between the surface of the earth and the bottom of the first heaven.

That the high gods resided in the heavenly realm where they lived as kings, queens, or nobles is common to most cultures of the ancient Near East. A few depictions of the heavenly realm have survived that indicate how the gods dwelled as kings. One such depiction is the ninth century tablet of king Nabuapaliddina (885–882 BCE) from the temple of the sun god Shamash in the city of Sippar.[71] The depiction on this tablet (figure 2.4)[72] shows Shamash enthroned as king in heaven. Shamash is the large figure on the right seated on a throne that has some zoomorphic characteristics. Above his head are the symbols of the celestial gods Sin (moon), Shamash (sun), and Ishtar (star). The wavy lines at the bottom of this scene indicate water, and beneath the waters is a solid base in which four stars are inscribed. These waters, then, are the celes-

Figure 2.4: Nabuapaliddina Tablet with the god Shamash on his throne; reproduced with permission from Leonard W. King, *Babylonian Boundary-Stones and Memorial-Tablets in the British Museum* (London: British Museum, 1912), plate XCVIII.

tial waters above the sky.[73] This tablet depicts the god Shamash enthroned as king in the heavenly realm above the stars and the celestial ocean. In front of Shamash is his symbol before which king Nabuapaliddina, a goddess, and a priest stand making offerings. This scene depicts the notion that when a human stands before the god's altar, symbol, or image on earth, that person is simultaneously appearing before the god in heaven itself. King Nabuapaliddina did not ascend to heaven, but while worshipping Shamash in his earthly temple, the king, or any worshipper for that matter, mythically appears before the god in heaven.

Assyrian and Babylonian Astronomy and Astrology

Speculation on the nature and structure of the celestial realm appears in both mythic and scientific texts. Astronomy, the scientific approach, was always closely linked to astrology in Mesopotamia.[74] Astrology was one of ancient Mesopotamia's divination techniques and was used to obtain information from the gods. Babylon was noted for its astronomy, and there were several observatories throughout the empire associated with temples and cult centers where the learned astronomer-priests observed the skies, recorded their observations, and made their calculations and predictions. Since they believed that the gods made revelations to humans through nature, observation of the skies was a natural focus, given that the high gods were believed to dwell in heaven above. The Mesopotamians believed that every event in this world is somehow related to other events. In one ancient diviner's own words, "The signs on earth just as those in the sky give us signals. Sky and earth both produce portents though appearing separately, they are not separate (because) sky and earth are related. A sign that portends evil in the sky is (also) evil on earth, one that portends evil on earth is evil in the sky."[75] Thus, the compilation of astronomical omens was not a purely scientific exercise based on empirical facts in the modern sense; it was a combination of scientific observation and myth. Astronomical omens make predictions of national interest based on the movements of celestial bodies. The horoscopic texts of the seventh through third centuries BCE correlate the date of birth with an astronomical observation to make a prediction regarding the child. Since these texts predate the Greek horoscopes, this form of astrology did not come about through Greek influence but was already a part of Mesopotamian religiosity.[76] All this astrological speculation arose once the people had identified the stars with gods. Since these gods were powerful and could influence a person's or nation's life, and since they might reveal the future, so the positions and movements of the stars might be harbingers of the future. These beliefs led them to observe the skies and correlate what they saw to what happens on earth.

Astrology superimposes two different complex systems: that of the heavens and that of the collective and individual destinies of the human beings on earth. Through the observation of the heavens (and the interpretation of those observations according to a framework of theoretical, nonobservational assumptions), these systems attempt to account for the changes within the human system, which are otherwise unpredictable, unobservable, and unsystematic.[77]

While their belief in the interconnection between the celestial and earthly realms seems absurd to the modern mind, their science is an honest attempt by these ancient human beings to bring structure to an otherwise unstructured world. It was only in the latter half of the first millennium BCE (i.e., during the Persian, Greek, and Roman periods) that Mesopotamian astronomy and astrology flourished. Until the latter part of the first millennium, astronomical observations were principally for the benefit of the king and state: a priest would observe the stars and make a prediction that concerned the welfare of the king or his empire. Only later did personal or private horoscopy develop.[78]

In ancient Mesopotamia there were two forms of astronomical speculation: mathematical and nonmathematical, sometimes referred to as "observational."[79] The mathematical texts are principally tables and calculations, while the nonmathematical texts lack this mathematical format and almost always contain a prediction about the future. A considerable collection of these scientific texts that demonstrate the ancient Mesopotamians' fascination with the celestial realm has survived from antiquity. "Astrolabes" are texts that divide thirty-six stars into three groups and identify when each star appears on the horizon in the course of the twelve months of the year. The three groupings are based on the three bands of the sky ascribed to the gods Enlil (northern path), Anu (central path), and Ea (southern path). These are the three celestial zones created by the god Marduk when he fashioned the cosmos.

Anu, Enlil, and Ea he [Marduk] made occupy their places.
He constructed stations for the great gods,
Fixing their astral likenesses as constellations.
He determined the year by designating the zones:
He set up three constellations for each of the twelve months.
After defining the days of the year [by means] of (heavenly) figures,
He founded the station of Nebiru to determine their (heavenly) bands,
That none might transgress or fall short.
Alongside it he set up the stations of Enlil and Ea. (Enûma Elish iv.146–v.8)

These three parallel paths of Enlil, Anu, and Ea roughly parallel the equator and span the sky from east to west.[80] The astrolabes are written either in circular tables or vertical columns that attempt to reckon the helical rising of thirty-six stars, three each month for the three paths of the sky. These devices, then, some of the earliest tools for systematizing astronomical data, provide a convenient catalogue of three stars that rise each month in the paths of Enlil, Anu, and Ea. They also calculate how long it takes for a star to return to its helical rising point through the course of a year.

The MUL.APIN ("plow-star") series represents another group of Akkadian texts that likely originated no later than the second millennium BCE[81] and that classify the celestial bodies according to the paths by which they traverse the sky (i.e., the paths of Enlil, Anu, and Ea).[82] The second tablet of MUL.APIN closes with several omens, demonstrating again the inextricable connection between astronomy and astrology in ancient Mesopotamia, and in fact such a dichotomy between astronomy and astrology did not exist until the seventeenth century CE (i.e., post-Kepler). A seasonal solar path and the accompanying predictions based on the sun's position in the sky according to a MUL.APIN text read as follows:[83]

> From the 1st of Adar to the 30th of Iyar, the Sun travels in the Path of Anu; breeze and warm weather.
> From the 1st of Sivan to the 30th of Ab, the Sun travels in the Path of Enlil; harvest and heat.
> From the 1st of Elul to the 30th of Arahsamnu, the Sun travels in the Path of Anu; breeze and warm weather.
> From the 1st of Kislev to the 30th of Shevat, the Sun travels in the Path of Ea; cold weather.

The Enûma Anu Enlil texts constitute the definitive collection of ancient Mesopotamian astronomical lore.[84] This is a series of approximately seventy cuneiform tablets containing astrological and meteorological omens where the opening line of the texts begins, "When Anu, Enlil and Ea, the great gods, by their decision laid down the design of heaven and earth . . ." These celestial omens contain two basic elements: a protasis that describes the celestial phenomenon, and an apodosis that predicts the event signaled by the celestial phenomena. Although these texts originated in the second millennium BCE, most all extant copies come from the neo-Assyrian versions recovered from the library of the great Assyrian king Ashurbanipal (668–627 BCE). Much like the other kinds of omen texts, these texts interpret natural phenomena, here celestial phenomena, as harbingers of events on earth.

> In month 11, the 15th day, Venus disappeared in the west, and it stayed away three days in the sky. Then in month 11, the 18th day, Venus reappeared in the east. This portends that springs will open; Adad will bring his rain, Ea his floods; one king will send messages of peace to another.[85]
> If Jupiter remains (in the sky) in the morning, enemy kings will become reconciled.[86]
> If Mars approaches the Scorpion: there will be a breach in the palace of the prince. If Mars approaches the Scorpion: the city will be taken through a breach.[87]

Discerning the meaning of celestial phenomena was crucial because what took place in the celestial realm among the gods who were identified with celestial objects was a harbinger of what might take place on earth among humans.[88] The horoscopic texts used astronomical data that had heretofore been used solely in service of the king and state and applied it to ordinary citizens. While the astronomers of ancient Greece have been remembered throughout history quite appropriately for their accomplishments in astronomy, it is clear that Babylonian astronomy was also rather advanced and preceded that of the Greeks. In many ways all subsequent astronomies depended upon Babylon. In fact, the term Chaldean was used for astrologers or learned people, as is evident in the biblical book of Daniel (chapter 2, כשׂדים) and among the Greeks and Romans (Strabo, *Geography* 16.1.16).[89] Note what the first century BCE Roman architect and engineer Vitruvius had to say about these Chaldeans:

> For the rest, as to astrology, the effects produced in the human course of life by the twelve signs, the five planets, the sun and moon, we must give way to the calculations of the Chaldeans, because the casting of nativities is special to them so that they can explain the past and the future from astronomical calculations. Those who have sprung from the Chaldean nation have handed on their discoveries about matters in which they have approved themselves of great skill and subtlety.[90]

Astronomical "diaries," another form of Babylonian astronomical texts that likely date back to the eighth century BCE, are virtually day-by-day accounts of celestial and meteorological observations as well as events on earth.[91] These observations were likely the basis of the mathematical predictions of celestial events as they provided the astronomers with the raw data regarding the movements of the celestial bodies.[92] Similarly, "Star almanacs" are records of the positions of the sun, moon, stars, planets, and zodiacal constellations as they appear on the first day of each month through the course of a year.[93] Early Mesopotamian astrology focused primarily on public or state matters. Only in the first millennium did personal astrology really become widespread in Mesopotamia, and that in association with advances in astronomy. The late Babylonian horoscopes, naturally, noted the positions of the celestial bodies at the time of a child's birth and than made a prediction regarding the child's future.

> Year 77 (of the Seleucid Era, month) Siman, (from?) the 4th (day until? some? time?) in the last part of the night (of?) the 5th (day), Aristokrates was born. That day: Moon in Leo. Sun in 12;30° in Gemini. The moon set its face from the middle toward the top; (the relevant omen reads:) "If, from the middle toward the top, it (i.e., the moon) sets its face, (there ensue) destruction." Jupiter . . . in 18° Sagittarius. The place of Jupiter (means): (His life? will be) regular, well; he will become rich, he will grow old, (his) days will be numerous (literally, long). Venus in 4° Taurus. The place of Venus (means): Wherever he may go, it will be favorable (for him); he will have sons and daughters. Mercury in Gemini, with the sun. The place of Mercury (means): The brave one will be first in rank, he will be more important than his brothers. . . .[94]

The ancient Mesopotamians apparently did not have a geocentric model with seven concentric spheres circling the earth at any stage in their astronomy, a model common in the Greek world after the middle of the first millennium BCE.[95] A series of Mesopotamian medical incantations use the phrase "seven heavens, seven earths" or "heaven seven, earth seven."[96] These do not necessarily indicate the number of heavens but more likely refer to the totality of heaven and earth or to the demons of heaven and earth. Since no other clear tradition of seven heavens appears in Mesopotamian texts, it would be safe to say that the phrase "seven heavens, seven earths" must refer to something other than beliefs about the structure of the cosmos. In other words, the ancient Mesopotamians did not view the sky as a seven-layered structure.[97] The number seven in this instance must have some symbolic or magical significance.

The ancient Mesopotamians contributed significantly to human understanding of the cosmos. Their astronomical texts demonstrate the advanced state of their learning about the celestial realm. Their interests were both theoretical and practical: they wanted to know about the cosmos, and they wanted to know if somehow the cosmos had something to tell them. Since the ancient Mesopotamians regarded the planets, sun, moon, and stars as gods, it was only prudent to record their movements and characteristics carefully to see what they might reveal about the future because the gods rule human affairs. Beginning with the Persian conquests in the sixth century BCE, this Babylonian science began to interact with Persian—and, later, Greek and Roman—astronomical traditions. What the Babylonians brought to the discussion were a long tradition of celestial observations, perhaps as long as two millennia, and the beginnings of mathematical calculations of the movements of the stars and planets. The Greeks, to be sure, were the ones to perfect the theoretical aspects of astronomy, but since a good deal of Babylonian science was known to the Greeks, it can safely be said that were it not for the Babylonian astronomers, the Greek advancements in astronomy would surely have been delayed.

Assyrian and Babylonian Images of the Afterlife

The ancient Mesopotamians clearly believed that there was a life after death, but this life was lived in the netherworld, a gloomy place that had a social and political structure much like the urban life of Mesopotamia.[98] Heaven was where the high gods resided, and even the best of humans could not, in fact would not, even begin to hope to join them there. The quality of one's postmortem existence depended not on how one lived one's life, but on one's status in life as well as on how lavishly one's family provided grave goods and how dutiful they were in performing the funerary cult.

As noted above, the Gilgamesh Epic—the tale of Gilgamesh, the legendary king of Uruk, and his quest for immortality—is one of Mesopotamia's most famous literary products. Gilgamesh set out to find the source of eternal life following the death of his comrade Enkidu, a tragedy that forced Gilgamesh to face his own mortality for the first time. His journey was fraught with dangers and setbacks. Ultimately, after a long journey to the east he arrived at the abode of Utnaphishtim, the Babylonian Noah, who lived in a remote, mythical place at the end of the earth and who alone knew the source of eternal life.

Gilgamesh convinced Utnaphishtim to tell him where to find the plant that gives eternal life, and he eventually obtained it. Unfortunately, Gilgamesh subsequently lost the plant of eternal life to a snake who ate it while Gilgamesh was bathing. The disappointing but unavoidable conclusion of this myth is that death awaits all humans: "O Gilgamesh, where are you headed? You will not find the immortality you seek. When the gods created humanity, they appointed death for humanity, and kept life in their own hands" (Old Babylonian version, x.iii.1–5). These traditions about Gilgamesh originated in the third millennium and were known in Sumer, but the fullest version of the myth dates from the late second or early first millennium BCE.[99] This indicates that there was a natural anxiety about death and that these people were interested in what happened after death. They imagined some murky existence in the netherworld, as was envisioned in the myths about the descents of Inanna and Ishtar to the netherworld.

The ancient Mesopotamian myths drew on and further developed Sumerian themes, as can be seen in the general dependence of the Akkadian myth of the Descent of Ishtar on its Sumerian precursor, the Descent of Inanna. The Descent of Ishtar aptly describes the Mesopotamian view of death and what lies beyond:

> To the Land of no Return, the realm of [*Ereshkigal*],
> Ishtar, the daughter of Sin, [set] her mind.
> Yea, the daughter of Sin [set] her mind
> To the dark house, the abode of Irkal[la],
> To the house which none leave who have entered it,
> To the road from which there is no way back,
> To the house wherein the entrants are bereft of li[ght],
> Where dust is their fare and clay their food,
> (Where) they see no light, residing in darkness,
> (Where) they are clothed like birds, with wings for garments,
> (And where) door and bolt is spread dust.[100]

The peoples of ancient Mesopotamia thought that human destiny was the dark, inescapable, and dusty realm of the dead. There was no celestial heaven awaiting deceased humans according to ancient Mesopotamian thought.

Ascent to Heaven in Assyrian and Babylonian Thought

The ancient Mesopotamians considered all natural phenomena as potential indicators of the future; thus, Mesopotamian omen literature abounds. Omens portending future events come from chance events or natural phenomena such as the appearance of the entrails of sacrificial animals, deformed newborn animals, the random movements of animals, and, of course, celestial events. Dreams were also a potential form of divine revelation—a tradition paralleled in ancient Israel[101]—so they collected records of dreams and their potential meanings. These "dream books" include a couple of texts suggesting that some people dreamt of ascending to heaven or descending into the netherworld.[102] "If a man flies from the place he is standing on and (rises) toward the sky: to <this> man one will restore what he has lost."[103] This does not refer to going into heaven, but to the theme of flying through the air, a common theme in dreams.[104] Other Mesopotamian dream accounts mention dreams of ascending to or toward heaven, but these are too fragmentary to provide a complete view of what these dreams involved and portended. In these dreams, however, the person may encounter the celestial gods or notice celestial phenomena. This shows that at least in some dreams people imagined that a human could ascend to or at least envision the heavenly realm. This reflects only a human aspiration to see what cannot be seen—the realm of the gods—and not a belief that people actually can ascend into the heavenly realm.

A series of Mesopotamian magical incantations entitled *Maqlû* contains nearly one hundred incantations that were used to ward off the powers of dead spirits or ghosts who might harm humans.[105] In the introduction to the *Maqlû* series the speaker appeals to the gods for the right to ascend into the heavenly realm.[106] It seems, however, that the speaker appears not in heaven per se but simply before the gods asking them to hear his petitions. This is very similar to Isaiah 6, which recounts Isaiah's vision of the divine throne room. If Tzvi Abusch is correct in his insightful reading of this passage from *Maqlû*, then some ancient Mesopotamians may have thought that a human could actually ascend into the heavenly realm to become a star or to appear in the presence of the divine assembly.[107] It seems to me, however, that the speaker is petitioning the gods to hear his prayer or to grant him special powers, not to admit him into the divine council itself.[108]

The only clear cases of people who were believed to have ascended into heaven are two ancient Mesopotamians who lived before the Flood. The first, Enmeduranki, the seventh king of Sippar in some versions of the *Sumerian King List*, was the king of the city of Sippar, the cultic center of the sun god Shamash. He was taken up into heaven and given the secrets of the gods.[109]

> Shamash in Ebabbarra [appointed] Enmeduranki [king of Sippar], the beloved of Anu, Enlil [and Ea]. Shamash and Adad [brought him in]to their assembly, Shamash and Adad [honoured him], Shamash and Adad set him on a large throne of gold, they showed him how to observe oil on water, a mystery of Anu, [Enlil and Ea], they gave him the tablet of the gods, the liver, a secret of heaven and [underworld], they put in his hand the cedar-(rod), beloved of the great gods.[110]

Enmeduranki learned all the secrets of divination in the divine council and thereby became the source of all human knowledge about how to obtain information from the gods. The second person believed to have been taken into the heavenly realm to receive secrets is Utuabzu, the seventh antediluvian sage and apparent contemporary of Enmeduranki.[111] Since both of these characters lived before the Flood, it appears that in Mesopotamian thought only very special people who lived before the Flood could be granted an ascent into the heavenly realm of the gods. After this long bygone era, humans were for the most part no longer allowed into the realm of the gods.

Another text that sheds some additional light on the ancient Mesopotamian images of the heavenly realm is the Legend of Adapa, versions of which date back to the time of king Hammurapi (eighteenth century BCE). This story is much like the Epic of Gilgamesh in that the hero squanders his chance to gain immortality. Here, however, instead of being defeated in his quest by fate, as Gilgamesh was, Adapa was prevented from gaining eternal life by the deceit of the gods who chose not to offer immortality to humans.[112] According to this myth, the god Ea endowed Adapa with all wisdom and learning, but he did not give him eternal life.[113] One day Adapa cursed the south wind after it had capsized his boat, and the wind ceased blowing for seven days. This affront to nature was noticed by the gods and they summoned Adapa to heaven to explain his actions. The god Ea came to Adapa and instructed him on what to say and how to behave when in the divine assembly in heaven. Ea's instructions, however, were clever deceptions meant to cause Adapa to do or say things that would prevent him from gaining eternal life when the great god Anu offered it to him. As a result, Adapa would remain a mortal and be available to be Ea's loyal servant, attending to the god's every need on earth. Anu sent his envoy to bring Adapa to heaven:

> The envoy of Anu arrived.
> "Send to me Adapa,
> Who broke South Wind's wing."
> He made him take the way of heaven
> And he [Adapa] went up to heaven.
> When he came up to heaven,
> When he approached the Gate of Anu,
> Dumuzi and Gizzida were standing in the Gate of Anu.[114]

Upon Adapa's arrival in heaven, the gods immediately recognized his superhuman wisdom and offered him eternal life. Unfortunately, relying on the deceitful advice given him by Ea, Adapa rejected everything the gods offered, including eternal life. Adapa's rejection surprised the gods and lost Adapa his only chance for immortality.

> "What can we do for him?
> Fetch him the bread of (eternal) life and let him eat."
> They fetched him the bread of (eternal) life, but he would not eat.
> They fetched him the water of (eternal) life, but he would not drink. . . .
> Anu watched him and laughed at him.
> "Come, Adapa, why didn't you eat? Why didn't you drink?
> Didn't you want to be immortal? Alas for downtrodden people!"
> "(But) Ea my lord told me: 'You mustn't eat! You mustn't drink!'"
> "Take him and send him back to his earth."[115]

Although the theme of the lost chance for immortality is similar to that in the Gilgamesh Epic, instead of traveling to some mythical place at the ends of the earth as Gilgamesh did to obtain the elusive secret to immortality, Adapa ascended to heaven with the help of a heavenly being sent by the high god to escort him. Once again, however, eternal life in the presence of the gods or in the company of the other superhumans was offered but lost.[116] The words of the Gilgamesh Epic again ring in our ears: "When the gods created humanity, they appointed death for humanity, and kept life in their own hands" (x.iii.4–5). The gods' ways are inscrutable. Heaven is the realm of the gods, and even an almost all-knowing superhuman like Adapa cannot hope to find a place there.[117]

The Legend of Etana narrates another story of a human ascending into or at least toward the realm of the gods.[118] Etana was the first king after the Flood according to the *Sumerian King List*,[119] where he is called "the shepherd who ascended to heaven." Etana intended to establish a dynastic kingship to provide security for his people in the aftermath of the Flood. His problem, however, was that he lacked an heir. He intended to ascend to heaven to obtain the "plant of birth" that would provide him an heir. An eagle whom he had earlier rescued from certain death repaid Adapa's kindness by carrying him aloft.[120]

The Ascent

After he had raised him one league,
the eagle addresses Etana:
Look, my friend, at how the land seems!
Gaze at the sea, peer at its sides!
The land is high ground at the side of the mountain.
After he had raised him two leagues,
the eagle addresses Etana:
Look, my friend, at how the land seems!
Land and waters . . .
After he had raised him three leagues,
the eagle addresses Etana:
Look, my friend, at how the land seems!
The land has turned into the garden of a gardener.
The sea has become like the waters of an irrigation ditch.

The Heaven of Anu

After they ascended to the Heaven of Anu,[121]
they passed through the gate of Anu, Enlil and Ea.[122]
The eagle and Etana bowed down together.
At the gate of Sin, Adad and Ishtar,
the eagle and Etana. . . .
After he had raised him one league,
Look, my friend, at how the land seems!

> The ... of the land murmurs,
> and the vast sea is as small as an animal pen.
> After he had raised him two leagues,
> Look, my friend, at how the land seems!
> The land has become a garden . . .
> and the vast sea is as small as a trough.
> After he had raised him three leagues,
> Look, my friend, at how the land seems!
> I am looking but I do not see the land,
> and the vast sea does not fill my eyes.
> My friend, I cannot go up into heaven.
> Stop the journey, let me go back to my city.

Etana was overcome by fear at this point in the ascent, so the eagle returned him to earth. This text concerns only two realms: the earth and the heaven of Anu. One can go directly from the one to the other without passing through any intermediate places. The three places where the eagle and Etana stop to observe the earth as they ascend are not localities in heaven or intermediate heavens such as the three heavens mentioned in *KAR* 307 above; rather, they are just points along the way where the two paused to look down upon the earth.[123] All this text reveals about the heavenly realm is that there are two gates in the heaven of Anu.[124] Etana and the eagle ascended three leagues in the heaven of Anu, but there is no account of the height of this realm. The myth of Etana was very popular, and an iconographic representation of this myth has been preserved. Etana appears on the upper right-hand corner of a seal from the city of Kish that shows Etana as he rides on the back of the eagle, clutching the bird by the neck (figure 2.5).[125] Etana's interrupted ascent into the heavenly realm reiterates the theme that a vast and for the most part uncrossable chasm separates the gods "up there" from humans "down here." Humans have no place in the divine heavenly realm, and even the great antediluvian king Etana was forced to declare, "I cannot go up into heaven!"

What were the Mesopotamian images of the heavenly realm? The ancient Mesopotamians imagined the universe as a three-tiered structure: heaven, earth, netherworld. The heavenly realm typically had only one level. One text (*KAR* 307), however, speaks of three levels, each consisting of a different type of stone.[126] The shape of these heavens seems to be that of a flat disk or perhaps a dome[127] whose perimeter matches the terrestrial horizons. The Mesopotamians had virtually no idea of deceased humans dwelling in the heavenly realm with the gods, although one might speak facetiously of humans feeling so positive that they might aspire to ascend to heaven as the Babylonian Job does when he writes, "In prosperity they speak of scaling heaven, Under adversity they complain of going down to hell."[128] The Mesopotamian creation myths recount the belief that humans were not created to enjoy the company of the gods in heaven but to serve them dutifully

Figure 2.5: Etana and the Eagle; drawing by Theodore W. Burgh
after Frankfort, *Cylinder Seals*, 138–39, plate XXIVh; used with
permission of the author.

in their temples on earth. At death all humans faced the same fate, the dark
and gloomy netherworld. Heaven or a Land of the Blessed was not part of
human destiny. Very few superhumans such as Utnaphishtim were transferred
to the Land of the Blessed. Two figures who might have taken residence in
heaven were thwarted—Adapa and Etana. The heavenly realm where the
gods reside was off-limits to humans. In the words of Gilgamesh to his friend
Enkidu, "Who can go up to heaven, my friend? Only the gods dwell with
Shamash forever. Mankind can number his days. Whatever he may achieve,
it is only wind."[129] Heaven as a place for humans, so it seems, cannot be found
in Mesopotamia.

Syria and Palestine

The perspectives of the people living in the eastern Mediterranean—Syria and Palestine—on death and the afterlife and on the structure of the cosmos parallel those of Mesopotamia in many ways.[130] For our purposes, we will consider the evidence from some brief inscriptions as well as from the considerable discoveries at the Syrian coastal city of Ugarit, modern Ras Shamra. This city was a major trading center in the Late Bronze Age and came to a cataclysmic end around 1200 BCE. Excavations at this site have produced many economic and religious texts. In fact, the Ugaritic texts are surpassed only by the Hebrew Bible in providing information about the religious beliefs and practices of the peoples who inhabited the eastern Mediterranean from the mid-second- through the mid-first millennium BCE.[131] Although not formally part of Canaan, Ugarit is part of Syria-Palestine, and it appears that its citizens' beliefs share essential features with those of the people we call Canaanites.[132]

The Divine Council in Heaven

As noted above, the idea of the gods residing in heaven emerged very early, likely coinciding with the development of kingship in the Near East. The Canaanites believed that the high gods lived as part of a great divine assembly in heaven or on the heights of tall mountains. The council of the gods met to decide the fates of both gods and humans.

> There [in the divine council] the gods sat down to eat; the Holy Ones to eat a meal; Baal was standing with El . . . Then the messengers of the Sea arrived; the mission of Judge River. They did not fall at El's feet; they did not bow before the assembly in council. They stood and delivered their speech, they repeated their message.[133]

While all the gods might participate in the deliberations, ultimate power and authority resided in the hands of the chief god. The Ugaritic Kirta Epic relates that the mighty god El was once the chief god at Ugarit and that he presided over the other gods in the Counsel of El. Another Ugaritic epic, the Baal Cycle, recounts how Baal eventually rose to replace El as chief god in the Ugaritic pantheon. Among Iron Age (1200–586 BCE) Israelites, Yahweh was the chief god of the divine council (see 1 Kings 22:19–23, and Job 1–2). As several biblical texts attest (Dan. 8:16; 9:13, 21; 12:1; Zech. 3:1–7), later tradition transformed this early council of gods into angels who were created by God and who unfailingly obeyed God's every command.[134] We will return to these matters in the history of ancient Israel's religions in the following chapter.

Syro-Palestinian Images of the Afterlife

The peoples of the eastern Mediterranean believed that death and the netherworld await every human, be they humble peasants or honored royalty. In a

dialogue that echoes the goddess Ishtar's proposal of marriage to Gilgamesh—
a marriage that, by the way, would have resulted in Gilgamesh's death—the
goddess Anat offered eternal life to Aqhat, the hero of the Ugaritic Epic of
Aqhat. Aqhat, however, already understood the inescapable nature of death.

> "If you want eternal life, Aqhat the Hero,
>> even if you want eternal life, I'll give it to you,
>> immortality—I'll make it yours.
> You will be able to match years with Ba'al,
>> months with the sons of 'El. . . .
> So will I give life to Aqhat the Hero."
> But Aqhat the Hero replied:
> "Don't lie to me, Virgin,
>> for with a hero your lies are wasted.
> A mortal—what does he get in the end?
>> what does a mortal finally get?
> plaster poured on his head,
>> lime on the top of his skull!
> As every man dies, I will die,
>> yes, I too will surely die!"[135]

The goddess's offer suggests that in special cases the gods might make immortality available to unique individuals, but in principle, death was the inescapable fate of all humans. There was a postmortem existence in the netherworldly
realm of the dead, a belief shared by the peoples of the Near East and the
Homeric Greeks. "Death is inescapable; but it is not something to be dreaded.
The infernal world may be gloomy and wet; but it is a far cry from burning
Hell."[136]

After death humans move from this world to the world ruled by Môt,
"Death," the ruler of the netherworld,[137] who sates himself by consuming
humans and gods: "Death will declare to himself, the Beloved One will in-
wardly exalt; I who alone will rule the gods, Who will become fat (feasting)
on gods and humans, Who will become sated on the masses of earth" (CTA
4:VII:47–52). There is no distinction between the just and the unjust; the same
fate awaits all. As in Mesopotamia, heaven is the place where the gods dwell,
and no human would even hope to ascend there after death. Some scholars
have suggested, however, that the royalty might be the lone exceptions to this
rule. The idea of a periodic revivification of the deified kings or privileged
dead has been adduced on the basis of several Ugaritic texts,[138] but this interpretation has been justly criticized.[139] In fact, the texts show no indication of
any deification of deceased kings at Ugarit.[140]

There is one bit of evidence that at least suggests that some of the peoples
of Syria-Palestine had an idea of an afterlife with the gods. An inscription of
the Aramean king Panammu I (780–743 BCE) found in northern Syria, may
indicate that this king hoped to join his god Hadad after death. "Should one of
my sons seize the scepter and sit on my throne and establish power and sacri-

fice to this Hadad, and say . . . and sacrifice to Hadad and memorialize the name of Hadad or . . . then may he also say, 'may the soul of Panammu eat with you and may the soul of Panammu drink with you.' Forever may he memorialize the soul of Panammu with Hadad."[141] Most ancient Near Eastern kings boast of their accomplishments and express their hope of reward by receiving a long life from their god. This text seems to suggest, however, that Panammu may have hoped to join his god personally in the afterlife, although it is not clear or certainly not explicit whether this communion with the god Hadad was to take place in heaven or the netherworld. It may be that this text is simply referring to the desire to be amply nourished in the tomb. The supplies of food stuffs and the other materials of life commonly put into ancient Near Eastern tombs would indicate that these people thought the dead needed sustenance in the afterlife. "By being allowed to eat and drink with the Hadad, Panammuwa's soul would be free from the confines of the Nether World, it would not be dead but would acquire life, nay . . . real personal immortality. Such was not the normal destiny of man."[142]

Finally, an inscription on the sarcophagus of Eshmunazar, the early 5th century BCE king of Sidon, indicates that after death the deceased found a "resting-place with the shades," that is with the spirits of the deceased.[143] The dead typically descend to the underworld after death. There is no idea of suffering or of joy; they are simply living in the dark, dusty netherworld. The archaeological evidence consists of the almost uniform treatment of the dead throughout the region of Syria-Palestine in the ancient periods. At the time of burial the living provided the dead with food, drink, and material possessions that the deceased would need in the next world. As elsewhere across the ancient Near East, the Canaanites appear to have had no idea of postmortem life with the gods in the heavenly realms.

Summary and Conclusion

The idea of heaven as a place for royal, righteous, or good people was unknown to most ancient Near Eastern peoples. Humans had no part in what took place in the heavenly realm. Early Jewish and Christian ideas of humans going to heaven are for the most part indebted to Greek ideals and not ancient Near Eastern ones. For the peoples of Mesopotamia and Syria-Palestine, heaven was the realm of the gods alone, while the netherworld was the ultimate destiny of all humans. To quote from the Gilgamesh Epic once again, "When the gods created humanity, they appointed death for humanity, and kept life in their own hands." Heaven was not an option for ancient Near Eastern peoples outside of Egypt. In Egypt at first the royal and privileged might hope to ascend to the celestial realm after death to join the cosmic circuit, and during the second millennium BCE this belief spread to other levels of Egyptian society. Admission into the heavenly realm was not based on any moral code. Rather, people could hope to gain admission into the celestial realms by using the appropriate funerary rites—prayers, incantations, and secret passwords.

Heaven as a place for humans to join the gods after death was, it seems, an Egyptian invention. The view of life and death for the other peoples of the ancient Near East is best summed up by the biblical verse that says, "This is what I have seen to be good: it is fitting to eat and drink and find good in all the work one does under the sun the few days of the life God gives us, for this is our lot" (Ecclesiastes/Qohelet 5:17). One might also cite the modern version of this verse: "Eat, drink and be merry for tomorrow you die."

3

ISRAELITE TRADITIONS

The heavens recount the glory of God, the sky proclaims his handiwork.
Day to day it speaks forth, and night to night it declares. There is no
utterance nor words whose sound goes unheard. Their cry goes out
through all the earth, their words to the ends of the world.

Psalm 19:1–5

Ancient Israelite ideas about the heavenly realms developed within the context of other ancient Near Eastern cultures. Thus, ancient Israel's notions about
the sky and the realm of the gods have many parallels among Israel's neighbors. This chapter examines the Israelite materials to determine how the ancient Israelites imagined the heavenly realms. I use the term Israelite to identify both peoples of ancient Israel—the Northern Kingdom of Israel and the
Southern Kingdom of Judah. The religious ideology promoted in a majority
of the texts that now form the Hebrew Bible represent the beliefs of only a
small portion of the ancient Israelite community; the late Judean individuals
who collected, edited, and transmitted the biblical materials were, for the most
part, members of a religious tradition centered in Jerusalem that worshipped
the god Yahweh exclusively.[1] The Bible is thus a curated artifact—it contains
a selective account of history and a biased religious perspective. Here we will
look at the biblical materials afresh in order to portray ancient Israelite views
of the heavenly realm. In addition to the Bible itself, there are numerous
extrabiblical texts, inscriptions and archaeological artifacts that will contribute
to a more complete perspective on these beliefs. Since this evidence does not
come to us through the hands of the biblical editors, it sheds additional, and in
some ways undistorted, light on what the ancient Israelites actually believed.
The goal here is more than simply recreating the "biblical" depiction of the
heavenly realms; rather, I hope to represent the ideas of a larger segment of
Israelite society in what may be termed the Israelite depictions of the heavenly
realms.

Biblical Views of the Cosmos

The Bible begins with a sentence that succinctly states the biblical editors' view of the cosmos: "In the beginning God created the heavens and the earth" (Gen. 1:1). Biblical texts from all historical periods and a variety of literary genres demonstrate that in Yahwistic circles, that is, among people who worshipped Yahweh as the chief god, God was always understood as the one who alone created heaven, earth, and all that is in them.[2] Yahweh, the Israelite god, had no rivals, and in a world where nations claimed that their gods were the supreme beings in the universe and that all others were subject to them, the Israelites' claim for the superiority of Yahweh enabled them to imagine that no other nation could rival her: "So acknowledge today and take to heart that Yahweh is God in heaven above and on the earth beneath. There is no other" (Deut. 4:39; cf. Josh. 2:11). Moreover, the belief of many Israelites that Yahweh had chosen them to be a special people (Deut. 7:6, 14:2), provided them with a sense of superiority over their neighbors. Phrases such as "Yahweh, God Most High, Creator of heaven and earth" (יהוה אל עליון קנה שמים והארץ) and related phrases for Yahweh as creator and almighty master of the cosmos have parallels in earlier Canaanite terminology for the god El.[3] In fact, the Israelites did not create these phrases but inherited them from earlier Canaanite civilizations. Moreover, later editors of the Hebrew Bible used them to serve their particular monotheistic theology: their god is the supreme god, and he alone created the universe.

The ancient Israelites used the phrase "heaven and earth" (השמים והארץ) for the modern idea of cosmos. The phrase stands for heaven, earth, and all that is in, on, between and around them.[4] The ancient Israelites imagined the universe as a tripartite structure: heaven or sky (שמים, *šāmayim*) above, earth (ארץ, *'ereṣ*) in the middle, and netherworld (שאול, *šᵉ'ôl*) below.

> You shall not make for yourself an idol or an image of anything that is in heaven above, or on earth below, or in the water under the earth (Ex. 20:4). Where can I go from your spirit; where can I flee from your presence? If I ascend to heaven, you are there; if I make my bed in Sheol, you are there (Ps. 139:8)

This ancient Israelite image parallels that of their ancient Near Eastern neighbors as the following excerpt from the Babylonian myth about creation and the flood indicates.

When the gods like men
Bore the work and suffered the toil—
The toil of the gods was great,
The work was heavy, the distress was much—
The Seven great Anunnaki (gods)

Were making the Igigi (gods) suffer the work.
Anu, their father, was king;
Their counsellor was the warrior Enlil;
Their chamberlain was Ninurta;
and their sheriff Ennugi.

The gods had clasped their hands
    together,
Had cast lots and had divided.
Anu had gone up to heaven,
[...] . . . the earth to his subjects.

[The bolt], the bar of the sea,
[They had given] to Enki, the prince.
[After Anu] had gone up to heaven
[And Enki] had gone down to the
    Apsû . . .[5]

From this Babylonian text we learn that the gods divided the cosmos into
heaven, earth, and netherworld, or "Apsû," the underworldly ocean. We may
depict the structure of this tripartite cosmos as follows.

Heaven—The Realm of the Gods and Celestial Bodies
_____

Earth—The Realm of Humans and Nature
_____

Netherworld—The Realm of Gods and the Dead

Ancient Mesopotamian sources indicate that these peoples thought that the
rightful place of the gods was in heaven or the netherworld while the rightful
place of humans was on earth. A similar theme is noted in the Bible: "Heaven
is Yahweh's heaven, but the earth he has given to humans" (Psalm 115:16).
When Abraham blessed his son Joseph he prayed that God would bless Joseph
"with blessings of heaven above, blessings of the deep that lies beneath, blessings of the breasts and of the womb" (Gen. 49:25). If, as seems likely, blessings
of the breasts and of the womb signify blessings on earth, then this is another
allusion to the tripartite universe. The Ten Commandments include an injunction against making idols[6] that also identifies three cosmic realms: "You
shall not make for yourself an idol, whether in the form of anything that is in
heaven above, or that is on the earth beneath, or that is in the water under the
earth" (Ex. 20:4; cf. Deut. 5:8). The prophet Amos mentions three levels of
the cosmos when he speaks of God's power to find all who would imagine
they could hide from him: "Though they dig down to Sheol, from there shall
my (i.e., God's) hand will take them; and though they ascend to heaven, from
there I (God) will bring them down; and if they should hide on the top of
Carmel, from there I will seek them and take them" (Amos 9:2–3a). The ancient Israelite image of the cosmos, then, was that the cosmos is divided into
three realms—heaven, earth, underworld.

Biblical Terms for Heaven or Sky

The Hebrew word שמים (šāmayim) can be translated into English as either
"heaven" (the realm of the gods) or "sky" (the atmosphere or celestial realm).[7]
The term שמים (šāmayim) is related to the Akkadian term šamû and has analogs
in other Semitic languages as well.[8] Although the Hebrew term appears to have
the standard dual ending (the Hebrew word ending "-ayim" typically signifies
things that occur naturally in pairs), the form is actually plural.[9] While some

have taken this to suggest that the Israelites had a notion of two or more heavens,[10] it is better to understand the plural form as expressing the sky's vastness or expanse. That is to say, by using the plural form heavens/skies, the Israelites intended to stress the sweep or vastness of the heavenly realm from horizon to horizon. The term's origin is unclear, but one suggestion is that שמים (šā-mayim) may go back to the Akkadian phrase ša-mê, "place of water."[11] One text provides just such an etymology for the term: šamê ša-mê meš "heaven, that which is of water."[12] The phrase "heaven of heaven" (שמי השמים) also does not indicate an Israelite belief in multiple heavens. Rather, this is how the Israelites expressed a superlative—"vast heaven," or "the highest reaches of the sky."[13] Furthermore, the Hebrew phrase literally rendered "heaven and the heaven of heaven(s)" (שמים ושמי השמים), has been thought by some to indicate that the ancient Israelites imagined that there were multiple heavens.[14] Closer examination, as we shall see below, reveals that there probably was no idea of multiple heavens in ancient Israel. As a result, the phrase "heaven and the heaven of heaven(s)" (שמים ושמי השמים) is probably best understood to refer again to the vastness of heaven.[15] It is probably best to translate the phrase as "heaven, indeed the vast heaven," or "the sky, even the furthest reaches of the sky." The Israelites perceived that the heavenly realm is incomprehensibly vast (Isa. 40:12; Jer. 31:37) and high above the earth (Isa. 55:9; Ps. 103:11). It extends down to and is coterminous with the surface of the earth (Deut. 4:32, 30:4; Neh. 1:9; cf. Isa. 13:5), so when one arrives at the farthest reaches of the earth, one has arrived at the boundary of the heavens (Deut. 4:32, 30:4; cf. Jer. 49:36). The term "firmament" (רקיע, rāqîaʿ) denotes the atmosphere between the heavenly realm and the earth (Gen. 1:6–7, 20) where the celestial bodies move (Gen. 1:14–17).[16] It can also be used as a synonym for "heaven" (שמים, Gen. 1:8; Ps. 19:2). This "firmament" (רקיע, rāqîaʿ) is part of the heavenly structure whether it is the equivalent of שמים ("heaven/sky") or is what separates it from the earth.[17]

As is echoed throughout the Bible and Jewish tradition, God created the heavenly realm (שמים, šāmayim). There are a few terms used for this creating—ברא (bārāʾ), קנה (qānāh), and עשה (ʿāśāh)—but these terms in themselves do not differ greatly in meaning, and the most frequent by far is עשה (ʿāśāh). The ancient Israelites also used more descriptive terms for how God created the celestial realm, and based on the collection of these more specific and illustrative terms, I would propose that they had two basic ideas of the composition of the heavenly realm. First is the idea that the heavenly realm was imagined as a vast cosmic canopy. The verb used to describe metaphorically how God stretched out this canopy over earth is נטה (nātāh) "stretch out," or "spread."[18] "I made the earth, and created humankind upon it; it was my hands that stretched out the heavens, and I commanded all their host (Isa. 45:12)." In the Bible this verb is used to describe the stretching out (pitching) of a tent.[19] Since the texts that mention the stretching out of the sky are typically drawing on creation imagery, it seems that the figure intends to suggest that the heavens are Yahweh's cosmic tent.[20] One can imagine ancient Israelites gazing up to the stars and comparing the canopy of the sky to the roofs of the tents under which they lived. In fact, if one were to look up at the ceiling of a dark tent with small holes in the roof during the daytime, the roof, with the sunlight shining through the holes, would look very much like the night sky with all its stars.

The second image of the material composition of the heavenly realm involves a firm substance. The term רקיע (rāqîaʿ), typically translated "firmament," indicates the expanse above the earth.[21] The root רקע means "stamp out" or "forge." The idea of a solid, forged surface fits well with Ezekiel 1 where God's throne rests upon the רקיע (rāqîaʿ).[22] According to Genesis 1, the רקיע (rāqîaʿ) is the sphere of the celestial bodies (Gen. 1:6–8, 14–17; cf. ben Sira 43:8). It may be that some imagined the רקיע to be a firm substance on which the celestial bodies rode during their daily journeys across the sky. Separating these terms into discrete images is not to deny the fact that the metaphors are mixed at times. Modern scholars look for slight differences in order to classify different images, yet it is likely that the ancient Israelites held these and other images together as part of a large complex of ideas about the heavenly realms.

Biblical Depictions of the Heavenly Realms

From the beginning two points must be made clear. First, there was no one biblical model of heaven (שמים), the realm of the gods; rather, there were several, and these various depictions cannot be reduced to one, unified model. The following discussion will attempt to trace the major features of biblical depictions of the heavenly realm and try to provide a sketch of the typical features of these models. Second, by distinguishing between biblical and Israelite views, this discussion follows recent scholarly tendencies to separate Biblical Israel, the theologically-oriented depiction of Israel in the Hebrew Bible, and Ancient Israel, the broader reconstruction of the various peoples of Syria-Palestine in the Late Bronze Age and the Iron Age available from textual and archaeological sources outside of the Bible, but not excluding the Hebrew Bible.[23] In the case of images of the divine realm, the biblical model has been a focus of past scholarship, while the second, the Israelite depictions, has been largely ignored.

When humans look skyward, they see the floor of heaven, and this floor is composed of stone according to some Israelite images of the heavenly realm. In Exodus 24:9–10 one reads that "Moses, Aaron, Nadab, Abihu, and seventy of the elders of Israel went up (to the top of Mt. Sinai). They saw the God of Israel and under his feet was an appearance like a lapis-lazuli (bluish) brick as clear as the sky itself." Furthermore, the prophet Ezekiel, in his description of the divine presence, mentioned that in his vision of God he saw "above the firmament which is over their (the cherubs) heads an appearance like a lapis-lazuli stone like a throne" (Ezek. 1:26; cf. 10:1). On this throne was seated "the appearance of the likeness of the glory of Yahweh" (Ezek. 1:28). These biblical texts indicate that at least part of the Israelite mythology conceived the floor of heaven, i.e., the base of the heavenly throne of God, as stone. The Akkadian text *KAR* 307, discussed in the preceding chapter, likewise imagined the base of the heavenly realms as a stony substance. This Israelite image has, therefore, parallels in the neighboring cultures.

This is only part of the picture, for in the biblical materials there is another description of the nature of the lowest level of heaven. Genesis 1:6–8 suggests that the lowest level of heaven serves as a barricade against the waters of heaven.

> And God said, "Let there be a firmament (רקיע, *rāqîaʿ*) between the waters. Let there be a division between water and water." And God made the firmament and divided between the water which is under the firmament and the water which is above the firmament. And it was so. And God called the firmament (רקיע) "sky" (שמים *šāmayim*). And there was evening and morning, the second day.

This text does not identify the substance of which this barricade (רקיע) is made; it is simply a water barrier. The description, however, indicates that the text is referring to the immense airy expanse between the heavenly realm and the earth. Like their neighbors, the ancient Israelites thought that there was a vast body of water above the sky that was the source of the rain. The rainwater— "the waters in heaven" (Jer. 10:13, 51:16) or "above heaven" (Ps. 148:4; cf. Gen. 1:6–8)—may also be stored in heavenly cisterns (נבלים, *niblîm*, Job 38:37) or storehouses (אצרות, *ʾōtṣārôt*, Deut. 28:12)[24] alongside the storehouses for the other meteorological phenomena such as wind, snow, and hail. The Flood story recounts that there are openings or windows in the sky through which this rainwater passes.[25] "In the six hundredth year of Noah's life, in the second month, on the seventeenth day of the month, on that day all the fountains of the great deep burst forth, and the windows of the sky were opened" (Gen. 7:11; cf. 8:2). In one biblical image, therefore, the lowest element of the heavenly realm is the barricade that prevents the celestial water from pouring down on earth.

The Babylonian Creation account, the Enûma Elish, recounts that the god Marduk created the floor of heaven from the carcass of the sea goddess Tiamat and used it as just such a water barrier.

> (Marduk) turned back to Tiamat whom he had bound.
> The lord trod on the legs of Tiamat,
> With his unsparing mace he crushed her skull.
> When the arteries of her blood he had severed,
> The North Wind bore (it) to places undisclosed.
> On seeing this, his fathers were joyful and jubilant,
> They brought gifts of homage, they to him.
> Then the lord paused to view her dead body,
> That he might divide the monster and do artful works.
> He split her like a shellfish into two parts:
> Half of her he shut up and ceiled it as sky,

> Pulled down the bar and posted guards.
> He bade them to allow not her waters to escape.
> He crossed the heavens and surveyed the regions.[26]

As in Genesis 1, the base of the heavenly realm in this model is a water barrier. So, it is clear from just these few texts that both the ancient Mesopotamian and the ancient Israelite images exhibit varying beliefs about the lowest level of the heavenly realm: it was either a rocky substance (Ex. 24:9–10; Ezek. 1:26, 10:1; cf. *KAR* 307) or another substance designed to restrain the rainwater (Gen. 1:6–8; cf. Enûma Elish iv.135–41). These multiple images warn against any attempt to reconstruct *the* image of the heavenly realms for any of these ancient cultures. There was never one image but several.

Israel and the "Heavenly Hosts"

The nighttime sky has always fascinated. From the dawn of human history to modern times the celestial phenomena have inspired awe. The Israelites certainly were familiar with astronomy, and in fact a few biblical texts mention stars or constellations by name. Unfortunately, the interests of the biblical editors did not include astronomy, and so there are no strictly astronomical texts in the Bible. As will be discussed in a later chapter, the third century BCE Jewish apocryphal work entitled the Astronomical Book of Enoch (1 Enoch 72–82), as well as several other early Jewish texts, attests to Jewish familiarity with at least a crude form of astronomy. It is unlikely that Jews learned astronomy only late in their ancient history. Rather, as several texts in the Hebrew Bible suggest, there were people in Israel who were well acquainted with astronomy. It is clear that just like their neighbors, the Israelites of all periods would look to the skies and imagine that the celestial bodies were divine beings.[27] These objects dominate the skies and make humans feel small in comparison. In Mesopotamia the goddess Ishtar was identified with the planet Venus; Sin was the moon god; and Utu/Shamash was the god of the sun. The Enûma Elish (v.1–8; vii.125–31) mentions that the stars are gods, and as gods they are fitting objects of devotion. The people of Israel were no different in this matter, and several biblical texts mention the predilection of Israelites to worship the celestial bodies.[28]

> Lest when you look up to the sky and see the sun, the moon, and the stars, all the host of heaven, and be led astray and bow down to them and serve them that Yahweh your God has apportioned to all the peoples everywhere under heaven. (Deut. 4:19)[29]

> He suppressed the idolatrous priests whom the kings of Judah had appointed to make offerings at the high places in the cities of Judah and around Jerusalem and those who made offerings to Baal, to the sun, moon, constellations, and all the host of heaven. (2 Kgs. 23:5)

You weary yourselves with your many consultations. Let those who study the heavens stand up and save you, those who gaze at the stars, and monthly predict what will befall you. (Isa. 47:13)

The ancients were led to worship the celestial bodies because their livelihood depended on nature, and these objects (i.e., their size, movements, etc.) are related to seasonal changes. Moreover, it is clear that the people thought that the stars were manifestations of gods or heavenly beings. Judges 5:20, part of a poem that may date as early as the tenth century BCE and that provides insight into early Israelite beliefs,[30] mentions that during Deborah's battle against the Canaanite king Sisera, the stars fought against one another as the human forces battled on earth. The stars, therefore, are gods fighting in heaven, and the outcome of their celestial battle determines the outcome of the battle on earth.[31] Job 38:7 mentions that when God created the world "the morning stars sang together and all the heavenly beings (בני אלהים, *běnê 'ělōhîm*, literally children of God) shouted for joy." The parallelism here of morning stars and heavenly beings indicates that this author equates the stars with the heavenly beings.

The Hebrew Bible seems to know of the constellation Orion and of the Pleiades, an asterism in the constellation of Taurus. Although one cannot show incontrovertibly that the terms כימה (*kîmāh*) and כסיל (*kěsîl*)[32] refer to these two constellations, this seems to be a reasonable assumption.[33] These terms always occur together, but only in three passages.

> . . . who made the Bear[34] and Orion, the Pleiades and the chambers of the south. (Job 9:9)

> Can you bind the chains of the Pleiades, or loose the cords of Orion? Can you bring out the Mazzarot in its season, and guide the Bear with its children. Do you know the laws of the skies or establish its rule on earth? (Job 38:31–33)

> The one who made the Pleiades and Orion, and turns deep darkness into morning, and darkens the day into night (solar eclipse?), the one who calls for the waters of the sea, and pours them out over the earth, Yahweh is his name. (Amos 5:8)

The prophet Amos knew of other stars worshipped by the Israelites:

> "You will carry Sikkuth your king and Kiyyun[35] your star-god, your images that you have made for yourselves,[36] when I exile you beyond Damascus," said Yahweh whose name is God of Hosts. (Amos 5:26–27)[37]

There is, therefore, clear evidence that worship of the astronomical elements was popular in ancient Israel.[38] Although there is no textual evidence of a developed astronomical science in ancient Israel parallel to that in Mesopotamia or Greece, it is clear that the Israelites believed that these celestial elements were created by God[39] and that God established the courses of their daily and annual travels.[40] The frequent references in the Bible to the Israelites' propensity to worship the celestial bodies suggests that there was a developed astronomical tradition in ancient Israel comparable to the other cultures of the Near East.[41] For strict Yahwists, however, the celestial bodies were not gods at all but were merely objects created by Yahweh and under his control.[42]

Solar worship was a part of Israelite religiosity as it was among other peoples of the ancient Near East.[43] That the peoples living in Syria-Palestine before the Israelites worshiped the celestial elements is apparent from the basalt stela uncovered at the Bronze Age cultic site in Hazor in northern Israel that shows a pair of hands raised toward a lunar crescent or a sun disk and a lunar crescent (figure 3.1).[44] In addition to the several biblical texts mentioned above that refer to the propensity of Israelites to worship the sun and other celestial bodies, archaeologists have uncovered several examples of "sun disks" that appear to have been part of the Israelite cult of the sun. One interesting object is the Taanach cult stand (figure 3.2).[45] The four registers of this tenth century religious object depict divine beings. The first and third registers clearly depict the goddess Asherah: the first register shows her as the mighty warrior defeating ferocious beasts, while the third register represents her in the form of her cultic image, the tree. Registers two and four appear to depict Yahweh: register four represents his solar features with the sun disk riding on the back of a horse, while the second register represents his "imageless" image. That is to say, register two depicts Yahweh flanked by cherubim but he is himself without physical representation. This agrees with the biblical injunction against representing Yahweh with an image. The Taanach cult stand, therefore, depicts both the imageless and solar aspects of Yahweh. One late biblical author actually caught people in the act of worshipping the sun: the prophet Ezekiel saw people worshipping the sun and other gods within the very precincts of Yahweh's temple in Jerusalem.

> Then he (God) brought me to the entrance of the northern gate of the house of Yahweh, and women were sitting there weeping for Tammuz. . . . Then he brought me into the inner court of the house of Yahweh. At the door of the temple of Yahweh, between the portico and the altar, were about twenty-five men with their backs to the temple of Yahweh and facing east they were worshipping the sun. (Ezek. 8:14, 16)

These people were facing the wrong way and, tellingly, they had turned their backs on Yahweh and his temple while they directed their prayers to the rising sun (cf. Jer. 2:27).[46]

The phrase "host of heaven" (צבא השמים) designates the vast assembly of heavenly beings and/or celestial bodies.[47] The phrase "Yahweh of Hosts" (יהוה צבאות) identifies Yahweh as the heavenly king presiding over the heavenly pantheon.[48] Yahweh of Hosts is also a designation of God as the creator and ruler of the heavenly forces, that is, the other heavenly beings or bodies, and

Figure 3.1: Hazor Stele with hand raised towards
a solar disk and lunar crescent; reproduced with permission from Yigael Yadin, *Hazor I* (Jerusalem:
Magnes Press/Hebrew University), 87–90, plate
XXIX,2.

may even identify Yahweh with the most prominent celestial body, the sun.[49]
It seems to be a militaristic epithet that Yahweh inherited from the Canaanite
god El as leader of the divine forces at the earliest stages of the Yahweh cult.[50]
Just as the heavenly hosts in Psalm 29:1–2 and 148:1–5 praise God, so do the
seraphim in the vision recounted in Isaiah 6. Isaiah himself exclaims, "Woe is
me for I am undone, for my eyes have seen the king, Yahweh of Hosts" (Isa.
6:3, 5).

The Hebrew Bible also knows of heavenly beings called "messengers" (מלאכים,
mal'ākim),[51] or "divine beings" (אלים *'ēlîm*, or בני אלהים *běnê 'ĕlōhîm*).[52] All these
beings reside in heaven but may come to earth to act on God's behalf. The
most common of these, however, is the "messenger" (מלאך, *mal'āk*). This

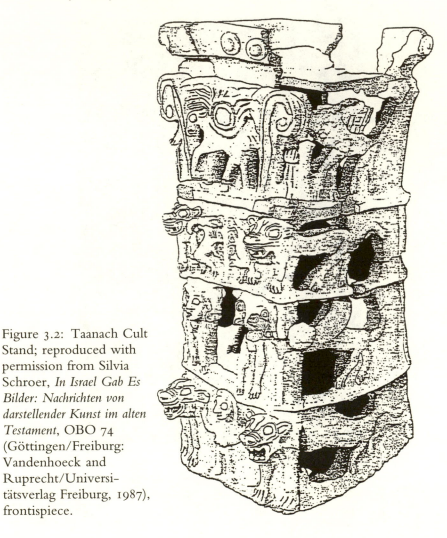

Figure 3.2: Taanach Cult Stand; reproduced with permission from Silvia Schroer, *In Israel Gab Es Bilder: Nachrichten von darstellender Kunst im alten Testament*, OBO 74 (Göttingen/Freiburg: Vandenhoeck and Ruprecht/Universitätsverlag Freiburg, 1987), frontispiece.

messenger is so closely related to God that at times they seem to merge. This messenger is the means by which God can act or be present in the material world.[53] These heavenly messengers can take human form, as the story about Abraham and his mysterious visitors in Genesis 18–19 suggests.[54] The patriarch Jacob had a dream in which he saw messengers of God going up and down on a "ladder" (סלם, *sullām*) that reached to heaven (Gen. 28).[55] The root of the term commonly translated as ladder or staircase is סלל (*sālal*)[56] and means to pile up or pave. This ladder is not a runged ladder but a stone staircase or paved path of some kind, perhaps even a structure like a ziggurat. This ladder is, therefore, a mountainous ladder much like the Ladder of Tyre, the steep coastal promontory at present-day Rosh HaNiqra on the Israel-Lebanon border. What Jacob saw, then, was a mountain reaching high into the sky. Joshua 5:13–15 describes an encounter that Joshua had with the "commander of hosts," apparently a heavenly being who was in charge of the heavenly armies that would fight on Joshua's behalf. Moreover, the distinction between this being and Yahweh is nearly lost because in Josh. 6:2 instead of the commander of hosts speaking to Joshua, Yahweh speaks to him. Moreover, just as Moses was commanded to take off his shoes on Mt. Sinai when he spoke with God (Ex. 3:5) so Joshua was instructed to take off his shoes because he too was standing on holy ground as he spoke with this commander of the hosts (Josh. 5:15).

Through the course of the biblical period, these nameless, opaque heavenly messengers began to be depicted as individuals with personal names and identities. Texts such as Psalm 68:18, Deuteronomy 32:2, and Daniel 7:10 all note that there is an innumerable host of celestial beings in heaven, but these beings receive personal names only beginning in the Second Temple Period (roughly 539 BCE–100 CE).[57] This can be seen in the book of Daniel, the latest book in the Hebrew Bible, where these beings—now called angels—appear with names.[58] This flowering of speculation on the heavenly beings during the Second Temple Period was due not simply to outside influences but to developments that had been going on within Israelite thought for some time.[59] The origin of the vast angelic orders known from early Jewish and Christian texts seems to derive both from the exegesis of biblical texts describing the heavenly entourage and from obscure cultic terms in the Bible.[60] The gods of the ancient Near East were subjugated over time in Israelite and emerging Jewish thought. The gods who at an earlier stage of Israelite religion were superior or equal to Yahweh were first made his peers, then subordinate gods, and finally angels created to serve him. These angels eventually developed independent identities and were organized into ranks.

Yahweh and the Other Gods in Heaven

Much of modern biblical scholarship assumes that Israel imported Canaanite or other foreign religious elements into its cult. "But Israelite religion did not *import* Canaanite. Israelite religion *was* a Canaanite religion!"[61] It is not surprising, therefore, to discover that some forms of Israelite religiosity have elements that would infuriate the strict worshippers of "Yahweh-alone." Israelite religion, in its early stages and even throughout the biblical period, had a pantheon with many gods, just like its Canaanite neighbors. The chief god in the Canaanite pantheon was the god El. The Israelites took some of the epithets and attributes of the Canaanite El and used them for their god Yahweh. The priest Melchizedek calls god "El the Most High, Creator of Heaven and Earth" while for the biblical patriarchs his name is "Yahweh-El, Creator of Heaven and Earth (Gen. 14:22)." This is just part of the transformation of ancient Israelite religion from its Canaanite roots to Deuteronomistic Yahwism.[62]

Many biblical texts admit that other gods exist besides Yahweh. First of all, there are the gods of the other nations: "For all the nations walk each in the name of its god; but we walk in the name of Yahweh our god for ever and ever" (Mic. 4:5). Several texts also acknowledge that there are other gods in heaven, although, naturally, these are always subject to Yahweh.

> Heaven praises your wonders O Yahweh,
>> even your faithfulness in *the assembly of the holy beings.*
> For who in the sky is comparable to Yahweh,
>> like Yahweh *among the divine beings?*
> A god dreaded in *the council of holy beings,*
>> awe-inspiring to all around him.
> Yahweh of the hosts,
>> who is like you, O Yahweh?
> Your might and faithfulness surround you. (Ps. 89:6–9)

The parallelism throughout Psalm 89 implies the identity of the "divine beings" (בני אלים, literally the "children of god") with beings in the heavenly realm. The psalmist defies anyone to find Yahweh's equal among any of these divine beings. Yahweh is so awesome that he is even dreaded among these holy beings. Moreover, Yahweh's title is "Yahweh of Hosts" (יהוה צבאות), a term also referring to celestial beings.

> Praise Yahweh!
> Praise Yahweh from heaven;
>> praise him in the heights!
> Praise him, all his messengers;
>> praise him, all his hosts!
> Praise him, sun and moon;
>> praise him, all shining stars!
> Praise him, O vast skies,
>> and waters above the sky!
> Let them praise the name of Yahweh,
>> for he commanded and they were created. (Ps. 148:1–6)

This psalm puts the hosts, the celestial bodies (sun, moon, and stars), and Yahweh's messengers in poetic parallelism. According to Hebrew poetic stylistics, such a parallelism indicates that these terms are identifying the same or very similar things—the celestial gods are represented in the celestial bodies and are regarded as Yahweh's messengers or servants. The point, of course, is to show that Yahweh controls all these powerful heavenly beings.

The Bible attests that ancient Israelites believed in the existence of and even worshipped other gods. While the late Deuteronomistic materials would go so far as to deny that these other gods are real (Deut. 4:28), several biblical texts contain allusions to the polytheistic milieu of the biblical traditions from all periods of Israel's early history. Recent trends in research on Israelite religion suggest that most Israelites worshipped a host of gods and worshipped Yahweh in forms other than those promoted by the Yahweh-alone movement. Just a brief survey of texts will be sufficient to show this.[63]

The first five books of the Bible—the Torah or Pentateuch—recount traditions about the early history of Israel's founding families, and these books include many stories about these people and their gods. Genesis 31 mentions Rachel's theft of the statuettes of her father's gods. Genesis 35:2–4 tells us of Jacob's dealing with his household's gods. The story of the Exodus from Egypt is full of rebukes to the Egyptian gods and the Ten Commandments begin with a proscription against worshipping other gods (cf. Ex. 20 and 23).[64] Exodus 32 is a classic example of how the Israelites were accustomed to worshipping many gods, and especially one in the form of a bull, the emblem of the Canaanite god El (figure 3.3).[65] The book of Deuteronomy is replete with commandments against worshipping other gods (e.g., 5:7; 6:14; 8:19; 17:13). Of course the other nations have their gods, but even these were created by Yahweh according to the Deuteronomistic editors of the Bible: "When the Most High apportioned the nations, when he divided humanity, he fixed the boundaries of the peoples according to the number of the gods" (Deut. 32:8). So, the Israelite tradition acknowledges, quite understandably, the existence of other gods. Nonetheless, Yahweh is above these gods and orders them as he wills: "For Yahweh your God is God of gods and Lord of lords, the great God, mighty and awesome" (Deut. 10:17; cf. Ex. 18:11; Ps. 86:8, 89:7).

The Deuteronomistic editors of the Bible molded their accounts of early Israelite history around the theme of religious devotion. They noted that the worship of other gods was the root of the problems during the so-called period of the Judges: "the Israelites continued to do what was evil in the sight of Yahweh, they served the Baals, the Astartes, the gods of Aram, the gods of Sidon, the gods of Moab, the gods of the Ammonites, and the gods of the Philistines. They abandoned Yahweh and did not serve him" (Judg. 10:6). This

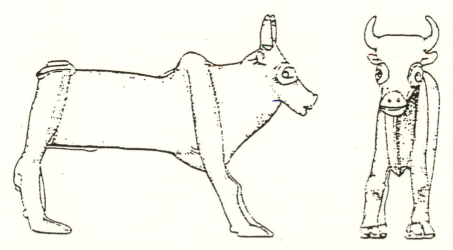

Figure 3.3: Bull, the cultic symbol of a god; reproduced with permission from Amihai Mazar, "The 'Bull Site': An Iron Age I Open Cult Place," *BASOR* 247 (1982): 27–42.

occurred during the time of Samuel as well: "Samuel said to all the house of Israel, 'if you return to Yahweh with all your heart, then put away the foreign gods and the Astartes from among you. Direct your heart to Yahweh and serve him alone . . .'" (1 Sam. 7:3; cf. 8:8). Even King Solomon, the builder of the magnificent Temple of Yahweh in Jerusalem, worshipped other gods: "when Solomon became old, his wives turned his heart away after other gods. His heart was not devoted to Yahweh his God as was the heart of David his father. Solomon went after the Astoret, the goddess of the Sidonians, and Milkom, the abomination of the Ammonites. . . . Solomon built a high place for Chemosh the abomination of Moab on the hill east of Jerusalem, as well as for Milkom the abomination of the Ammonites. And he did this for all his foreign wives who offered incense and sacrificed to their gods" (1 Kings 11:4–8). Many of the subsequent kings of Israel and Judah likewise worshipped the other gods: "after Amaziah came from attacking the Edomites, he brought the gods of the people of Seir and set them up as his gods, worshipping and making offerings to them. Yahweh became angry at Amaziah, so he sent a prophet to him who said to him, 'why are you inquiring of the gods who could not deliver their own people from your hand?'" (2 Chr. 25:14–15). The point is clear. How could Amaziah turn to seek the help of the gods of the people whom he had just defeated? If these gods could not protect their people from the onslaught of Amaziah, what aid could they provide Amaziah?

The Deuteronomistic historians, the final editors of major portions of the Hebrew Bible, went so far as to claim that the other gods were nonbeings with no power or influence: "their gods . . . in fact are not gods at all, but only the work of human hands, just wood and stone" (2 Kings 19:18).[66] According to the Chronicler (1–2 Chr.) who also follows Deuteronomistic principles, "Great is Yahweh, and worthy of great praise; he is revered above all gods because all the gods of the peoples are just idols, while Yahweh made the sky" (1 Chr. 16:25–26; Ps. 96:5). The prophet Jeremiah continues this theme: "Can humans make gods for themselves? These are not gods!" (Jer. 16:20; cf. Jer. 10:1–16). Several of the Psalms reflect an awareness of the reality of other gods in spite of the Deuteronomistic tendency to deny their effectiveness or existence: "God stands in the divine assembly; amid the divine beings he passes judgment" (Ps. 82:1).[67]

This worship of other gods besides or in addition to Yahweh persisted in the late sixth century BCE and is presented in the Bible as one of the causes for the Babylonian invasion and conquest of Judah.

> I will declare my judgments against them for all their wickedness in forsaking me. They made offerings to other gods and worshipped the works of their own hands. (Jer. 1:16)

> Do your eyes not see what they are doing in the cities of Judah and in the streets of Jerusalem? The children gather wood, the fathers kindle fire, and the women knead dough to make cakes for the Queen of Heaven, and they pour out drink offerings to other gods in order to provoke me. (Jer. 7:17–18)[68]

The worship of Baal was widespread throughout most all of Israelite history. In fact, the impassioned words of Hosea 2 express the hope that although Israel devotedly worships the various Baals, one day Israel will turn away from them. As a husband woos back the adulterous wife, so will Yahweh woo Israel back from worshipping the Baals. The rebukes for worshipping the Baals are numerous in the Hebrew Bible and extend throughout Israelite history (e.g., Deut. 4:3; Judg. 10:6; Jer. 2:8; 1 Kings 16:31–32; Hos. 2:15, 11:2). It is indeed rare when the narrators can recount that "Israel put away the Baals and the Astartes, and they served Yahweh only" (1 Sam. 7:4).

The prophet Ezekiel witnessed inappropriate worship as people within the sacred area of the Temple of Yahweh in Jerusalem were worshipping the sun—and likely other celestial gods—instead of Yahweh. That these people were able to do this within the sacred area of the temple indicates that what they were doing was at least tolerated by the priests. Furthermore, the textual and archaeological data converge to indicate that there was a vibrant Yahwistic cult that thrived outside the central temple in Jerusalem: this was the worship of Yahweh at the "high places" (bamôt) scattered throughout the country.[69] This was further augmented by *naoi* or "house shrines," a place set aside in the home for small, box-like shrines modeled after temples and other cultic paraphernalia where people would worship Yahweh and/or other gods (figure 3.4).[70] A

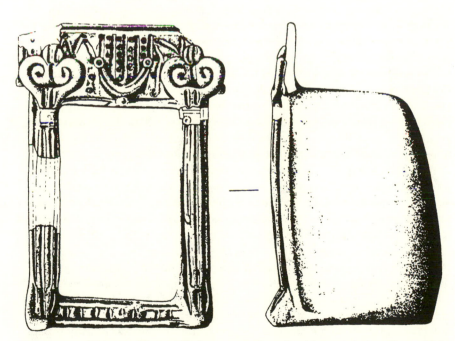

Figure 3.4: Naos or House Shrine; reproduced with permission from Alain Chambon and Henri de Contenson, *Tel el-Far'ah I: L'Age du Fer* (Paris: Editions Recherché sur les civilisations, 1984), plate 66.

close look at figure 3.4 reveals that this Iron Age *naos* has astronomical symbols. Above the lintel is a lunar crescent and four or more columns with several circles in each column. This is likely depicting the moon and several paths of stars rather like the three stellar paths of Enlil, Anu, and Ea known from ancient Mesopotamia.

The exclusive worship of Yahweh in Jerusalem was the focus of a group of people who have been dubbed the Yahweh-alone group.[71] It is important to note that Amos, the earliest writing prophet (ca. 750), does not seem to have a strict Yahweh-alone agenda. This theme first emerges with Hosea (ca. 740) and his opposition to Baalism.[72] The Yahweh-alone group forbade the worship of gods other than Yahweh and promoted a form of Yahwism that was centered in Jerusalem. The rise and ultimate domination of the Yahweh-alone ideology within the circles that came to define what was later to become "nominative" Judaism[73] took place as part of an attempt to define Judaism in late biblical and early second temple periods. The people who remained in Judah during the Babylonian Exile (ca. 586–539 BCE) went along just fine without the many Yahweh-alone Jerusalemites and others who had been carried off to exile in Babylon by Nebuchadnezzar and his army. These remaining Judeans lived according to their traditional Yahwistic practices after the Yahweh-alone officials in the Jerusalem Temple left. That is to say, they worshipped Yahweh in their homes[74] and at the high places, and likely worshipped other divinities such as Baal and Asherah. Jeremiah, Third Isaiah (Isa. 55–66), Ezekiel, Ezra, Nehemiah, Haggai, and Zechariah all represent the religious views of Yahweh-alone groups, and they continually denounce these Judeans for their religious practices. Zechariah 14:21 mentions Canaanites in the temple, and this surely identifies non-Deuteronomistic people who continued to have influence over the temple and its cult. In fact, Jeremiah suggests that the people who fled to Egypt to escape the invading Babylonians thought that the restrictive measures taken in the religious reforms of Josiah were the cause of their exile. Therefore, with an attitude that must have completely appalled the Yahweh-alone group, they vowed to continue sacrificing to gods other than Yahweh in the hope that this would reverse their misfortunes (Jer. 44:15–19).

Texts mentioning Jews or written by Jews living outside of Israel/Palestine proper indicate that these people, too, worshipped other divinities. The Murashu Documents, a collection of Persian period administrative cuneiform texts from Nippur in southern Mesopotamia, indicate that the Jews who had been transported and settled there adapted themselves to local conditions. They appear to have found employment at all levels of society. Some even gave their children non-Yahwistic names. Now this might not necessarily indicate that the parents of these children with non-Yahwistic names worshipped the gods whose names they gave to their children, but this at least indicates that they were thoroughly integrated into the social fabric of the local society. These non-Yahwistic names include elements with the names of well-known Babylonian gods—Bel, Nabu, and others.[75]

The situation is similar in Egypt where Jews settled as early as the eighth century BCE. At the island town of Elephantine located at the first cataract of the Nile, Jews settled as mercenaries in service of the Pharaoh. Jewish names here include Akkadian, Egyptian, Persian, and other elements.[76] These people also had their own temple in Elephantine, directly in contradiction to Deuteronomistic, Yahweh-alone policy. These people seem to have worshipped, in addition to Yahweh, the gods and goddesses Anat and Bethel, as well as the Egyptian god Chnum.[77]

Within the groups aligned with the Yahweh-alone movement, Yahweh was the supreme being in heaven without rival. There are other beings in heaven, but these are always subordinate to Yahweh. In fact, a strong bias in the biblical traditions would have us believe that the worship of divinities other than Yahweh was a corrupting influence that entered into Israelite religiosity from outside rather than being an element that was always an integral part of the cult, as it actually was. Part of the triumph of the Yahweh-alone movement can be seen in the fact that in the process of Yahweh gaining ascendancy over the other gods, the people used the epithets previously associated with these other gods and attributed them to Yahweh. As a result, people who were accustomed to worshipping these other gods would find an easy transition to the worship of Yahweh alone. For example, Baal is described in the texts from the Syrian coastal city of Ugarit as "O Prince Baal, . . . O Rider of the Clouds" (*CTA* 2.4). Yahweh was similarly described in the Hebrew Bible as the one who "rides on the clouds" (Deut. 33:26; Isa. 19:1; Ps. 68:5, cf. Ps. 18:10–15). The Canaanite high god El sits with his heavenly court: "El sits enthroned with Attart; El sits as judge with Haddu (i.e., Baal) his shepherd."[78] Yahweh, too, is enthroned in heaven with his court surrounding him (1 Kgs. 22:19–23; Isa. 6:1–7; Ps. 82:1; Job 1:6–12; Dan. 7:9–14).

Like El or Baal, Yahweh had a consort, the goddess Asherah. She appears throughout the Bible as a feminine deity mostly associated with trees. It appears that late in the biblical period the astral imagery of the Babylonian/Assyrian goddess Ishtar was used in Israel for the goddess Asherah. Thus the goddess came to be represented by a star.[79] Recent textual and archaeological studies have indicated that Asherah was more than simply a feminine deity. She was, for many Israelites anyway, the consort (wife) of Yahweh.[80] The "queen of heaven," probably Asherah, may have been a complex feminine deity who combined the attributes of several goddesses of the Levant and who was worshipped by Israelites.[81] Asherah, perhaps the queen of heaven, is depicted in several poses commonly used for ancient Near Eastern goddesses. When ancient Israelites imagined her in heaven, they would have pictured her in any of several images: as the nurturing mother or fertility goddess either naked grasping her breasts (figures 3.5–3.6)[82] or holding a cake in her hand (figure 3.7a–b);[83] as the mighty warrior holding her prey or mounted on a powerful animal (figures 3.8–3.9);[84] or as an enthroned deity (figure 3.10).[85]

It is very clear that Israelite religiosity was multifaceted. The biblical tradents—those people who did the final collecting and editing of the materials that became the Hebrew Bible/Old Testament—believed that there was only one god and that this god alone created and sustains the universe. This is the voice of the Yahweh-alone movement. It experienced times of prominence and times

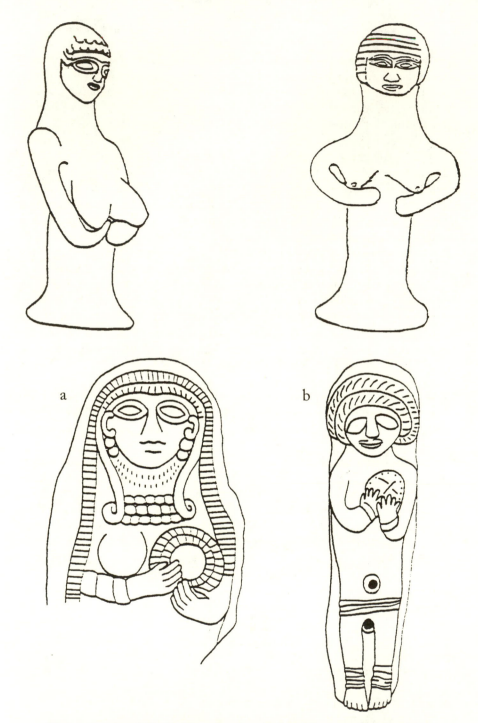

Figure 3.5: *(top left)* Goddess figurine (Asherah?); reproduced with permission from Winter, *Frau und Göttin*, 30. Figure 3.6: *(top right)* Goddess figurine (Asherah?); reproduced with permission from Winter, *Frau und Göttin*, 33. Figure 3.7a–b: *(bottom)* Goddess figurines (Asherah?) holding a cake; reproduced with permission from Winter, *Frau und Göttin*, 63.

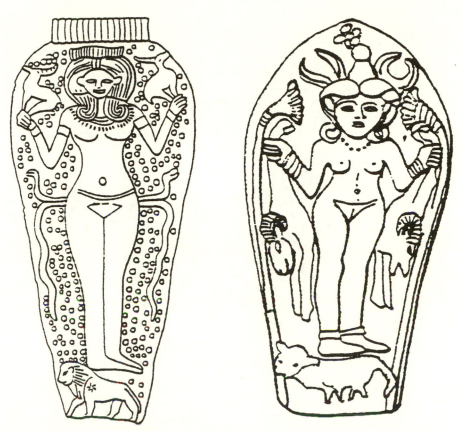

Figure 3.8: *(left)* Goddess figurine (Asherah?); reproduced with permission from Winter, *Frau und Göttin*, 41. Figure 3.9: *(right)* Goddess figurine (Asherah?); reproduced with permission from Winter, *Frau und Göttin*, 42.

of decline. It was centered in Jerusalem where it was controlled by powerful priests. Its real heyday began in the wake of the Persian conquests of the Near East in the mid-sixth century BCE. The Deuteronomistic priests who had been exiled to Babylonia after 586 further refined their Yahweh-alone ideology during their exile. In 538 they began to return to Judah with the blessings of the Persians, and they brought with them an even more militant monotheism. Because they were supported by the Persian state, these people came to control the religious institutions of the Judaean nation. As they began assembling and editing the documents that became the Hebrew Bible, they included materials that fit their own rigidly monotheistic views, and as a result, the biblical materials reflect this bias. Theirs, however, was most likely a minority opinion at that time. The majority of people who had never been exiled continued to worship Yahweh along with the other gods and goddesses, just as they had since even before the temple was destroyed in 587/586 BCE. Any attempt to understand the ancient Israelite and Judean visions of the divine realm,

Figure 3.10: Kuntillet Ajrud pithos with seated Asherah; from Ze'ev Meshel, "Kuntillet 'Ajrud—An Israelite Site from the Monarchical Period on the Sinai Boarder," *Qadmoniot* 9 (1976): 118–24 [Hebrew], and "Did Yahweh Have a Consort?" *BARev* 5:2 (1979): 24–36; reproduced with author's permission.

therefore, must include this more cosmopolitan approach to religion. Heaven, so it seems, was for most Israelites and Judeans a much more thickly settled region than the strict Yahweh-alone group could have imagined!

Yahweh As King of the Divine Counsel

The peoples of the Near East typically imagined that many gods resided in heaven and functioned in a heavenly assembly.[86] Heaven, the realm of the gods, is a dynamic place teeming with beings and activity. The chief god—whoever that may be, depending on the tribe, city, or nation—presided over this heavenly assembly. This assembly was thus a royal court with the chief god ruling as the king. The Israelites shared this imagery of God as king in the divine assembly attended by other gods.[87] The Psalmists can proclaim: "God has taken his place in the divine council; in the midst of the gods he passes judgment" (Ps. 82:1); or "Yahweh sits enthroned as king forever" (Ps. 29:10). The clearest narratives on the topic are two visions of the divine counsel in action. The prophet Micaiah ben Imlah had a vision of the heavenly assembly in which God interacts with the other members of the council.[88]

> Then he (Micaiah) said, "Therefore hear the word of Yahweh: I saw Yahweh sitting on his throne and all the host of heaven standing beside him on the right and on the left. Then Yahweh said, 'Who will entice Ahab so that he will go up and fall at Ramoth-gilead?' And one said one thing and another said another until a spirit came forward and stood before Yahweh and said, 'I will entice him.' Then Yahweh said 'How?' He (the spirit) replied, 'I will go out and be a lying spirit in the mouth of all his prophets.' Then he (Yahweh) said, 'You shall indeed entice him. Go out and do it.'" (1 Kings 22:19–22)

Micaiah saw Yahweh sitting on his throne in heaven with all the other divine beings standing to his right and left. A similar description of a divine assembly in session appears in the beginning of the Book of Job where the narrator recounts a heavenly scene as God extols the piety of Job (Job 1). Just then, one of the council's members, "the satan,"[89] or "adversary" steps forward to indict Job.

> One day the heavenly beings (בני האלהים *běnê hā'ĕlōhîm*) came to present themselves before Yahweh, and the Adversary also came in their midst. Yahweh said to the Adversary, "Where are you coming from?" The Adversary answered Yahweh, "From roaming about on the earth, and from walking around on it." Yahweh said to the Adversary, "Have you noticed my servant Job? There is no one like him on the earth, a blameless and upright man who fears God and turns away from evil." The Adversary answered Yahweh, "Does Job fear God for nothing? Have you not put a fence all around him and his house and all that he has? You have blessed the work of his hands, and his possessions have increased in the land. But stretch forth your hand and strike all that he has, and he will surely curse you to your face." Yahweh said to the Adversary, "Behold, all that he has is in your hand! Only do not stretch forth your hand against him!" Then the Adversary went out from the presence of Yahweh. (Job 1:6–12; cf. 2:1–7)

Job's subsequent misery is a well-known motif in western culture. The *Book of Job* is a late composition, and this passage, along with Daniel 7:10, 26—where the "ancient of days" sits on a throne surrounded by myriad heavenly beings—suggest that the theme of Yahweh presiding over a heavenly council continued in Jewish circles for some time. Since the Canaanite god El from whom Yahweh derived many of his epithets was imagined as king of the gods already in the Late Bronze Age, it appears that Yahweh was similarly imagined among Israelites as king of the heavenly court early in Israelite history. Fortunately, one sketch of the god El sitting on his throne has been recovered. It is very likely that some early Israelites pictured Yahweh in a manner much like this (figure 3.11).[90]

Figure 3.11: El seated on his throne; reproduced with permission from C. F.-A. Schaeffer, "Les Fouilles de Ras Shamra-Ugarit, Huitième campagne," *Syria* 18 (1937): 129, plate XVII.

According to Psalm 82, which is best understood against the background of a Canaanite pantheon,[91] God presides over a heavenly council and excoriates the other, lesser gods for not fulfilling their responsibilities. While the tenor of the Psalm clearly indicates that the Israelite god is supreme, the imagery is not far removed from a polytheistic context.

> God stands in the divine council;
>   in the midst of the gods he passes judgment.
> "How long will you judge perversely,
>   and show favor to the wicked?"
> "I had said that you were divine,
>   children of the Most High, all of you;
> but you shall die like any human,
>   and fall like any prince." (Ps. 82:1–2, 6–7)

This Psalm, as elsewhere in the Hebrew Bible, assumes that God resides in heaven,[92] or above it,[93] but that he does not live alone, for the other members of the heavenly council reside there as well.[94] In fact, one of the names that the Israelites used for their god Yahweh was "God of heaven."[95] The title god of heaven is also the name of the Syrian/Phoenician god Baal Shamayim, the "lord of heaven."[96] The title designates the supreme god of the heavenly realm and was applied to several gods in Syria-Palestine and the eastern Mediterranean. After the Babylonian exile, while the lord of heaven was Baal in one place, Hadad in another, and so forth, in Israel and for Jews elsewhere the title was used exclusively for Yahweh.[97] It was the typical epithet of Yahweh at the Jewish military colony on the island of Elephantine in the Nile River across from present-day Aswan.[98] This use of a divine epithet common among Israel's neighbors enabled the Jews of the post-exilic community in Palestine as well as those of Elephantine to accommodate their conceptions of god to their socio-religious environment. This even hints at a competitive theology: "our god is the true 'God of Heaven'!" Moreover, the title itself suggests the shift of a local, national god to cosmic levels: Yahweh is no longer simply the god of Abraham, Isaac, and Jacob, or even the god of Israel, but has become the God of heaven, ruling the entire universe. Eventually, as part of the development in Judaism of preferring not to use the divine name out of respect for its holiness, and since Yahweh lived in heaven, in later periods the term heaven became a metonym for the divine name.[99] So, rather than say "God," one could say "heaven" as in the modern phrase "heaven forbid!"

The peoples of the ancient Near East imagined that a god's temple on earth was a reflection or incarnation of the god's heavenly residence: to approach the temple of a god was to approach the presence of the god. The principle Hebrew term for Yahweh's residence is היכל (hêkāl), "palace."[100] This term is used both for a king's royal residence (e.g., 1 Kings 21:1; 2 Kings 20:18, 39:7), as well as for Yahweh's heavenly residence.[101] The Hebrew term היכל (hêkāl) is related to the Akkadian term ēkallu, "palace," as well as to the Sumerian é-gal, "large house."[102] In addition, the term מקום (māqôm, "place") is a technical term for the special place, that is, Jerusalem, where Yahweh's temple was located.[103] King Solomon's speech dedicating the Jerusalem temple in 1 Kings 8 makes an explicit link between the "place" on earth (Yahweh's temple) and the "place" in heaven (Yahweh's palace). The connection could not be any clearer: Yahweh simultaneously dwells in his temple in Jerusalem and in his heavenly palace.[104] The ancient Israelites, therefore, conceived of God as a king ruling over the universe from his heavenly palace.[105]

Although descriptions of the divine presence in the Bible and early Jewish literature have features that draw on motifs of the cult and priesthood—holy servants, sacrifices, holy place[106]—it seems that the connections with kingship and the court are much more pronounced and certainly had a long life in other ancient Near Eastern cultures.[107] Ancient Mesopotamian images of the divine presence were patterned in many clear features after that of the king. As William Hallo has noted, already in ancient Sumer a god's temple was modeled after the king's palace: ". . . the temple assumed essentially the appearance of the contemporary palace . . . once arrived at the cella, the worshipper was confronted by a life-size, seated statue of the deity looking for all the world like an enthroned king!"[108] Why did these ancients imagine the heavenly realm after the pattern of the palace of their king? What they have done is project their greatest expectations onto the heavenly realm. Since the king is the highest authority on earth and lives in the most marvelous mansion humans can design, so, they reasoned, the gods must live in similar splendor. By transferring their images of the magnificence of the royal palace by analogy onto the heavenly realm, they show that, in Hans Küng's terms, their love of this life has inspired their images of the divine realm.[109] Humans have the tendency to foist onto the heavenly realm their highest hopes and aspirations, and when it comes to the overall administrative structure, what better image could the ancients have chosen than the king and his palace? The heavenly king and his realm is analogous in almost every way to an earthly king and his realm.

The prophets Isaiah and Ezekiel had visions of Yahweh in his heavenly residence, and the imagery they used was inspired by the features of contemporary royal palaces, entirely in keeping with the perception of Yahweh as the cosmic king who rules the universe with the assistance of his heavenly court.[110] The central feature of Iron Age palaces in Syria-Palestine was the throne room. One entered this room after passing through a colonnaded entrance and then a large foyer. Figure 3.12 presents a *bit hilani*–style palace complex uncovered in northern Syria.[111] Palace J was built by king Kilamuwa in the late ninth century BCE. The entrance to this palace is marked by a single pillar just beyond which is the foyer (J1) that led into the throne room (J3). The dominating feature of the throne room was of course the raised platform on which sat the royal throne. Rooms J4–12 in the illustration are the residential parts of the palace complex. About a century later, king Barrakib built his own palace (K) adjacent to palace J, and it is another magnificent example of the *bit hilani* palace style. Seven steps lead up to a tricolonnaded foyer (K1). Beyond this is the throne room (K2) where the king could be found ruling his realm from his elevated throne. Throne rooms such as these must have been imposing sights. From just such a room in the Jerusalem palace, as we know from 1 Kings 7:1–12, Solomon ruled his kingdom. The structural form of the Jerusalem temple itself was also based on Syrian and Phoenician patterns (figures 3.13–14).[112] The entryway of the temple was flanked by pillars as was the outer foyer of the *bit hilani* palaces. The divine throne room was entered only after passing through the long main hall. As one passed through the long Holy Place and into the Holy of Holies, so in real life subjects proceeded through the colonnaded entrance and then the large entrance hall before appearing before the king sitting on his throne on a raised platform. As a king, Yahweh has a throne in heaven, and the image of this heavenly throne was certainly patterned after the cherubim throne Solomon had his Phoenician craftspeople fashion for the temple (1 Kings 6:23–28). This immense throne was placed in the Holy of Holies inside the temple.[113] The winged beings (cherubim and seraphim) described as part of the throne or as the means of transport in Isaiah 6,[114] and Ezekiel 1 and

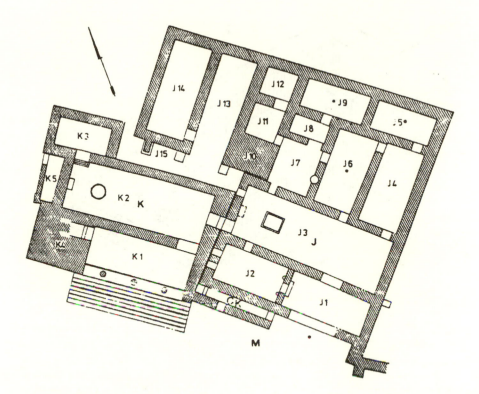

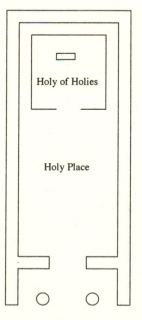

Figure 3.12: *(above)* Palace complex of kings Kilamuwa and Barrakib; reproduced with permission from David Ussishkin, "King Solomon's Palaces," *BA* 36:3 (1973): 87, figure 5. Figure 3.13: *(left)* Plan of the Jerusalem Temple; based on Volkmar Fritz, "Temple Architecture: What Can Archaeology Tell Us about Solomon's Temple?" *BARev* 13:4 (July–August 1987): 41.

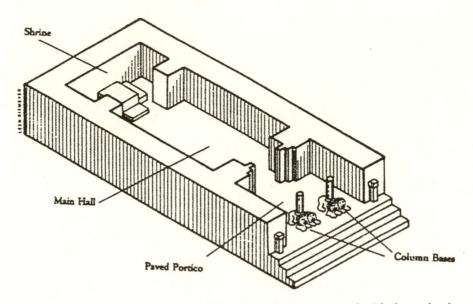

Figure 3.14: Plan of a Syrian Temple by Leen Ritmeyer; used with the author's permission.

10[115] are common features in the iconography associated with ancient Near Eastern thrones (figures 3:15–3.16).[116] Like any earthly king, Yahweh, too, sits on a winged cherubim throne (figure 3.17).[117] The throne the prophet Ezekiel saw in his vision was made of lapis-lazuli,[118] a bluish stone that was widely used on the thrones of ancient Near Eastern kings.[119] What Ezekiel saw was a typical portrayal of a god enthroned in heaven, and this image was inspired by knowledge of actual throne rooms.[120] The temple, therefore, is the palace of God as king, and this heavenly king, like his earthly counterparts, also had a royal court, the hosts of heaven.

The Apadana (hall of pillars) was the central hall in the palace complexes of the Persian kings in Babylon, Ecbatana, Susa, and Persepolis.[121] On the north and east sides of the Apadana in Persepolis are mirror depictions of king Darius (521–486 BCE) and the crown prince Xerxes (486–465 BCE) giving an audience to an official who is leading or officiating at a ceremony (figure 3.18).[122] Behind the king and crown prince stand a host of court officials, and their depictions ". . . project an impression of a rather mannered courtly intimacy."[123] The scene is of the court in session with the king receiving the tribute of subject nations. These staircase reliefs from Persian Persepolis reflect distinctly Persian ideals and present an ideal as opposed to an actual scene regarding court practice and the ideology of kingship.[124] As these scenes clearly illustrate, to approach the king, likely a rare event in the lives of most people, was a daunting experience.[125] The architecture and protocol are intended to inspire awe. The entire event, from the architecture of the palace to the attending ceremonies,

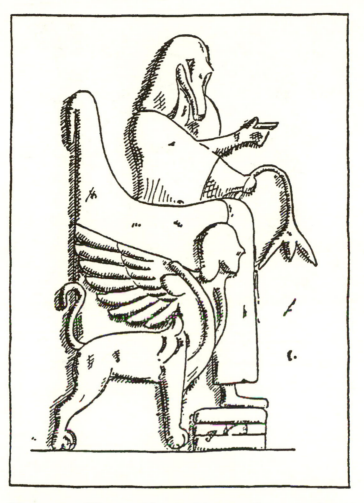

Figure 3.15: Throne with animal imagery from sarcophagus
of King Hiram of Byblos by A. H. Detweiler; reproduced with
permission from W. F. Albright, "What Were the Cherubim,"
BA 1:1 (Feb. 1938): 1–3.

was meant to convey a sense of separation between the majestic king and the
lowly subjects. The Greek historian Herodotus's description of the palace of
Median king Deioces (ca. 700 BCE) in Ecbatana and the protocol with regard
to the king captures the essence of the ideology of the royal throne room.

> He allowed no one to have direct access to the king, but made all communi-
> cations pass through the hands of messengers, and forbade the king to be seen
> by his subjects . . . whereas if they did not see him, they would think him
> quite a different sort of being from themselves. (*Persian Wars* I.99)

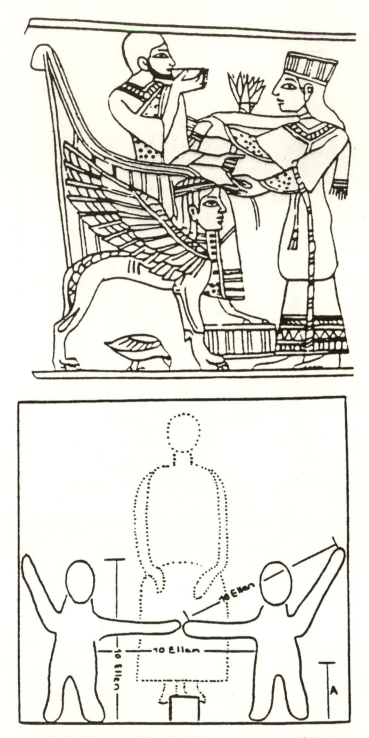

Figure 3.16: *(top)* Throne with animal imagery on carved ivory panel from Megiddo; reproduced with permission from Gordon Loud, *The Megiddo Ivories* (Chicago: University of Chicago Press, 1939); plate 4:2b. Figure 3.17: *(above)* Yahweh on his throne according to Othmar Keel; reproduced with author's permission.

In his court the king was surrounded by court officials and royal family.[126] The biblical book of Esther, set in the Persian period, also exhibits some familiarity with Persian court protocol. Several times in the book one reads of Esther fearfully approaching the king (Xerxes I, 485–465 BCE?) as he sits on his throne (4:11, 5:1–2, 8:3–4). The text relates that one dare not enter the throne room without first having been officially summoned, for not everyone was welcome in the king's presence. Moreover, people must not approach the king unless he first extends his golden scepter to bid them to come forward. The depictions in the book of Esther, then, reflect the awe-inspiring sense of what it was like to come into the presence of the Persian king. These narratives accord with the scenes illustrated on the Apadana staircases. Note, for example, that as the Persian king Darius sits on his throne, he holds a long scepter in his right hand (see figure 3.18). This may indeed be the type of scepter mentioned in the story of Esther. Moreover, the banquet described in Esther 1 accords with other known banquets hosted by Persian and other ancient Near Eastern kings.[127]

These images of an earthly king sitting on his throne approximate what the ancient Israelites imagined when they spoke of Yahweh as king. Of course God's throne was in the heavenly realm, the totally other world beyond our own. Nonetheless, their images of the divine throne room were created by analogy to the throne rooms of earthly kings. As the king was enthroned in an imposing room with all manner of attendants, so God was analogously enthroned in a similarly imposing room and was attended by innumerable heavenly courtiers. Moreover, just as Queen Esther was aware of a fixed protocol for entering into the presence of the king, so too would the ancients have been aware

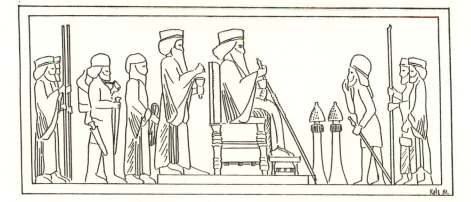

Figure 3.18: Persian Throne Room scene; drawing by Katharine Mackay after Oriental Institute photograph #P57121; used with permission of the author.

that only the properly prepared could enter into the presence of the divine king. This fact was mentioned by the prophet Isaiah in describing his vision of the divine throne room:

> In the year King Uzziah died, I saw the Lord seated on a high and lofty throne, and the skirts of his robe filled the Temple. Seraphs stood attending him. . . . And I said, "Woe is me! I am doomed! For I am a man of unclean lips, and I live among a people of unclean lips. Yet my eyes have seen the king, Yahweh of the heavenly Hosts!" One of the Seraphs flew to me carrying in his hand a burning coal which he had taken from the altar with tongs. He touched my lips with it and said, "Behold, this has touched your lips, your guilt has been removed and your sin purged." (Isa. 6:1–7)

The narrative continues with God's address to the prophet and the prophet's response. This ceremony made the prophet fit to be in God's presence. Just as Esther had to be prepared before entering into the presence of the king by going through an elaborate year-long ritual (Esther 2:12), and as the decorations on the staircases of the Apadana indicate the preparations before entering into the king's presence to pay tribute, so in his vision Isaiah had to be made fit to enter into the divine presence; that is to say, his lips were purified, his guilt removed, and his sin purged. The king was a superhuman and was not to be treated commonly. This imagery was analogously transferred to the heavenly realm when speaking of the divine.

Biblical tradition typically views Jerusalem as the city of Yahweh and the temple's cherubim throne as the earthly representation of Yahweh's heavenly throne. Yahweh is present simultaneously in both of his palaces. This is how most ancient Near Eastern peoples imagined the gods and their connection with their temples. A scene from the tablet of the ninth-century BCE Babylonian king Nabuapaliddina demonstrates that the earthly temple of a god is in a sense "heaven," or heaven on earth (figure 2.4).[128] Here the king stands before the image of the sun god Shamash as a priest and a goddess assist him in making a sacrifice to the great god. The god himself sits on his throne on the right-hand side of the drawing. That Shamash's throne is in heaven is made clear from the fact that the wavy lines below it represent the celestial ocean and underneath these are four stars. So, as the king stands before the symbol of the god on earth, he is at the same time appearing before the god in heaven in a cultic sense; heaven and earth are thus united. In fact, the ancient Egyptians referred to the Karnak Temple in Luxor as heaven on earth.[129] The images of a temple are equivalent to images of heaven because in the ancient Near Eastern mythopoetic imagination the two were not only intimately connected but were one and the same. To approach or offer prayers toward the earthly temple of a god is to approach or have one's prayers heard in the god's heavenly throne room. Just as the king listens to his subjects or their representatives from his throne on a raised platform, so the god listens to his worshippers from his exalted throne in heaven. The shrine on earth is a mirror of the god's residence in the heavenly realm. The Bible recounts stories of several shrines dedicated to the worship of Yahweh; but the one that came to dominate was the temple in Jerusalem built by Solomon, described in a dedicatory prayer attributed to Solomon that expresses a late Israelite perspective on the temple of Yahweh in Jerusalem.[130]

> Then Solomon stood before the altar of Yahweh in front of the whole community of Israel and spread out his hands toward heaven and said, "O Yahweh, God of Israel, there is no god like you in heaven above or on earth below who keeps the covenant and the loyal love for your servants who walk before you with all their heart. . . ."
>
> "But will God really dwell on the earth? Behold, heaven, even the vast heaven, cannot contain you, much less this *temple* that I have built! Turn to your servant's prayer and his plea, O Yahweh my God, and hear the cry and the prayer that your servant prays to you today so that your eyes will be open toward this *temple* night and day, toward the *place* of which you said, 'My name shall be there,' so that you may hear the prayer that your servant prays toward this *place*. Hear the plea of your servant and your people Israel that they pray toward this *place*. *Hear in heaven your dwelling place*, hear and forgive." (1 Kgs. 8:22–23, 27–30) (emphasis mine)

The phrase at the end of verse 30, "Hear in heaven your dwelling place," punctuates the rest of Solomon's prayer in 1 Kings 8.[131] This repetition indicates that though prayers are directed to the Jerusalem temple as the "*temple/ place*" where Yahweh dwells between the cherubim, Yahweh actually dwells in "heaven your dwelling *place*," and it is from there that the Israelites expect him to hear and respond. The temple is the link between the Israelites on earth and their god Yahweh in heaven. While the temple on earth is where people perform their cultic duties before God, since his presence rests there between the cherubim, his actual dwelling is in the heavenly realm. Isaiah 63:15 and 66:1–2, written in the postexilic era, are unambiguous on this point: Yahweh dwells in heaven, not in the temple on earth.[132] The focus on heaven as Yahweh's dwelling place in 1 Kings 8 and Isaiah 63 and 66, all late biblical texts, reflects a theological adjustment occasioned by historical reality: in 587 BCE the Babylonians conquered Jerusalem and leveled the temple. Although the people of Jerusalem and Judah were defeated, Yahweh was not. By capturing the temple of Yahweh in Jerusalem, the Babylonians had not "captured" Yahweh, as many of them likely thought, for Yahweh does not actually dwell in the temple; he dwells in heaven, far above the earthly realm where he remains forever unassailed as the enthroned king of the universe.

Cherubim or other beasts appear regularly as part of the thrones on which ancient Near Eastern kings sit.[133] Large versions also guard palace gateways in Mesopotamia[134] such as the winged beasts at the doorway of Ashurnasirpal's palace at Nimrud (figure 3.19).[135] Such ferocious, even bizarre beasts bring a sense of awe to the scene, and any person encountering such beasts, whether in real life as they approached the environs of the king or as they envisioned god in their religious imagination, would be struck with fear and immediately

Figure 3.19: Winged beast guarding Ashurnasirpal's Palace; reproduced with permission from *ANEP* 212, figure 646.

reminded of their humble position. Yahweh, like any earthly king, sits on a cherub throne.[136] That some Israelites imagined that Yahweh resided in heaven on a throne is evident from statements such as the following: "Yahweh has established his throne in heaven, and his kingdom is over all" (Ps. 103:19); "Yahweh is in his holy palace; Yahweh's throne is in heaven" (Ps. 11:4); "Yahweh sits enthroned forever" (Ps. 29:10b); and "Heaven is my throne, the earth my footstool. What kind of a house could you build for me, and what place could be my abode?" (Isa. 66:1). The vision of Ezekiel 1, a vision that would later inspire a vast Jewish mystical tradition,[137] portrays Yahweh in heaven seated on a chariot drawn by "living creatures" (cherubim?), over whose heads is a "firmament" (רקיע) that looks like "ice." This is a mirror image: Yahweh resides symbolically on a cherubim throne in his temple on earth with the earth's "firmament" above him, just as he resides on a cherub-driven throne in heaven with a symbolic firmament above him there.[138]

Ascent to Heaven in Biblical Thought

Two verses from the Book of Psalms summarize the biblical conceptions of the afterlife and of humans' place in the heavenly realm: "Heaven is Yahweh's heaven, but the earth he has given to humans. The dead do not praise Yahweh, nor all those who go down to silence" (Ps. 115:16–17). These verses pointedly indicate what the biblical tradents thought about humanity's place in the heavenly realm—they have no place there! In biblical thought, ever since the expulsion of Adam and Eve from the Garden of Eden, God and humans have been separated: the divine retreated to the heavens and humans scattered across the face of the earth. Moreover, as elsewhere in the ancient Near East, there is nothing beyond the grave. While people may be said to "live" in the grave, this "life" is only in the dust and gloom of the netherworld. Israelite attitudes toward death and the afterlife parallel those of their neighbors, and as one would expect, the funerary practices of the Israelites differed little from their Canaanite precursors and neighbors.[139] At death a person entered into the netherworld, that dark, gloomy mirror of the earthly world typically termed "Sheol" (שאול).[140] The Israelites believed that the dead continued to exist and that they could be either persuaded to help the living or dissuaded from harming them. As a result, ancient Israelites performed rituals in honor and memory of the dead.[141] The cult of the dead had a central place in ancient Israel, although the Deuteronomists tried to suppress this activity as part of their program of centralizing the cult in Jerusalem. For them, only Yahwistic priests and prophets were legitimate intermediaries between humans and God. They proscribed offerings to the dead (except funerary items) because this took away from revenues that could otherwise go to the "legitimate" priests and prophets at the Jerusalem temple. Although forbidden by the strict Yahwists, necromancy, or "consulting the dead," was popular in ancient Israel, and even king Saul did this (1 Sam. 28).[142] The cult of the dead was vibrant in Israel and Judah until the mid-eighth century when it drew the wrath of the religious reformers under kings Hezekiah and Josiah.[143] Necromancy and the cult of the dead were not late, foreign imports from outside Israel;[144] rather, they were important parts of the cosmopolitan Israelite cult.

As mentioned in the previous chapter, the inscription of the Aramean king Pannamu (*KAI* 214) may suggest that the dead king may have hoped to enjoy his god's care in the afterlife. This text and biblical passages such as Deuteronomy 26:14, 2 Samuel 18:18, and Psalm 21 evoke the idea of a blessed afterlife. But as Smith and Bloch–Smith have noted, "(t)he difficulty lies with whether such language reflected a real belief in a royal heavenly afterlife. With the presently known data, it is impossible to establish this hypothetical development."[145] Some have suggested further that Isaiah 26:14,19,[146] Numbers 23:20, Ezekiel 37, and Psalms 49 and 73 all suggest, and rather early at that, that the seeds of a belief in a blessed afterlife existed in Israel.[147] There may have been life after death, but all the evidence suggests that this life was not in heaven with the divine but in the netherworld or perhaps in the land of the Blessed at the mythical ends of the earth. There is no compelling reason to find in these texts a belief in a beatific afterlife in heaven with God. The clearest suggestions of an ancient Jewish belief in the idea of a beatific afterlife in heaven with God appear only vaguely in the later biblical materials (i.e., Psalms 16, 73, 49; Ecc. 3:21; Dan. 12:1–3).[148] The earliest Jewish idea of the dead joining god in the heavenly realm emerges only in the Hellenistic period (Dan. 12:2; 2 Macc. 7:9, 11, 14, 23; 1 Enoch 51:1, 61:5; 2 Esdras 7:32). It appears most unlikely that in the biblical period anyone thought they could or would ascend to heaven. Outside of Enoch (Gen. 6:21–24) and perhaps the prophet Elijah (2 Kings 2:1–2), no matter how desirable or laudatory it might seem (Amos 9:2; Ps. 139:8), ascent to heaven does not figure into ancient Israelite piety (cf. Deut. 30:12; Prov. 30:4). In fact, to intend to ascend to heaven is evidence of wickedness not piety as the prophet Isaiah noted: "You said in your heart, 'I will ascend to heaven! I will raise my throne above the stars of God! I will sit on the mount of assembly on the heights of Zaphon! I will mount on the tops of a cloud! I will be like the Most High.'" Instead, the fate of the king of Babylon is just the opposite: "Sheol below was excited to greet your arrival; rousing the shades of all the princes of the earth; raising from their thrones all the kings of the nations. All say to you, 'even you are afflicted like us; you have become like us. Your pride has been brought down to Sheol, to the throng of your victims. Worms are your bed, maggots your blanket'" (Isa. 14:9–10; cf. Ezek. 28:2, 6). And as the rhetoric of Proverbs further indicates, to go into the heavenly realm and know heavenly secrets is far beyond human ken. "Who has ascended to heaven and come back down? Who has gathered the wind in the palm of his hand? Who has wrapped up the waters in a garment? Who has established all the ends of the earth? What is his name? And what is his child's name? Surely you know!" (Prov 30:4). Deuteronomy 30:11–13 also inveighs against the idea that a human could ascend to heaven or cross to the mythical regions beyond the ocean.

> This commandment that I am commanding you today is not too difficult for you, nor is it far from you. It is not in heaven that you should say "who will ascend to heaven for us and get it for us and declare it to us so that we can do it?" Neither is it beyond the ocean that you should say "who will cross over to the far side of the ocean and get it for us and declare it to us so that we can do it?"

The passage states that God's commandments are near at hand, and that mortals need not expend extraordinary efforts to learn or follow them. The commandments are neither in heaven above in the realm of the gods, nor are they at the ends of the earth where, according to ancient Mesopotamian traditions, the supermortals like Gilgamesh reside. The general ideology of the Hebrew Bible, then, is that God's rightful place is in heaven while humanity's is on earth (Ps. 115:16; Ecc. 5:1). The prophets Micaiah ben Imlah, Isaiah, and Ezekiel all had visions of the divine presence, but their feet remained firmly on earth; they did not "ascend" into heaven.

The Hebrew Bible begins with narratives about humanity's frustrated quest for eternal life (Adam and Eve) and frustrated attempt to enter heaven (Tower of Babel).[149] In Mesopotamia the quest for eternal life was undertaken by Gilgamesh, while the ascent to heaven motif figures in the myths of Enmeduranki, Etana, and Adapa. The Bible also has two people who, like Adapa and Etana, ascended into heaven (Enoch and Elijah), and one who, like Utnaphishtim, received eternal life (Noah). Regarding what happens to a person at death, perhaps the biblical view is best summarized by the following.

> Remember that my life is a breath; my eye will never again see good. The eye that beholds me will see me no more; while your eyes are upon me, I shall be gone. As the cloud fades and vanishes, so those who go down to Sheol do not come up; they return no more to their houses, nor do their places know them any more. (Job 7:7–10)[150]

So, apart from a couple of suggestive but unfortunately ambiguous passages, the Hebrew Bible does not attest a belief that humans during life or even in the afterlife can ascend to heaven; for the biblical tradents heaven is the realm of the gods and earth is the realm of humans. The only biblical texts to suggest a belief in the heavenly ascent of the righteous are Ecclesiastes and Daniel.

> For in the matter of fate, human and animal have one and the same fate: as the one dies so does the other. Both draw the same breath. The human is in no way superior to the animal since both come to nothing. Both go to the same place—both came from the dust and both return to the dust. Who knows if a man's spirit rises upward and if a beast's descends downward to the earth. I saw that there is nothing better for humans than to enjoy their possessions since that is their lot for who can enable a human to see what will happen afterward? (Ecc. 3:19–21)
>
> At that time the great prince Michael, who stands besides your compatriots will appear. There will be anguish such as has never been since they became a nation and until that time. But at that time your people will be delivered, everyone whose name is written in the book. Many of those who sleep in the dust of the earth will awake, some to eternal life, others to reproaches and eternal abhorrence. The knowledgeable will shine like the splendor of the firmament, and those who led many to righteousness will be like the stars forever and ever. (Dan. 12:1–3)

Admittedly, Ecclesiastes is much more ambiguous than Daniel, but it does seem to at least hint at an awareness of the idea of the postmortem ascent of the soul. If this interpretation is correct, then Ecclesiastes in some sense and Daniel very clearly break with the strong biblical tradition against heavenly ascent. This deviation is completely understandable, however, since Ecclesiastes was composed in the Persian period[151] and Daniel in the Hellenistic era (ca. 165 BCE).[152] By that time many Jews had adopted Persian and Greek ideas of heavenly ascent and models of the cosmos. Ecclesiastes seems aware of the idea of heavenly ascent and Daniel adopts it. This was only the beginning, for during the Hellenistic era Jews adopted the newer images of the cosmos and the idea of heavenly ascent of the soul, and created new articulations of Judaism.

A New Depiction of the Israelite Heaven

The preceding discussion about the diversity in Israelite images of the heavenly realm calls for a reexamination of scholarly descriptions of the biblical images of heaven. The previous attempts to provide a description of the biblical views of the heavenly realm are just that—biblical; they do not account for the views of most Israelites whose religiosity was much more variegated than that of most of the biblical editors. Traditionally, biblical scholars have focused on the literary, linguistic, religious, and historical contexts. These traditional tools of biblical and ancient Near Eastern scholarship rely most prominently on the textual evidence that has survived from antiquity. These texts either have been passed on within religious traditions (i.e., the Hebrew Bible/ Old Testament) or have been retrieved from the dustbin of history by the archaeologist's trowel. We cannot, to be honest, completely understand the ancient people's views of the cosmos. Nonetheless, I think that we can, and must, attempt to comprehend at least the basics of their views of the world. The goal all scholars have in mind is to reconstruct ancient history and the behaviors, beliefs, and institutions of ancient peoples. No matter how reliable his or her techniques nor how vast his or her knowledge, no scholar would claim complete understanding of any ancient people, and this includes the topic of ancient images of the universe.

Cornelius Houtman, who has written the most extensive treatment on the "Old Testament" images of heaven has suggested that Israel had no real, integrated image of the heavenly realm but only a collection of images that expresses its awe for the power and beauty of the celestial realm.[153] Houtman's careful analysis of the biblical materials has yielded valuable insight into the various biblical images of the cosmos. Nevertheless, he has mostly ignored the comparative evidence from the rest of the ancient Near East. There exists, as he notes, not one conception of the heavenly realm in the Hebrew Bible but several images that seemingly at times conflict with one another. This does not mean that Israel had no integrated image of the cosmos that made sense to them. If they did not, they would have been unique among ancient Near Eastern cultures. Houtman further notes that recent scholarly representations of the biblical images of the cosmos are simply too western, too modern. These depictions are the products of modern minds trying to create a coherent and logically consistent system where there was none in ancient Israel. Houtman's pessimism about being able to reconstruct ancient Israelite cosmography is excessive. He is surely correct to maintain that we cannot describe their cosmographies in detail but we can outline the general features. He is further correct to maintain that there was not one cosmography but several. Perhaps the problem is just that we cannot achieve the precision in delimiting all these different images as Houtman seemingly would like, and that is why he abandons the quest. Although we may not have all the details in order, I think we must try to sketch at least the broad contours of their images of the heavenly realm.

In fact, it is common to offer such hypothetical reconstructions of ancient Israelite images of the cosmos in Bible commentaries, handbooks, and dictionaries. Nahum Sarna has offered a visual representation of how he thinks the ancients imagined the cosmos (figure 3.20).[154] What initially strikes the observer is the symmetry of Sarna's diagram.[155] Also—and this is crucial—there is (are) no god(s) in the picture. Surely this is due to the belief that God is beyond the imaginable universe or that it is forbidden to depict the divine (Ex. 20:4). Although he does not provide much of a narrative explanation of this depiction, Sarna does a good job of drawing on a wealth of biblical passages and motifs to represent the biblical image of the cosmos. Alas, Sarna's depiction of the heavenly realm seems artificial; and this may be what Houtman is warning against when he claims that the biblical materials do not provide the kinds of information that allow modern scholars to depict the biblical conception of the heavenly realm or that when used to create such a depiction these materials produce a largely modern, western image. Other portrayals of ancient Near Eastern and Israelite images of the heavenly cosmos are much like Sarna's. Alexandra Schober's representation (figure 3.21) of the heavenly realms likewise accounts for many of the items that the Hebrew Bible locates in the heavenly realms.[156] Again, however, in Schober's illustration there is no attempt to render the ancient Israelite image of the divine presence itself. Matthews and Benjamin have attempted to depict the Israelite cosmos more recently (figure 3.22).[157] Their depiction, however, lacks explanation and represents the barest minimum of the details we know about the Israelite and ancient Near Eastern views of the cosmos. They, too, fail to indicate how these ancients imagined the realm of the gods.

In addition to the more traditional fields of biblical research, one area that has been receiving more attention recently is the iconographic or art-historical context. These efforts have been largely inspired by the work of Othmar Keel, Christoph Uehlinger and the so-called Fribourg School. Keel, drawing on his extensive work in ancient Near Eastern iconography and biblical studies, has provided his own representation of how the ancient Israelites imagined the heavenly realm (figure 3.23);[158] above the cosmic ocean sits the empty throne of God attended by two flying seraphs (#2 in fig. 3.23). Keel's most important contribution, however, is in noting that the heavenly scene is repeated in the temple on earth (#3 in fig. 3.24) where again appears the empty throne of God attended by the two flying seraphs. This observation is crucial and finds a close parallel in Mesopotamia. The scene depicted on the tablet of Nabuapaliddina

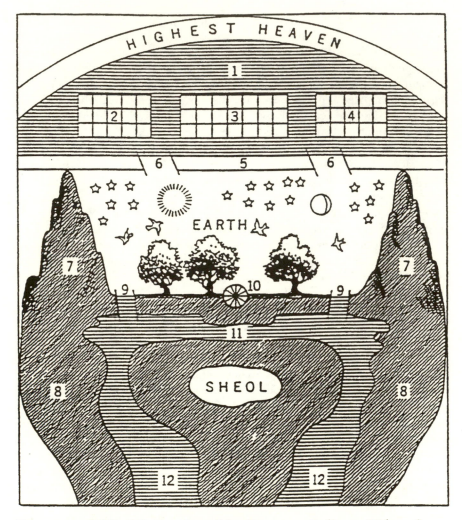

Figure 3.20: Biblical Conception of the Cosmos according to Nahum Sarna; reproduced with permission from Sarna, *Understanding Genesis: The Heritage of Biblical Israel* (New York: Schocken Books, 1966), 5.

(figure 2.4)[159] shows the priest and his cultic assistants making his offerings in the temple of the sun god Shamash in Sippar. The Nabuapaliddina tablet shows that as these people stand in the earthly temple of Shamash they are at the same time appearing before the god in his heavenly abode. This is clear from the representation of the cosmic ocean under the throne of the god and the petitioners' feet. At the base of this cosmic ocean are represented stars. The right-hand side of this scene on the Nabuapaliddina tablet, therefore, takes place in heaven. The Israelites imagined that exactly the same thing is happening when the high priest enters the Holy of Holies in the Jerusalem Temple once a year:

Figure 3.21: Biblical Conception of the Cosmos according to Alexandra Schober; reproduced from T. Schwegler, *Probleme der biblischen Urgeschichte* (Munich: 1960), plate 1.

as he stands in the Temple on earth he is also appearing before God whose actual residence is, naturally, in the heavenly realm.

Surely no one is better qualified than Keel to comment on the iconography of the peoples of the ancient Near East. Keel and his colleagues of the Fribourg School have transformed the modern study of ancient Near Eastern iconography. Nonetheless, Keel's depiction of the heavenly realm leaves one asking, "where is everyone?" That is to say, this depiction does not actually represent any divine being. His caution is surely due to the biblical injunction against representations of the divine (Ex. 20:4). The biblical injunction and the entire aniconic tradition were responding to what was a real issue in ancient Israelite society: some people were not only imagining the physical appearance of the

Figure 3.22: Biblical Conception of the Cosmos according to Victor H. Matthews and Don C. Benjamin; reproduced with permission from Matthews and Benjamin, *Old Testament Parallels: Laws and Stories from the Ancient Near East* (Mahwah, NJ: Paulist Press, 1991), 22, figure 10.

divine but they were even making physical representations of the divine! The injunction makes no sense unless people were actually doing this. What Keel has offered, then, is indeed the biblical image of the divine realm. This image represents Yahweh only in the form of the empty cherubim throne, precisely the empty throne to be found in the Holy of Holies in the Jerusalem Temple. However, it seems probable that this biblical image was not the only image that came to the minds of many Israelites.

All of these depictions depend almost exclusively on the late Deuteronomistic statements about the contents of the heavenly realm. The Deuteronomists, strict observers of the Yahweh-alone ideology, maintained that Israel must worship only Yahweh, only in Jerusalem, and only according to the dictates of the Yahwistic priests in Jerusalem. It has become clear, however, that the Deuteronomists were only one group within ancient Israel, and probably not a majority at that. If we intend to recreate an Israelite depiction, we need to consider several features that are not part of the Deuteronomistic worldview, for it seems that the Yahweh-alone theology was not the principal religious orientation of most Israelites. These features become evident as we read between the lines and against the grain of the Deuteronomistic ideology behind much of the biblical materials.

The principle feature of a more broadly representative Israelite image of the heavenly realm is that there are many gods in heaven. That the ancient Israel-

Figure 3.23: Biblical Conception of the Cosmos according to Othmar Keel; reproduced with permission from Keel and Christoph Uehlinger, *Altorientalische Miniaturkunst* (Mainz am Rhein: Verlag Philipp von Zabern, 1990), 15, figure 6.

ites worshipped more than Yahweh alone is clear at least from the prophetic indictments against such behavior and from what we can reconstruct of early Israelite religion.[160] So, to create a truly representative Israelite depiction of the heavenly realms one must first add the other gods worshipped by many Israelites. A god that can be reliably depicted and who was surely worshipped in ancient Israel is Baal (figure 3.24). In addition to Baal, archaeological evidence and a close reading of the biblical materials suggest that many ancient

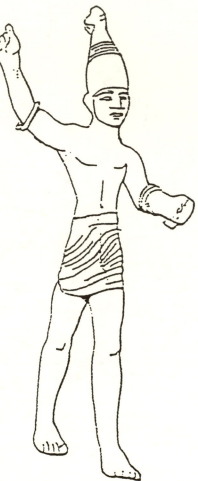

Figure 3.24: The god Baal; drawing
by Theodore W. Burgh and used with
permission of the author.

Israelites worshipped Yahweh's consort, the goddess Asherah (figures 3.5–3.10).
Israelite inscriptions from the ninth-century caravanserai Kuntillet Ajrud in the
Negev, and from the eighth-century Khirbet el-Qom inscription, suggest that,
at least for some Israelites, Asherah was Yahweh's wife.

> I bless you by Yahweh of Teman and by his Asherah.[161]
>   Amaryaw says, "say to my lord, 'is it well with you? I bless you by Yahweh
> of Teman and by his Asherah. May he bless and protect you and be with my
> lord. . . .'"[162]
>   Uriyahu the rich man wrote it. Blessed be Uriyahu by Yahweh for he saved
> him from his enemies by his Asherah. . . .[163]

Moreover, the materials from Kuntillet Ajrud may have preserved a depiction
of the goddess (figure 3.10).[164] Adding just these elements of Israelite images

of the heavenly realm reveals that the Israelite heaven was much more dynamic than the typical modern reconstructions based solely on Deuteronomistic or Yahweh-alone texts of the Hebrew Bible suggest. That is to say, we must distinguish between the limited, even sterile, images of the heavenly realm offered by Isaiah and Ezekiel and those more cosmopolitan depictions of the divine assembly presented by Job and Micaiah ben Imlah, who describe Yahweh as he oversees a vast heavenly court. Thus, there is on the one hand how many ancient Israelites imagined the heavenly realm and on the other hand what became the orthodox, or traditional, conceptions of heaven. Strict Yahwistic theology eventually took the several gods that were in the early Israelite pantheon—that is to say, the gods of the neighboring nations as well as the other gods of Israel (i.e., El, Baal, and Asherah)—and made them first of all into subservient gods and ultimately transformed them into angels, the laborers of heaven. Later Jewish and Christian ideas depend on the strictly monotheistic Deuteronomistic theology that depicted the heavenly realm with God served by a host of subservient heavenly beings. Many of the ancient Israelites would not have had such a view. In fact, they may well have thought it blasphemous to ignore the other gods in such a depiction—just as some of the opponents of Jeremiah thought that it was because they had neglected the worship of the other gods that Judah fell to the Babylonians (Jer. 44). The depictions discussed above that put only one god in heaven or those that leave out any heavenly attendants would not have been acceptable to a good many ancient Israelites.

The focal point of an ancient Israelite image of the heavenly realm would have been Yahweh, the divine king. Since some of the epithets describing Yahweh in the Bible were originally used for the god El, many have concluded that early Israelites imagined Yahweh as an El figure. If they used El's epithets for Yahweh, they likely also imagined Yahweh physically in a form that was much like that of El. Fortunately, archaeologists have recovered a depiction of El sitting on his throne (see figure 3.11). This throne has slight zoomorphic features that hint of the seraphim and cherubim associated with the divine presence in the Bible. I propose that a more inclusive picture of an Israelite view of the heavenly realm must show at a minimum Yahweh enthroned above the heavenly ocean and joined by his consort Asherah and other gods such as Baal (figure 3.25). Although they are not included here, one should also imagine a multitude of other gods—the hosts of heaven and the gods of the other nations—surrounding the throne as part of the heavenly council much like that described by Micaiah ben Imlah in 1 Kings 22:19. Such an image reflects the ideas of the multitudes of ancient Israelites who did not adopt the strictly monotheistic and aniconic ideology of the Yahweh-alone movement.

Summary and Conclusion

The image of heaven in the Hebrew Bible, the foundation document of subsequent Judaism and Christianity, is a multifaceted image. To be sure, there is a strictly monotheistic depiction that dominates the Bible. On the other hand,

Figure 3.25: An Israelite image of the Divine Throne Room; drawing by Katharine Mackay and used with permission of the author.

however, there is abundant archaeological and textual evidence to show that for some of the people of ancient Israel, as was the case for their neighbors as well, heaven was populated by myriad gods and goddesses. Judaism and Christianity inherited one of these models; the other was largely suppressed by the biblical editors and nearly lost. This was the heaven of the poly-Yahwists, the people who worshipped Yahweh *and* the other gods. For them Yahweh was just one of the gods or perhaps chief among the gods. The traditional depictions of the biblical image of heaven represent the views of the few parochial and perhaps elitist editors who curated the biblical materials into what became their canonical shape. This was the monotheistic conception of heaven that was inherited by later Judaism and Christianity and that in the course of time would become norminative. The depiction offered here should give life to the voices of those whose views were marginalized, discredited, or otherwise silenced in the course of the Persian and Hellenistic periods when what was later to become "normative" Judaism began to emerge.

The ancient Israelites, like their Near Eastern neighbors, imagined the cosmos as a tripartite structure: heaven, earth, netherworld. Also like their contemporaries, the Israelites believed that heaven was for the gods, earth for humans, and the netherworld for the mortuary gods and deceased humans. Humans, with the possible exception of Enoch and Elijah,[165] did not ascend to heaven during life or after death. Humans shared the same, inescapable fate—death and the netherworld. The netherworld (Sheol) was not a place for terrible punishments, at least not yet;[166] it was simply a dark, dusty place where one continues in a shadowy form of one's life on earth. Heaven was not the postmortem destiny of humans. Heaven was for the gods, and humans were not welcome. As Daniel 12:1–3, the latest book of the Hebrew Bible, suggests, however, this idea underwent a dramatic change as the Jews began to interact more intimately with the Persians and Greeks.

4

PERSIAN, GREEK, AND
ROMAN TRADITIONS

But looking at the stars makes me dream as simply as I dream over the black
dots representing towns and villages on a map. Why, I ask myself, should
the shining dots of the sky not be as accessible as the black dots on the map
of France? As we take the train to get to Tarascon or Rouen, so we take
death to come to a star. There is one thing certainly true in this reasoning,
namely that we while still alive cannot get to a star no more than we when
dead can take the train.

Vincent van Gogh, Letter to Theo, 1888 (#506)

A shift took place in Jewish views of the universe in the period from Cyrus the
Great to Alexander the Great (ca. 540–333 BCE). This transformation occurred
because of the new ideas that were imported into Syria-Palestine by the Persians and Greeks in the wake of their conquests of the region. To be sure, the
Jews were not alone as the entire Mediterranean, Egyptian, and Mesopotamian
civilizations experienced similar transformations. The old ways of defining and
describing the universe and how humans relate to it and to the gods gave way
to new formulations. The cosmos became vastly larger and the gods seemingly
more transcendent. Such transformations have been termed "Axial Age Breakthroughs."[1] For Jews, this meant creating new ways to imagine their God, to
conceive of their place in the world, to understand the flow and direction of
history, and to interact with neighboring peoples. Their reconceptualizations
of the heavenly realm fit within this process of evolving self-understanding. In
this new, increasingly cosmopolitan world, their image of heaven transformed
to fit this new world order, and they—most likely only the *literati* at first—
sought to bridge the chasm between this world and the totally other, transcendent realm of the divine.

Astronomy and the "Scientific" Views of the Heavenly Realm

Greece

Sometime around the middle of the first millennium BCE, the Mesopotamian astronomical speculations discussed in chapter 2 spread westward.[2] This interest then, if not even earlier, diffused across the Near East and Greek world along with the spread of Hellenistic culture.[3] All Babylonian astronomy presupposed a flat earth and either did not recognize or ignored the influence of latitude on celestial observation. To notice the difference in the rise and set azimuths of the sun and moon, one would need to travel over 110 miles due north or south and remain there for some time to make observations. For the rise and set azimuths of the stars, one would need to travel over 660 miles due north or south. Since Greek astronomical observations were spread across a vast empire that extended from Europe to North Africa,[4] comparing and compiling observations from such different latitudes enabled the Greeks to develop the idea of a spherical earth that could account better for the variety in stellar observations. The Greeks made significant, lasting contributions to astronomy. Although he might be charged with overstatement, Otto Neugebauer, well known for his work on the history of ancient sciences, has made the following claim: "Up to Newton all astronomy consists in modifications, however ingenious, of Hellenistic astronomy."[5]

Greek astronomical thought in the Homeric Age (ca. 1200–700 BCE) as attested in Homer's *Iliad* and *Odyssey* as well as in Hesiod's *Works and Days* and *Theogony* conceived of the earth as a flat land mass encircled by water, the "Okeanus."[6] The celestial bodies rose in the eastern part of Okeanus, ran their daily courses through the sky, and in the evening descended into the western part of Okeanus. Thus, the earliest Greek conceptions of the universe were very much like those of the peoples of the Fertile Crescent. The Ionian philosophers of the pre-Socratic Age (i.e., those who lived on the western coast of modern-day Turkey from ca. 600–400 BCE) broke away from the mythological thought that characterized all preceding Greek philosophy. These scholars sought to explain the origin and development of the universe in physical terms as opposed to the mythological explanations of their predecessors and contemporaries. Generally, these scholars believed that the earth was flat and surrounded by air in the middle of the universe. The heavenly bodies move as they do because they are fixed to a sphere that encircles the earth. One of the first of these philosophers, Thales (ca. 624–547 BCE), viewed the earth after a model that closely resembles those of the Mesopotamians and Egyptians—a land mass completely surrounded by water. Anaximander (ca. 611–547 BCE), a student of Thales, described the earth as a flat cylinder suspended freely in the center of the universe with all the heavenly bodies rotating around it in three orbits: the stars nearest, the moon in the middle, and the sun farthest away. Anaximenes (ca. 585–526 BCE), a student of Anaximander, maintained that the earth was a flat disk supported in the middle of the universe on air and that some heavenly bodies (i.e., sun, moon, and planets) ride through the air while others (i.e., the fixed stars) were affixed "like nails" to a crystalline vault above the earth. These three astronomers were all from the town of Miletus on the western coast of modern-day Turkey. They made significant advances, but for them the earth was flat and the stars were affixed to a celestial vault. In other words, they did not advance much beyond ancient Near Eastern models.

The famous philosopher Pythagoras (ca. 575–500 BCE) was born on the island of Samos slightly south of Miletus.[7] He eventually moved to southern Italy where he founded a school that lasted for nearly two hundred years. According to his mathematical construction of the universe, he and his followers, the Pythagoreans, imagined the earth, the heavenly bodies, and the universe itself to be spherical. All these exist and move in harmony, producing sounds as they move. Humans are unable to hear these sounds because they have tuned them out through the years and because these sounds have become obscured by the sounds of everyday life.[8] The Pythagoreans also introduced, along with the Orphics, the idea of the immortality of the soul, an idea that was later widely popularized by Plato.[9] After death the immortal soul attempts to reunite itself with the universal soul from which it originated in the heavenly realm. This contribution would eventually evolve into the idea that humans themselves have a place in the heavenly, immortal realm. Likely speaking of the Orphics or the Pythagoreans, Plato writes: "They say that the human soul is immortal. At one time it comes to an end, which they call dying, at another time it is reborn, but it never perishes; therefore one must live one's life as piously as possible (*Meno*, 81b)."

Anaxagoras (ca. 500–428 BCE) took his place in the history of astronomy by discovering that the moon was illuminated by the sun. He seems to be the first to have arranged the planets in the following order from the earth: moon, sun, the five planets (Venus, Mercury, Mars, Jupiter, and Saturn), and the fixed stars.[10] The universe consisted initially of air and ether. The ether was the lighter, drier, hotter, rarer substance found at the extremity of the universe while the air further divided or condensed and became matter—water, clouds, soil, and rocks. The celestial bodies travel about in the ether far away from the earthly realm and continue their movements under the flat earth that itself is suspended in the center of the universe. Eventually, Philolaus (end of the fifth century BCE), one of the Pythagoreans, introduced an entirely different conception of the universe that was in some ways a precursor to the Copernican model. His theory proposed that at the center of the universe was an immense fire, the "Hearth of the Universe" (ἑστία τοῦ παντός). This fire rests in the center of the limitless universe, and the earth as well as the rest of the heavenly bodies all orbit around this central fire in the following order: "the counter-earth" (ἀντίχθων), earth, moon, sun, the five planets,[11] and finally the fixed stars (figure 4.1). The central hearth and counterearth cannot be seen from earth because the surface of the earth is always pointed away from them out toward the stars and planets that reflect light emanating from the central hearth. As one can readily see, this system displaces the earth from the center of the universe, a remarkable theory in its day. Although we today find the central hearth and the counterearth

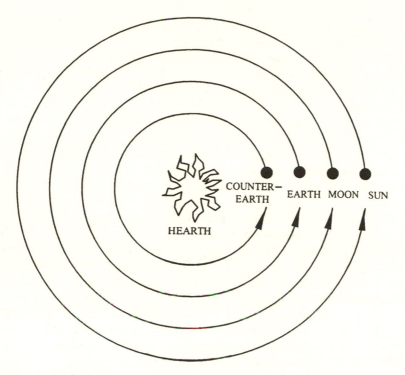

Figure 4.1: Pythagorean cosmos; drawing by Farzad Nakhai and used with permission of the author.

to be curious oddities, they were revolutionary ideas in Philolaus's days. This system did not, however, find many adherents outside of the Pythagorean school.

Plato (ca. 427–347 BCE) followed the early Pythagoreans in describing the earth as a sphere (*Phaedo*) around which revolved, each in its own orbit, the moon, sun, Venus, Mercury, Mars, Jupiter, Saturn, and finally the fixed stars.[12] Plato described the harmonious workings of the cosmic machine in book 10 of his *Republic*, but he offered more details on the nature and movements of the celestial bodies in the *Timmaeus*. Plato's cosmography was purely geocentric with each of the seven celestial bodies traveling alone in its own simple orbit around the earth. Eudoxus of Cnidos in Asia Minor (ca. 408–355 BCE), a brilliant mathematician and a younger contemporary of Plato, was the first to move beyond the model of the Pythagoreans and mere philosophical reasoning to propose a theoretical, geometrical model wherein the various heavenly bodies encircle the earth each in its own sphere.[13] Thus, he theorized that there were several concentric spheres encircling the earth that account for the movements of the celestial bodies. The celestial bodies were fixed in the center of their respective spheres, but Eudoxus added additional intervening spheres between the spheres housing the celestial bodies themselves. The total number of spheres in his system was twenty-seven (three each for sun and moon, four each for the five planets, and one for the fixed stars). According to this complex system, the sphere housing a celestial body is immediately surrounded by blank spheres rotating at different speeds and in different directions. All these intervening spheres allow each celestial body to follow its own path at its own speed without being affected by the movement of the next orbiting body.[14]

Aristotle (ca. 384–322 BCE) wrote a four-volume treatise entitled "On the Heavens" that deals with our subject, but only the second volume deals with the structure of the cosmos and the movements of the celestial bodies.[15] Aristotle generally adopted the system of Eudoxus but transformed it from a theoretical model into an actual physical mechanism.[16] Moreover, to improve upon the movements of the celestial bodies in the Eudoxian model, Aristotle added to it an additional number of intervening spheres, bringing their total to fifty-five.[17] The celestial bodies remain stationary in their spheres and move only as the sphere itself rotates around the earth. Since the actual rotation of these now physical spheres would affect the rotation of the adjoining spheres, Aristotle added additional spheres to Eudoxus's model to account for the different speeds and directions in which the celestial bodies move. Aristotle's additional "reacting" spheres allow the physical system to work without interference between the several celestial spheres: the empty spheres between the spheres housing the celestial bodies act as differentials, enabling each celestial body to rotate at its own speed.

For Aristotle the divine sphere was the farthest away from the earth that itself sat at rest in the center of the cosmos. "As far back as human tradition goes there has never been any change in the outermost heaven or any of its parts. The upper region, therefore, already in ancient times was called ether (αἰθήρ) because it "always runs" (ἀεὶ θεῖ)."[18] According to Aristotle, the heavenly realm—the ethereal realm from the vast outer limits of the universe down to the level of the moon—is characterized by perfection and unchanging order. Each lower realm suffers from increasing disorder and corruption.[19] In his understanding, therefore, the earth was the realm where imperfection, impurity, and disorder reigned, while the heavenly realm was perfect, pure, and entirely orderly. Aristotle's physical explanation comports completely with his metaphysical understanding of the universe. The gods ultimately reside in the ethereal realm of purity and stasis, while humans dwell in the impure and chaotic realm, earth.

Even though it is popularly associated with the work of sixteenth-century scholar Nicolaus Copernicus,[20] the heliocentric view of the cosmos was actually developed by ancient Greeks.[21] This theory was propounded as early as the fourth century BCE by Aristarchus of Samos (ca. 310–230). Aristarchus proposed that the sun was the center of the universe and around it revolved all the other celestial bodies including the earth. The theory was as revolutionary in his day as it was some seventeen hundred years later in Copernicus's day, and because of it Aristarchus was charged with impiety by Cleanthes the Stoic.

> Aristarchus of Samos published a book of certain hypotheses from which he concludes that the cosmos is very much larger than it is now imagined to be.

He hypothesizes that the fixed stars and the sun remain motionless, that the earth revolves around the sun in a circular orbit, that the sun sits at the center of the circuit, and that the sphere of the fixed stars, set on the same center point as the sun, is of such great size that the circle in which he hypothesizes the earth to revolve is as comparable in distance to the fixed stars as the center point of the sphere is to the [earth's] surface.[22]

Unfortunately for Aristarchus, the geocentric model with its surrounding concentric circles as propounded by the Platonists, Aristotelians, and Stoics continued as the dominant view of the cosmos.

The peoples of the Near East interacted with these "scientific" developments. That some of these peoples adapted their speculations about the structure of the cosmos is pointedly demonstrated by a depiction of the goddess Nut from the Ptolemaic period (ca. 304–30 BCE). This depiction presents the goddess twice as she bends over the earth (figure 4.2).[23] The Egyptians of the Ptolemaic period, as part of their attempt to blend native Egyptian and Greek myths, took ancient Egyptian customs, beliefs, and motifs and tried to wed them to Hellenistic modes of expression. They were at least partially successful in this attempt of "Egypto-Greek symbiosis."[24] Figure 4.2 represents the

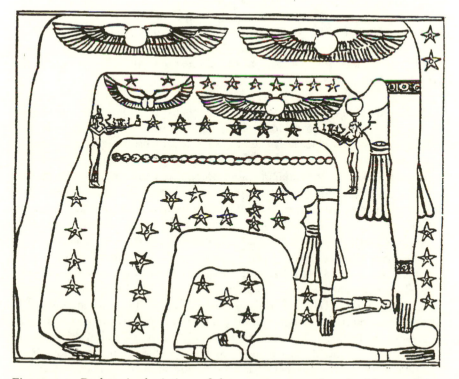

Figure 4.2: Ptolemaic depiction of the cosmos; reproduced with permission from Keel, *Symbolism of the Biblical World*, 34, figure 30.

idea of multiple heavens common to the Greeks and expresses it with an iconographic image that had been commonly used by ancient Egyptians (see chapter 1, figures 1.2–1.5). Thus, the Egyptian sky-goddess Nut appears twice, once
as the celestial sphere of the moon, that is, the lower Nut, and once as the
celestial sphere of the sun, or the upper Nut. The earth god Geb was typically depicted stretched out beneath Nut, but he here appears contorted into
a ball, perhaps reflecting the Greek idea of the earth as a sphere.[25] Although
the ancient Egyptians did not conceive of multiple levels in the celestial realm
or of the earth as a sphere, the Greeks did, and so they adapted the much
older Egyptian motifs of Nut and Geb to fit their astronomy. The Greeks influenced the cultures of the peoples they conquered, and part of this influence
extended to how people imagined the heavenly realms.

Rome

In spite of Aristotle's fame and in spite of the fact that others had already developed models based on the geocentric theory,[26] this theory for the structure
of the cosmos is most readily identified with Claudius Ptolemy of Alexandria
(ca. 100–170 CE).[27] In Ptolemy's system there was a total of eight planetary
spheres that account for the daily rotation of the seven planets and the fixed
stars, and beyond these there was the ethereal realm.[28] That such a schema of
the cosmos was popularly known already in the mid-first century BCE is evident from Cicero's "Dream of Scipio" narrated in *Republic* 6:9–26. Cicero
recounts Scipio Africanus's dream in which he saw his deceased grandfather,
Africanus the Elder, who elevated Scipio above the earth and showed him the
structure of the cosmos.

> As I gazed still more fixedly at the earth, Africanus said: "How long will your
> thoughts be fixed upon the lowly earth? Do you not see what lofty regions
> you have entered? These are the nine circles, or rather spheres, by which the
> whole is joined. One of them, the outermost, is that of heaven; it contains all
> the rest, and is itself the supreme God, holding and embracing within itself
> all the other spheres; in it are fixed the eternal revolving courses of the stars.
> Beneath it are seven other spheres which revolve in the opposite direction to
> that of heaven. One of these globes is that light which on earth is called
> Saturn's. Next comes the star called Jupiter's, which brings fortune and health
> to mankind. Beneath it is that star, red and terrible to the dwellings of man,
> which you assign to Mars. Below it and almost midway of the distance [be-
> tween heaven and earth] is the sun, the lord, chief, and ruler of the other
> lights, the mind and guiding principle of the universe, of such magnitude that
> he reveals and fills all things with his light. He is accompanied by his com-
> panions, as it were—Venus and Mercury in their orbits, and in the lowest
> sphere revolves the Moon, set on fire by the rays of the Sun. But below the
> Moon there is nothing except what is mortal and doomed to decay, save only
> the souls given to the human race by the bounty of the gods, while above the
> Moon are all things eternal. For the ninth and central sphere, which is the

earth, is immovable and the lowest of all, and toward it all ponderable bodies are drawn by their own natural tendency downward. (*Republic* 6.17)[29]

Africanus the Elder here mentions nine spheres because in addition to the customary seven he includes the realm of the fixed stars and the earth. Between heaven and the earth there are seven spheres each with its own planetary body: the fixed stars, Saturn, Jupiter, Mars, Sun, Venus, and Mercury, and Moon (figure 4.3).[30] Beyond the stars is the heavenly (*caelestis*) realm.

Ptolemy's geocentric model remained prominent until the time of Copernicus, but it was being continually refined. The two most important adjustments to the model of the concentric spheres were those known as epicycles and eccentric circles.[31] According to the epicycle model, the planets rather than simply encircling the earth actually revolve in their own orbit, the center of which encircles the earth (figure 4.4). According to the eccentric circles model, the planets orbit the earth, but the earth is not located in the center (c) of this orbit (figure 4.5). As a result, the planets at times are closer to the earth and appear to be moving fast, while at other times are farther away from the earth and appear to move more slowly. These refinements to the simple geocentric

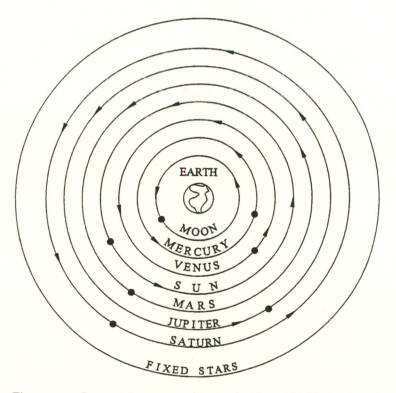

Figure 4.3: Geocentric cosmos; drawing by Farzad Nakhai and used with permission of the author.

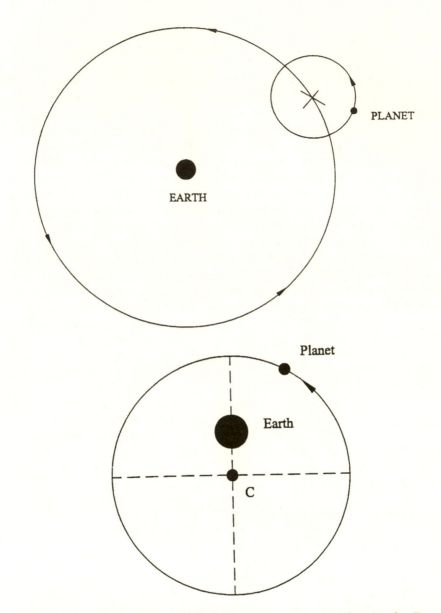

Figure 4.4: *(top)* Epicycle model of planetary movement; drawing by Farzad Nakhai and used with permission of the author. Figure 4.5: *(above)* Eccentric model of planetary movement; drawing by Farzad Nakhai and used with permission of the author.

model were becoming popular with astronomers and mathematicians as early as the third century BCE as a way to account for the irregular movements of the planets. Clearly, however, these theories were so complex that they likely were not very well known—and certainly not well understood—by common folk.[32] For them, the model of concentric spheres rotating around a stationary earth adequately explained the cosmos.

Ptolemy's further refinements of this system made him the one we most closely associate with the geocentric model of the universe. This association is due to the fame of his most important work, the vast collection of astronomical speculations and computations known as the Almagest.[33] To be honest, all medieval and early modern astronomy really began with Ptolemy, who used both the eccentric circles and the epicycles to account for the movements of the celestial bodies. The motionless earth situated in the middle of the universe with all else whirling around it, the geocentric model, thus became popularly known also as the Ptolemaic model. The influence of Babylonian astronomy on Hellenistic ends at least with Ptolemy, if not earlier, as the Greco-Roman world developed models that were vastly more complex than anything from ancient Mesopotamia. The old three-story universe common to so many of the cultures of the ancient Near East was displaced, slowly and only partially in some places, by a Hellenistic model that made the universe even more vast and complex.

This brief survey of Greco-Roman astronomy should make it clear that the Greeks far surpassed the astronomical speculations of the Mesopotamians and Egyptians. These civilizations did indeed make many significant contributions to the history of astronomy, but it was the Greeks whose mathematical genius presaged most all subsequent astronomical "discoveries" until those of Johannes Kepler in the seventeenth century. Almost all astronomy is driven at least in part by human awe at the starry night, and this awe has been described by none other than the great Roman astronomer Ptolemy himself.

> Mortal though I be, yea ephemeral,
>> if but a moment I gaze up to the night's starry domain of heaven,
> Then no longer on earth I stand;
>> I touch the Creator,
>> And my lively spirit drinketh immortality.[34]

This is part of the motivation of astronomy and astrology. It can be understood by anyone who goes out on a clear night to gaze up at the starry night sky: the vision overhead confirms one's finiteness amidst the vastness of the universe. It can heighten one's sense of alienation: "mortal yet immortal," says Ptolemy. Humans who witness the dust-to-dust nature of life on a daily basis also feel a connection and longing to be united with the divine. For the ancients the stars were gods, and to know about the stars is to know something about the gods. Immortality, then, came to be associated with living with the stars and the hope to somehow join the celestial realm.

Persia

The Persians rose to dominate the Near East in the mid-sixth century BCE.[35] Cyrus the Great was the first Persian leader to conquer vast stretches of the Near East, and his successors built on his achievements. After vanquishing the Babylonians, the Persians marched across the Near East from India in the east to Asia Minor in the north and to North Africa in the south. Their conquests stretched even to mainland Greece where they tried to conquer the Greeks with only moderate success. The Greeks ultimately defeated the Persians and eventually began their own march to dominate the world under the leadership of Alexander the Great. The Persian Period in Syria-Palestine is typically defined as the period from 538–333 BCE, or from Cyrus to Alexander.[36] Although this roughly two-hundred-year period is called the Persian Period, it was likely during this time, if not even before, that Greek ideas began to have an influence on the articulation of some forms of Judaism, for Greek culture, language, and literature had been present in Palestine for centuries.[37]

Cuneiform texts from the Persian period evidence the advanced state of mathematical precision regarding the movements of the celestial bodies.[38] It was also in the period 600–300 BCE that the zodiac was invented in Babylonia and that Babylonian horoscopy developed.[39] This form of astrology focused not simply on the movements of celestial bodies but on their precise locations at specific times as the basis of predictions. Moreover, it was in this period that the predictions based on celestial phenomena began to be applied to private individuals. Prior to this, astrological predictions were principally for the benefit of the state or the king; private individuals did not consult the stars for themselves.[40] The omens in the great collection of Babylonian astronomical information known as Enûma Anu Enlil (see chapter 2) were superseded by this more sophisticated horoscopic astrology of the Persian period.[41] The rise of personal horoscopy must surely be related to the use of astronomy in fixing or determining calendrical issues. Although the Persian period developments in astronomy built on earlier Assyrian and Babylonian traditions, these changes were clearly of a new, more precise and advanced order.[42]

Persian religious ideas spread throughout the expanding Persian empire. According to Persian Zoroastrianism, world history is a product of an eternal enmity between the forces of good and evil. In the end, good will triumph and there will be a final fiery cataclysm that will destroy all evil. In Zoroastrian thought, the cosmos is a living thing, not simply the physical creation of a god. Like the Greeks, the Persians believed that the soul was immortal and that its true home was in the great celestial beyond. Zoroastrians believed that a person crosses a bridge after death, and for the good and just, the bridge widens to allow them to pass easily and go on to heaven; for the wicked, however, the bridge narrows to a hair's breadth and they fall into hell.[43] While in Persian myth the good soul ascends through three levels to reach the divine level, the Greeks and Romans imagined seven levels apparently corresponding to the seven planetary spheres (cf. Plato, "Myth or Er," and Cicero, "Dream of Scipio"). "Traditionally Zoroastrianism are the three cosmic layers, or 'heavens,' that the visionary crosses—corresponding to *humata*, 'fair thoughts' (the stars); *hûkhta*, 'fair words' (the Moon); *hvarshta*, 'fair deeds' (the sun)—to arrive at *anagra raoca*, or Paradise, the layer of 'infinite lights.'"[44] This suggests a roughly contemporary parallel development in Persia and Greece about the origin and post mortem fate of the human soul: after death the soul returns to its place of origin, the cosmic regions of purity. That the Persians believed such a myth is clear from a Middle Persian text (ninth–tenth century CE) about the birth of Zarathustra.

> As revelation mentions it: When Aûharmazd had produced the material of Zaratûst, the glory then, in the presence of Aûharmazd, fled on towards the material of Zaratûst, on to that germ, from that germ it fled on . . . ; from the endless light it fled on, on to that of the sun; from that of the sun it fled on, on to the moon; from that moon it fled on, on to those stars; from those stars it fled on, on to the fire in the house of Zôish and from that fire i[t] fled on, on to the wife of Frâhîmvana-zôish, when she brought forth that girl who became the mother of Zaratûst.[45]

Apart from the somewhat odd configurations of the celestial bodies, this text is describing the descent of the soul of Zarathustra from the heavenly realm into this world. At the end of life, as one would expect, the soul desires to return to its pre-incarnate state, a motif with parallels in Pythagorean and Platonic thought. This idea of the soul's return to the heavenly realm, therefore, was common to both Persia and Greece. Since the Persian ideas are preserved only in much later texts, it would seem appropriate to attribute the origins of this idea to the Greeks, although it may be that the idea developed roughly simultaneously and stems from developments in astronomy and philosophy that were occurring at the same time.

Persian astrology also spread throughout the Mediterranean world, and astrology had become so popular in Rome by 139 BCE that the authorities tried to curtail it.[46] Astral religions became popular, for this form of piety offered people the opportunity to join the pure cosmic realm after death. This form of piety was expressed most profoundly in the "mystery religions" (Isis and Osiris, Mithraism, Gnosticism, and others), which seem to have begun in the late Persian and early Hellenistic periods and which addressed this yearning to join the great celestial beyond. If the soul's true home is somewhere in the pure heavenly realms or beyond, one needs a way to prepare one's soul to be fit for such a place after death. The heavenly realm, therefore, was becoming a focus of postmortem hope for many people.

Tradition and the Religious Views of the Heavenly Realm

The Homeric poems provide a good deal of information about the ancient Greeks' view of the cosmos in the times that preceded the great philosophers of Greece. These classic poems, set within late Mycenaean society (thirteenth–

twelfth centuries BCE), but actually dating from no earlier than the eighth or seventh century BCE,[47] demonstrate that the authors believed that the gods were intensely humanlike in their actions and attitudes. They often take on human form and interfere in human history (*Iliad* VI, 128–43). As Herodotus noted, "Homer and Hesiod were the first to compose genealogies and give the gods their epithets, to allot them their several offices and occupations, and describe their forms" (*Persian Wars* II, 53).[48] Just as the king in Homer's world lived in a palace set on an acropolis, so the gods by analogy dwelled in palaces on the heights (*Iliad*, 1.595–610). In early Greek thought Zeus resides in his royal court on Mt. Olympus with a host of lesser gods to do his bidding.[49] He also is described as "Zeus who lives in air on high" (*Works and Days*, 21), and when he came to battle with the Titans "he came from Heaven and from Olympus, lightening as he came . . . to the ear it sounded and to the eye it looked as though broad Heaven was coming down to earth" (*Theogony* 692–700). Many gods have palaces in heaven, but they also dwell in palaces on Mt. Olympus (*Iliad* 1.219–21; (*Odyssey* 6.41–47). In fact, as one character in the Odyssey points out, the gods' courts resemble the splendid courts of the richest and most powerful kings (*Odyssey* 4.71–75). In addition, among Romans, Jupiter was regarded as residing in a palace (*palatia*) with his divine court as the ruler of a heavenly empire.[50] Such descriptions of the divine abode parallel the ancient Near Eastern and biblical traditions of imagining the divine presence in the form of a royal court, a motif that patterns speculation on the divine realm by analogy with the highest, most powerful institutions known to humans.

As far as cosmography is concerned, for the early Greeks the earth was considered to be equidistant between heaven and the netherworld. For the Homeric Greeks, the universe had a three-tiered structure, and each tier was generally governed by individual gods— Zeus (heaven), Poseidon (sea), Hades (netherworld)—but the gods could move between these realms (*Iliad* 15.184–204). At the ends of the earth there were approaches to the netherworld,[51] and beyond these Tartarus, "where is the deepest gulf beneath the earth, the gates whereof are of iron and the threshold of bronze, as far beneath Hades as heaven is above the earth" (*Iliad* 8.14–16), and where Zeus sends gods who oppose his decrees.

The Greeks were profoundly interested in astrology and created a vast horoscopic tradition.[52] The earlier astrological sources in cuneiform lack the orientation of the Hellenistic astrological texts with their belief in the unalterable influence that celestial events and the position of celestial bodies have on individuals or groups. While the Mesopotamians thought that the gods put signs in the stars and planets portending things to come, the Greeks thought that relative positions of the stars and planets were themselves responsible for current and future events on earth.[53] In the Hellenistic period, Greek and Babylonian astronomy combined with new religious ideas about the nature of the human soul, and one of the outcomes of this combination was the development of astral religions in which the transient, disharmonious, unsure nature of this realm is balanced by the hope for an afterlife in the predictable, harmonious, and safe realm of the stars. Ours is an impure and transitory world of disorder; the soul longs for purity and order, to be restored to its original state, and this can be accomplished only by returning to the divine realm whence it came.[54] Many of the mystery religions that began during the Greek period and flourished during the Roman period have an astral focus. The worship of Demeter in the Eleusian Mysteries, and the religion of Isis and Serapis (or Osiris), as well as Gnosticism, all promised the devotee the opportunity to gain eternal life. Mithraism, a Roman mystery religion that was very popular among the army, has, like most of the other mystery religions, left no texts explaining its basic ideas, but a vast amount of iconography has come down to us. The most prominent feature of Mithraism is the Tauroctony, the bull-slaying scene (figure 4.6).[55] The difficulty lies in interpreting these symbols without any texts. Mithraism was Christianity's major rival in the Roman Empire until the fourth century CE. It spread throughout the Near East and Mediterranean worlds as far as Great Britain. Although for most of the twentieth century the interpretation of Mithraism by Franz Cumont as an Iranian religion that was transplanted to Rome has dominated the field, it has become clear that Mithraism is predominantly a Roman phenomenon[56] and was based on astronomical speculations.[57] The initiate was brought into a secret community that knew the secrets of the cosmos and because of this knowledge would be admitted into the astral realm after death and there obtain immortality. Astral immortality thus became the chief conception of life after death during Greco-Roman

Figure 4.6: Tauroctony, Mithras slaying the Bull; reproduced with permission from *Études Mithriaques: Actes de Congrès IV* (Acta Iranica 17; Leiden: E. J. Brill, 1978), plate XXI, fig. 9.

times. The "Mithras Liturgy" contains a spell that was intended to enable a Mithraic initiate to ascend into the heavenly realm.[58]

> Be gracious to me, O Providence and Psyche, as I write these mysteries handed down [not] for gain but for instruction; and for an only child I request immortality, O initiates of this power . . . which the great god Helios Mithras ordered to be revealed to me by his archangel, so that I alone may ascend into heaven as an inquirer and behold the universe.[59]

Likewise Gnosticism, more of a movement than any one individual religion,[60] promised the initiate who learned the secrets the opportunity to have his or her soul rejoin the pure celestial order after death.[61] Moreover, all mystery religions (Isis and Serapis, Eleusian, Mithraism, Gnosticism, etc.) provided the initiate with an unambiguous worldview: they knew their place in society and the cosmos; they had a powerful ritual to dramatize their initiation into the community of the saved; and, most important, they now had a clear hope for immortality. In the Isis cult the goddess was conceived as the controlling power in the universe. The words of Lucius, the hero of Apuleius's *Metamorphoses* (also known as "The Golden Ass"), indicate the nature of this piety.

> You chase away the storms and dangers of life by your outstretched hand. You unravel the hopelessly tangled threads of Fate. You mitigate the tempests of Fortune and restrain the malicious courses of the stars. The heavenly gods honor you; the infernal gods revere you. You rotate the earth, illume the sun, and rule space. . . . The stars answer to you.[62]

Such words suggest a deep longing for a personal connection to a power capable of overcoming the chaotic forces of the cosmos that controlled human fate. The goal was to ascend to the celestial realm and become part of the cosmic order either as a spirit, angel, or some kind of heavenly being.[63]

Images of the Afterlife

Book eleven of the *Odyssey* recounts Odysseus's journey into Hades, "the place where there is no joy" (*Odyssey* 11.92–94),[64] where he encountered the souls of a multitude of the deceased. It seems clear that in Homeric thought people died and went, if properly interred, immediately into Hades.[65] Extraordinary people such as Odysseus could visit Hades and return to report about it with the help of the gods, but this was not for everyone. While Odysseus journeyed to an island at the end of the earth in order to descend into Hades, the dead descend immediately down into "the house of Hades beneath the depths of the earth."[66] We read of no corresponding Homeric journey into the heavenly realm, except for the case of Ganymedes, who, because he was the handsomest of humans, was taken up by the gods to dwell with them and become Zeus's cupbearer (*Iliad* 20.231–35). Thus, a god or goddess may come to earth and take on a human form—a frequent motif in Homeric epics—but humans do not commonly go into heaven (cf. *Odyssey* 7.199–206): "Bethink thee, son of Tydeus, and give place, neither be thou minded to be like of spirit with the gods; seeing in no wise of like sort is the race of immortal gods and that of men who walk upon the earth" (Iliad 5.440–42). While humans went down to "the house of Hades" after death, no one, living or dead, went into heaven, the realm of the immortal gods, without some special act of the gods to make that person immortal. There is no distinction among the dead in Hades: ". . . death for all the purely human shades is morally neutral."[67] The dead wander about as spirits or ghosts with personality but no physical form.[68] Theirs is a gloomy existence to be sure. There is no good whatsoever in death as Achilles's well-known lament indicates: "Never try to reconcile me to death, glorious Odysseus. I should choose, so I might live on earth, to serve as the hireling of another, some landless man with hardly enough to live on, rather than to be lord over all the dead that have perished" (11.488–91).

There are exceptions to this general rule, however. Already in Homeric times the Elysian Fields or Isles of the Blessed was where the souls of truly exceptional people were thought to go after death.[69] These regions were believed to be located at a mysterious, distant place at the ends of earth. Gods may transport exceptional people to these Elysian Fields: "But for yourself, Menelaus, fostered by Zeus, it is not ordained that you should die and meet fate in the horse-pasturing Argos, but to the Elysian plain and the ends of the earth will the immortals convey you . . . where life is easiest for men. No snow is there, nor heavy storm, nor ever rain, but always Ocean sends up blasts of the shrill-blowing West Wind that they may give cooling to men. . . ." (*Odyssey* 4.561–568). Hesiod notes that some of the people of the period of the Trojan War were a special race of humans, demigods really, who were allowed by Zeus to leave the realm of the mortals and go to the Isles of the Blessed at the end of the earth where they lived a carefree life.

> A godlike race of heroes, who are called the demi-gods—the race before our own. Foul wars and dreadful battles ruined some; some sought the flocks of Oedipus, and died in Cadmus's land, at seven-gated Thebes; and some, who crossed the open sea in ships, for fair-haired Helen's sake, were killed at Troy. These men were covered up in death, but Zeus the son of Kronos gave the others life and homes apart from mortals, at Earth's edge. And there they live a carefree life, besides the whirling Ocean, on the Blessed Isles. (*Works and Days* 160–70)

This paradisical Isles of the Blessed motif turns up among the sixth- and fifth-century worshippers of Dionysus, the Orphics. The Orphics in their sacred poems—Orpheus was believed to be a musician/poet—preached a new gospel, as it were, one that promised eschatological salvation.[70] In order to attain to the postmortem life of purity, one must follow a strict purity code in this life. The human problem is that the pure, immaterial soul is encrusted in an impure, physical body, but it longs to rejoin the realm of purity and immateriality. One of Pindar's *Olympian Odes*—poems written in praise of athletic heroes—describes just such a blessed realm.

If one has it [i.e., wealth and virtue] and knows the future, that the helpless
spirits of those who have died on earth immediately pay the penalty—and upon
sins committed here in Zeus' realm, a judge beneath the earth pronounces sentence with hateful necessity; but forever having sunshine in equal nights and in
equal days, good men receive a life of less toil, for they do not vex the earth or
the water of the sea with the strength of their hands to earn a paltry living. No,
in company with the honored gods, those who joyfully kept their oaths spend
a tearless existence, whereas the others endure pain too terrible to behold. But
those with the courage to have lived three times in either realm [i.e., earth and
Hades] while keeping their souls free from all unjust deeds, travel the road of
Zeus to the tower of Kronos, where ocean breezes blow round the Isle of the
Blessed, and flowers of gold are ablaze, some from radiant trees on land, while
the water nurtures others; with these they weave garlands for their hands and
crowns for their heads. . . . (*Olympian Ode* 2.56–74).[71]

The early Greeks were hesitant to imagine that any earthling could enter
the heavenly realm. Book eleven of the Odyssey recounts a tale of the giants
Otus and Ephialtes who intended to stack mountain upon mountain in order
to climb into heaven (11.305–20), and had they reached manhood, they might
even have accomplished this. Their plans were thwarted when they were killed
in their youth by one of Zeus's sons. This story appears to be a polemic about
ascending into heaven, much like the tale of the Tower of Babel in the Hebrew Bible (Gen. 11:1–9). For the early Greeks, Mt. Olympus and the heavenly realm were the homes of the gods alone. Humans might become immortal through an offer from the gods, but even these offers were most often
thwarted, thus maintaining a clear separation between mortals and immortals.
For example, Calypso offered immortality to her lover Odysseus, and Demeter
attempted to immortalize her "step-son" Demophoon. At least by the fourth
century in Greek thought, however, the postmortem residence of the human
soul was transferred to the heavenly realms. This belief stems from Pythagorean
and Platonic ideas that the human soul originated in the ethereal realm, became imprisoned in the earthly body, and will return to the spiritual realm again
at the death of the body.[72] An example of this belief in Plato's own writings is
the Myth of Er recounted at the end of the *Republic*.[73] The hero Er died, but
before his funeral his soul left his body to visit the underworld and the heavens
where it witnessed people being rewarded or punished according to their behavior while on earth. Er's soul returned to his body on earth after this heavenly tour; he revived and told his contemporaries what the other world was
like. This myth is based on the belief that the soul will survive the body, and
although it aspires to rejoin the pure spiritual realm, it also fully expects to suffer
or be punished for its earthly sins after death. Cicero's "Dream of Scipio," relates that Romans in the first century BCE imagined that people would find an
eternal home in the heavenly realm in reward for having lived nobly.

But, [Scipio] Africanus, be assured of this, so that you may be even more
eager to defend this commonwealth: all those who have preserved, aided, or

enlarged their fatherland have a special place prepared for them in the heavens, where they may enjoy an eternal life of happiness.

Consequently, if you [Scipio] despair of ever returning to this place [i.e., the heavenly realm], where eminent and excellent men find their true reward, of how little value, indeed, is your fame among men, which can hardly endure for the small part of a year? Therefore, if you will only look on high and contemplate this eternal home and resting place, you will no longer attend to the gossip of the vulgar herd or put your trust in human rewards for your exploits. Virtue herself, by her own charms, should lead you on to true glory.

Strive on indeed, and be sure that it is not you that is mortal, but only your body. For that man whom your outward form reveals is not yourself; the spirit is the true self, not that physical figure which can be pointed out by the finger.

And as a spirit is the only force that moves itself, it surely has no beginning and is immortal. Use it, therefore, in the best pursuits! And the best tasks are those undertaken in defense of your native land; a spirit occupied and trained in such activities will have a swifter flight to this, its proper home and permanent abode [i.e., in heaven]. And this flight will be still more rapid if, while still confined in the body, it looks abroad, and, by contemplating what lies outside itself, detaches itself as much as may be from the body. For the spirits of those who are given over to sensual pleasures and have become their slaves, as it were, and who violate the laws of gods and men at the instigation of those desires which are subservient to pleasure—their spirits, after leaving their bodies, fly about close to the earth, and do not return to this place except after many ages of torture. (*Republic* 6.13, 23, 24, 29)[74]

So, according to Cicero, the human spirit or soul desires to return to its true home in the heavenly regions beyond the cosmos, but to do so it must have first prepared itself through living a life devoted to "the best pursuits" while also avoiding all manner of sensual pleasures. Otherwise, the soul will undergo punishment to purge it of the earthly vices that prevent its ascent into the higher, purer realms. These disqualifying vices indicate the belief that there are qualifications one must meet in order to attain to the heavenly realm. While later Jewish and Christian texts will develop this theme of prerequisites for admission into heaven as a tool to encourage obedience to behavioral and theological codes, here the goal is to encourage valiant patriotism and moral conduct.

A memorial commemorating the Athenians who died in the battle at Potidaia in 432 BCE succinctly depicts the idea of the soul obtaining immortality after the death of the body: "the ether has received their souls, while the earth has their bodies."[75] A similar idea appears in a first century CE Jewish funerary inscription from Leontopolis, Egypt. This epitaph for a deceased girl reads, "this grave hides in its bosom my chaste body, but my soul has flown to the holy ones."[76] The same theme appears in a version of the Egyptian Book of the Dead dating to the Ptolemaic period (ca. 323–30 BCE): "Heaven hath thy soul, earth hath thy body."[77] Although the idea of a personal existence beyond the grave was available to the heroes of the early periods in Greek history, after the fifth century BCE the idea of an afterlife in the heavenly realms became prominent in myriad mystery religions. The old civic religions were being gradually eclipsed by these newer personal religions. Eventually, as Cicero noted, postmortem punishment was thought to take place in the heavenly realms as the sin-encrusted soul tried to relieve itself of its corrupting burdens in order to ascend higher and higher toward the divine realm, the realm of absolute perfection. Now, postmortem punishment would take place as one's soul attempted to ascend into the heavenly realms. This is a much different conception of the afterlife than what we encountered in the ancient Near East and in early Greece. This conception of the heavenly realms and of humans' postmortem experience appears commonly in early Jewish and Christian beliefs. Jews, and eventually Christians, had new ways of imagining the physical and spiritual worlds that conflicted somewhat with the images they inherited from their religiously authoritative ancient writings.

Summary and Conclusion

The impact of the Persian, Greek, and Roman cultures on Jews and Judaism cannot be overstated. The fourth and third centuries BCE were especially important centuries in early Jewish history.[78] In this era the ideas of the Persians and Greeks were already influencing how some Jews articulated their Judaism. As Jews became increasingly aware of the rest of the Near Eastern and Mediterranean cultures, so those worlds became aware of the Jews who lived in the "dispersion."[79] Greek influence or at least familiarity with various aspects of Greek culture began in the Bronze Age in the eastern Mediterranean and Syria-Palestine.[80] Archaeologists have found traces of Greek pottery in major cities and small villages across the region. Although the political power rested in Persian hands, and Persian ideas surely filtered into the area, the material culture indicates that the people were increasingly oriented to Greece.[81] All levels of Jewish society in Palestine would have been affected by Hellenistic culture to some extent. The palaces of the Hasmonean kings were the first Jewish palaces to be built following the fall of Judah, and these were patterned after Hellenistic models.[82] Greek language was used to one extent or another by most all levels of Jewish society in Palestine. "The degree of a person's Hellenistic culture depended on his social standing. Probably the upper class knew Greek literature, the middle class was less conversant with it, while the knowledge of the lower class was limited to the vernacular only."[83] Even later rabbinic literature exhibits many connections with various aspects of Hellenistic culture and learning.[84] From the conquests of Cyrus the Great and Alexander the Great to the era of Herod the Great, Jews participated fully in vast, cosmopolitan empires. They were influenced by the cultural values of their overlords, to be sure, and they began to express their religions, culture, history, and values in manners that reflect their participation in these larger societies. The following chapters explore how early Jews and Christians reacted to the new ways of imagining the cosmos and their place in it.

5

EARLY JEWISH AND CHRISTIAN TRADITIONS I

The Persistence of Biblical and Ancient Near Eastern Models

This grave hides in its bosom my chaste body,
but my soul has flown to the Holy Ones.

Jewish Epitaph, Leontopolis Egypt

The previous chapters have examined how ancient Near Eastern and Mediterranean cultures imagined the heavenly realm and humans' potential to have a place in it. The ancient Israelites and their neighbors imagined a three-storied universe: netherworld, earth, and heavenly realm. While the various gods inhabit and can move from one realm to the other, humans are not so mobile and are for the most part restricted to the earth during life and to the netherworld in death. Humans did not normally have a share in the heavenly realm after death and certainly not before. In some cases, however, exceptional humans could visit or join the heavenly realm. In the fifth century BCE belief in a heavenly afterlife developed and spread across the Mediterranean world and the ancient Near East. Segments in Judaism and Christianity eventually adopted the belief that humans could have a place in the heavenly realm, but this was normally limited to a select few, and depending on one's ideology, the numbers could be indeed few.

Several scholars have grappled with the issue of the postmortem ascent into the heavenly realms. Probably the most important works are those of Bietenhard, Segal, Tabor, and Himmelfarb.[1] This chapter builds on and is somewhat related to these previous works; but my goal here is to trace how Jews and Christians imagined or depicted the heavenly realms themselves. During the Greco-Roman Period Judaism adopted and adapted cosmological views and ideas of the afterlife that were common in the region, and this had a major formative impact on the various expressions of Judaism. The emerging Jewish conceptions of the universe and the ideas about what happens to a person after death were not the natural outgrowth of biblical religiosity but were the product of the fruitful interaction of the ancient biblical traditions with new trends in religion and science during the Greco-Roman period. Early Christianity, initially just another of the many Jewish sects of the period, inherited aspects of both the biblical traditions and the newer Hellenistic expressions of Judaism.

This chapter will explore the early Jewish and Christian texts that mention the structure of the cosmos, focusing on those that seem to present a single heaven structure. This is the model of the cosmos that dominated the biblical traditions. As should now be clear, this model became "obsolete" in the course of the Persian, Greek, and Romans periods as Jews reacted to newer images of the size and shape of the cosmos. Nonetheless, some texts continued to describe the cosmos as a simple three-tiered structure—heaven, earth, netherworld. The reason for the continued use of the biblical model is the abiding power of religiously authoritative biblical texts to shape people's views on just about every topic, including astronomy. Through the course of this and the following chapter, it will become clear that there never was only one dominating view of the structure, contents, and population of the heavenly realm in early Judaism and Christianity but several.

What seems to be at issue is a particular text's overall goals. That is to say, when most ancient Jewish authors describe heaven, their primary intention is not to provide an accurate depiction of the universe. The authors apparently did not feel constrained to conform to any specific system. So, when separate texts attest to different numbers of heavens or to different contents in the various heavens, it may be that (1) they had different scientific knowledge regarding the structure of the cosmos, or (2) they depicted the cosmos in a manner that augmented their overall literary or theological goals. Accepting the general consensus about the date and provenance of the individual texts discussed in this chapter, I will attempt to present these texts in the best approximation of their chronological order. Determining a text's original community setting remains a vexing problem.[2] Moreover, we have yet to develop agreed-upon criteria for distinguishing clearly between a Jewish and a Christian work. Therefore, these issues will not be deciding factors in the following discussions. Nonetheless, as all would agree, even a clearly later Christian text may draw on originally Jewish traditions, beliefs, or cosmological speculations.

Most of the texts discussed in this chapter are part of a very large body of early Jewish extrabiblical literature known as apocrypha and pseudepigrapha. These are texts that were not part of the Hebrew Bible but that nonetheless enjoyed varying degrees of popularity in early Jewish and Christian communities. These texts provide important new insight into the great diversity that characterized early Judaism and emerging Christianity. Although not well known outside of academic circles, this literature has become an area of specialization within the broader academic fields of early Jewish and Christian studies. The study of early Christianity is no longer focused exclusively on the

New Testament, nor the study of early Judaism on rabbinic literature. As the field continues to grow, we gain new insights into the history, literature, and cultures of these communities.

1 Enoch

Enoch is one of the most prominent figures in this pseudepigraphical literature. Genesis 5:18–24 presents Enoch as a person who lived before the Flood and whose exceptional piety inspired God to "take him." Although precisely where God "took him" is not specified in the text, later Jewish and Christian traditions have assumed that he was taken to heaven to join God, a fitting reward for his piety. An enormous wealth of material was pseudepigraphically attributed to Enoch, and much of it has to do with the secrets that he learned while in the heavenly realm. Several of these stories appear in a text traditionally designated "First Enoch." Rather than being a book, 1 Enoch is actually a collection of five separate texts attributed to Enoch.[3] It is more fitting, therefore, to speak of this as an "Enochic Collection." The following discusses a few of these five books separately because they stem from different social and historical contexts.

Book I: The Book of the Watchers (1 Enoch 1–36)

The Book of the Watchers dates to the early part of the second century BCE and focuses on the theme of the rebellion of angels in heaven. This section opens with a declaration of the earth's corruptness and an announcement of its impending judgment (chapters 1–5).[4] 1 Enoch 6:1 begins a long narrative that explains the cause of all the earth's problems: rebellious angels descended from heaven to have sex with human women whom they impregnated and taught heretofore unknown secrets about cosmetics, metallurgy, and the making of weapons.[5] The offspring of these women eventually turned against humans and began devouring them. All of this was viewed by other heavenly angels who heard the cries of those suffering on earth and who then implored God to intervene. These angelic Watchers instructed righteous Enoch to inform the "Watchers of heaven who have left the high heaven and the holy eternal place" that they will be punished for their evil actions (12:4). According to this passage there is only one heavenly realm that is designated either high heaven or, more commonly, heaven.[6] The only other realm is the earth, and a being should reside only in one or the other.[7] The initial sin of these "fallen angels" was that they crossed the boundary between heaven and earth. They forsook their rightful home in the heavenly realm and brought potentially harmful secrets from that realm and gave them to humans.

Later in the narrative (1 Enoch 14:8–16:3) Enoch ascended to heaven where he learned how God would punish these Watchers, and the account of his ascent reveals something about the structure of the heavenly realm presupposed in this work. Enoch ascended to the heavenly realm by being lifted up by strong winds in the midst of lightning, clouds, and fog (14:8), and after arriving in the heavenly realm, he approached a wall of hailstones surrounded by fire. Enoch passed through the wall and entered a brilliant house whose floor looked like snow, and whose ceiling looked like water with lightning, stars and cherubim flashing across it. Inside the house it was simultaneously as hot as fire and as cold as snow; there was neither pleasure nor life in it. This whole event induced awe, and Enoch fell to the ground in fear (14:9–13). The account of the vision continues with Enoch seeing a second house that was larger and more splendid than the first. It had open doors and was built of fire. The floor was aflame, and, like the first house, the ceiling had lightning and stars flashing across it. Inside he saw God sitting upon a shining throne and wearing gleaming raiment. The throne had rivers of fire flowing from under it and a vast sea of fire surrounding it. Tens of thousands of angels stood before God singing perpetually. God then addressed the cowering Enoch, lifted him up, and brought him near the door where he told him what to say to the rebellious Watchers (15–16).[8]

This narrative portrays Enoch's ascent to a heavenly temple.[9] The beings, their activities, and their surroundings all suggest that the biblical ideology of the Jerusalem Temple thoroughly influenced the portrayal of this divine residence in heaven. Quite naturally, the place where the divine being dwells is a temple that corresponds to its earthly analogue. As was noted in the previous chapters, the ancient Near Eastern cultures customarily imagined the divine presence after the images, symbols, and protocol of the king enthroned in his royal palace. Postbiblical Jewish literature adopted, for the most part, the biblical images of God in his Jerusalem Temple because of the formative influence that the religiously authoritative texts of the Hebrew Bible had on later generations. Enoch, having ascended to the presence of God, and having there received his commission in a manner resembling that of the biblical prophets, then toured the cosmos where he saw that the regions of punishment and reward were already in place (17–36). So far, then, Enoch has ascended to heaven into the presence of God where he was commissioned to travel through the cosmos to see its sights and then to report back to the fallen angels on earth.

ENOCH'S FIRST EARTHLY JOURNEY

Enoch returned to earth and began a journey to the west escorted by angels (chapters 17–19).[10] As he traveled west, he crossed a vast dark region and came to a mountain whose summit reached heaven (17:2, 8).[11] He eventually arrived at the ends of the earth where he saw the storehouses of the winds and the foundations of the earth (18:1–2). Here, too, is where the firmament of heaven rests on the earth (18:2, 5).[12] He learned that the sky remains in place because the winds that blow on the earth function as the pillars of heaven, holding it in its place (18:3).[13] There are also other winds that cause the movements of the starry host (18:4).[14] Enoch saw a vast chasm where the rebellious angels and the stars that have deviated from their appointed courses are all confined and punished (18:12–19:2). This phase of the journey culminates with the following proclamation: "And I, Enoch alone saw the sight, the ends of everything; and no man has seen what I have seen" (19:3). Although he had been "lifted up" by the angels, Enoch was not in the heavenly realm, but appears to have flown with them above the surface of the earth to the mythical ends of the earth. The earth, therefore, is here conceived of as a flat surface upon which one can travel to a certain point where it ends and drops off into a vast chasm—the classical ancient Near Eastern model of the earth.

ENOCH'S SECOND EARTHLY JOURNEY 20–36

Chapter 20, a list of the names and functions of the archangels, interrupts the account of Enoch's journeys, and the travelogue resumes in chapter 21. Some scholars have proposed that chapters 21–36 represent a second journey by Enoch into the heavenly realms.[15] More accurately, this section is a continuation of the earthly journey begun in chapter 17, or at least a supplement of additional traditions about Enoch's fantastic journeys.[16] Without giving any notice of the direction in which he traveled, Enoch arrived at a desert place where neither heaven nor earth are visible but where he saw seven stars of heaven bound together (21:1–6). Uriel, Enoch's angelic companion, explained to him that this is the place where the stars that abandoned their divinely appointed course are kept until the completion of their punishment.[17] This is a clear example of "repetitive resumption" linking back to 18:12–16.[18] In other words, this passage returns the reader to the place where the text left off before the insertion of the list of archangels in chapter 20. This literary technique indicates that the following should be read as the continuation of the earthly journey interrupted at the end of chapter 19.

Enoch saw a large mountain in the west where the souls of the dead go until the day of judgment (22:1–14).[19] These souls are separated according to whether they did good or evil during their lifetime.[20] Enoch then proceeded to the "ends of the earth" in the west where he saw a perpetually burning fire that gives the lights of heaven their brightness (23:1–4). While this image of fires at the mythical ends of the earth whose light illumines the celestial bodies seems odd, this may represent a transformation of the Pythagorean belief in the "hearth of the universe" at the center of the cosmos (see figure 4.1). The Pythagoreans thought that the planets and stars do not produce their own light but only reflect light emanating from the fire of this cosmic hearth. Enoch, however, locates the fires that illuminate the celestial bodies not at the center of the cosmos but at the mythical ends of the earth. Enoch's cosmography acknowledges that planets and stars reflect light, but it eschews the discredited Pythagorean idea of a central hearth. Most importantly, Enoch has not displaced the earth from the center of the cosmos. Although he had presumably reached the ultimate ends of the earth before (18:14), this section describes other phenomena that were thought to be at this mythical place. The author has added this material here without concern for the fact that it was a place visited earlier in the journey. Next, without specifying the direction in which he traveled or the route by which he arrived there, Enoch came to a place where he saw a mountain ablaze day and night (cf. 18:6). Near this mountain he saw a range of seven other mountains (24:1–3). From the descriptions of these mountains it appears that they are located at the extreme northwest ends of the earth (cf. 18:7–8): three of the mountains extend to the south and three to the east, while the seventh is located at the corner where they converge. All are made of precious stone and all are enormously tall. The seventh mountain is the throne where God will sit when he comes to the earth in the eschaton (25:3). Aromatic trees (24:3c–5) that bear a special life-giving food for the righteous surround the tall mountain (25:4–7, cf. 17:4). The description of this place recalls the place visited by Enoch at 18:8. It seems, therefore, that this text is attempting to narrate a journey throughout the earth by Enoch. The author creates this journey by integrating many different traditions into the journey scheme. The journey seems to turn back on itself at times because the author has incorporated disparate traditions about Enoch's journeys without fully integrating them into a consistent, linear format.

Enoch then began an eastward journey starting from Jerusalem (28–33).[21] He traversed the Wilderness of Judah (28), and entered a mountainous and aromatic land (29:1–31:3). Turning to the northeast,[22] Enoch eventually crossed the Red Sea (= Indian Ocean?),[23] a vast region of darkness,[24] and finally entered the "Garden of Righteousness" (32:2–6).[25] This is clearly the Garden of Eden, for here Enoch saw the beautiful "tree of wisdom" from which Adam and Eve ate and were subsequently expelled from this place. From this Garden of Righteousness Enoch went to the "ends of the earth" where he saw various kinds of very large beasts and birds (33:1). Continuing his journey eastward, Enoch came to the place where he saw "the ends of the earth on which heaven rests, and the open gates of heaven" (33:2; cf. 36:2–3). These gates are the ones through which the stars pass to begin their daily journeys through the sky. Enoch recorded the number, names, positions and courses of these stars (33:3–4). Afterward Enoch journeyed to the west where he saw three gates in heaven corresponding to the three gates he saw in the east (35:1). Because of this connection to the gates in the east, these gates must be for the celestial bodies to exit the sky at the end of their daily journeys. These gates are precisely the gates encountered in other ancient Near Eastern traditions about how the celestial bodies enter and exit the visible sky. This is clear indication of the dependence of 1 Enoch on an ancient Near Eastern model of the cosmos: the earth is flat and the celestial bodies enter and exit the sky via gates at the ends of the earth. Enoch's rather impressive knowledge of astronomy will be more fully revealed in "the Astronomical Book" (see below).

Having completed his tour to the extreme ends of the earth, Enoch responded with the following words that also close this first book of the Enochic collection:

And when I saw, I blessed, and I will always bless the Lord of Glory who has made great and glorious wonders that he might show the greatness of his work to his angels and to the souls of men, that they might praise his work, and that all his creatures might see the work of his power and praise the great work of his hands and bless him for ever.[26]

This passage presents the overall purpose the author had in writing and disseminating this text—to display the marvelous deeds of God so that people might revere him. In addition, the fact that the places of torment for evildoers are already in place and that the fallen angels are already being punished serves to encourage people to live according to traditional values in order to avoid similar postmortem punishments.

The cosmography of this text involves only one heaven. When Enoch ascended into the presence of God he went immediately into his presence without passing through any intermediate heavens (12:4; 14:8). The central interest of this text, however, is to describe the mythic regions of the earth. If one travels far enough toward any of the four points of the compass, one will arrive at the place where the surface of the earth drops off into a vast chasm (17–19). The places of punishment are located at these extreme ends of the earth. Also visible at the ends of the earth are the "gates" through which the celestial bodies and the meteorological elements pass. This flat earth model was not only an ancient Near Eastern view, however, for the early Greeks, too, had an ancient tradition that the surface of the earth was flat and completely surrounded by water.[27] At least since the days of Aristotle in the mid-fourth century the idea of a spherical earth was known.[28] Furthermore, the geographer Eratosthenes[29] in the mid-third century BCE and the astronomer Hipparcus[30] a century later attempted to draw maps of the world on globes. Nevertheless, the cosmography and geography of this text finds its closest affinities with long-standing traditions that originated in the ancient Near East and that were shared by all the biblical tradents. This tendency to adopt and transmit old traditions in spite of the existence of more advanced models indicates that these people lived in a world where there were competing models of cosmography and geography. They appear to have perpetuated the traditional views because they were an important part of their cultural heritage. Their view of the cosmos depended more on ancient Near Eastern traditions than on the more recent developments in the Greco-Roman intellectual world. This persistence of an "obsolete" image of the cosmos in a Jewish text is due to the author's dependence on the biblical image of the cosmos. The Hebrew Bible's authoritative knowledge for this author extended even to astronomy. There was, in his mind anyway, no need to adopt the newer Hellenistic models.

Book II: The Parables of Enoch (1 Enoch 37–71)

This section of 1 Enoch was not found among the many 1 Enoch texts and fragments of the Dead Sea Scrolls at Qumran, and this initially created some debate about the origins of this material.[31] It seems from its linguistic and ideological features that the Parables of Enoch is a Jewish sectarian composition from the first century BCE whose ideas for some reason did not find a welcome home in the Qumran community. Our concern here will be, once again, to examine this text as a literary unit[32] to determine what the heavenly realm looks like according to its author(s).

I ENOCH 38–44, THE FIRST PARABLE

The cosmography of the Parables agrees with that of the Book of the Watchers. The wicked angels descended from "the high heavens" to cohabit with human woman (39:1, cf. 12:4). The designation is the equivalent of the Hebrew phrase שמים עליונים ("high heavens"), and is of no significance because the plural is the standard form for heaven in Hebrew and Aramaic and does not necessarily indicate multiple heavens. Enoch reported that when he learned about the fall of the Watchers, ". . . clouds and a storm-wind carried me off from the face of the earth, and set me down at the end of heaven" (39:3; cf. 52:1). This description is obviously inspired by the vocabulary of Elijah's ascent (2 Kgs. 2). Likewise, the cosmography is also biblical: Enoch went directly to the heavenly realm without passing through any intervening spheres. Enoch appears to have ascended to the heavenly realm or perhaps to have journeyed to the outermost boundary of earth where heaven and earth intersect. If this is a journey to the ends of the earth and not an ascent account, then what he recounts is a vision of the heavenly realm and not a visit to it. He saw "the dwelling places of the righteous" with the angels (39:4, 6) and learned that he was destined by God to join this multitude (39:8–14). This is a clear statement of the belief that the righteous have a place with God in the heavenly realm. Although the cosmography of this text is based on the biblical model, the religious ideology is clearly Hellenistic. At this place he also saw four beings surrounding the "Lord of the Spirits": the angels Michael, Raphael, Gabriel, and Panuel (40:1–10). Interestingly, although four beings (beasts) customarily attend the divine presence, here there is no mention of God's throne.[33] Also, as will become customary for Enoch, he learned astronomical secrets (41, 43–44). So, Enoch here relates traditional material, but the central focus, the throne of God, is not mentioned. Enoch either has ascended directly to the heavenly realm or has come to the boundary between heaven and earth and has had a vision of the heavenly realm. If this is an account of a journey to the mythical ends of the earth and not an ascent account, then for this author all these things exist at or can be seen from that mythical place where heaven and earth intersect.

I ENOCH 58–69, THE THIRD PARABLE

The Second Parable (1 Enoch 45–57) does not speculate on the appearance of the cosmos. According to the Third Parable, Enoch learned of the secret cosmic laws regulating the lightning and thunder (59:1–3), although he does not say where he was when he "saw" these mysteries. Enoch[34] then had a vision of the divine throne surrounded by myriad angels (60:1–4, cf. 61:8, 62:2–3, 5). He learned of the impending day of judgment when the two ancient mythic monsters—Leviathan and Behemoth—will be separated from one another (60:7–8, 16, 24).[35] Leviathan, the female monster, dwells in the depths of the sea, while Behemoth, the male monster, lives in the vast desert "to the east of the garden where the chosen and righteous dwell" (60:8). So, according to this depiction, there is a vast desert beyond the earthly garden where the righteous live.[36] The Leviathan-Behemoth discussion is interrupted by a catalog of cosmological secrets that Enoch learned regarding the functioning of the celestial and meteorological phenomena (60:11–23).[37] Again, Enoch was the focus of early Jewish astronomical speculation. Who better than Enoch, who lived 365 years—the number of days in a solar year—and who was "taken" by God (Gen. 5:24), to know about the celestial realm. Enoch also learned a secret oath that reveals how God created the earth and that bestows divine powers to the one who learns it. The text's description of the process of creation reveals the author's image of the earth's structure: ". . . heaven was suspended before the world was created and for ever. And through it (the oath) the earth was founded upon the water. . . ." (69:16–17). This passage reflects an ancient view of the cosmos that imagined that the surface of the earth floated upon water (cf. Ps. 24:1–2; 136:6). The statement that "heaven was suspended before the world was created and forever" appears to depend on a careful reading of Genesis 1:1—"In the beginning God created heaven and earth." Because this verse reads "heaven and earth," the author of this Parable may understand Genesis 1:1 to mean that God created heaven first and then the earth. This secret oath, Enoch learned, also causes the sun, moon, and stars to follow unerringly and perpetually their designated courses (69:20–21), and it sustains the storehouses of the meteorological elements, that is, the hail, frost, mist, rain, and dew (69:23, 25). The Third Parable, then, also adopts the ancient Near Eastern model of the cosmos. Enoch also saw how the righteous would be rewarded in the eschaton while the powerful would be punished (61–63). This vision of eschatological judgment mentions that the wicked rulers will be cast down into Sheol and there suffer terrible punishment (63:10). This Hellenized version of Sheol transforms the morally neutral biblical Sheol into a place where the wicked undergo horrific punishment. This eschatological separation of the righteous and the wicked is meant to give the readers hope and to encourage them to live just lives, knowing that one day they will be rewarded by God with heavenly bliss for their fidelity and, conversely, that those who oppress them will one day be punished for their wickedness. Enoch's vision, therefore, serves a larger theological purpose by encouraging people to remain faithful to their religious traditions.

Book III: The Astronomical Book (1 Enoch 72–82)

This section of the Enochic corpus[38] details additional cosmological secrets disclosed to Enoch regarding the operation of the celestial bodies.[39]

The book of the revolutions of the lights of heaven, each as it is, according to their classes, according to their (period of) rule and their times, according to

their names and their places of origin, and according to their months, which
Uriel, the holy angel who was with me and is their leader, showed to me;
and he showed me all their regulations exactly as they are, for each year of
the world and for ever, until the new creation shall be made which will last
for ever. (*1 Enoch* 72:1)

Paleographic analysis of the fragments of the Astronomical Book from
Qumran (4QEn[ast]) indicate that this is the earliest attested Jewish apocalypse,
dating at least to the third century BCE.[40] The detailed astronomical speculation in this work reveals that one of the formative influences in early Jewish
apocalyptic ideology was an interest in astronomy.[41] Theophrastus (ca. 372–
288 BCE) in describing Jews says that while they celebrate festivals at night they
contemplate the stars.[42] Although this is not a direct reference to early Jewish
astronomy, it at least suggests such an interest already in the late fourth or early
third century BCE.

Genesis 5:21–23 records that Enoch lived 365 years, the exact number of
days in a solar year, but this brief passage does not necessarily reflect the existence of traditions associating Enoch with detailed calendrical or astronomical
speculation.[43] As was noted in chapter 3, there was certainly considerable interest in astronomy in ancient Israel, although the biblical editors decided not
to include this feature in their materials. During the late Babylonian and Persian periods, Jewish astronomical speculation was often associated with Enoch,
and the growth of his persona in early Jewish literature included considerable
astronomical speculation. The figure of Enoch was based, as has long been
known, on Mesopotamian antecedents, and part of these Mesopotamian traditions included astronomical secrets. The extra- or postbiblical evolution of
the figure of Enoch, because of his biblical association with the solar year,
naturally attracted astronomical features. The scientific data presented in 1 Enoch
72–82 is precisely this kind of ancient Mesopotamian science,[44] and in the
Astronomical Book we encounter an Enoch who is in every respect a true
astronomer.

Enoch first learned the Laws of the Sun (72). He learned that the sun crosses
the sky in a chariot driven by winds (72:5)[45] and that there are six gates on the
eastern and western horizons through which the sun passes to begin and complete its daily course (72:2–4).[46] Enoch, ever the careful astronomer, traced the
location of the sun at sunrise and sunset as it entered and exited through the
six gates. These calculations are very systematic and demonstrate a thorough
acquaintance with the apparent north–south movements of the sun throughout an annual cycle (72:5–37).[47] In addition, 72:5 notes that once the sun and
the moon set in the evening, they return to the east via a northern route (cf.
41:5).[48] The authors of this section of the Enochic corpus imagined that the
earth was flat and that the nighttime courses of the sun, moon, and stars did
not continue in a straight line under the earth. Rather, as in the ancient Near
Eastern models, they exit the visible sky through gates and then make their
way back to the east. Clearly, although this section of the Astronomical Book
is intimately interested in astronomy, its astronomy is largely ancient Near

Eastern in character. The author or authors of this material have not adopted, or were unacquainted with, then-contemporary Greek astronomy. For them, Enoch was not a modern Greek astronomer but an ancient Mesopotamian one: Enoch's wisdom had a decidedly ancient Near Eastern flavor!

Enoch then learned the Laws of the Moon (73–74).[49] He learned that the moon uses the same six gates the sun uses when it enters and exits the sky (cf. 74:17; 75:6; 78:2–17; 83:11). The moon, too, rides in a chariot driven by the wind (73:2). The moon and the sun are equal in size (78:3), although the moon when fully illuminated is only one-seventh as bright as the sun (72:37; 73:3; 78:4). Persian, Hellenistic, and Roman astronomical texts tend to provide zodiacal reference points when tracing the movements of the celestial bodies, but this is entirely missing from this Enochic material. In fact, the schematic nature of this text's calculations betray a notable lack of interest in quantitative or observational astronomy.[50]

The Astronomical Book's descriptions of the cosmos contain little that directly describes the structure of the cosmos. It describes the workings of the celestial bodies and the winds—where they come from, the courses in which they travel, and how they move about. It provides no detail on the physical or geographical features of the heavenly realms. Such matters did not interest the purveyors of this Enochic material. The descriptions presuppose a view of the earth as a flat plane that comes to an end in each direction. The whole description echoes Babylonian cosmic speculation and only faintly indicates any knowledge of Greek mathematical astronomy.[51] Since the celestial bodies enter the sky via gates, a feature common to ancient Near Eastern conceptions of the celestial realm, it appears that the author either does not know or has shunned the multiple heaven models where these bodies orbit each in their own sphere. Having looked at the Mesopotamian and Greek astronomical materials in the preceding chapters, it is clear that 1 Enoch 72–82 is very basic observational astronomy and vastly inferior to that in both Mesopotamia and Greece during the fourth and third centuries BCE.[52] The central issue here is acquiring the knowledge about the secret workings of the sun, moon, stars, and so forth. This is a basic function of an apocalypse— to transmit information that apart from divine revelation would otherwise remain unknowable.[53] This section does not so much provide information regarding the appearance of the heavenly realm as it provides information on the inner workings of the cosmos itself. This, our earliest Jewish apocalypse, is interested simply in scientific information about the celestial bodies and meteorology. To this strictly scientific interest, however, the author has added an ethical and eschatological component: humans should be as consistent in their behavior as the celestial bodies are consistent in theirs, following the plans God laid out for each of them. Otherwise, just as God punishes errant celestial bodies, so he will punish erring humans. Although the astronomers were interested in the mechanics of the heavenly realms when they looked skyward, the Jewish apocalyptists who created and transmitted this material were interested in ethics as well. For them, observations or knowledge of the heavenly realms, no matter what the specific object may be, must always lead to ethics; the heavens have something to say about God! As the celestial bodies unfailingly follow God's prescribed rules for them, so humans ought to obey God's laws for them.

The Dead Sea Scrolls

The people of the Qumran or Dead Sea Scrolls—they referred to themselves as "the Community of the Renewed Covenant"[54]—many of whom lived for at least a time at the site of Qumran on the northwestern shore of the Dead Sea, were by no means religious or cultural innovators; they were largely unattracted to the many aspects of Greco-Roman culture. Their piety was of a largely conservative nature, albeit decidedly apocalyptic in many ways.[55] As one might expect, the texts use the Hebrew and Aramaic terms for "heaven" (שמים and שמיא) in much the same way they were used in the Hebrew Bible. Moreover, their texts adopt the traditional biblical model of the cosmos, and this is not surprising given the conservative nature of their religious beliefs.

In spite of the apocalyptic orientation of the Qumran sectarians' world view, one finds remarkably little speculation about the world beyond. This is especially significant since these people imagined themselves as a community of angels whose rigidly pious life was thought to imitate that of the angels in heaven.[56] These people also believed themselves to have access to divine mysteries, just as the angels did, via their group's inspired leaders. This group could produce documents, such as the *War Scroll* (1QM, the War of the Sons of Light Against the Sons of Darkness) that speculates on the cataclysmic, eschatological battle of good and evil; the *Serek HaYahad* (1QS, the Community Rule) that outlines in detail how the faithful must live "in the last days" (1QSᵃ 1.1); and texts on the "New Jerusalem" (especially 4Q554–55) that speculate on the appearances of the eschatological version of the Holy City, to name just a few. Nevertheless, these people apparently did not speculate on what awaited them after death and what the world to come looked like. Clearly, they expected either to live on the renewed earth in the New Jerusalem or to take their place in the heavenly realm along with the other angels. For some reason, speculation about the appearance and nature of the heavenly realm was not a driving force in their religious imagination.

They were not completely disinterested in the cosmic realm, however. Several texts attest to their fascination, much like their contemporaries in the rest of the Greco-Roman world, with the celestial bodies. The Qumran sectarians paid particular attention to the movements of the celestial bodies and developed their own versions of astronomy. One text (4Q317) traces the phases of the moon through the course of nearly a month. Another (4Q318) discusses the positions of the moon in relation to the signs of the zodiac and appends an astrological prediction to these observations. This text in many ways formally resembles the earlier astrological texts from Mesopotamia and Greece discussed in chapters 2 and 4; these people's astronomy, therefore, draws on long-standing ancient Near Eastern astronomical and astrological traditions. Such astrology at first glance seems rather unbecoming of these religiously traditional Jews, for one would think that biblical passages such as Isaiah 47:13–14 and Amos 5:26–27 would have led them to limit the practice of astrology. The Qumran text 4Q318 and other early Jewish texts, however, demonstrate that many Jews of the Greco-Roman world were familiar with astrology and even practiced it.[57] Thus the people of Qumran were in this way much like their contemporaries. To be sure, they would have confessed that the "signs" put in the heavens were put there by their God alone. Yet another text (4Q319) provides a painfully detailed reckoning of the conjunctions of the sun and moon over a period of nearly 300 years. These few texts, in addition to the fragments of the Enochic Astronomical Book (1 Enoch 72–82) that were found in the Qumran caves but were not composed by the sectarians, indicate the sectarians' interest in accurately tracking the movements of the celestial bodies. Their interest in this form of astronomy was not simply academic: these astronomical speculations provided the foundation for their calendrical calculations. Interestingly, what appears to be a small sundial or possibly even a crude astrolabe was found at Qumran.[58] To be honest, whether in fact this device is a sundial or some kind of astrolabe is not certain, but if it is, its presence at Qumran situates the astronomical speculations of the Qumran sectarians within long-standing ancient Near Eastern astronomical traditions.

The Qumran calendrical texts (4Q320–30) in conjunction with calendrical references in other sectarian documents indicate that these sectarians followed a different calendar than their co-religionists in Jerusalem and elsewhere, and it was this difference in calendar that irrevocably separated the Qumran community from the rest of Judaism. That is to say, they used a crude form of astronomy to develop or at least justify a solar calendar of 364 days while the rest of the Jewish community in Palestine adhered to a lunar calendar of 354 days. Their solar calendar would have put their festivals on different days than those sanctioned by the religious leaders in Jerusalem, and these calendrical differences put the Jews of Qumran at odds with the rest of Judaism. Judaism could and did absorb all manner of philosophical and cultural differences, but celebrating festivals on the "wrong" days would have put the people of Qumran out of the mainstreams of early Jewish life. On the other hand, the people of Qumran would have thought that everyone else was observing the wrong calendar.[59] The calendar of the Qumran sectarians, therefore, was probably the single matter that most set them apart from the rest of the Jewish community.

The people of Qumran apparently did not expend much if any effort on speculating on the appearances of the heavenly realm. Their eschatologically oriented sect was more concerned with defining and promoting holy living in the here and now. Regarding the structure of the cosmos, however, one text does call for some attention—4QMysteries[a]. One fragment of this text (column 8, line 10) mentions the "heaven above heaven" (שמים ממעל לשמים).[60] The text deals with the theme that all knowledge comes from God, and that God enables people to understand divine mysteries—presumably the peculiar teachings of the group. The text then reads:

ה]סגיר בעד עד⁶¹ מים לבל]תי
[שמים ממעל לשמים
] he shut them up before (the) waters, so as [not to
] heaven above heaven [

What the author meant by this phrase is unclear due to the fragmentary nature of this text, but the phrase "heaven above heaven" does not seem to refer to multiple heavens. If the author intended such, the expected phraseology would be "the second (etc.) heaven," or "the higher heaven." Also, as Schiffman notes, the first letter of the first word in the second line, that is the Shin (שׁ) of the word שמים (šāmayim = heaven), is partially obscured. It may be that the term is not שמים (šāmayim = heaven) at all but simply מים (mayim = water). Given that the previous line mentioned stopping something up until or before the waters, it may be that the text is referring to the waters which are "above the sky," or "in heaven above the sky" (i.e., מים ממעל לשמים). Such a phrase is close to Ps. 148:4: הללוהו שמי השמים והמים אשר מעל השמים, "Praise Him, O vast heavens, and O waters that are above the sky." If this is indeed the case, then this text does not suggest that the Qumran sectarians adopted the widely held Hellenistic notion of multiple heaven. Like their traditional though peculiar religious ideas, their astronomical ideas were based on biblical prototypes.

The Old Testament Apocrypha

The Greek term for heaven, οὐρανός (ouranos),[62] was used just as the Hebrew and Aramaic terms (שמים and שמיא) to designate both the sky, the physical universe, and heaven, the abode of the gods. It would be well to note that this term (οὐρανός) appears more than 670 times in the Septuagint, the Greek translation of the Hebrew Bible made by Jews and for Jews during the last several centuries BCE. By far the most frequent form is the singular οὐρανός (ouranos, 621). The plural form, οὐρανοί (ouranoi), on the other hand, appears 52 times, and 29 of those in Psalms alone! Again, the use of the Greek plural form does not necessarily indicate a belief in multiple heavens, but appears to be an example of "translation Greek" or biblical imitation, based on the Hebrew and Aramaic plural forms שמים and שמיא, and is not native Greek usage, where οὐρανός (ouranos) appears consistently in the singular.[63] The Septuagint, then, follows typical Greek usage, where the singular form is by far the most common.

One looks in vain for clear references to a multiple heaven schema in the books traditionally identified as the Old Testament Apocrypha. The few possible exceptions are: "For your dwelling is the heaven of heaven (οὐρανὸς τοῦ οὐρανοῦ, both singular), unapproachable by human beings" (3 Macc. 2:15); "Even heaven and the highest heaven of God (ὁ οὐρανὸς καὶ ὁ οὐρανὸς τοῦ οὐρανοῦ τοῦ θεοῦ, all singular), the abyss and the earth tremble at his appearance" (ben Sira 16:18); and "Bless the Lord, O heavens (οὐρανοί, plural); praise him and highly exalt him forever" (Prayer of Azariah 35). All these passages can be understood within the context of the traditional or biblical perspectives from which they appear to have originated. What these phrases signify is not multiple heavens but the vastness of heaven or the heights of heaven. True, they could be taken to mean multiple heavens, but their dependence on the biblical usage seems to indicate that these Jewish texts, like those of the Hebrew Bible, present a single heaven cosmography. The early Jewish books in the Apocrypha, although written in the Hellenistic era when the most prominent image of the cosmos in the many cultures of the Mediterranean basin was that of multiple heavens, continue to use the biblical image of the tripartite cosmos: heaven-earth-netherworld. Ben Sira 1:3 explicitly mentions this model: "Who can search out the height of heaven, the breadth of the earth, the netherworld, and wisdom?" This biblical image, described as it is in the religiously authoritative books of the Hebrew Bible, was adopted by people who also adopted the Hebrew Bible's religious and cultural prescriptions.

Joseph and Aseneth

This fanciful tale belongs to a vast body of early Jewish literature that attempts to rewrite biblical stories, making them more relevant to Greco-Roman audiences. The book of Joseph and Aseneth is a tale about the conversion of Joseph's Egyptian wife Aseneth to Judaism.[64] The story seeks to fill in the information about Joseph's wife that is lacking from the story in Genesis 41:45–50: it recounts her conversion to Judaism and shows Joseph's unfailing fidelity to Jewish customs. As part of her conversion, Aseneth repents of her former ways and turns to God in confession and praise.[65] In 12:2 Aseneth praises God "who lifted up the heaven (οὐρανόν) and founded it on a firmament (στερέωμα)[66] upon the back of the winds." The image and vocabulary depend on the narrative of the creation story in Genesis 1. It would seem from this, therefore, that the author of this tale believed in a single heaven. In chapter 15 (verses 7 and 12) there are three occurrences of the term heaven in the plural form, the only plural forms in the book. However, in 22:13 we read that Levi, as a person with insight into matters in the heavenly realm, saw that Aseneth's place of rest (heavenly abode) was in the highest places. The term ὕψιστος means "highest, loftiest of places."[67] The plural form, as in Joseph and Aseneth 22:13, is rarer than the singular but still carries the same idea as the singular. Interestingly, a variant to Joseph and Aseneth 22:13 adds that this place was located in the seventh[68] heaven. It seems that the variant was inspired by the copyist's own cosmography as well as the occurrence of the plural here. That is to say, the copyist transformed the original single heaven cosmography into a multiple heaven cosmography because that model fit his or her own image of the cosmos. In the end, it appears that the story of Joseph and Aseneth originally presented a single heaven cosmography that depended on the old biblical model. The tale of Joseph and Aseneth confirms in its own way that heaven awaits the faithful.

Fourth Ezra

The book of Fourth Ezra recounts a dialogue between Ezra and God in which the two argue over the issue of theodicy, that is why the righteous suffer and the wicked go unpunished. Chapter 7 recounts a debate over what happens when a person dies and when God comes to judge the world in the eschaton. Ezra learned that after death a person's soul wishes to return to God but must be judged first (7:32, 75–101).[69] If the person has lived a righteous life, then it is allowed to ascend to its heavenly habitation (7:32, 80, 95; cf. 4:35). If, on the other hand, it has been evil, then it must suffer punishment. Michael E. Stone has suggested that 4 Ezra 7:75–101 is actually an ascent account.[70] The text describes the seven "ways" (vias) of the wicked and the seven "orders" (ordines) of the righteous in the context of what happens to a soul after death. This passage may suggest an ascent through seven heavens, but the vocabulary does not explicitly identify these ways or stages as heavens.[71] Nonetheless, the postmortem ascent of the righteous soul is the main point of this passage, and this shows that by the late first century CE this originally Greek idea was well known in Jewish circles. Still, why has the author been so ambiguous? Surely this was a most appropriate place to describe how a soul ascends though the several heavens to return to the divinity. Were such an account to be found here, it would not seem out-of-place. The author's use of the terms "ways" and "orders" instead of "heavens" may be due to his or her rejection of a seven heaven schema. That is to say, the author accepted the Hellenistic idea of the postmortem ascent of the soul but rejected the Hellenistic cosmography in favor of the traditional cosmography of the Bible. As Stone has amply demonstrated in his commentary on this book, the actual author of Fourth Ezra was a conflicted individual. Another of his many conflicts was between the traditional biblical view of the cosmos and the modern Hellenistic models. The author has used terms that hint at familiarity with the Hellenistic model, but the text stops short of a complete adoption of the Hellenistic image.

The New Testament

Generally speaking, the singular and plural forms of the Greek term for heaven (οὐρανός and οὐρανοί) are not used consistently in the New Testament. "The singular and plural are used so interchangeably, that we can hardly suppose any difference of meaning between them."[72] While almost all commentators note 2 Corinthians 12:2 in this regard (see chapter 6), several other New Testament passages may also suggest multiple heavens, none more clearly than Revelation 12:12: "Therefore rejoice O heavens (οὐρανοί, plural) and those that dwell in them (αὐτοῖς, plural)!" The problem is most vexing and shows how the simple distinction between the plural and singular forms of the noun cannot alone suffice to identify which model of the heavenly realm the particular author holds. The plural form outnumbers the singular in Matthew, Hebrews, and

2 Peter, while the two forms appear equally in Pauline texts. Nonetheless, the following passages appear to betray adoption of a single heaven cosmography.

GOSPELS

The New Testament Gospels purport to be accounts of the life of Christ written by eyewitnesses or compiled from reports by eyewitnesses. As elsewhere in the New Testament, the singular and plural forms of the Greek term for heaven are used interchangeably. The Gospel of Matthew's phrase "kingdom of heaven" (ἡ βασιλεία τῶν οὐρανῶν) uses the plural form of the term heaven, literally "the kingdom of the heavens." Of the fifty-five occurrences of the plural form of this term in Matthew, twenty-five occur in this phrase. This phrase is unique to Matthew and is rendered as "kingdom of God" in Mark and Luke.[73] In Luke and Acts the ratio of singular to plural is about ten-to-one in favor of the singular. The fact that the singular and plural forms are used interchangeably in the Synoptic Gospels is apparent in the following verses:

> In the resurrection people neither marry nor are given in marriage but are like the angels in heaven (Matt. 22:30, singular; parallel in Mark 12:25 has plural).
> Heaven and earth will pass away . . . (Matt. 24:35, singular; parallels in Mark 13:31 and Luke 21:33 also singular).
> Concerning that day and hour no one knows, not even the angels in heaven . . . (Matt. 24:36, plural; parallel in Mark 13:32 singular).

ELSEWHERE IN THE NEW TESTAMENT

The Greek term for heaven (οὐρανός) appears about equally in the singular and plural in texts attributed to the Apostle Paul. Given what the apostle says in 2 Corinthians 12:2, however, it is clear that he held to a cosmography with multiple heavens. In the rest of the New Testament (Hebrews, James, 1–2 Peter, and 1–3 John) the ratio is somewhat in favor of the plural form.

The book of Revelation at the end of the New Testament is presented as a Revelation to John by Jesus Christ (1:1) and was likely written in the second century CE.[74] The book's descriptions of the horrifying eschatological woes are well known. All the descriptions of the heavenly realm, however, provide no indication that the author imagined that there was more than one heavenly realm. Revelation uses the singular form fifty-one times as opposed to one occurrence of the plural. One verse does seem to indicate that the author believes in a multiple-heaven schema. In 12:12 we read: "Rejoice [εὐφραίνεσθε, plural], therefore, you heavens [οὐρανοί, plural] and those who dwell in them [αὐτοῖς, plural]!" Interestingly, this is the only occurrence of a plural form of heaven (οὐρανός) in the book. The passage is clear. The author calls on the heavens (plural) and those who dwell in them (plural) to rejoice at the fact that the Devil/Satan and his cohort have been expelled from the heavenly realm.

Neither here nor anywhere else in the book do we find a description of various heavens. This passage seems to intimate that the author believes that there is more than one heaven inhabited by heavenly beings. However, it may be that the author is recalling the phrase "rejoice O heavens" from the Septuagint where the plural form of the word heaven (οὐρανοί) is paired with the word rejoice (εὐφραίνειν; e.g., Deut. 32:43; Isa. 44:23, 49:13; Ps. 96:11; but cf. 1 Chr. 16:31 and Isa. 45:8 with the singular). If such is the case, then the plural is due to the plural in the Septuagint passages which in turn has been influenced by the customary use of the plural form in the original Hebrew. The plural form of the term stems not from a particular cosmographical schema but from the vocabulary of the Greek Septuagint, which in turn depends on the vocabulary of the underlying Hebrew text.

All of the activity described in this apocalypse takes place on earth or in heaven. The author's visionary experience begins in 4:1:

> After these things I looked and behold a door was open in heaven and the voice that I had first heard as a trumpet was now saying "come up here and I will show you what must take place after these things." Immediately I was in the spirit and there in heaven was a *throne* with someone sitting on it. The one who was sitting on it looked like jasper and carnelian. A emerald-like rainbow encircled the *throne*. Around the *throne* were twenty-four other *thrones* and upon them were seated twenty-four elders dressed in white and wearing golden *crowns* on their heads. From the *throne* came flashes of lightning and peals of thunder. Seven lamps, representing the seven spirits of God, were burning before the *throne*. In front of the *throne* was a crystalline or glass-like sea. (Rev 4:1–6)

The literary connections back to the prophet Ezekiel's vision in Ezekiel 1 are striking. As here, Ezekiel 1:1 mentions that "the heavens were opened" and the prophet saw "visions of God." In fact, the symbolism of the entire vision recounted in Revelation 4 seems to have been inspired by the prophetic visions recorded in Isaiah 6 and Ezekiel 1. This is unmistakably a vision of the divine throne room. The author stands in a long tradition of people who imagine the divine presence after the model of a throne room. David Aune has shown that the depiction of the divine throne room in Revelation is based on the appearance and protocol of the Roman imperial court.[75] This is not surprising given the long tradition of imagining the divine presence in royal terms and images. "The Lamb" (i.e., Jesus) comes into this throne room scene and seizes control of the action in the rest of the narrative. Eventually a vast multitude of the righteous join the scene and give praise to "God who sits on the throne and to the Lamb" (7:10; cf. 19:4). The focus of this text, then, is the celestial throne of God. The author does not present a multiple heaven schema. Rather, the narrative action takes place either in heaven where the divinity, the heavenly beings, and the righteous all reside, or on earth where humans live and where God's eschatological wrath will one day be vented. The author was commanded to "come up" (4:1) to heaven, and he did so without passing through any intermediary heavenly realms. Likewise, the two prophets of chapter 11 were commanded to "come up," and they, too, ascended immediately into heaven (11:12).

The book also describes God's sanctuary or temple (11:19; 14:15,17; 15:5; 16:1). In fact, the vocabulary of Revelation 11:19 suggests that the heavenly temple is closely associated with the heavenly throne of God. In describing each, the author notes that "a door in heaven" (4:1; "the temple of God in heaven" 11:19) "was opened" (4:5; 11:19) and from the throne (4:5; "ark of his covenant within the temple" 11:19) came forth "flashes of lightening and peals of thunder" (4:5; 11:19). So, for the author of the Book of Revelation, the central element in his vision of heaven was the divine presence. God and Christ rule over the world from the heavenly throne room/temple. Decisions that affect the cosmic order and the lives of humans issue from this throne room/temple. The mixing of temple and royal images is just what one would expect because the image of the heavenly residence of god was analogically shaped by both royal and priestly traditions: the cosmic king's palace is also the divinity's temple.[76] Since this text was written after 70 CE when the Jerusalem Temple was destroyed by the Romans, the complete domination of royal/priestly imagery for the divine presence is striking, especially because this is a Christian document and the Christians had no necessary interest in the Jerusalem Temple and its cult. The combined royal/priestly imagery for God appeared long ago in the biblical materials. Christianity inherited this imagery from its Jewish roots and continued to use it. It seems likely, however, that the Christian communities who lived under the mighty hand of Rome were much more attracted to the powerful royal symbols than to the priestly images. For them, God was the great king on his throne, and the respect and awe shown him was mostly a consequence of his cosmic power.

The New Testament usage of the singular and plural forms of the Greek term for heaven (οὐρανός) is inconsistent. Authors use both forms without any clear distinction between the two. This ambiguity frustrates any attempt to draw firm conclusions about these authors' cosmographies. In general, as one might expect, the New Testament continues traditions with long histories in Judaism: God is in heaven and resides there in a palace/temple.

Greek Apocalypse of Ezra

This Christian text was composed in Greek sometime between 150 and 850 CE,[77] and although it is a Christian composition as it now stands, it likely drew on earlier Jewish traditions. At 1:7 Ezra recounts: "I was taken up into heaven and I saw in the first heaven a great company of angels and they led me to the judgments." It appears that there are several sources behind this text that have conflicting statements regarding the location of these punishments:[78] in chapter 1 they are located in heaven (1:7), while in chapters 4 and 5 they are located in Tartarus, that is, the netherworld (4:4–5:6). Rather than being simply the result of the author's inelegant splicing together of different sources, how-

ever, it should be noted that punishments in the heavenly realm are part of the
development of the ideas about reward and punishment after death that takes
place either in the infernal regions or in the heavenly realms.[79] An author may
believe that there are postmortem punishments in both the infernal region and
the heavenly region.

At some stage in its literary history this apocalypse knew of multiple heavens, although this schema has been reduced to one heaven in the form in which
it has been preserved. The confusion over the allusion to a multiple heaven
cosmography (i.e., "the first heaven," τῳ πρώτῳ οὐρανῷ)[80] may be explained
in one of two ways. First, it may be that the inelegant incorporation of different sources into the text has produced the confusion about the exact number
of heavenly realms. On the other hand, a later editor may have inserted the
term "first" (πρώτῳ) into this phrase because he or she wished to clarify that
what was being described took place in the first of several heavens. That is to
say, originally the text may have not specified the number of the heavens, but
a later editor introduced the designation "first" here because he or she held a
multiple heaven cosmography and wanted to "clarify" the text. Moreover, as
we have already discussed, in this period the Greek term for heaven appears in
both singular and plural without any intention of indicating the number of the
heavenly realms. So, the three cases in this text where the plural form occurs
(1:14; 5:7; 7:6) may not be determinative for the number of heavens in the
cosmography of this text. In fact, given that the plural and singular are not used
consistently, the phrase "the first heaven" (τῷ πρώτῳ οὐρανῷ) in 1:7 is the
only place in this text that unambiguously suggests a multiple-heaven schema.
It could be explained, therefore, as an insertion prompted by an editor's desire—conscious or unconscious—to make the text conform to his or her
multiple-heaven schema. That is to say, the Greek Apocalypse of Ezra originally had a single-heaven cosmography, but somewhere during the text's transmission the term "first" was added to the term "heaven" in 1:7 by someone
attempting to update the text's cosmography. Therefore, what was once a single
heaven cosmography was transformed somewhat inelegantly and incompletely
into a multiple-heaven schema.

While in heaven, Ezra saw the punishments of the wicked and felt compassion for their sufferings. He also saw that the righteous receive their reward in
the heavenly realm. Ezra then asked to go down into Tartarus to see the punishments of sinners. He went down innumerable "steps" in six stages, and
after descending through the first two stages, he stopped at each of the remaining
stages to see the punishments being inflicted on people. The structure of this
descent into the infernal regions has been patterned after an ascent narrative:
the seer moves through several stages in his journey to another realm. When
he finished his tour of the netherworld, a cloud enveloped Ezra and returned
him directly to the heavenly realm (5:7) where he again saw Paradise and some
punishments (5:20–22).

> The prophet said, "Lord, reveal to me the punishments and Paradise!" Then
> the angels led me to the east, and I saw the Tree of Life. I also saw there Enoch

and Elijah and Moses and Peter and Paul and Luke and Matthew and all the righteous and the ancestors.

The narrative is somewhat confused at this point and it is unclear whether this "Paradise" is in the east of heaven or on earth.[81] Since the "Tree of Life" is there, it appears that Ezra has journeyed to the mythical ends of the earth. Here, too, is where the immortals or righteous live (i.e., Enoch, Elijah, and the rest).

The Greek Apocalypse of Ezra provides little detail regarding the structure of the cosmos and the appearance of heaven. It adopts a traditional three-tiered universe: the netherworld, the inhabited surface of the earth, and the heavenly realm. At least one source behind the present text had a multiple-heaven schema and from this came the "first heaven" mentioned in 1:7. Other than this one verse, the text adopts the ancient Near Eastern three-tiered model. The text's reference to the "four corners" of the earth (3:6) and its suggestion that the righteous live in "Paradise" at the mythical ends of the earth indicate that the text presupposes an earthly geography that imagines the earth as a flat plane with mysterious regions at its outermost edges. This is quite revealing because even this text, the latest to be discussed here, imagines the earth and the cosmos after obsolete ancient Near Eastern models. Clearly for this author the biblical images were more reliable than those of the Greco-Roman astronomers and philosophers. The power of the images of the heavenly realm in the Hebrew Bible/Old Testament overrode any model put forward by their contemporaries. Nonetheless, they did adopt some of the religious innovations that developed in the Greco-Roman era. Now, unlike in the Bible, people went either to punishment or reward after death. The afterlife was no longer imagined as the morally neutral Sheol of the Bible. Judaism in all of its varieties had to compete in a much more competitive, cosmopolitan spiritual marketplace. To do so many created new articulations of Judaism that presented the religion in Greco-Roman terms. Thus, as it was earlier formulated among the Persians and Greeks, heaven became a very exclusive club where only the truly deserving would go after death to join the Divine. To prove one's merit, one must observe a prescribed way of life, and, obviously, the prescriptions varied from community to community. Obedience to God's laws now determined the nature of one's postmortem existence. Heaven, or the hope of joining the righteous in God's presence in heaven, was now becoming a powerful religious tool to promote conversion to or steadfast persistence in a religious system.

Summary and Conclusion

The texts discussed in this chapter all seem to presuppose a single heaven cosmography. Throughout the many centuries represented by these texts the dominant "scientific" depiction of the universe was that which imagined multiple heavenly realms above or around the earth. Why do these texts not adopt this model? One explanation for this might be that although the texts do not mention multiple heavens explicitly, their authors nonetheless held to a multiple-heaven schema. The multiple-heaven schema does not appear in these texts because the authors were not interested in providing a complete description of the heavenly realms. Their interests were in discussing what went on in the heavenly realms and in the immediate vicinity of the divine. Their interests were not so much cosmographical as they were theological: they wanted to tell their readers what awaited them after death. These authors would then use this information to convince their audience either to adopt or to persist in a particular lifestyle or belief system.

A second explanation for the single-heaven cosmography in these texts would suggest that some of these authors did not in fact hold a multiple-heaven cosmography. These authors continued to describe the heavenly realm in terms of the ancient model handed down to them in the religiously authoritative writings of their Jewish or Christian communities (i.e., the Bible). That is to say, these authors either did not know or consciously ignored the more "modern" Greco-Roman models of the heavenly realms. Astronomical knowledge did not pass quickly or evenly among all peoples of the ancient Mediterranean world. These authors held on to ancient conceptions of the universe in spite of the developments in modern astronomy. For them even the depictions of the heavenly realm in their religiously authoritative writings were likewise authoritative. This would have created an intellectual conflict between the obsolete models they inherited from their religious tradition and the more modern models of their scientists. The authors of the texts discussed in this chapter appear to have rejected the newfangled Greco-Roman models of the cosmos because they conflicted with the model presupposed in the Bible. Their reaction to this aspect of Hellenistic culture, therefore, was rather negative. To be honest, some of the models proposed by the ancient astronomers were simply too complex to have been understood by most people. Nonetheless, the cosmography of Ptolemy with all its complexities did come to dominate the discussion, and many of these authors must have been familiar with at least some version of the multiple-heaven models.

EARLY JEWISH AND CHRISTIAN
TRADITIONS II
The Adoption of Hellenistic Models

Therefore, fear not death! For that which is from me, namely the soul,
departs for heaven. But that which is from the earth, namely the body,
departs for the earth from which it was taken.

Greek Apocalypse of Ezra 7:3

Some early Jews and Christians reacted to new information about the size and
shape of the cosmos by adopting contemporary Greco-Roman images of the
cosmos. The seeming conflict between the model of the cosmos presupposed
in their religiously authoritative texts and the newer models of their contemporary scientists did not inhibit them, so they chose to express their religious
ideas about the heavenly realms according to these more modern notions. The
"scientific" perception of the structure of the universe had changed, and these
people found no ultimate conflict between their inherited religious traditions
and the new ways of imagining the cosmos. In fact, the new ideas about the
structure of the cosmos fit nicely with newer ideas about the relationship of
humans to God and to the cosmos. The idea that the Divine resides far beyond the several planetary spheres that encircle the earth does not suggest that
these people imagined that God had somehow become further removed from
the world—the Divine had always completely transcended human perceptions.
The new images of the cosmos simply gave more definition to the space that
intervenes between the human and divine realms. Moreover, as was discussed
in chapter 4, the Persian and Greco-Roman ideas that the human soul originated in the divine realm and longs to return to that pure realm after death
comport with these newer images of the cosmos: the soul must ascend through
these intervening spheres in order to reach its ultimate goal. Judaism and Christianity inherited an ancient Near Eastern religious tradition that did not have
such an idea of souls ascending to the heavenly realm. This idea became part

of Judaism, and thus Christianity, as a result of the Jews absorbing Persian and Greek ideas during the Hellenistic period. This is why the only biblical book displaying any familiarity with the idea of astral immortality is the book of Daniel, a book written in the mid-second century BCE. The texts discussed in this chapter all come from the Greco-Roman era and exhibit varying degrees of familiarity with the multiple-heaven schema that became common during this period. This chapter will examine these texts to show how they depict the heavenly realms and what goes on in them. As in chapter 5, the texts are discussed in the best approximation of their chronological sequence.

1 Enoch

The discussion of 1 Enoch in the previous chapter noted that rather than being a book as such, 1 Enoch is actually a collection of five separate texts. Most of these Enochic works adopt a single-heaven cosmography. An appendix to the second unit of this collection, the Parables of Enoch (1 Enoch 37–69), however, suggests that its author(s) held a multiple-heaven cosmography. This appendix, 1 Enoch 70–71, recounts Enoch's ascent into the heavenly realm. The narrative states that Enoch was transported on "the chariots of the spirit" to the northwest region of the earth where he saw the patriarchs and the saints of old who dwelt in that place (70:1–4). This is the abode of the righteous and is the place where Noah went when he wanted to talk with his grandfather Enoch long after Enoch had ascended into heaven (65:1–3). Noah was concerned with the increasing evil in the land and Enoch descended from heaven to tell him about the impending Flood (65:4–66:2). From this place Enoch's *spirit* "was carried" into the heavens where he saw the fiery appearance of the holy angels in their white garments (71:1; cf. 60:8). The angel Michael showed him "all the secrets of the ends of heaven and all the storehouses of all the stars and the lights, from where they come out before the holy ones" (71:3–4). In other words, Enoch's cosmological training was now complete: he knew all the secrets of the cosmos! After these revelations "the spirit carried Enoch off to the highest heaven" (71:5). The phrase "highest heaven" is the equivalent of the Hebrew phrase שמים עליונים (highest heavens) and is of little significance because the plural is the standard form for heaven in Hebrew and Aramaic and does not necessarily indicate multiple heavens. However, there are additional indicators in the passage that suggest that a multiple-heaven schema may underlie this passage. Enoch was lifted up to the heavenly realm where he encountered many angels and then was lifted up again to appear in the vicinity of the Divine. If this is the case, then Enoch experienced a two-stage ascension: first he ascended to a lower heaven where he received revelations about the cosmos from the archangel Michael, and then he ascended to the "highest heaven" where he encountered the Almighty and his retinue (71:9–17).

> And the spirit carried Enoch off to the highest heaven, and I saw there in the
> middle of that light something built of crystal stones, and in the middle of

those stones tongues of living fire. And my spirit saw a circle of fire which surrounded that house; from its four sides (came) rivers full of living fire, and they surrounded that house. And round about (were) the Seraphim, and the Cherubim, and the Ophannim; these are they who do not sleep, but keep watch over the throne of his glory. And I saw angels who could not be counted, a thousand thousands and ten thousand times ten thousand, surrounding that house; and Michael and Raphael and Gabriel and Phanuel, and the holy angels who (are) in the heavens above, went in and out of that house. And Michael and Raphael and Gabriel and Phanuel and many holy angels without number came out from that house; and with them the Head of Days, his head white and pure like wool, and his garments indescribable. (1 Enoch 71:5–10)[1]

This appendix provides the climax of the Parables: Enoch has become one of the angels (71:9–17). In the highest heaven Enoch saw God sitting on a throne attended by myriad angelic beings in the heavenly palace. Although the phrase "highest heaven" alone does not necessarily indicate a multiple-heaven schema, in this case the passage provides additional information that makes such an interpretation possible: Enoch ascended to heaven (71:1) and then ascended again to the heaven where the divinity resided (71:5). If this is the case, then the place where Enoch met the angel is in one of the lower, if not the lowest, of the heavens, and the residence of God is in the highest heaven. This two-stage ascent may depend on a literal exegesis of the biblical phrase שמי השמים "heaven of heavens," which seems to suggest two heavenly realms. Enoch learned cosmological secrets in the first heaven since it was the heavenly realm that humans can observe directly. The reliability of this information provides the reader with additional reasons for believing the heavenly secrets that Enoch claimed to learn in the highest heaven, the realm that humans could never observe directly. The presence of a throne in God's "house" in the highest heaven indicates that this is no typical house; this is the heavenly palace of the divine king, an image that as the previous chapters have shown has deep roots in ancient Near Eastern depictions of the gods, and, most pertinently, the biblical narratives themselves have provided religiously authoritative warrant for describing God's heavenly residence as a great palace or temple (1 Kgs. 8; cf. chapter 3). Enoch was then welcomed by God and his angels into heaven where would remain forever. The text then suggests that what happened to Enoch prefigures what awaits all who are as righteous as Enoch.

And that angel came to me, and greeted me with his voice, and said to me: "You are the Son of Man, who was born to righteousness, and righteousness remains over you, and the righteousness of the Head of Days will not leave you." And he said to me: "He proclaims peace to you in the name of the world which is to come, for from there peace has come out from the creation of the world; and so you will have it for ever and for ever and ever. And all . . . will walk according to your way, inasmuch as righteousness will never leave you; with you will be their dwelling, and with you their lot, and they will not be separated from you, for ever and for ever and ever. And so there will be length of days with that Son of Man, and the righteous will have peace, and the righteous will have an upright way, in the name of the Lord of Spirits for ever and ever." (71:14–17)[2]

These closing sentences of the ascent narrative appended to the "Parables" present Enoch as an example of what can happen to anyone who follows Enoch's pattern of righteous living. In other words, this appendix takes a tradition about Enoch's ascent and personalizes it: "you, too, can expect to be warmly welcomed into heaven by God and his angels as long as you 'walk with God' (Gen. 5:24) as Enoch did!" Postmortem residence in the heavenly realm with the Divine is the reward offered to the faithful who have proven themselves morally qualified. By appending this ascent tradition to the Parables, the author makes the reader's choice clear: live righteously like Enoch, and heaven awaits you; live wickedly, and you will have hell to pay!

Treatise of Shem

The Treatise of Shem is an astrological text that predicts the nature of the coming year based on the sign of the zodiac in which the year begins. This text may have been composed as early as the first century BCE in Alexandria.[3] The following is a brief excerpt from this astrological treatise.

If the year begins in Aries: The year will be lean . . . the river Nile will overflow (at) a good rate. . . . And if the year begins in Taurus: Everyone whose name contains a [B, Y, or K] will become ill, or be wounded by an iron (weapon). . . . And if the year begins in Libra: there will be spring rains. And the year will be transformed. And people will be spared from the east wind. And fig trees will not produce fruit. But date and oil will be plentiful.[4]

This text, if early and Jewish, demonstrates that in some Jewish circles astrology was common practice. Although the astrological notions of this text seemingly contravene the ancient traditions about Yahweh's control of the natural elements, as was discussed in chapter 3, astrology was likely a significant component of some ancient Israelites' religious system. This element was not part of the accepted traditions passed down by the biblical and rabbinic tradents, but it was surely once very popular. Additional evidence of Jewish interest in astrology comes from the Dead Sea Scrolls (4Q186, 317–319). One fragmentary text (4Q186 I.1.5–9) contains a horoscope and a reference to the zodiac: ". . . and his thighs are long and slender, and the toes of his feet are slender and long. He is from the second column. He has a spirit with six parts in the house of light and three parts in the house of darkness. This is the sign in which he is born: the period of Taurus. He will be poor. This is his animal: a bull."[5]

It would be incorrect to assume that astrology such as this was the product of some Hellenistic Jews who ". . . compromised ancient traditions as they became accommodated to foreign lands and customs."[6] This had long been a part of Israelite piety or "science" and can be imagined as some form of cultural or religious compromise only from the standpoint of much later standards of Jewish orthodoxy or from the parochial perspectives of the latest biblical tradents (see chapter 3). The Treatise of Shem and similar texts are simply fortuitous remnants of Israelite and early Judaism's ancient astronomical and astrological traditions. The text does not describe the heavenly realms per se, but the fact that the foundation of this text is the zodiac suggests that the authors were positively predisposed to Greco-Roman astronomy/astrology. This form of heavenly speculation surely captivated a good many ancient Jews. In fact, even the rabbis admit familiarity with speculation on how the astronomical bodies might affect a person (b. Shabb. 156a). So, when some ancient Jews looked to the heavens, what intrigued them was not what the divine presence or the world beyond looked like but what the stars could tell them, a fascination they share with almost all human cultures. One thing is certain, while humans live at different times, in different places with different climates, and have different languages and cultures, they all share one thing in common, the stars.

Testament of Levi

The traditions about the patriarch Levi are amazingly complex. In addition to the Hebrew Bible and the many references to Levi in several early Jewish and Christian texts, there are two related Levi documents.[7] First, the Greek Testament of Levi (Gk. Test. Levi) is part of a larger work entitled The Testaments of the Twelve Patriarchs. These Testaments purport to be records of the last words of the patriarchs to their descendants. They are either Jewish compositions that were subsequently edited by Christians, or Christian documents that depend heavily upon earlier Jewish sources.[8] Either way, they surely preserve early Jewish traditions.[9] Second, the Cairo Geniza and the Qumran caves (the Dead Sea Scrolls) have yielded another document, the Aramaic Levi Document (ALD).[10] This separate Levi document[11] was one of the sources behind the Greek Testament of Levi[12] and was composed no later than the second century BCE.[13]

Because of the fragmentary nature of the Aramaic Levi Document, and because Levi's heavenly ascent is narrated fully only in the Greek Testament of Levi, this discussion will focus on the latter. Since the early Levi traditions preserved in the Aramaic Levi Document do not include this elaborate heavenly ascent, the attribution of this ascent to Levi may have occurred sometime after the mid-second century BCE. Levi's vision of the heavens is recounted in the Greek Testament of Levi 2:1–5:3. The manuscripts for this section of Greek Testament of Levi divide into two groups, each attesting a different cosmography. The most convincing reconstruction of the textual stemma for this text is that proposed by H. J. de Jonge,[14] while the reconstruction by R. H. Charles is inferior in many ways.[15] The cosmographic schemas found in these two editions of the Greek Testament of Levi differ significantly: De Jonge's edition has a seven-heaven cosmography, while Charles's edition has a three-heaven cosmography. Furthermore, Charles claims that ancient Jewish cosmographic speculation evolved from a schema with three heavens to one with seven heavens.[16] As will become clear, the evidence from the edition of the Greek Testament of Levi by de Jonge indicates just the opposite: the copyists of the manuscripts used by Charles abbreviated an original seven-heaven schema to a three-heaven schema.

Levi's vision of the heavenly realms began when "the spirit of understanding of the Lord" came upon him and made him painfully aware of humanity's wickedness (Gk. Test. Levi 2:3). Levi prayed to be saved and then fell asleep while grieving over his and humanity's sin (2:4–5a). In his sleep he had a vision of the heavens (2:4–5:7). This heavenly vision, then, came in response to Levi's prayer for salvation from wickedness.[17]

One manuscript (designated "e") has a slightly different setting for the onset of the vision.[18] This expanded form of Levi's prayer is part of a fragment incorporated into the Greek Testament of Levi possibly from the Aramaic Levi Document or a text very much like it.[19] In this form of the prayer Levi ritually cleansed himself (verses 1–2) and then prayed to God for protection and wisdom (verses 6–18). This form of the prayer reads as an attempt to induce a vision or to make Levi fit for receiving a vision. The features here are (1) ritual cleansing of clothes and body, (2) prayer for forgiveness, (3) request for wisdom, and (4) a request for admission into to the divine presence. Does this expanded version of Levi's prayer belong here? There are several internal indications that some form of this prayer provides a fitting introduction to the ascent narrative. First, the response of the angel to Levi's astonishment in Greek Testament of Levi 2:9b–10 links directly back to Levi's request for divine wisdom and admission into the divine presence as recounted in the expanded prayer: "when you ascend there you will stand near the Lord, and will be his minister, and will declare his mysteries to men, and will proclaim concerning him who will rescue Israel" (2:9b–10).[20] Second, just prior to Levi's entrance into the divine presence, the angel told Levi that the Most High will grant his requests for deliverance, to become a priest, and to be a "son of God" (Gk. Test. Levi 4:2). Only two of these requests in 4:2 appear in the expanded prayer. The granting of deliverance from wickedness in 4:2 corresponds to the request in the expanded prayer:[21] "Make far from me, O Lord, the wicked spirit." The promised appointment to the priesthood in 4:2 corresponds to another request in the expanded prayer: "bring me forward to be your servant and to minister to you well." The third element, to become a "son of God," has no connection to any version of the prayer. Together these correspondences indicate that the vision came in response to the very things Levi requested according to the expanded version of the prayer found in the "e" manuscript of the Greek Testament of Levi and reflected in the Qumran fragments of the Aramaic Levi

Document. The internal connections between the prayer of the "e" manuscript and the subsequent narrative strongly suggest that either the prayer of the "e" manuscript or one very much like it formed the original introduction to the vision.[22]

The following is a reconstruction of the description of the heavens in Charles's version of the Greek Testament of Levi.

2:7: And I entered into the first heaven and I saw there much water hanging.[23]

2:8: Then I saw a second heaven far brighter and more luminous and indeed there was boundless height in it.

2:9–11: I said to the angel, "Why is this so?" And the angel said to me, "Do not marvel at this for another heaven more luminous and incomparable you shall see, and when you enter it you shall stand near to the Lord and shall become his servant. You shall declare his mysteries to men and herald the one coming to rescue Israel.

3:1–2: Hear, therefore, concerning the heavens shown to you: The lower for this reason is more gloomy, since it sees all the unrighteous acts of men. It has fire, snow, and ice prepared for the day of judgment by the righteousness of God. In it are all the spirits of persecutions for vengeance on men.

3:3: In the second (heaven) are the hosts of the armies who are appointed for the day of judgment to perform vengeance on the spirits of error and of Beliar. Above these are the holy ones.

3:4–6: In the highest (heaven) of all dwells the Great Glory above all holiness. In it (the heaven) with them are the archangels who minister and make atonement to the Lord for all the sins of ignorance of the righteous. They offer to the Lord a pleasant savor, an appropriate and bloodless sacrifice.

3:7–9 In the one (heaven) below are the angels who bear answers to the angels of the Lord's presence. In it (the heaven) with them are thrones and authorities.[24] In it hymns are always being offered to God. When, therefore, the Lord looks upon us, we all tremble; not only us, but also heaven and earth and the abyss shake from the presence of his greatness."

After 3:9 Charles's reconstruction returns to basic agreement with the other versions. According to this account of the ascent, Levi saw three heavens. An angel summoned him to the first heaven (2:4–6) while he was standing on the otherwise unknown mountain called "Abel-Maoul," apparently the place where heaven and earth intersect or where the entrance into the heavenly realm was located.[25] After Levi saw each of the heavens, his guiding angel explained to him what he had seen.[26] Levi entered the first heaven and saw there much water (2:7).[27] He peered into the second heaven which was extremely high and luminous (2:8). Marveling at the sight, he asked his accompanying angel to explain the vision (2:9a), and the angel told him not to be amazed at this for he was about to see another heaven even more brilliant (2:9b). The angel further told Levi that once he ascended to the next heaven he would stand near the Lord, become his minister, and proclaim his mysteries to mankind (2:10).

Although the angel had told him not to marvel at the sight, the angel continued to focus attention on the sight by explaining it to Levi (3:1–8). The angel's explanation, however, does not agree with the vision. A detailed interpretation of what Levi reportedly saw in the first two heavens appears nowhere in the angel's explanations. Instead, the angel identifies and explains several elements that Levi himself never mentioned. The angel described the first heaven as gloomy—a feature unnoticed by Levi—because it witnesses the wicked deeds of humanity (3:1). In addition, the natural elements of fire, snow and ice are stored here for use on the day of judgment (3:2). Levi himself did not see these natural elements in the first heaven, nor anywhere else; he learned of them only through the angel's revelations. While it is not unusual to encounter natural elements such as these in the lowest heaven, they are not typically associated with eschatological judgment.[28] According to the angel, the armies prepared for the day of judgment are in the second heaven (3:3), but Levi never mentioned having seen these either. The angel's explanations indicate that his interests were in the eschatological judgment of the wicked, and it appears, therefore, that this material has been forced upon the account of Levi's vision.[29] Whatever Levi's observations were, the angel's explanations transform the focus of the text to an interest in eschatological judgment. The angel's explanations do have a coherence of their own, but they do not relate to the things Levi reportedly saw. The angel's interpretations must be secondary; they have been incorporated into the text of the vision in order to emphasize the theme of eschatological judgment. This added material takes Levi's simple descriptions of the items he saw during his ascent and transforms the text into an exhortation to ethical living.[30] Moreover, the angel's concern with the punishment of sinners harkens back to Levi's concern for sin in his preparatory prayer (2:3–4). Literarily, the angel's refocusing of the ascent narrative is designed to teach Levi that the evil that so troubled him will eventually be punished by God. The angel then described the heavens in descending order starting with the highest heaven (3:4–8). Thus, Charles's reconstruction of the Greek Testament of Levi attests a three-heaven structure. Levi saw water in the first heaven (2:7), but the angel described it as a gloomy place (3:1). Levi saw intense brightness in the second heaven (2:2), but the angel described it as the place where the heavenly armies stand prepared for the day of judgment (3:3), and where angels praise God (3:7–8). The third heaven, "the highest," which Levi had not yet seen, is where God dwells along with the archangels who make atonement for the sins of humanity (3:3–6).[31]

De Jonge's edition improves upon that of Charles in many ways, and this edition explicitly attests a seven-heaven cosmography. Levi entered the first heaven and went immediately to the second (2:7). Between the first two heavens he saw the vast celestial sea (2:7). In the angel's account of the heavens the first is a dark place, a darkness due to the sins of humanity that corrupt it (3:1b). In the second heaven are stored the means of God's judgment—fire, snow, ice, and "all the spirits of affliction"—ready for the day of God's judgment (3:2). In the third heaven, which is brighter than the first and measureless in height (2:8), the divine armies stand prepared for the day of judgment (3:3a). The text becomes obscure at 3:3b where the fourth heaven is concerned. De Jonge's edition reads "and those in the fourth who are above these are holy."[32] Hollander and de Jonge render it as "but the (heavens) down to the fourth above these are holy."[33] Hollander and de Jonge's identification of ἅγιοι, "holy ones," with the heavens[34] is unwarranted since the term ἅγιοι, "holy ones," is best understood as referring to a class of angels. The immediate context both preceding and following this statement is concerned with the contents of the various heavens. Perhaps a better translation would be "but those in the fourth (heaven) above these are holy ones." The Greek particle δὲ introduces a contrast first between these holy ones and the beings and instruments of judgment encountered in heavens one and two, and second between these holy ones and "the Great Glory in the holy of holies far beyond all holiness" (3:4). Although the angelic beings in the fourth heaven are indeed holy, they cannot compare with the ultimate glory of God.

Oddly, at this point the angel reverses direction and explains the heavenly realms in descending order starting with the seventh (3:4–8). Following the text of de Jonge carefully, one finds that in the highest heaven (i.e., the seventh, 3:1) dwells the "great glory in the holy of holies of all holiness" (3:4). In the next lower heaven, the sixth, the angels of the Lord's presence offer savory sacrifices before God (3:5–6). In the fifth heaven (i.e., "in the heaven below") are the angels who communicate with the angels of the Lord's presence (3:7). Finally, in the fourth heaven are the "thrones and authorities" (3:8).[35]

After explaining the contents of the seven heavens to Levi and giving some eschatological predictions, the angel opened the gates of the highest heaven so Levi could see God sitting on the throne (5:1–2). It is not clear whether Levi actually entered the highest heaven or simply stood outside the gates and peered into this realm. The Greek Testament of Levi 2:10 assumes that he will enter into this heaven and stand next to God, while 5:1–3 seems to leave him standing at the gates when God addressed him from the throne. What is being depicted is a heaven surrounded by a gated wall that separates the beings who have access to this heaven from the actual dwelling place of God. Levi may thus be on this heavenly plane and yet not in the immediate presence of God. God then commissioned Levi to the priesthood and to the task of declaring transcendent knowledge upon his return to earth (2:10–12, cf. 4:2–5:3). After God addressed Levi and appointed him as a priest,[36] the angel led him back to earth (5:3).

Ascent accounts can serve to authorize many things,[37] but here the central interest is in validating Levi's priesthood and not in detailing the structure or contents of the heavens. While the second century BCE "Aramaic Levi Document" mentioned Levi's vision of heaven, it did not describe any heavenly ascent; this original "vision of heaven" was later transformed into an "ascent to heaven." The manuscripts of the Greek Testament of Levi describe either a three-heaven[38] or a seven-heaven cosmic schema. Such variations are likely due to the copyists trying to make the text conform to their own particular cosmographies. Whatever the reason for these differences, the seven-heaven structure seems to be original. Charles's claim that the original text had three heavens that were eventually expanded to seven is based on his adoption of the so-called "α" (alpha) family of texts as the earliest and most reliable. The work of Hunkin and de Jonge have demonstrated that Charles was wrong in this textual decision.[39] The Greek text did not evolve from a three-heaven to a seven heaven schema as Charles, Bietenhard, and Kee assume.[40] The shorter versions are a corruption of an earlier seven-heaven schema. It is very possible that a later Christian hand revised the original seven-heaven schema to a three-heaven schema in light of the Apostle Paul's ascent to the "third heaven."

2 Corinthians 12:1–4

> It is necessary to boast. Although there is nothing to be gained, I will go on to visions and revelations of the Lord. I know a person in Christ who fourteen years ago was caught up to the third heaven. Whether this was in the body or out of the body I do not know—God knows. I know that such a person—whether in the body or out of the body I do not know, but God knows—was caught up into Paradise and heard things unutterable, things no person is permitted to talk about.

Saul the Pharisee became Paul the apostle after a visionary experience in which he saw Christ (Acts 9:1–9; 22:3–16; 26:9–18), and from his writings it appears that he had several other visions.[41] One might say, then, that Paul was a visionary in the true sense of the word. Despite the hesitant nature of Paul's words in 2 Corinthians 12:1–4, most all agree that the apostle is here speaking of one of his own ecstatic experiences in the early part of his ministry, fourteen years prior to writing this letter (12:2).

Paul equates the third heaven with paradise.[42] All Paul recounts is that he heard "things unutterable"; he does not elaborate on what he saw or heard. This passage appears in a context where Paul is trying to prove his superiority to those teachers who oppose him and his teachings. Paul expresses the overwhelming awe of what he experienced by noting that he did not know whether this took place in or out of the body. That is to say, he could not determine whether he had bodily ascended to heaven or had simply had a vision. The psychological dynamics of heavenly ascent are profoundly expressed in a passage from the Ascension of Isaiah. According to this apocryphal story, the prophet Isaiah had come into Jerusalem to speak to king Hezekiah and a crowd of prophets gathered to hear him.

> And when Isaiah spoke with Hezekiah the words of righteousness and faith, they all heard a door being opened and the voice of the Spirit. And the king summoned all the prophets and all the people who were to be found there, and they came. And Micah, and the aged Ananias, and Joel, and Josab were sitting on his right. And when they all heard the voice of the Holy Spirit, they all worshipped on their knees, and they praised the God of righteousness, the Most High, the One who (dwells) in the upper world and who sits on high, the Holy One, the One who rests among the holy ones, and they

ascribed glory to the One who had thus graciously given a door in an alien world, had graciously given it to a man. And while he was speaking with the Holy Spirit in the hearing of them all, he became silent, and his mind was taken up from him, and he did not see the men who were standing before him. His eyes indeed were open, but his mouth was silent, and the mind in his body was taken up from him. But his breath was (still) in him, for he was seeing a vision. And the angel who was sent to show him (the vision) was not of this firmament, nor was he from the angels of glory of this world, but he came from the seventh heaven. And the people who were standing by, apart from the circle of the prophets, did [not] think that the holy Isaiah had been taken up. And the vision which he saw was not from this world, but from the world which is hidden from the flesh. And after Isaiah had seen this vision he recounted it to Hezekiah, and to Josab his son, and to the other prophets who had come. (Asc. Isa. 6:6–16)[43]

This passage dramatically depicts how a trance state appears to those observing it. This is obviously a literary creation, but some real knowledge or experience of the physiological and psychological components of altered-state experiences seems to have influenced the narrative.[44] Although the visionary was sitting in the midst of other prophets, what was going on in his mind was beyond the perceptions of those watching. According to this narrative only those members of Isaiah's inner group perceived that he was having an encounter with the divine realm. One might guess that this perception was due to peculiarities in his behavior or vocabulary or to their belief in Isaiah as a true prophet and mediator between the divine and mundane worlds. A similar altered-state experience appears to have happened to Paul. For this reason he does not know whether his ascent into the third heaven was in the body or not. Whatever the mode, the experience was overwhelming.

How did the apostle Paul imagine the heavenly realms? In 2 Corinthians 12:1–4 we are simply not provided with enough information. He obviously adopted a multiple-heaven model, but precisely how many heavens he thought there were is not certain.[45] It seems that if Paul were trying to impress people with the greatness of the things that God had done for him, it would have been fitting that he be ushered into the divine presence in the highest realm. Beyond this, however, one cannot determine exactly how many heavens Paul thought there were—three, four, seven, more? If the third heaven is not the highest, as would support his polemics against his detractors, then nothing more can be known about Paul's image of the heavenly realm other than that he believed in multiple heavens. Moreover, Ephesians 4:10 may provide an additional hint of Paul's cosmography. In describing Christ's descent from heaven and his subsequent return to the heavenly realm, this verse says that "he who descended is the one who ascended far above all the heavens (ὑπεράνω πάντων τῶν οὐρανῶν [plural]) so that he might fill the universe." The use of "above all the heavens" suggests multiple heavens, but as was noted before, the New Testament authors use the singular and plural forms of the term for heaven (οὐρανός and οὐρανοί) almost interchangeably.[46] Ephesians 4:10 only suggests that the apostle conceived of multiple heavens. Unfortunately, the other New Testament texts attributed to the apostle Paul provide little additional detail into his image of the heavenly realm. Nonetheless he clearly adopted a multiple-heaven model. Paul, betraying the Greco-Roman character of his piety, wrote to his followers that their ultimate destiny, their true citizenship, was not in any earthly empire but in the heavenly realm (2 Cor 5:1–5; 1 Thess 4:15–17). Paul's idea that Christians long to abandon this mortal world of decay and corruption to ascend to the heavenly realm of perfection and there rejoin the company of the Divinity is a Christian adaptation of beliefs and motifs from long-standing Greco-Roman astral religions. Paul, no matter how devout a Pharisee he may have been (Phil 3:4–6), articulated his new religion with a recent convert's zeal and a decidedly Greco-Roman tone. Heaven for him was the kingdom whither the righteous Christians would ascend to join their God, and there inherit heavenly bodies and inhabit celestial mansions (1 Cor. 15:20–57; 2 Cor. 5:1–5; Eph. 2:6; Phil. 3:20–21). Paul's thoroughly Greco-Roman image of immortality has influenced all subsequent western Christian images of heaven. Christian theologians to this day speculate on the mansions, streets of gold, and so forth that await the faithful. It is a powerful image. The pains and limitations of this world are to give way to unlimited fulfillment.

Philo of Alexandria

Philo of Alexandria, that great first century CE Jewish philosopher, unabashedly ascribed to a Greco-Roman model of the universe, and his version of Judaism was likewise thoroughly Hellenized. Philo was familiar with traditional Jewish thought and was thoroughly versed in most all aspects of Greco-Roman philosophy. His works represent an attempt to commend Jews and Judaism to the rest of the Greco-Roman world as well as to show Jews how his Hellenized interpretation of Judaism can be favorably compared with the best of contemporary philosophy. Philo's adoption of the seven-heaven model is apparent in several passages, but the following examples will suffice. In each case, Philo's description of the universe is prompted by his allegorical interpretation of items mentioned in the Bible: the seven-branched candelabra in the Temple and the Cherubim who guard the entrance to the Garden of Eden.

> The holy candlestick and the seven candle-bearers on it are a copy of the march of the choir of the seven planets. How so? perhaps we shall be asked. Because, we shall reply, each of the planets is a light-bringer, as the candle-bearers are. For they are supremely bright and transmit the great luster of their rays to the earth, especially the central among the seven, the sun. I call it central, not merely because it holds the central position, which some give as the reason, but because apart from this it has the right to be served and attended by its squires on either side, in virtue of its dignity and magnitude and the benefits which it provides for all that are on the earth. Now the order of the planets is a matter of which men have no sure apprehension—indeed is there any

other celestial phenomenon which can be known with real certainty?—and therefore they fall back on probabilities. But the best conjecture, in my opinion, is that of those who assign the middle place to the sun and hold that there are three above him and the same number below him. The three above are Saturn, Jupiter and Mars, and the three below are Mercury, Venus and the Moon, which borders on the lower region of air. So the Master-craftsman, wishing that we should possess a copy of the archetypal celestial sphere with its seven lights, commanded this splendid work, the candlestick, to be wrought. (Who is the Heir of Divine Things 221–24)[47]

We must now examine what is symbolized by the Cherubim and the sword of flame which turns every way. I suggest that they are an allegorical figure of the revolution of the whole heaven. For the movements assigned to the heavenly spheres are of two opposite kinds, in the one case an unvarying course, embodying the principle of sameness, to the right, in the other a variable course, embodying the principle of otherness, to the left. The outermost sphere, which contains what are called the fixed stars, is a single one and always makes the same revolution from east to west. But the inner spheres, seven in number, contain the planets and each has two motions of opposite nature, one voluntary, the other under a compelling force. Their involuntary motion is similar to that of the fixed stars, for we see them pass every day from east to west, but their own proper motion is from west to east, and it is in this that we find the revolutions of the seven governed also by certain lengths of time. These lengths are the same in the case of three whose course is equal, and these three which have the same rate of speed are known as the Sun, the Morning-star, and the Sparkler (or Mercury). The others have unequal courses and different lengths of time in revolution, though these too preserve a definite proportion to each other and the above-named three. One of the Cherubim then symbolizes the outermost sphere of the fixed stars. It is the final heaven of all, the vault in which the choir of those who wander not move in a truly divine unchanging rhythm, never leaving the post which the Father who begat them has appointed them in the universe. The other of the Cherubim is the inner contained sphere, which through a sixfold division He has made into seven zones of regular proportion and fitted each planet into one of them. He has set each star in its proper zone as a driver in a chariot, and yet He has in no case trusted the reins to the driver, fearing that their rule might be one of discord, but He has made them all dependent on Himself, holding that thus would their march be orderly and harmonious. For when God is with us all we do is worthy of praise; all that is done without Him merits blame. This then is one interpretation of the allegory of the Cherubim, and the flaming turning sword represents, we must suppose, their movement and the eternal revolution of the whole heaven. (On the Cherubim 21–25)[48]

Philo clearly understood Greco-Roman models of the cosmos: he knew that there were seven spheres encircling the earth and that each sphere housed one celestial body. He even knew of the Pythagorean notion that the celestial spheres make sounds as they rotate (Heir of Divine Things 207–14). Since his cosmography is one of the few that displays a good understanding of Greco-Roman astronomy, and since he was unquestionably a very well-educated person, Philo is a good example of our thesis that although the Greco-Roman models were known to early Jewish and Christian writers, they either did not understand them completely or they chose to adapt these astronomical models to fit their own particular literary agenda or religious perspectives. Philo's version of Judaism was unmistakably Greco-Roman, and because of his vast learning and intellectual acumen, Philo was able to express Jewish images of the cosmos in virtually flawless Greco-Roman terms.

Not surprisingly, Philo also believed in the immortality of the soul and that at death it would return to the celestial realm whence it came. Again, a couple of examples make this clear.

> Why does Abraham say "I am an immigrant and sojourner among you? (Gen 23:4)" But does not every wise soul live like an immigrant and sojourner in this mortal body, after having for habitat and country the most pure substance of heaven, from which it migrates to this habitat by a compelling law? Perhaps this was in order that it might carefully inspect terrestrial things, that even these might not be without a share in wisdom to participate in the better life, or in order that it might be akin to created beings and not be continuously and completely happy. (Questions on Genesis 4.74)[49]

> A fine lesson is given us when he represents the good man not as dying but departing, in order that the kind of soul that is fully purified be shown to be inextinguishable and immortal, destined to undergo a journey from hence to heaven, and not dissolution and corruption, which death appears to bring. (Who is the Heir of Divine Things 276)[50]

Philo's Hellenized form of Judaism knew well both Greco-Roman astronomy and philosophy. Surely he was not alone in this as all aspects of Jewish life in the first century BCE were affected to one degree or another by Hellenistic culture. Nor were such Hellenistic interpretations of Judaism limited to areas outside of Judaea such as Philo's Alexandria.[51] In fact, the Jewish sect of the Essenes, traditionalists to be sure, lived in Palestine and held clearly Hellenistic beliefs about the heavenly origin and postmortem destiny of the soul (see chapter 7). Philo fittingly represents, therefore, the ideas of Jews with a thorough exposure to and personal affinity for Greco-Roman thought and culture. Their images of the heavenly realm, therefore, accorded very well with those of their non-Jewish neighbors.

Testament of Abraham

This early Jewish text recounts Abraham's tour through the places of judgment and is, strictly speaking, not a tour through various heavens.[52] The story recounts that when the archangel Michael told Abraham that he was about to die, the famous patriarch asked to see the entire inhabited world.

And now, O Lord, I do not oppose your power because I know that I am not immortal but mortal. Since, therefore, at your command everything submits and shakes and trembles before your power, I too fear. But one request I ask of you. Now, Master, Lord, hear my petition, for while I am in this body I wish to see all of the inhabited world and all the creations which by one word you, O Master established. When I have seen these things, should I then depart from this life, I shall be without sorrow.[53]

The text has been preserved in two recensions: "long" (A) and "short" (B).[54] According to recension A, God instructed Michael to take Abraham "upon a cherubim chariot and elevate him to the ether of heaven so that he might see all the inhabited world."[55] This ether is the expanse above the atmosphere of the earth according to popular Greco-Roman cosmography.[56] After viewing the earth from the ethereal realm and rashly condemning sinners, the archangel escorted Abraham to the east to the first gate of heaven (10:15–11:1A).[57] The ancient Greeks identified the ether as the rarefied air in which the planets and stars traveled. Mentioned first by Anaxagoras in the fifth century, the idea gained prominence through the work of Aristotle (384–322 BCE). The ethereal realm is the space from the level of the moon upward. The reference to ether in recension A displays the author's acceptance of this popular Greco-Roman conception of the universe. However, since according to the Greco-Roman understanding of the ethereal realm no earthly substance can exist in this realm, this author either misunderstands this concept or is attempting to portray Abraham as so completely righteous that he, unlike anyone else, can ascend to this level and not perish.

At the easternmost regions of the ethereal realm is a gate leading up to heaven. At this gate there is a division in the road: on the right is a wide gate leading to destruction, while on the left is a narrow gate and path leading to Paradise (11:1–4A). At this fork in the road sits a man (Adam) weeping over the souls being driven down the wide path to destruction, but rejoicing over the few souls being led by angels down the narrow path to Paradise (11:4–12:3A).[58] Inside the broad gate another man (Abel)[59] sits on a throne behind a table with a book lying on it. This man is attended by two angels; one angel holds a pen and papyrus while the other carries a light and a set of scales (12:4–8A). The man is the judge of human souls, and he consults the book on the table while the angels on either side record the person's righteous and wicked deeds (12:11–18A). Michael then returned Abraham to his house where he began to prepare for his death (15:1A).

This story is based on the belief that there is a place at the easternmost region of the ethereal realm where heaven and earth intersect. Here a soul's fate is decided. Although the narrative never explicitly identifies the direction in which the sinners travel to arrive at their ultimate destination, the righteous go "up" from this place to "the garden" or "Paradise" (13:13A; 14:8A). For this author the heavenly abode or the paradise of the righteous, as well as the realm of punishment, is accessed from a gate at the easternmost region of the ethereal realm. No one can enter heaven without first facing a review of their life. This "life review" serves an an obstacle to prevent the undeserving from ascending into heaven. That Abraham saw only a few people entering into "Paradise" indicates that heaven is a very exclusive place into which only the truly qualified may enter.

The shorter B recension of the Testament of Abraham has a slightly different portrayal of Abraham's travels. Here Michael transported Abraham on a cloud instead of a chariot,[60] and their first stop was the earth-encircling "river Okeanus" where the righteous and wicked souls are separated (8:3B). This place was not mentioned in recension A. So, part of the difference between the two recensions of the Testament of Abraham involves the cosmography. The separation of the righteous from the wicked takes place at the first gate of heaven in the easternmost reaches of the heavenly realm according to recension A, while recension B locates this event at the river Okeanus at the mythical ends of the earth. Functionally, these two places represent the boundary between the earthly and heavenly realms. However, while the places are rather different, the event that takes place at these two places is the same: the just and the unjust are finally separated. Such a theme appeared already in Plato's "Myth of Er:"

> He (Er) said that when his soul went forth from his body he journeyed with a great company and that they came to a mysterious region where there were two openings side by side in the earth, and above and over against them in the heaven two others, and that judges were sitting between these, and that after every judgement they bade the righteous journey to the right and upwards through the heaven . . . and the unjust to take the road to the left and downward. (*Republic*, x, 614).[61]

This image of separation is meant to inspire the readers to adopt a way of life that will ensure that they receive reward when they arrive at this place after death. There is an entrance to heaven, to be sure, but not all are granted admission.

The next difference between the two versions of the Testament of Abraham is that in recension A Abraham and Michael followed an angel who forced souls to pass through the broad gate leading to destruction. On the other side of this gate they saw a judgment scene in which Abel and some angels judged souls (12:1–14:15A). In recension B, however, Michael transported Abraham on a cloud to "the garden," and there they saw Abel separating the souls (10:1–11:10B).[62] Here Enoch and not an angel records the deeds of humans (11:3–10B). So, according to recension A, this judgment of souls takes place inside of the broad gate located just inside the gate leading to heaven. Recension B, on the other hand, locates this same judgment scene in "the garden" located at the mythical ends of the earth some distance beyond the river Okeanus.

The conception of the structure of the universe in recension A assumes that Abraham journeyed to the ethereal realm in the sky where no earthly being can exist because of its rarefied air. This Greco-Roman model involves concentric planetary spheres encircling the earth beyond which is the realm of purest ether. Either the author misunderstands the astronomical model or has chosen to have Abraham travel about this realm without dying in order to emphasize Abraham's righteousness. The presentation in recension B assumes that Abraham journeyed to a place at the mythical ends of the earth. The cosmographical structure assumed by this text is the ancient, traditional flat earth model that was common throughout the Near East and that persisted in Jewish tradition because of its place in the religiously authoritative biblical materials.

From the differences between the two recensions, one may conclude that the people who produced the final forms of these two recensions of the Testament of Abraham held differing views of the structure of the universe and of the location of postmortem judgment. They have transformed certain details in the text to make it conform to their own ideas about the cosmos's structure. This text, then, shows how diverse cosmographic views have influenced the depiction of the cosmos. Thus, the diversity in how ancient Jews and Christians depicted the cosmos is apparent not only between different texts and authors but, in the cases of the Testament of Levi (see above) and the Testament of Abraham, even in different versions of a single text. These differences in cosmography between the two versions of the Testament of Abraham are introduced into these texts in a manner that parallels how verbal or theological differences are introduced into different versions of a text: thus in the case of the Testament of Abraham, the two versions differ not only over issues of theology[63] but also over cosmography. Just as editors might introduce new theology or ideology into a text, so they can change the cosmography to fit their own personal views. The Testament of Abraham's theological goal of inspiring people to live moral lives could have been furthered by speculating more on the bliss of the heavenly realm. Instead, the focus is on punishment and judgment, the sufferings to be avoided. In the end, however, Abraham's soul was escorted into the divine presence in heaven where it worshipped God (20:11–13). Then angels took Abraham's soul into "Paradise, where the tents of my righteous ones and the mansions of my holy ones Isaac and Jacob are in his bosom, where there is no distress, no sorrow, no groaning, but peace and joy and unending life" (20:4). The text ends, fittingly, with a description of the good fortune that awaits the righteous in heaven. Although there are no details on the appearance of the heavenly realm, the nature of the life enjoyed there is attractive enough to encourage the reader to heed the ethical admonitions of this text. This author uses the prospect of having to face an inescapable and frightful critique of one's life and of enjoying eternal bliss in heaven to inspire people to live righteous lives.

Apocalypse of Zephaniah

This appears to be a Jewish apocalypse written sometime between the first century BCE and the mid–second century CE but transmitted in Christian circles.[64] Apart from the Coptic text treated below, the heavenly journey of the prophet

Zephaniah is mentioned also in a couple of ancient sources, the most note-worthy being a fragment preserved by Clement of Alexandria (ca. 150–215 CE).

> Are these statements not like those of Zephaniah the prophet? "And a spirit took me, and brought me up to the fifth heaven. And I saw angels called 'lords', and the diadem had been set upon them by the Holy Spirit. And each of them had a throne seven times brighter than the light of the rising sun;[65] and they dwelt in temples of salvation, and they praised the ineffable Most High God." (Stromata V.xi.77)[66]

Zephaniah was transported by a spirit to the fifth heaven where he saw angels wearing crowns and sitting on thrones. This text has neither a detailed account of the journey nor any description of the contents of the individual heavens. This lack of detail is likely to be accounted for by the fact that this fragment is a quotation in a secondary source whose own interests were not in issues of heavenly speculation. The mention of diadems (i.e., crowns) and thrones in-dicates that this Zephaniah fragment imagined the heavenly realm after the pattern of a royal palace, a model that had been the most common image of the divine presence for millennia.

The longest version of the Apocalypse of Zephaniah is preserved in Coptic, but this, too, is incomplete. The text recounts how the angel of the Lord raised Zephaniah up to hover over Jerusalem to observe the people below. The angel then led Zephaniah to Mt. Seir where he saw the angels of God and the angels of the Adversary sitting "at the gate of heaven" and recording people's good and wicked deeds (3:5–9). The angel accompanying Zephaniah took the records of the just and brought them to "the Lord Almighty" who then transcribed the names into "the Book of the Living." Similarly, the angels who wrote down the wicked deeds reported these to "the Accuser." This text, then, demon-strates a belief that angels sit and record human deeds "at the gate of heaven." Although the text explicitly states that the seer has ascended to the top of Mt. Seir, this is a much more significant place than simply the top of a moun-tain. Zephaniah is just outside of the divine abode, and this mountain is the place where heaven and earth intersect; it is nothing less than the entrance to the heavenly realm.[67] But why Mt. Seir? This imagery is dependent upon an ancient biblical tradition of Mt. Seir as the mountain of God.[68] It was believed by some ancient Israelites that this was the place where God once resided. The mention of Mt. Seir, therefore, is due to the use of the name Seir in the He-brew Bible in connection with the mountain of God.

Zephaniah then walked on with the angel of the Lord to a place where he saw fearsome beings identified as the "servants of all creation" who enter into the souls of the ungodly to lead them to the place of eternal punishment (4:1–10). The angel and Zephaniah then passed through bronze gates and entered a spectacular city square, apparently the city of the righteous (5:1–6). Zephaniah could not describe anything about this place, however, because, like the apostle Paul in 2 Cor 12:1–4, he was unable to speak (5:6). Although the text is vague about the movements of the seer, it appears that Mt. Seir functions here as the boundary or intersection between heaven and earth. At this place the angels make a complete record of humans' deeds and decide who may proceed to the place of the righteous and who must go to the place of punishment. This place, therefore, is the intersection between heaven, earth, and netherworld much like those described in Plato's Myth of Er and the Testament of Abraham (11–14 [A]; 8–11 [B]). This is further indicated by Zephaniah's subsequent movements because from here he made brief visits to heaven and hell. He "walked" with his angelic guide from Mt. Seir to a place where he saw the angels who lead sinners to punishment (4:1–10) and then accompanied the angel to the gates of the city of the righteous (5:1–6).

After brief visits to the realms of punishment and blessing, Zephaniah returned to the realm of punishment, Hades (6:1–17), where he appears to have had his "life review" by a fearsome angel. Happily, he passed the review: "Then I arose and stood, and I saw a great angel before me saying to me, 'Triumph, prevail because you have prevailed and triumphed over the accuser, and you have come up from Hades and the abyss. You will now cross over the crossing place.'" (7:9). This passage recounts that Zephaniah ascended out of Hades and returned, presumably, to Mt. Seir, the intersection between heaven and earth. What happened next is unknown because this portion of the text has been lost. A likely conjecture is that after he ascended from the infernal regions to Mt. Seir, Zephaniah proceeded to the ends of the earth. The text resumes with Zephaniah standing on the shores of a vast body of water where he boarded a boat, changed into angelic garments,[69] and prepared to cross over this watery divide. This body of water is the earth-encircling cosmic ocean that one must cross to enter the abode of the righteous. Once in the land of the righteous Zephaniah saw Abraham, Isaac, Jacob, Enoch, Elijah, and David (8:1–9:5).

Although the fragment from Clement mentioned an appearance by Zephaniah in the fifth heaven, the apocalypse itself, as preserved in the Coptic text, takes place entirely on the earthly plane, albeit at the mythical ends of the earth. Although it is possible that an ascension to a heavenly realm was once recounted in this text, as it has been preserved the text does not include such a journey and may never have included an ascent. The author of this text believed that there was a mythical place on earth where heaven and earth intersect and that at this place the postmortem fate of every soul was irrevocably decided. The righteous could enter heaven, but only after an examination of their deeds and an extremely dangerous ordeal at the hands of the Accuser and his minions. This motif of a postmortem trial to ascertain or prove one's worthiness was common in many Greco-Roman religions. This motif surfaced long before in ancient Egypt (see chapter 1) where the ancient Pyramid Texts, Coffin Texts, and the Book of the Dead all describe similarly dangerous postmortem trials. While the ancient Egyptians believed that knowing the correct passwords would enable one to negotiate these trials successfully, the Jewish and Christian traditions of the Greco-Roman era transformed this into an ethical matter—only those who lived righteously while on earth would succeed.

Clement of Alexandria's reference to an ascent by Zephaniah into the fifth heaven suggests that the single-heaven cosmography of the extant *Apocalypse of Zephaniah* was revised into a multiple-heaven cosmography in some circles.[70] Although he may have entered heaven in the version of the apocalypse known to Clement of Alexandria, according to the Coptic version Zephaniah entered the land of the blessed somewhere on the earthly plane. This is not a vision of heaven, but a vision of the place of the blessed at the mythical ends of the earth. Although Zephaniah put on an "angelic garment" (8:3), he boarded a boat to cross over to the place where he saw the righteous ones of old, the patriarchs, Enoch, Elijah, and David (9:4–5). This does not seem to be a transposition to the heavenly realm; rather, Zephaniah has come to the realm of the righteous at the end of the earth. Later, a great angel blew a golden trumpet "up towards heaven," and then Zephaniah saw heaven open up above him. This further suggests that Zephaniah remained on the earthly level.

The motifs of judgment and punishment depict God in the role of royal judge meting out decisions in his court;[71] thus heaven is a place where ultimate justice is obtained. This is where people can vent their anger at their enemies. Beyond the personal level, however, the belief that God will one day (at death or in the eschaton) mete out punishment to all evildoers functions as a source of hope for many people. It is this hope for eventual justice that provides hope for some people in a world that otherwise seems to be most unjust. For those who lack access to or who have distrust of the institutions of justice in this world, one way to maintain hope in the face of what is perceived as hopeless injustice is to transfer the hope for justice from this world to the next. There, God, who is impartial and obviously on the side of the righteous, will mete out ultimate justice. Thus the pains of this life are transitory injustices that will one day be made right. This view of heaven provides hope for all who feel wronged but cannot get the justice they desire.

Ascension of Isaiah

The text commonly designated the Ascension of Isaiah is actually three books combined into one: the Martyrdom of Isaiah (1:1–3:12, 5:1–16),[72] the Testament of Hezekiah (3:13–4:22), and the Ascension of Isaiah (6:1–11:43).[73] The Martyrdom of Isaiah does not mention the structure of the cosmos, but seven heavens are mentioned several times in the Testament of Hezekiah (3:13; 3:18; 4:14), although it lacks any detail about the appearance and inhabitants of these heavens.

The prophet Isaiah's heavenly journey in the company of an angel from the seventh heaven is the central focus of the Ascension (6:1–11:43). The account of the ascension begins with a description of the onset of the ecstatic experience, an account which is striking in the detail about the appearance of the event to those observing it (text quoted on pp. 148–49).[74] Isaiah describes the seven heavens and their contents in a detailed but schematic fashion. Each heaven is more glorious than the one below it, and located in the center of each of the first five heavens is a throne with an angelic being sitting on it. In the seventh heaven Isaiah met all the righteous and witnessed the descent, earthly life, and ascent of Jesus.[75] Other than the basic seven-heaven schema, the text displays no interest in other heavenly phenomena, save for the angelic praises and the degree of glory in each heaven. The author's interests were simply in narrating an ascent without adding information about the contents of the various heavens. This cosmographical structure is dependent on the Hellenistic view of several superimposed layers above the earth. Because this text does not refer to the spheres of the planets, the seven heavens are not those in which the planets move. The number seven certainly derives from the seven spheres of Hellenistic astronomy, but there is no indication in this text of any familiarity with the details of Greco-Roman astronomy. Texts such as this suggest that while some early Jews and Christians knew of the seven-heaven cosmography, they did not understand it fully.

This text presents heaven as the ultimate goal of the righteous. The fact that each heaven is more spectacular than the previous suggests that the Christian author and his or her community hoped to attain to the highest levels and become more glorious than all the angels after death. Such a belief provides not only a hope for future reward but also the motivation to live the kind of life that will warrant eventual inclusion in such a heavenly company. These texts are trying to persuade people to follow a certain religious life or belief system. The very fact that a person claims to have visited the heavenly realms and seen the actual punishments that await the wicked and the rewards that await the righteous serves to authorize that person's religious claims. Knowledge of the heavenly realm, therefore, is used in many texts as a tool to persuade, even coerce, people into adopting or remaining loyal to certain belief and ethical systems.

Apocalypse of Paul

This third century CE Christian apocalypse recounts the fictitious journeys of St. Paul to heaven and hell.[76] If one were to follow the reconstructed text and translation of Duensing and de Santos Otero,[77] Paul ascended to the third heaven at §11; however, the Latin text does not mention an ascent to the third heaven at this point.[78] Duensing and de Santos Otero's reconstruction of the text is unwarranted. Without their addition of a sentence suggesting an ascent to the third heaven, §11 places the following events in the firmament, the boundary between the earthly and heavenly spheres.

> The angel answered and said to me: Follow me and I will show you the place of the just where they are brought when they have died. After that I will take you to the abyss and will show you the souls of the sinners and the kind of place where they are brought when they have died. And I went on behind the angel and he led me toward heaven (*in celum*) and I beheld the firmament and I saw there the power and the forgetfulness that deceives and leads to itself the hearts of men, and the spirit of slander and the spirit of fornication and the spirit of wrath and the spirit of impudence were there, and the princes of wickedness were there. These I saw under the firmament of heaven.

Paul does not move from this place until he actually ascends to the third heaven at §19. It seems that this place is the entrance into the heavenly realm, perhaps on the outskirts of or at the entrance to the first heaven. From here Paul can "look down" (*deorsum*) and see people on earth below (§§13, 15). Paul saw angels escorting righteous souls toward this place, but they were being opposed by wicked angels as they ascended. This angelic opposition is due to the fact that humans are impure, they even smell acrid according to some texts, and they are thereby unfit to be in the heavenly realm.[79] Eventually, a soul was proved righteous and was escorted on into the divine presence and given its place in the "paradise of exaltation" (§14). A wicked soul encountered similar opposition during its postmortem ascent through the heavens, but unfortunately for this soul, its sins were discovered and it was forced to descend to Tartarus after a brief appearance before God (§§15–16). This "firmament" where Paul stands is the place on the outskirts of the heavenly realm where the initial judgment determining the relative righteousness or wickedness of a person's soul is made.[80] From here the righteous ascend to their heavenly abode while the wicked descend to their place of punishment.

The account of Paul's ascent into the heavenly realms in the Apocalypse of Paul actually depends on the account of this ascent in 2 Cor. 12:1–4.

> The angel answered and said to me: "Have you understood everything?" And I said: "Yes, lord." And he said to me: "Follow me again and I will take you and show you the places of the just." I followed the angel and he lifted me up to the third heaven (*tercium celum*) and set me at the door of a gate. I contemplated it intensely: it was a golden gate with two golden pillars full of golden letters on top. The angel turned to me again and said, "blessed are you if you enter through these gates, because only those are allowed to enter who have goodness and purity of body." (Apoc. Paul §19)

This passage indicates that the gates leading to the heavenly relam serve to limit entrance to those who are qualified, those who either are free of sin or whose bodies have been purified of their earthly sins. When Paul passed through the gates of the third heaven he entered "Paradise" (§20; cf. 2 Cor. 12:2–4 and 2 Enoch 8:1–10:6). Just inside these gates Paul met Enoch, "the scribe of righteousness" whose face "shone as the sun." Paul's escorting angel informed him that he was about to learn things that he must not repeat to anyone on earth (§21), a warning clearly inspired by the statement in 2 Cor. 12:2–4 that Paul heard things that he was unable to recount. After learning the heavenly secrets, the angel led Paul back down to earth.

> He brought me down from the third heaven and led me into the second heaven. Then he led me again to the firmament, and from the firmament he led me to the gates of heaven. There was the beginning of its foundation over a river that watered the whole earth. Then I asked the angel and said: "lord, what is this river of water?" And he said to me: "this is the Ocean." Then I

came out under heaven and understood that it is the light of heaven that gives light to the entire earth. (Apoc. Paul § 21)[81]

Paul landed in the "Land of Promise" (§§21–22), but he did not recognize the place so he asked his guiding angel, who told him that "the souls of the righteous, therefore, when they come out of the body are sent for a while to this place" (§21; cf. § 14). Moreover, this verdant place is the region of the earth that will be renewed when Christ returns to establish his millennial kingdom (§21; cf. Rev. 20:1–6). It seems that this place is the classical Land of the Blessed at the mythical ends of the earth. While many of the classical and ancient Near Eastern traditions discussed in previous chapters know of a place at the ends of the earth where the righteous or superhumans live, this text has transformed the image of this place into a place where righteous souls go for a short time before they ascend to their permanent residences in the heavenly realm. The author of this text has thus slightly transformed the old Land of the Blessed image: this mythical place at the ends of the earth is just a temporary residence for the righteous souls, not their ultimate destination.

The angel then led Paul to Lake Acherusia where he saw its milk-white waters. Paul learned that the righteous are cleansed by being baptized in this water after their death.[82] From the waters of Lake Acherusia the angel took Paul aboard a golden boat for a long journey to the "City of Christ" (§23). This city is surrounded by twelve walls, and the distance between each of the walls is "as great as between the Lord God and men on earth." Four rivers encircled this city, a motif clearly drawing on Genesis 2: Pishon (a river of honey), Euphrates (a river of milk), Gihon (a river of oil), and the Tigris (a river of wine). Some people are not allowed to enter the city because they are not sufficiently righteous and must await the return of Jesus to escort them inside (§24). Paul toured the city with the angel and met various righteous people (§§25–30). So, according to this text some of the righteous are not given access to the inner parts of the city because they were not righteous enough. Such a theme suggests that for the author of this text as well as for some other early Christian communities, there will be a division even among the righteous, and only the exceptionally righteous will receive extra privileges because of the advanced level of their piety.

Having completed his tour of the Land of the Blessed, Paul set out with his angel to learn about the places of punishment of the wicked.

Then he led me to the ocean that bears the foundations of heaven. The angel answered and said to me: "do you understand that you are going away from here?" I said, "yes, lord." Then he said to me: "come and follow me and I will show you the souls of the impious and sinners so that you may know what the place is like." Then I set out with the angel and he brought me to the setting of the sun, and I saw the beginning of heaven founded on a great river of water, and I asked, "what is this river of water?" And he said to me: "this is the ocean that encircles the whole earth." When I was beyond the ocean I looked and there was no light in that place, but darkness and sorrow and distress; and I sighed. (Apoc. Paul §31)

This narrative provides geographical details that correspond to the depiction of the earth given during his descent from the third heaven in §21. The land mass of the earth is completely surrounded by water, the cosmic ocean. The heavens rest on the ocean at or near the place where the sun sets in the evening. The thought that the heavens rest on the oceans stems from the natural observation that the blue sky extends all the way down to the ocean on the horizon. Beyond the ocean and the place of the sunset is where the dark netherworld begins. Paul then visited the places where sinners are punished (§§31–44). This place of punishment, or at least the entrance to it, is located at the mythical western ends of the earth. Paul next learned about the rewards of the righteous (§§45–51) by following his angelic guide into paradise, the place where Adam and Eve sinned. This is the terrestrial paradise, not the mythical Land of the Blessed he had just visited (§14) nor the paradise in the third heaven he will visit presently (§45). The text provides no geographical information about the location of this place. Since Paul will enter the paradise in the third heaven presently, and since the location of the infernal region is beyond the cosmic ocean in the west, a reasonable conjecture is that this "earthly Paradise" is located beyond the cosmic ocean at the mythical eastern ends of the earth. This place then balances with the infernal region at the western ends of the earth. In this paradise Paul met several biblical heroes.[83]

The apocalypse ends abruptly at this point. In some manuscripts the narrative continues with Paul's return to the third heaven where he witnessed myriad angels perpetually praising God. Then the angel brought Paul into the heavenly paradise and showed him his own throne. But Paul's heavenly residence is not in the same heaven with the divinity. The text already made it clear that the author believed that there were seven heavens, for in §29 it states that "Christ, the Son of God, sits at the right hand of his Father . . . in the seventh heaven." It seems that although the author himself knew of additional heavens above the third, he did not speculate on them because the account of Paul's ascent to the third heaven in 2 Corinthians 12 limited him to only the first three heavens. The author's purpose was to expand on what happened to Paul during his ascent to the third heaven. According to the author of the Apocalypse of Paul, the apostle did not ascend to the highest heaven but to the third heaven where he could learn secrets of the transcendent world unknown to other mortals. The author understands Paul's ascent as recorded in 2 Corinthians 12 as an ascent to the third of seven heavens. In his own account in 2 Corinthians 12, however, Paul did not specify the total number of heavens. It would seem that the author of the Apocalypse of Paul has simply wedded the material from 2 Corinthians 12 to a seven-heaven cosmography. The text further attests the combination of old ancient Near Eastern conceptions of earthly geography with a Greco-Roman multiheaven cosmography. That is to say, the author describes the earth as a land mass encircled by the cosmic ocean, but layered above it are seven heavens. Thus, the old traditional view of the cosmos has been wedded to a more modern image. Moreover, this text is apparently concerned with division between the righteous. Clearly not all Christians are admitted into the City of Christ because they are not worthy enough, although when Jesus returns he will lead them in. Furthermore, one suspects that Christians are also spread out between the heavens based on their character. All this is meant as a forewarning to the readers: make sure you live a righteous life, or in the end you will suffer the punishments of Hades or at least be denied immediate entrance into the City of Christ. Again, this image of punishment and reward is designed to motivate people to adopt or maintain a certain form of Christian comportment. These Christian authors are using powerful images of heaven and the afterlife to promote their religious agendas.

Gnostic Apocalypse of Paul

This Christian apocalypse, a text possibly originating as early as the second century CE,[84] is a Gnostic version of the Apostle Paul's ascent to heaven, and is not genetically related to the Latin *Apocalypse of Paul*, although it, too, is inspired by 2 Corinthians 12:1–4. At the outset of this apocalypse the apostle Paul meets a child (Jesus?) who leads him on his journey. In this account Paul ascended immediately to the third heaven and continued up to the tenth. In the fourth heaven Paul looked down toward earth and saw the twelve apostles, other people, and, oddly, even himself on the earth (19:26–20:5). Apparently the author of this text understood Paul to have ascended to heaven in a spiritual form, leaving his physical body on earth (cf. 2 Cor 12:1–4). This version of Paul's ascent, then, was an out-of-body experience much like that described in the Ascension of Isaiah. This description explains how a human can ascend to heaven prior to death, an experience claimed by many mystics: when a person ascends to heaven they leave their physical body behind as they mount to the heavenly realms in their minds.

In the fourth and fifth heavens Paul saw angels torturing a soul for the sins it committed while in a body on earth (20:5–22:12). This suggests that after death all souls will ascend to the heavenly realms but some will undergo punishment there. As has been discussed in previous chapters, this motif stems from the Greek and Persian belief that souls originate in the ethereal or heavenly realm and are only briefly imprisoned in human bodies. Upon their release from the body, these souls wish to return to their rightful place; however, their return is impeded by the impurities they have absorbed while on earth. These impurities come from their physical incarnation and from the evil deeds committed by the bodies in which they were imprisoned. Because of these sins, souls must be purged of their impurities before they are able to ascend to the higher, purer heavenly realms. In fact, when Paul got to the seventh heaven, an old man (God) asked him where he was going. This "ancient of days" figure (cf. Dan. 7:13) in gleaming white raiment and sitting on a brilliant, large throne is clearly God himself, for Creation is called "his Creation" (23:27). Paul replied, "I am going to the place from which I came" (23:8–10). The apocalypse ends with Paul entering the tenth heaven, where he says "I greeted my fellow spirits" (24:8).

This apocalypse describes the heavenly realm as having ten levels.[85] This multilevel structure is an elaboration of Hellenistic models, but the description of the contents of the various heavens depends on ancient religious myths and not on Greco-Roman astronomy. Once again, this text demonstrates how some early Jews and Christians could adopt modern ideas about the structure of the universe and integrate them with their traditional religious beliefs about what is found in the heavenly realms. Gnostic speculation also includes schemas involving 8,[86] 72,[87] and 365 heavens.[88] One unique feature of this text is that because of Gnostic ideas about the nature of the God (the Demiurge) who created the physical universe, Paul encountered this God in the seventh heaven but continued to ascend higher to the tenth heaven where the righteous dwell. At first glance it seems odd that the Creator of this world should live below the righteous. Describing God as dwelling in the seventh heaven would be expected in a traditional seven-heaven cosmography. Here, however, the God who created this world dwells in a lower region (seventh heaven) than the righteous (tenth heaven) because this God is not the highest or purest spirit being in Gnostic thought.[89] This God is in fact partially corrupted by his contacts with the material realm. In Gnostic thought, the highest being is so pure it cannot have any contact with the material realm, and as a result, the God who created this world is only an offshoot from the purest, highest divinity. Moreover, since souls were originally from the highest, purest realms, they seek to return to these pristine realms after departing from their earthly bodies, ascending far beyond the realm of the partially limited or defiled creator God. Since the strict dualism of Gnosticism maintains that anything associated with this material world is corrupt, all vestiges of materiality must be shed to ascend to the highest heaven. In Gnostic images of the heavenly realms, then, the truly righteous are even more spiritual than the God who created the universe.

3 (Greek Apocalypse of) Baruch

Like Enoch and Ezra, Baruch ben Neriah, the prophet Jeremiah's scribal assistant, was made the pseudepigraphical author of several early Jewish and Christian texts.[90] 3 Baruch's narrative setting is in the aftermath of the destruction of Jerusalem by the Babylonians in 586 BCE. As is customary in pseudepigraphic literature, this fictional setting stands for another time, and that time is clearly the late first or early second century CE in the wake of the Roman destruction of Jerusalem in 70 CE. 3 Baruch is an ascent apocalypse and in the form in which it has been preserved it has a five-heaven schema. M. R. James, the scholar who produced the first modern edition of 3 Baruch, assumed that this five-heaven schema is an abbreviation of an original seven-heaven schema, and many have followed him in this.[91] James's conclusion rests on the presupposition that early Jewish and Christian cosmic speculation involved only a seven-heaven schema. Moreover, when the Church Father Origen mentions an ascent by Baruch through seven heavens in De Principiis ii.3.6, James assumed that Origen was referring to 3 Baruch.[92] As James's assumption that early Jewish and Christian cosmic speculation knew only a seven-heaven cosmography is wrong, so too is his claim that Origen refers to it in De Principiis misinformed. It is more likely that Origen knows of another Baruch text that has a seven-heaven cosmography.[93]

The initial focus of this text is the question "why do the righteous suffer?" Although the apocalypse does not answer this question directly, Baruch's tour through the heavenly realms does seem to assuage his anxiety. Contemplation of the heavenly realms and the activities that take place there in part enables Baruch to transcend his present troubles. Unlike most of the preceding texts, 3 Baruch contains rather detailed descriptions of the contents of the various heavens. Baruch's angelic guide Panael gave him a first class tour!

First Heaven: 3 Baruch 2:1–7

3 Baruch opens with Baruch weeping over the destruction of Jerusalem and tormented with the question of why God would allow the wicked to oppress the righteous. Baruch prayed for an explanation, and God sent the angel Panael to lead Baruch on a guided tour through the heavenly realms. The first stop in Baruch's ascent was the place "where heaven was set up and where there was a river that no one could cross" (2:1). Baruch had come to the farthest reaches of the earth where the sky rests on the ocean.[94] This impasse symbolizes the great divide between the earthly and heavenly realms. The heavenly ascent, however, bridges this seemingly insurmountable separation between the human and divine realms by showing that one can, if he or she is holy and righteous enough, make contact with the other realm. After they had crossed this vast ocean, Baruch and his angelic guide arrived at an enormous gateway leading into the first heaven. The gateways into the various heavens indicate that at the edge of each heaven there is a large gate or door outside of which one may stand and through which one must pass to enter into the heaven itself. This image is natural, for just as one would pass through gates to enter an ancient city, so one must pass through gates to enter the divine realm. These gates serve as the borders demarcating the limits of heaven and perhaps even as barriers to keep out the undeserving. Moreover, the image of "gates" into the heavenly realm is an image with a long history in the ancient Near East going back to the ancient Egyptian and Mesopotamian cultures (see chapters 1 and 2).

The first thing Baruch encountered in the first heaven was a group of beastly people living on a vast plain. A vast plain appears in each of the first four heavens (cf. 2:3; 3:3; 4:3; 10:2), and these vast open spaces are inhabited by different types of people. Although the beasts in the first heaven catch the reader's attention, Baruch's first question to the angel, surprisingly, is about the size of the heaven and not about these strange inhabitants: "tell me, I ask of you, what is the thickness of this heaven in which we have traveled, or what is its dimension, or what is this plain, so that I might report it to the sons of men" (2:4). Several texts discuss the dimensions of the heavenly realm,[95] and the general purpose of these descriptions is to indicate the vast separation between the heavenly and earthly worlds. This vast separation suggests that under normal circumstances there can be no bridging of the two realms. This fact makes the people claiming to have ascended to heaven and to have brought back information from there very important indeed: without them and the information they can provide, people on earth could not know anything about the heavenly realm.[96] Baruch was believed to have ascended to heaven, and part of his legacy is to inform others about what happens there.

The grotesque, beastly inhabitants of the first heaven receive only brief attention from the angel. As striking as these creatures are to the modern reader, they are only of secondary interest to the author. Baruch's question about their identity is, seemingly, tacked on after the angel's call for Baruch to continue journeying with him to see "greater mysteries" (2:6). The angel answers Baruch's question by stating that "these are the ones who built the tower of the war against God and the Lord removed them" (2:7).[97] Nothing further is said about them—no explanation of their appearances, and no details about the conditions of their punishment.[98] The first heaven, then, like each of the first four heavens, is a vast plain. This heaven is a place of punishment for those who, like the builders of the Tower of Babel, oppose God. Thus, the initial lesson the author presents is that those who oppose God will suffer certain punishment for their behavior. The sympathetic readers are supposed to cheer the punishment of the wicked while at the same time examining themselves to make sure they are not opposing God in any way and thereby making themselves liable to similar punishments.

Second Heaven: 3 Baruch 3:1–8

The accounts of Baruch's ascents into the first, second, fourth, and fifth heavens use the same vocabulary: "the angel took me and led me to the (first-second-fourth-fifth) heaven." The description of how the angel transported Baruch to the ends of the earth also used the same format: "the angel took me and led me" to where heaven is founded (2:1). In fact, the basic structure of the account of Baruch's ascent to and travels in each of the heavens is fairly consistent and contains the following elements:

1. The angel "takes" and "leads" (λαμβάνω and ἄγω) Baruch (first heaven, 2:2; second heaven, 3:1; fourth heaven, 10:1; fifth heaven 11:1).
2. The angel shows Baruch a large door or gate (first heaven, 2:2; second heaven 3:1; fifth heaven, 11:2).
3. Baruch and the angel undertake a long journey to pass through the gateway (first heaven, 2:2; second heaven, 3:2; third heaven 4:2).
4. Baruch sees a large plain (πεδίον) in the midst of the heaven (first heaven, 2:3; second heaven, 3:3; third heaven, 4:3; fourth heaven, 10:2).

5. Baruch inquires about the inhabitants of the heaven (first heaven, 2:3–7; second heaven, 3:3–8; third heaven, 4:3–9:8; fourth heaven, 10:2–9; fifth heaven, 11:2–17:1).

In the second heaven Baruch saw people who look like dogs with deer feet (3:3). The angel said that these bizarre beasts are those who laid the plans for building the tower of Babel (3:5) and who attempted to discover heavenly secrets (3:7). This group is distinguished from the group of beastly people in the first heaven who did the work of actually building the tower. Not only did the group in the second heaven lay the plans for the tower, but they also brutally forced people to make the bricks used in constructing the tower (3:5–8). The theme of forced brick-making stems from a creative reading of the Exodus tradition about the Israelites making bricks for Pharaoh (Ex 1:15; 5:6–19) into the Tower of Babel story about making bricks for the Tower (Gen 11:3). In addition to having their languages confused (cf. Gen 11:7–9), 3 Baruch 3:8 notes that they were struck with blindness, a punishment that may harken back to the ninth plague against the Egyptians (i.e., darkness; Ex 10:21–29). This creative reshaping of biblical themes makes the planners of the tower appear as supremely wicked people: they are as wicked as the Egyptians who mercilessly oppressed the Israelites, and they deserve a similar punishment. This difference accounts, therefore, for the separation of the workers from the overseers; the former suffer in the first heaven and the latter in the second heaven. This second group was also punished for trying to uncover the secrets of heaven without divine approval (3:7–8). Their punishment warns others who would try to learn these secrets. Again, the lesson is that certain punishment awaits the wicked, and just as the wicked people of ancient history could not escape God's punishment, so, too, will wicked people of all generations suffer at the hand of God.

Third Heaven: 3 Baruch 4:1–9:8

After they entered the third heaven, Baruch and his angelic guide found themselves in a vast plain where they saw a stone-like serpent (4:3a) that drinks a cubit of water from the ocean every day (4:6b). The ocean never lacks water, however, because it is continually replenished by the many rivers that God created on earth (4:7; cf. Qoh 1:7).[99] The enormous belly of this serpent is "Hades" (5:3).[100] After an aside about the vine that led Adam astray (4:8–17), the angel led Baruch to the eastern part of this heaven (6:1). Not only does 6:1 mark a transition to another location in the third heaven, it also marks a transition to an altogether different subject—speculation on the celestial bodies. In 3 Baruch 6:1–9:8 is a long discussion of the characteristics and movements of the sun and moon. This section reminds one immediately of the Enochic Astronomical Book (1 Enoch 72–82). Although the biblical tradents were not interested in astronomy, the Enochic cycle, this section in 3 Baruch, and other texts (e.g., Treatise of Shem, 4Q317–319, etc.) point to the continued popularity of astronomy/astrology in some Jewish circles. Oddly, this text puts both the sun and the moon in the same heaven. Such a blunder indicates that the author was not well informed at all about astronomical models current in his or her day. The multiple heaven schema informed the cosmic speculations in 3 Baruch, but the author did not understand all the intricacies of Greco-Roman astronomy. The author adopted the overall model and infused it with his or her religious ideas quite apart from any truly astronomical concern: not astronomy but religion and teaching religious values were the driving forces behind this and most all other early Jewish and Christian ascent texts.

At the eastern edge of the third heaven where the sun enters the sky at dawn,[101] Baruch saw "a chariot drawn by four horses and fire underneath it, and a man wearing a crown of fire was sitting on the chariot. The chariot was being drawn by forty angels. And behold, a bird was running ahead of the sun, as large as nine mountains" (6:2).[102] Since he did not understand what he was seeing, Baruch asked the angel to explain this marvelous sight (6:3–6). The rest of the section dealing with the sun (6:1–8:7) actually concentrates on the bird and not on the sun, its chariot, or the horses or angels that pull it on its daily course. The bird is the phoenix,[103] the guardian of the world whose wings absorb the intense heat of the sun (6:3–6). Baruch's initial perception of the sun was as a man wearing a fiery crown[104] and sitting in a chariot drawn either by four horses or by forty angels (6:2).[105] This picture stems from a transformation of older Jewish motifs through the influences of newer Hellenistic ideas. As discussed in chapter 3, recent reevaluations of ancient Israelite religion indicate that this depiction of the sun depends upon long-standing Jewish practices of solar worship and of using solar images for God.

After having learned the identity of the celestial bird, the angel told Baruch that he was about to see the glory of God (6:12). Baruch and the angel were still standing at the place where the sun rises when they heard thunder and felt the earth shake under their feet (6:13). This tumult was caused by the opening of 365 gates to allow the sun to begin its daily course. The astronomical speculations in 1 Enoch 72 and 2 Enoch 13–14 describe six gates for the sun on the eastern and western horizons and trace the sun's path through the course of a year. Baruch's 365 gates relate to the solar calendar, and indicates that the author thinks that there is one gate for each day of the year. That is to say, the sun passes through a different gate each morning, and, although the text does not mention it, there are presumably 365 corresponding gates on the western horizon through which the sun exits each evening. The Enochic six-gate system is much more economical and sophisticated than Baruch's 365 which, to be honest, appear rather amateurish. It seems that the author knows that seers typically learn of the movements of the celestial bodies during a heavenly ascent, but the model created by the author is most unwieldy. Moreover, 3 Baruch has mixed the ancient Near Eastern idea of the sun rising through gates with the Greco-Roman astronomical model of multiple heavens. Again, this demonstrates that though the author is aware of the multiple-heaven model, he or she does not fully understand it. As the day dawned Baruch heard a voice crying out, "Light giver, give light to the world" (6:14). This verse and the entire passage of 6:14–16 depend clearly on the same tradition as 2 Enoch 15:1–2 (J):

And then the solar elements, called phoenixes and khalkedras, burst into song. That is why every bird flaps its wings, rejoicing at the giver of light. And they burst into song at the LORD's command: "The light-giver is coming, to give radiance to the whole world; and the morning watch appears, which is the sun's rays. And the sun comes out over the face of the earth, and retrieves his radiance, to give light to all the face of the earth."[106]

The angel then led Baruch to the west of the third heaven to watch the sun set (8:1). As the sun sets angels remove its crown and take it "to heaven" to renew it because it becomes defiled each day as it looks down on all the unrighteous behavior on earth. The idea that the celestial bodies are repulsed at the sight of human wickedness is found in several early Jewish and Christian texts.[107] In a text associated with the prophet Jeremiah, God decries the moral faults of humans with the following words: "However, because you have transgressed my commandments, the sun and the moon hate to rise upon you as they look down upon the abominations which you do and all your idolatries."[108]

After the sun had set, darkness came over the place and the moon and stars shone, prompting Baruch to inquire about the operations of the other large celestial body, the moon (9:1–2), but the angel put Baruch off until the next morning (9:3). Although the text does not explain the reason for the delay, the delay may allow Baruch to observe the moon during its overnight journey. The next morning Baruch learned that the moon, depicted as a woman, rides on a chariot drawn by angels who appear in the form of oxen and lambs (9:3–4). Baruch's next question (9:5) is about the phases of the moon: "Why is it that at times it waxes and at times it wanes?" The discussions about the moon in 1 Enoch 73–74 and 2 Enoch 16 contain just such descriptions about the phases and movements of the moon. The information 3 Baruch provides is nothing like the detailed calculations of 1 and 2 Enoch, for 3 Baruch's interests lie elsewhere. The author knows, presumably from familiarity with other ascent texts, that a person who ascends to the heavenly realms learns about the operations of the sun and moon, but for this person mathematical calculations were less important than the mythical traditions about the celestial world. Rather than discuss the movements of the sun in mathematical terms as in the Enochic materials, the author of 3 Baruch was more interested in the mythical figures attending the sun. With regard to the moon, Baruch learned that the dimmed light of the moon stems from its involvement in the sin of Adam.

> And again I asked, "Why is it that at times it waxes and at times it wanes?" "Listen, O Baruch, this which you see was designed by God to be more beautiful than any other. And when the first Adam transgressed, it gave light to Samael when he took the serpent as a garment. It did not hide but rather waxed. So God was enraged at it, and punished it, and shortened its days." (9:5–7)[109]

Obviously, the reader is supposed to draw the appropriate religious conclusion: God punishes sinners, be they celestial bodies or humans! Since the moon shines brightly only at night, Baruch asked why this is the case (9:8). The angel answered this question with an analogy:

> Listen, just as servants cannot speak openly before the king, likewise neither can the moon or stars shine before the sun. For the stars are permanently fixed, but are diffused by the sun. And the moon, although being safe, is exhausted by the heat of the sun. (9:8)

Although the author stated that "the stars are permanently fixed," the idea is not that they do not move. Even this author who betrays a terrible lack of understanding of astronomy in its Greco-Roman forms knows that the stars move at night. This statement seems to relate to ideas that appeared in the words of the Greek astronomer Anaximenes (585–526 BCE) who imagined that some stars were affixed "like nails" to the crystalline vault above the earth (see chapter 4). Again, the author of 3 Baruch betrays familiarity with Greco-Roman astronomy, imprecise as it may be. With this the discussions about the sun and the moon end. These discussions indicate that the cosmic interests of 3 Baruch are not like those in the Enochic literature where considerable attention is given to mathematical calculations of the movements of the celestial bodies. In 3 Baruch, on the other hand, the interest is more in passing on certain religious myths associated with these bodies. The mathematical calculations did not contribute to the author's goals who was instead interested in answering the question of why Israel was suffering (3 Baruch 1). These myths about the sun and the moon show how these bodies are affected by human wickedness. Since the sun is defiled when it witnesses sin on earth (8:4–5), God established a means to counter the effects of these sins: the angels of heaven take the sun's crown to heaven at night to renew it (8:4). The moon, on the other hand, was an active participant in sin. Because the moon let its light shine when the evil one led humans into sin, God punishes it by decreasing its light. The point is that God has ways to deal with sin. Not even the moon can escape punishment for its deeds. The renewal of the sun from the effects of human sin demonstrates that God has ways to reverse the effects of sin. Those who like Baruch were lamenting the fall of Jerusalem to sinners do not get a direct response to their laments. Instead this section of 3 Baruch suggests that all sin will be punished and God will reverse its effects. Just as the moon was punished, so too will those who are oppressing the readers of this apocalypse be punished. Likewise, just as the sun is renewed from the effects of sin, so too can these readers hope for renewal.

Fourth Heaven: 3 Baruch 10:1–9

Although the text does not explicitly say so, it is clear that at 10:1 Baruch and the angel entered the fourth heaven. They entered a vast, verdant plain where they saw a lake (10:2) and several species of birds not found on earth (10:3). The angel explained that this is the place where the souls of the righteous come after death (10:5). The birds, in fact, are these souls who continuously praise the Lord (10:7). As others have noted,[110] this lake is likely to be identified as Lake Acherusia. According to the Apocalypse of Moses 37:3 this is the place where angels washed Adam before escorting him into Paradise, and according to the Apocalypse of Paul this is the place where Michael washes sinners after death (Apoc. Paul §22; cf. Apoc. Pet 14). According to 3 Baruch the habitations of the righteous are in the fourth heaven immediately below the heaven where the Divine dwells. The image of the vast plain and the large lake indicate that the author views this place as the equivalent of the earthly Fields of the Blessed or the Island of the Righteous known from classical sources.[111] The influence of the classical image is clear, but when it came into Judaism cannot be ascertained, although surely no later than in the wake of Alexander's conquests of the Near East in the fourth century BCE. Other early Jewish and Christian sources (e.g., 1 Enoch) continued to imagine a region of the blessed on earth, but 3 Baruch has transformed the image so that this place is now found in one of the heavenly realms and not at the farthest reaches of the earthly plane. Once again, the old traditions are reinterpreted in the light of newer ideas gained as Jews interacted with the cultures surrounding them.

Fifth Heaven: 3 Baruch 11:1–17:1

When Baruch and the angel ascended to the fifth heaven, they found the gateway closed and were unable to enter (11:1–2a). This depiction suggests that the author's conception of the structure of each heaven involves (1) an area outside of the gates, (2) the gate complex proper, and (3) the realm within the gates.[112] Moreover, the accounts of Baruch's entrance into heavens one and two explicitly say that he arrived in the heaven, saw a large door, and passed through it into the inner part of the heaven. The angel told Baruch that they could not enter through the gate of the fifth heaven until Michael, the "gatekeeper of the kingdom of heaven," came to open the gates and receive people's prayers (11:2). Once Michael opened the gates, he greeted Baruch's angelic guide affectionately (11:6–8a) and then took hold of an enormous bowl into which he received people's virtues or prayers—here represented as flowers—so that he might present them to God (11:8–9).[113] This narrative indicates that at a certain hour angels present human prayers to God. If the liturgical schedule (horarium) preserved in the Testament of Adam is based on early Jewish models, then the following account of the activities of the human and heavenly realms during the night may reflect the activities described in 3 Baruch 11.

> The ninth hour is the praise of the cherubim. The tenth hour is the praise of human beings, and the gate of heaven is opened through which the prayers of all living things enter, and they worship and depart. And at that hour whatever a man will ask of God is given to him when the seraphim and the roosters beat their wings. The eleventh hour there is joy in all the earth when the sun rises from Paradise and shines forth on creation. The twelfth hour is the waiting for incense, and silence is imposed on all the ranks of fire and

wind until all the priests burn incense to his divinity. And at that time all the heavenly powers are dismissed. The End of the Hours of the Night.[114]

It is clear, therefore, that angels were believed both to report the good and bad deeds of people and to present their prayers to God on a regular basis. In 3 Baruch Michael used an enormous bowl to carry the virtues/prayers to God (11:4, 9; 12:5; cf. Rev 5:8). The Greek term used here (φιάλη) is a fairly common term for a bowl, and the Septuagint translation of the Hebrew Bible uses precisely this term to translate the Hebrew word מזרק (mizrāq), the basin used for sprinkling liquids on the altar (Ex. 27:3, 38:3). This basin is being presented to God in a form resembling an offering. This presentation of prayers, therefore, is being depicted with imagery associated with the temple cultus. The Divine is here depicted in terms and images associated with the temple. Although the Jerusalem Temple had long since been destroyed by the time 3 Baruch was written, this author continued to imagine the divine presence in the terms of the temple. As Michael returned to God and closed the gate behind him, there was a thunderous roar just as when he opened the gate and came out to meet the angels (14:1, cf. 11:3–5). The vocabulary used to describe Michael's movements indicates that the place where God dwells is somehow "above" the place in the fifth heaven where Baruch and the angels stood awaiting the divine response. At 11:4 Michael descended (κατέρχομαι) to receive the prayers or virtues. After he had received these into the large basin, he left (ἀπέρχομαι) to appear before God (14:1) and then came down again (κατέρχομαι) to deliver the divine response (15:1). It remains unclear, however, whether the author understood Michael to ascend to a higher heaven, or whether the divine residence was located in the fifth heaven just beyond the gates. Baruch and the other angels never passed through the gates but waited outside of them. Therefore, God may reside in the fifth heaven in the region beyond the gates. Baruch and his angelic guide clearly arrived at the outskirts of the fifth heaven (11:1), but they never passed through the gates to enter into the region inside these gates.

This is precisely where the problem regarding the cosmography of this text arises. Most assume that there were additional heavens in the cosmography of this book.[115] These heavens were either never described or have somehow dropped out of the text during the process of its transmission. It seems that the vocabulary is decisive in this issue. As was discussed above, the formula for Baruch's ascension into the successive heavens has the following structure: (1) Baruch is taken by the angel and led (λαμβάνω and ἄγω) into the next heaven; (2) Baruch sees a large door or gate (θύρα or πύλη); (3) Baruch and the angel undertake a long journey (πορείας ὁδοῦ) through the door or gate;[116] (4) Baruch sees a large plain (πεδίον) in the midst of the heaven; and (5) Baruch sees and inquires about the inhabitants of the heaven. The account of Baruch's visit to the fifth heaven includes elements one (λαμβάνω and ἄγω, 11:1) and two (πύλη, 11:2ff). Elements three and four do not appear because Baruch and his angel never passed through the gates. The fifth element, the questions about the beings he saw in the heaven, may be identified with his questions about the angels and activities he saw outside of the gates. All this indicates that Baruch entered the outskirts of the fifth heaven but was not allowed to pass through the gates that lead to the interior of the fifth heaven. This, it seems, is the place where God resides, and only Michael is allowed to enter into this part of the fifth heaven.[117] There need not be additional heavens above the fifth. God resides in the fifth heaven but is beyond the gates through which only Michael can pass. The author of 3 Baruch, like the authors of most of the other texts discussed here, was no astronomer, and his five-heaven cosmography is admittedly odd.[118] It seems that this author's cosmographical model for some reason had only five levels. The absurdity of this model is clear from the fact that the author locates the sun, moon and stars together in the third heaven (cf. 6:1, 7:1–9:8). On the literary side, Picard and Harlow have discovered convincing internal evidence to suggest that this text has not suffered from intentional or accidental abbreviation.[119] It appears, therefore, on both literary and cosmographic grounds that the Greek text is complete in the form in which it has come down to us and that its cosmography included only and originally five heavens.

When Michael returned from the divine presence he rewarded each group of angels with oil[120] in proportion to the quantity or quality of their prayers or virtues (15:2–4). After this the gates closed again and Baruch and his angelic guide departed (17:1). Baruch never personally entered into the divine presence. This is not because the text has been truncated, however. Baruch's journey was complete. It reached its climax without disappointment, since Baruch, who had been praying over Jerusalem at the beginning of the book, learned at the outskirts of the fifth heaven that God attends daily to human prayers and rewards the righteous for their behavior. That the gates are locked and that only Michael can pass through them is significant. Neither the human Baruch, his angelic guide, nor the angels who report on the prayers and deeds of humans can enter through these gates. The author believes that other than through Michael's mediation, no one can directly approach God, not even angels. Michael attends God in heaven much like the high priest attends God on earth: only the high priest can go into God's immediate presence in the Jerusalem Temple, and that only at a specified time—the Day of Atonement. God resides alone in the interior of the fifth heaven. Only Michael can approach him, and that apparently only at the set time for receiving prayers. To suppose that the ascent was incomplete because Baruch did not see God or the throne may be to expect the text to meet one's preconceptions based on what other seers who ascended to heaven are reported to have seen. If the seer's purpose was to learn about God's attention to prayers and to the administration of justice, then an audience with the divine would be, strictly speaking, unnecessary. Baruch learned what he desired to learn without having to stand before God: God attends to the prayers of the saints, and even though they may seem to go unnoticed, God is aware and will reward acts of virtue.

3 Baruch imagines heavens one through four as vast plains, but the defining feature of the fifth heaven is the heavenly temple wherein God resides, unapproachable by all but the archangel Michael who presents human prayers and

virtues to the Divine. In a sense, 3 Baruch reaffirms the theology of 1 Kings 8:27–30:

> Will God indeed dwell on the earth? Behold, heaven in all its vastness cannot contain you, how much less this house that I have built! Turn to your servant's prayer and his supplication, O Yahweh my God, and hear the cry and the prayer that your servant prays to you today. May your eyes be open toward this house night and day, toward the place of which you said, "My name will be there." May you hear the prayer that your servant prays toward this place. Hear the supplication of your servant and of your people Israel that they pray toward this place. Hear in heaven your dwelling place; hear and forgive.

According to the prologue to 3 Baruch, Baruch had gone to the ruins of the Jerusalem Temple to pray for Jerusalem and his compatriots who had suffered at the hands of the Babylonians (3 Baruch 1). While praying and weeping there, Baruch had a vision that transported him ultimately to the gates of the heavenly temple of God, the heavenly counterpart of the now ruined earthly temple, and there he learned just what he wanted to know: although the temple, the central institution of Judaism for centuries, was in ruins, God was still active, hearing prayers for forgiveness and justice in his heavenly temple. Thus, Solomon's prayer is still being answered, and God is still attentive to his people (1 Kgs. 8:56–57). And concomitantly, people are still encouraged to live virtuous lives, just as Solomon had hoped: "May He incline our hearts to Him so that we will walk in all His ways and keep His commandments, rules, and laws that He commanded our ancestors" (1 Kgs. 8:58). Just because the earthly temple is gone does not mean that God is any less attentive to human actions and needs, nor does it mean that people are any less responsible to follow God's ways. Where some could potentially see the "death of God," 3 Baruch would proclaim that God is alive and well in his heavenly abode. Baruch's tour of the heavenly realms, then, reassures the faithful in three ways. First, God is still present in his heavenly temple, and in spite of any reports of his death or deafness, he hears and responds to the prayers of the righteous. Second, a certain, horrible punishment awaits the wicked for their sins against the righteous. Third, and perhaps most important for the faithful, God rewards the faithful for their virtue. The ultimate reward of the righteous is to ascend to the fourth heaven like some exotic bird and take their place alongside the host of righteous souls. All traces of earthly existence have been erased. There are no mansions, no human forms, no grief, pain, or oppression. This vision of the heavenly realms assuages any anxiety present circumstances may cause. There is hope.

2 Enoch

2 (Slavonic Apocalypse of) Enoch is another of the many texts pseudepigraphically attributed to Enoch. This Enochic text is preserved only in Old Church Slavonic manuscripts.[121] These manuscripts separate into two recen-

sions, and it has proven difficult to determine which of the two recensions is the more original.[122] The "J" or longer recension will serve as the basis for my observations, and any cosmographical differences in the shorter "A" recension will be integrated into the discussion where appropriate. Determining a date for the composition of this text is also difficult; nonetheless, I guardedly follow Andersen, who concludes, "The present writer is inclined to place the book— or at least its original nucleus—early rather than late; and in a Jewish rather than a Christian community."[123]

First Heaven: 2 Enoch 3–6

On his 365th birthday, the day God took him from the earth (Gen 5:21–24), Enoch was lying on his bed and he began to dream.[124] In his dream Enoch saw two gigantic angels who had come to escort him to heaven (1:3–9). These two angels "took me (Enoch) up onto their wings and carried me up to the first heaven" (3:1–2). The first thing Enoch saw in the first heaven was "a vast ocean, much bigger than the earthly ocean" (3:3; cf. 3 Baruch 2:1, Test. Abr. 8:3(B).[125] This is the celestial ocean believed since ancient times to be just above the atmosphere. This text thus incorporates the ancient Near Eastern traditions about the celestial ocean into the Greco-Roman multiple heaven model. Enoch also saw the angels who govern the stars and constellations (4:2).[126] This heaven also holds the storehouses of the snow, ice, clouds, and dew as well as the angels who stood watch over them (5:1–6:1). The first heaven, then, is the place where the heavenly beings who control the movements of the stars reside and where the meteorological elements are stored. Again, this strange collocation of items indicates that the author is mixing old biblical and ancient Near Eastern images with Greco-Roman astronomy.

Second Heaven: 2 Enoch 7

The two angels then brought Enoch up to the second heaven where he encountered "darkness greater than earthly darkness" and saw angels being held under guard and awaiting punishment (7:1). These angels had disobeyed God in order to follow "their prince." They now weep unceasingly and ask Enoch to pray for them, something Enoch says he was unable to do (7:2–5; cf. 1 Enoch 13:4–7.). The second heaven, then, is a place where some of the fallen angels are punished.

Third Heaven: 2 Enoch 8–10

In the third heaven Enoch saw "Paradise,"[127] a place he describes as "inconceivably pleasant" (8:1b) where he saw the beautiful "tree of life" (8:3–4) and angels perpetually singing praises to God (8:8). Enoch learned from his angelic guides that this pleasant place is reserved exclusively for the righteous "as an eternal inheritance" (9:1). The two angels then "carried me (Enoch) to the northern region" to a terrible place of gloomy darkness where angels are inflicting all manner of torture and punishment on people (10:1). The people suffering these punishments are those who throughout their lives scorned God and committed impious acts (10:2–6). In the third heaven, then, one finds both the region of the blessed and the region of the wicked. Based on their behavior while on earth, the one group receives rewards while the other receives punishment. The shocking juxtaposition of the rewards awaiting the righteous and the sufferings awaiting the wicked vividly remind the reader that how one lives one's life on earth will determine one's postmortem fate.

Fourth Heaven: 2 Enoch 11–17

In this heaven Enoch learned the secrets about the movements of the celestial bodies: "those two men (i.e., angels) took me (Enoch) and they carried me up to the fourth heaven. And they showed me there all the movements and sequences, and all the rays of solar and lunar light. And I measured their movements and compared their light" (11:1–2a). The information Enoch learned here is much like that recorded in 1 Enoch 72–82, the Astronomical Book. Enoch learned the secrets about the sun's movements, size, and the intensity of its light (11:2b–d; cf. 1 Enoch 72). A multitude of celestial beings, including phoenixes,[128] accompany the sun as it rides in its chariot on its daily journey.

The two angels then "carried me (Enoch) away to the east" to view the six gates through which the sun passes when it enters the sky each morning (13:1–2a; cf. 1 Enoch 72:3). Enoch measured the size of the gates and calculated the number of days the sun uses each of the gates in its apparent annual north-south migrations (13:2b). The two angels then carried Enoch to the western region of this heaven to see the six gates where the sun sets each day (14:1). Enoch learned that after the sun sets in the evening it travels under the earth to return to the eastern gates (14:2–3). When the sun sets, 400 angels remove its crown of light, carry it to the Lord, and guard it there. For seven hours the sun remains in the darkness, and at the eighth hour the four hundred angels return to crown him with his radiant crown and then the blazing sun rises again (14:3b). As the sun rises, the "phoenixes and khalkedras" burst into song, awakening all the other birds on earth who sing merrily at sunrise (15:1–2). Enoch then saw the movements and phases of the moon as it enters and exits the sky via twelve gates (16:1–8; cf. 1 Enoch 73–74). The number twelve is unusual—six is the expected number—and the entire arrangement seems rather artificial.[129]

The fourth heaven, then, is the realm of the larger celestial bodies. 2 Enoch, although either directly dependent upon material in 1 Enoch or on data very similar to it, does not strictly agree with the cosmography of 1 Enoch. 1 Enoch speculates at length on the sun and moon, but it does not identify specifically in which heaven these celestial bodies are located. 2 Enoch, therefore, evidences a slightly different "scientific" tradition than 1 Enoch in this regard. All of this appears as an attempt by the tradents of 2 Enoch to conform more to Greco-Roman astronomical models. Still, the fact that 2 Enoch, like 3 Baruch, locates the sun and moon in the same heaven indicates that its author does not completely understand the Greco-Roman multiple-heaven model. Moreover, the gate complex used by the celestial bodies to enter and exit the visible sky is an idea that belongs to the ancient Near Eastern image of the cosmos and does not fit the Greco-Roman model. Again, this indicates a serious misunderstanding of the multiple-heaven model. This and other authors know that a person who ascends to heaven should learn about the workings of the cosmos, but they do not know Greco-Roman astronomy well enough to put things in their proper places.

Fifth Heaven: 2 Enoch 18

The two angels then "took me (Enoch) up on their wings and placed me on the fifth heaven" (18:1). The fifth heaven is a place for the punishment of the "Watchers" or fallen angels who are being held for judgment (18:1–5). These are the angels whose rebellion against God and departure from heaven were narrated in 1 Enoch 6–14. The rest of this group of angels was being punished in the second heaven. The fifth heaven is a sad place in which there is no liturgy or praise being directed to God (18:2). Enoch encouraged these unfortunate angels to start singing praises so that God might forgive them, so they responded with a sincere yet pitiful attempt at praising God (18:6–9). The events described in the fifth heaven show that sin against God does not go unpunished. The unstated implication for the readers is that they ought to obey God and practice virtue now lest after their death they suffer the same fate as these rebellious angels. If God does not spare angels who sin, he will not spare human sinners either.

Sixth Heaven: 2 Enoch 19

The angels then took Enoch up to the sixth heaven (19:1) where he saw seven groups of angels who "carefully study the movements of the stars, and the revolution of the sun and the phases of the moon, and the well-being of the cosmos" (19:2). These are the archangels who supervise all the other angels and who ensure that the cosmos functions properly (19:3–5). They also keep records of all human deeds, records that will be used by God to judge them either after they die or in the eschaton (cf. 40:13; 52:15; 65:4). The sixth heaven, then, is a place where angels try to control matters in heaven and earth and make note of everything that fails to follow the divine plan. The author's point is that there is a place in the heavenly realm where God's agents keep track of all that takes place and record all deviations from the divine plan so that God might one day have all the evidence he needs to mete out appropriate punishment. The image is almost unnerving; no human, angelic, or cosmic act goes unnoticed or unrecorded! Big brother is watching!

Seventh Heaven: 2 Enoch 20

The two angels then brought Enoch up to the seventh heaven (20:1) where he saw a large group of heavenly beings singing praise to God. Although he was at first terrified at this sight, his angelic escorts assured him that he was not in danger (20:2). From this heaven Enoch could see God sitting on his exceedingly high throne in the tenth heaven (20:3a)[130] with the angelic hosts standing according to their ranks on ten steps, singing the Trisagion, "Holy, Holy, Holy, Lord Sabaoth, Heaven and earth are full of his glory" (20:4–21:1; cf. Isa. 6:3, Rev. 4:8).[131] At this point the two escorting angels left Enoch standing alone, and he was struck with fear and fell to the ground crying "Woe is me!" (cf. Isa. 6:5). He was immediately comforted by the archangel Gabriel who escorted him up to the tenth heaven, allowing him only fleeting glances into the eighth and ninth heavens (21:2–6).

The shorter "A" recension of 2 Enoch has a seven-heaven cosmography and does not mention any journey through the eighth, ninth, or tenth heavens. All the things mentioned about what Enoch saw in these higher heavens according to the longer "J" recension are located in the seventh heaven according to the "A" recension. It could be that the parts of the text mentioning the different heavens have dropped out somewhere during the transmission process of the "A" recension. It seems unlikely, however, that just these details could have dropped out so fortuitously. It is more likely that those who transmitted the "A" recension and those who transmitted the "J" recension held different models of the cosmos, and at some point one recension underwent purposeful changes in the descriptions of the structure of the universe. In both recensions the ascent is complete: Enoch arrived finally in the presence of the divine in the highest heaven. The differences between the two recensions are due not to inadvertent errors creeping in during the process of transmitting the text but are the result of changes introduced purposefully by those transmitting the text. The rationale behind these editorial adaptations is based on the editors' views of what they believed to be the true structure of the cosmos—seven or ten heavens.

Eighth and Ninth Heavens: 2 Enoch 21:6 (J recension only)

The angel Gabriel took Enoch to the tenth heaven to stand before the Lord but on the way Enoch saw into the eighth and ninth heavens.

> And Gabriel carried me up, like a leaf carried by the wind. He moved me along and put me down in front of the face of the Lord. And I saw the eighth heaven, which is called in the Hebrew language Muzaloth, the changer of the seasons, of dry and wet, and the 12 zodiacs, which are above the seventh heaven. And I saw the ninth heaven, which in the Hebrew language is called Kukhavim, where the heavenly houses of the 12 zodiacs are. (21:5–6)

Enoch saw the regulator of the seasons (cf. 19:3–5) and the twelve zodiacs in the eighth heaven (2 Enoch 21:6). It may be that the stars of the zodiac are inscribed in the underside of the eighth heaven, but what the "heavenly houses of the 12 zodiacs" in the ninth heaven are is unclear.[132] That the zodiac was acceptable in early Jewish circles is evident from its appearance in Jewish texts

(4Q186, 318; magic amulets; Treatise of Shem) and in mosaics from several early Palestinian synagogues.[133] Initial reaction to the presence of such astrological features in these Jewish contexts is typically one of amazement, yet it is wise to remember that while Jews used this iconography, they subsumed it under a theology that maintained that their God was nonetheless the ultimate creator and controller of everything in the cosmos. Use of zodiacal themes and images becomes a statement about God's power over even those celestial bodies that other people thought controlled or influenced human fate.

Tenth Heaven: 2 Enoch 22 (J recension only)

Enoch saw God in the tenth heaven but struggled to provide any description of the divine being. (22:1–3; cf. 39:1–8)

> And on the 10th heaven, Aravoth, I saw the view of the face of the LORD, like iron made burning hot in a fire and brought out, and it emits sparks and is incandescent. Thus even I saw the face of the LORD. But the face of the LORD is not to be talked about, it is so very marvelous and supremely awesome and supremely frightening. And who am I to give an account of the incomprehensible being of the LORD, and of his face, so extremely strange and indescribable? . . . Who can give an account of his beautiful appearance, never changing and indescribable, and his great glory?

God then commanded his angelic servants to initiate Enoch into the heavenly assembly, and Enoch became exactly like one of the holy angels (22:6–10). Enoch sat down with a pen and, over a period of thirty days and thirty nights,[134] wrote 366 books at the dictation of the archangel Vrevoil (22:11–23:6). The contents of these books deal with the mysteries of the cosmos, the elements of the earth, and the nature of human existence, precisely the kinds of secrets that were typically associated with Enoch throughout the literature pseudepigraphically attributed to him. These books were, however, not all the secrets revealed to Enoch (24:1–32:2).[135] Some of these secrets involve a recasting of the Genesis creation story in terms of Greek physics. Moreover, the picture of the universe depicted here is not at all like the seven- or ten-heaven schemas encountered in the first half of this book. According to the account of the creation in 2 Enoch 25–26, the universe has this overall structure:

Nothing
Great Light
Darkness
Nothing

In the middle, between the "great light" and the "darkness," God caused the light and the darkness to coalesce forming water (27:1–3a). God then surrounded the water with seven crystalline circles or "heavens"[136] in each of which a planet travels in its own particular path (27:3b–4; cf. 48:1–4).[137] The author, in the midst of an extended commentary on the biblical creation account in 2 Enoch 28–33, notes that on the fourth day God created the celestial bodies that orbit in seven circles around the earth: the star Kronos (κρόνος, Saturn) in the first or highest circle, Afridit (ἀφροδίτη, Aphrodite, Venus) in the second, Arris (ἄρης, Mars) in the third, the sun (ἥλιος, Helios) in the fourth, Zeous (ζεύς, Jupiter) in the fifth, Ermis (ἑρμῆς, Mercury) in the sixth, and finally the moon (σελήνη) in the seventh and lowest circle.[138] Below all these God placed the stars in the air (30:3–6). As the names of the planets clearly indicate, this account of the planetary spheres is based on Greco-Roman astronomy. The location of the planets in their different spheres does not agree completely with the Ptolemaic model, for Ptolemy located Jupiter in the sixth sphere and Venus in the third sphere, while 2 Enoch 30 reverses the order. Moreover, although the Ptolemaic model located the stars above the highest sphere, 2 Enoch 30 locates them in the air below the moon. In several respects, then, the cosmography of 2 Enoch 30 is idiosyncratic. Apart from the works of the learned and thoroughly Hellenized Jewish philosopher Philo, this part of 2 Enoch is the only text discussed here that truly understands, albeit somewhat imperfectly, the Greco-Roman models of the cosmos. Yet this section seems to have been tacked on to the rest of the narrative. This thoroughly "modern" conception of the cosmos has not influenced the descriptions of the cosmos elsewhere in the text.

His revelation of secrets to Enoch complete, God returned Enoch to his people so that he might reveal to them the things he had learned (33:3–9). Following a last impassioned exhortation (56–66), Enoch was enveloped in darkness and taken to the "highest heaven" where he became like the rest of the angelic host in appearance and stood before the face of the Lord forever (67:1–3, cf. 22:10, 55:1–2). Slavonic Enoch evidences in one text the tensions already encountered in several of the preceding early Jewish and Christian texts regarding the issue of the structure of the universe. Were there ten (J recension) or seven (A recension) heavens? The seven-heaven schema of the shorter "A" recension seems to have been the original cosmography. The tradents of longer "J" recension expanded the seven-heaven schema to a ten-heaven schema, and their revisions stem from their desire to make the text conform to their own cosmography. They were updating what must have appeared to them as an inaccurate or obsolete cosmography. Another tension involves the overall structure of the multiple heavens. Were these heavens layered successively one on top of the other as in the old ancient Near Eastern and biblical conception (chapters 1–21), or were they a set of concentric circles each with its own planet surrounding the earth as in the Greco-Roman models (chapters 22–73)? This confusion could be due to the accidental corruption of the manuscripts during the transmission process, but it seems more probable that these are editorial alterations purposely introduced into the text. The motivation for the alterations was the desire to make the text conform to the editors' own cosmography. Several different conceptions of the universe have been incorporated into the two recensions of this text as it has been preserved. The earliest was likely the seven-heaven schema. This schema was then expanded to a ten-heaven schema. The seven-heaven schema and the account of Enoch's ascent indicate that these multiple layers were stacked one on top of the other above the earth. This schema was augmented by the Ptolemaic planetary spheres model in chapters 22–73. In the end, this text intends to show that the heavenly realm is very complex and teeming with activity.

Enoch's tour through the heavens enabled him to report back to his companions that God does indeed ultimately control everything in the astonishingly complex universe. Moreover, since all the instruments for the punishment of sinners are already in place and working efficiently, humans would do well to lead moral lives lest they too one day fall prey to the angels in charge of postmortem punishments. On the positive side, those who imitate Enoch's piety can expect to receive a similar heavenly reward: "I had become like one of his glorious ones, and there was no observable difference" (22:10). As has been the case in almost every other early Jewish or Christian description of the heavenly realms, the authors' goals focus more on proper ethical conduct than on accurate astronomy.

Apocalypse of Abraham

This apocalypse has been preserved only in Slavonic manuscripts but it may date from the first or early second century CE.[139] According to this apocalypse, Abraham, after fasting for forty days and offering a sacrifice (9–14), ascended into the heavenly realms seated on the wings of a sacrificial bird.[140] Abraham's first stop was in the "heaven that is fixed on the expanses" (15:4), a place he later learned to be the seventh heaven (19:4). Oddly enough, Abraham traveled immediately to the divine presence and saw God's fiery throne and a multitude of fiery angels in this heaven. Abraham then looked down and only then did he see the contents of the lower heavens. Abraham saw a multitude of angels in the sixth heaven (19:5–8), and when the sixth heaven rolled back to reveal the fifth heaven (19:9) Abraham saw the angels who govern the stars and the natural elements on the earth. Abraham marveled at the vast number of stars (20:1–5) and saw the surface of the earth where the course of human history was being played out (21:1–29:21). As Abraham watches history unfold from on high, the reader marvels at how the heavenly realm is beyond time, and that from a heavenly perspective the present and future are as certain as the past. The rest of the text focuses on the course of human history and records all the private and public acts of impiety people commit. Oddly, the text never returns to describe heavens four through one. The reader expects the text to continue describing the appearance and the contents of the heavens in the descending order as the author has done with heavens seven through five, but it is clear that the author's interests were other than strictly cosmographical. The author has used the ascent motif as the narrative framework in which to relate his ideas about social, ethical, national and eschatological issues. The text is an apocalyptic expansion of Abraham's sacrifice described in Genesis 15. Although most visionaries weave their interpretations of the ancient texts into their apocalypses, this text is actually a sustained commentary on Genesis 15. The result is an apocalypse that speaks afresh to the issues of the day that most concerned the author. Or to look at it from another perspective, the seer had a vision that was influenced by traditional literary forms and ideology, but he integrated them in a new way. The religious and social concerns that weighed heavily upon the seer influenced the contents of his vision, and the traditional literary forms influenced the structure of the vision. Thus the text teaches its readers that God sees everything humans do and will one day hold everyone accountable.

It is clear that the interests of the author of this text were not in cosmographical speculation. The author has used traditional ascent imagery regarding a seer's journey to heaven but has not included in the narrative a detailed account of the contents of the separate heavens. In fact, although the author conceptualized the cosmos in terms of a seven-heaven structure, the text includes information only on heavens five through seven. The author simply used the ascent motif to transport the seer into the divine presence. What could have been learned along the way regarding the contents of the various heavens simply did not interest the author of this unusual apocalypse.

Apocalypse of Sedrach

In its final form this apocalypse is clearly Christian, although it seems to have drawn upon earlier Jewish materials.[141] The text as we have it consists of a Christian homily on love and a narrative of Sedrach's ascent to heaven.

> And the voice said to him, "I was sent to you that I may carry you up to heaven." And he [Sedrach] said, "I want to speak to God face to face, but I am not able, Lord, to ascend into the heavens." But the angel, having stretched out his wings, took him and went up into the heavens, and he took him up as far as the third heaven, and the flame of divinity stood there. (2:2–5)[142]

God welcomed Sedrach and the two debated the topic of theodicy. There is no further movement of the seer, except at the end of the narrative God carried Sedrach's soul into Paradise (16:6). There are no details to indicate whether Paradise is in the third heaven or somewhere else. The seer himself did not move about in the third heaven, nor did he travel to any heavens above or below. In the author's view of the cosmos, God resided in the third heaven. This apocalypse is primarily interested in moving directly to the debate between Sedrach and God; speculation about the contents of the intermediate heavens and the heaven wherein God resides did not interest this author. Since God resides in the third heaven, it seems likely that there are no additional heavens above the third. Paul's ascent to the third heaven in 2 Cor. 12:1–4 appears to have influenced the cosmography of the Apocalypse of Sedrach. If Paradise is in fact in the third heaven in the Apocalypse of Sedrach, then it joins 2 Cor. 12:1–4, 2 Enoch, Apocalypse of Paul, and, possibly, 3 Baruch in this regard (cf. Apocalypse of Moses). The overall theme of the homily on love and the ascent focuses on God's great mercy to all, and the goal is to inspire people to use the opportunity afforded by God's mercy to repent of their evil ways. Again, an ascent text wherein the seer learns of God's expectations of people is being used to promote ethical, moral behavior. As in almost all of the preceding texts, the ascent to heaven is not simply or primarily an opportunity to learn about the secrets of the cosmos. The ascent provides the opportunity to learn that no matter how chaotic the world may seem, God is still in control and has already put into place all the instruments necessary to punish all who do not follow his intended designs be they celestial bodies, angels, or humans. These devout authors, therefore, use their "visions of heaven" to promote moral, virtuous behavior on earth.

Summary and Conclusions

The texts discussed here have for the most part not received much interest in traditional Jewish and Christian circles. Together these texts shed enormous light on early Jewish and Christian history, religion, and culture. Both early Judaism and nascent Christianity were vibrantly diverse in the Greco-Roman period. These texts fill in the picture that the traditional texts of these two communities provide only in part. Beyond the many details that these texts provide about how people imagined the heavenly realms, two matters are significant. First, the texts discussed here adopt some form of the Greco-Roman models of the cosmos. While the biblical texts that were religiously authoritative for both Jews and Christians viewed the cosmos as a simple tripartite structure—heaven, earth, netherworld—these texts adopted an entirely different image of the heavenly realm with multiple heavens above or encircling the earth. To be honest, nearly all of these texts demonstrate a misunderstanding of the Greco-Roman models to one degree or another. Instead of having each heaven or sphere contain a separate planet, these texts (with the exception of Philo and a part of 2 Enoch) tend to put the planets, sun, moon, and stars in one or two different heavens. Moreover, several still speak of "gates" through which the celestial bodies enter and exit the visible sky. These "gates" were common in the older biblical and ancient Near Eastern images of the celestial realm but are technically incompatible with the Greco-Roman models. Thus, although adopting a multiple-heaven schema, these texts misunderstand the model and transform it into a schema whose true organizing principle centers around theological interests. The heavenly realms have become little more than places where people receive postmortem punishment or reward.

Second, the overall goal of these visions of heaven is to inspire people to live an ethical or moral life. That the places for postmortem punishment are already in place and functioning effectively serves as a warning: do what God expects of you or you will suffer as some of these people, angels, or celestial bodies are currently suffering! In contrast, the visions of heavenly bliss that await the righteous appeal to basic human egocentrism. No matter what one's station in life may be, for most people there lurks just under the surface a longing for something more, something better. This angst is especially acute for people who are actually suffering in some way. For those who are suffering from physical pain, are alienated from the power structures of their society, are being oppressed by people or institutions outside of their control, or even only sense that they are being somehow oppressed, these visions of a blessed afterlife inspire hope and thereby ameliorate their pain. For these people, the hope of receiving heavenly rewards and watching the wicked receive their deserved punishments makes the pain of this world a little more tolerable.

These images of heaven, therefore, become powerful tools in promoting obedience to a theological agenda or particular way of life. Those who do not live according to the moral guidelines of these texts can expect to suffer for it, while the obedient can expect a fitting reward. These religious authors looked to the vast skies and marveled at how the celestial bodies, not to mention the seasons and even the ocean tides, follow what they thought was the divine design. These authors' goal was similar to a portion of the Pater Noster or Lord's Prayer, "thy will be done on earth as it is in heaven." Many religious communities thought that they alone knew the divine will for humans, and so in their theological speculations they devised rather specific requirements for who could be admitted into heaven. In the beliefs of some, therefore, heaven, the incomprehensibly vast realm of the Divine, was not big enough to allow others with differing belief systems or cultural patterns to enter. Heaven was becoming a place with rigorously exclusive admission standards.

EARLY JEWISH AND CHRISTIAN TRADITIONS III

Common Themes and Motifs

So it is for the Therapeutae, who so diligently contemplate nature and the things in it and live by the soul alone, citizens of heaven and the world, presented faithfully to the Father and Maker of all by Virtue, who has procured for them God's love and added a fitting gift—noble character, a blessing better than all good fortune and indeed tantamount to true happiness.

Philo of Alexandria, *The Contemplative Life*, 90

In the course of the Second Temple Period (most broadly defined as ca. 539 BCE-135 CE), as their ancestral homeland came under successive waves of foreign domination or as they spread across Asia, Africa, and Europe, Jews encountered many different cultures. This interaction affected how they expressed their religion, history, and customs. A prime example of this is Philo of Alexandria whose works reflect his familiarity with other cultures and his efforts to commend Jews and Judaism to a Roman audience. Ezekiel the Tragedian is another well-known example. His *Exagoge* retold the story of the Exodus from Egypt in the form of a Greco-Roman tragedy. Examples could be multiplied. The point is that in the wake of the Persian, Greek, and Roman conquests of the Near East, Jews were introduced to myriad new ways of imagining the world and their place in it. Part of this reimagining the world involved their image of the cosmos itself. The common ancient Near Eastern model of the cosmos was that it was a tripartite structure: heavenly realm of the gods, earthly realm of humans, plants and animals, and netherworldly realm of gods and deceased humans. Ancient Israel shared this ancient Near Eastern view of the cosmos. As a consequence of their interactions with the Babylonians, Persians, Greeks and Romans, however, the Jews learned new ways to imagine the heavenly realm. The vast astronomical and astrological interests that were common to most all cultures of the ancient world are not explicitly attested in ancient Israelite sources. Astronomy and astrology were surely part of ancient Israelite culture, but the editors of the Hebrew Bible choose not to include this material in their works, although the Hebrew Bible itself as well as extrabiblical sources provide occasional hints of this interest. The early Jewish communities were affected by the myths and science of the cultures that dominated them. In the Greco-Roman period all Jews were Hellenized to one extent or another. Even before the conquests of Alexander the Great, Jews were aware of the Greeks and their culture. Slowly, even imperceptibly at first, Jews were being drawn into the Greek orbit. Although it has been common to pit traditional Jews against Hellenized Jews in this period, most ancient Jews would not have so strictly compartmentalized their culture. It was not a question of who was Hellenized and who was not. Everyone was. The issue was the extent to which a person adopted Hellenistic traditions, religions, culture, and so forth. A person such as ben Sira, the author of the apocryphal book of Ecclesiasticus (Ecc. 50:27), could be thoroughly Hellenized on outward appearances but at the same time be completely traditional in many aspects of religious beliefs.

As the preceding chapters have indicated, there was some tension in how Jews and eventually Christians imagined the heavenly realm. On the one hand these communities inherited a religious tradition and a religiously authoritative body of writings (the Hebrew Bible/Old Testament) that imagined and described the cosmos according to the obsolete Near Eastern models. The texts from the Greco-Roman world attest entirely new and vastly more complex ways to imagine the heavenly realm. Early Jewish and Christian authors were caught between these newer Greco-Roman models and the images of the cosmos found in their religiously authoritative texts and traditions. New patterns of belief typically do not completely efface the old; rather, the old may live on in a revised version in the new, or the old and new may persist alongside one another in spite of their sometimes considerable logical incompatibility.[1] Some early Jews and Christians adopted the Greco-Roman models wholeheartedly, others did so only partially, and still others maintained the old biblical views. In each case, these texts exhibit several features that were shared by the different models of the cosmos existing and even competing in this period.

The Geography of Heaven

Historically, all aspects of Jewish culture are based at least in part on the biblical traditions. If the Bible, their foundational, religiously authoritative document, imagined the universe in the customary ancient Near Eastern tripartite model, how could later generations of Jews abandon that in favor of the newer models? Justification for adopting newer Greco-Roman models can readily be found in the fact that the Hebrew term for "heaven" or "sky," שמים (šāmayim), is a form that appears on the surface to indicate plurality (i.e., the -ayim ending indicates more than one). The Jewish religious and intellectual leaders—priests and scribes—surely justified their speculations on the observation that since the word for heaven or sky suggests plurality, the heavenly realm must be plural in some way. Thus, later authors had ample justification for adopting and adapting Hellenistic models.

What does a person find in heaven? As one might well imagine, God dwells in heaven along with his angelic entourage. In the biblical and Israelite conceptions of the heavenly realm, God lived in the heavenly realm immediately above and beyond the stars, planets and visible dome of the skies. In the course of the Second Temple Period, however, as Jews absorbed and modified the cosmographical speculations of the Persians, Greeks, and Romans, the heavenly realms became vastly more complex and teeming with activity. The Divinity's abode thus became seemingly more distant, more removed. Too much, however, has been made of this observation. The several intervening heavens did not make God any more distant, for he already was unfathomably distant from the human realm: in the Psalmist's words, "Heaven is Yahweh's heaven, but the earth he has given to humans" (Psalm 115:16). The book of Isaiah echoes similar thoughts: "For my thoughts are not your thoughts, nor your ways my ways . . . For just as the heavens are high above the earth, so are my ways high above your ways and my thoughts above your thoughts" (Isa. 55:8–9). The addition of multiple heavens simply suggested how incomprehensibly complex the cosmos is and gave definition to the chasm between God and humanity. Each text's speculations only rarely conform to those in other texts, yet there are some consistent features.

Storehouses for the Meteorological Elements

The Bible notes that meteorological elements (wind, rain, snow, lightning, etc.) are stored in the heavenly realm (e.g., Deut. 28:12; Jer. 10:13, 51:16; Ps. 135:7; Job 38:22). The pseudepigraphical texts and traditions attributed to Enoch describe how he learned all manner of cosmological secrets regarding these celestial storehouses. Because the story of the ascent of Enoch into heaven was an early and formative element in the development of Jewish cosmic speculation, learning about these elements in the course of an ascent became fairly standard elements in accounts of what a visionary encounters when viewing the secrets of the cosmos (1 Enoch 17–18, 41:1–9, 44:1; 4 Ezra 3:18–19; 2 Enoch 5:1–6:1; Gk. Apoc. Ezra 6:23).[2] In texts with multiple heavens these elements are typically though not exclusively found in the lowest heaven. Their location in the lowest heaven makes complete phenomenological sense because simple observation indicates that these meteorological elements come from the sky.

The Gates of Heaven

Several texts mention that one enters heaven via gates. This motif comes from the realia of the ancient world: one had to pass through gates in the walls to enter a fortified city. The idea that there were gates leading into the heavenly realm began early in the Bible's narrative history. In Genesis 28:17 Jacob dreamed of a ladder or mound extending into heaven, and he thought that he was looking at the gate of heaven: "How awesome is this place. This is none other than the 'house of God' (Beth-el), and this is the gate of heaven." He then named the place, quite naturally, "Beth-el," literally, "the house of God"; this was where heaven and earth intersected. Moreover, the people who tried to build a tower reaching into heaven named it "Babel" (Gen. 11:1–9), which in Akkadian can be rendered as "the gate of god" (bab-il). Both of these stories associate the entrance into heaven with a gate. Postbiblical materials imagined that some kind of angelic beings sat at the "gate of heaven" where they could hear the pleas of humans on earth (1 Enoch 9:2,10). Likewise, the archangel Michael receives the prayers of humans at the gate of the fifth heaven (3 Baruch 11:4). According to 3 Macc. 6:18, God opened the gates of heaven and sent two angels down to fight the Greeks on behalf of Jews (cf. 4 Macc. 4:10). Some believed that heavenly beings sat at a gateway located at the end of the world or just outside the entry into heaven and decided the postmortem fate of souls based on their conduct during their lives (e.g. Test. Abr. 11:4–12:3 [A]; Apoc. Zeph. 3:5–9; Apoc. Paul 13–16). Probably the clearest statement about gates leading into the heavenly realm is 3 Baruch where Baruch and his angelic guide pass through one gate complex after another to enter the successive heavens. Other gates into the heavenly realm are used by the celestial bodies—sun, moon, planets, and stars—to enter and exit the visible sky. This gate image as the means by which to enter or exit the heavenly realm can be traced back well before the time of the monarchies of Israel and Judah. The Egyptian and Mesopotamian cultures all used this image (see chapters 1 and 2). The Jews of the Greco-Roman period had, based on Genesis 11 and 28, ample biblical warrant to imagine that the heavenly realm could be accessed through gates. The entrances to the heavenly realm, like most all images of this realm, are patterned analogically on what people encounter on earth. Heaven is in many ways, therefore, glorified projections of mundane things from human experience.

Heaven as a Verdant Garden—Paradise

Several texts describe places in the heavenly realms as verdant gardens (e.g., 2 Enoch and 3 Baruch, cf. Life of Adam and Eve). This idea was created by transposing themes about the Garden of Eden from Genesis 1–3 to the heavenly realm.[3] "Paradise" (παράδεισος) is a loan-word from Persian (paridaida, pardez, pairidaeza) meaning "verdant garden." The Septuagint, the Greek translation of the Hebrew Bible, used the term paradise (παράδεισος) to translate the Hebrew term for garden (גן, gan). Since this term occurs in the phrase "garden of Eden" in Genesis 2–3 (cf. Neh. 2:8; Ecc. 2:5; Song 4:13), the term paradise became a technical term for the Edenic place of the blessed. In the Hebrew Bible, however, it had no such technical connotation.[4] Over the course of the Second Temple Period this idea came into Judaism in conjunction with Greek and Persian ideas of the immortality of the soul and the theme of the paradisical dwelling place of the immortals. Paradise was no longer simply the place where Adam and Eve lived but the place where the deceased righteous will reside eternally. The question remains, is this place to be found on earth or in heaven? It may be that the idea of paradise as a blessed place is Persian (i.e., Zoroastrian) in origin. But since Mesopotamia, Egypt, and Greece all had ideas of a blessed place for the righteous, it may be that while the idea was common to many cultures, the Persian terminology came to dominate. The location of paradise varies from text to text. As was detailed in chapters 5 and 6, some texts imagine the universe after the ancient Near Eastern tripartite model—heaven, earth, netherworld—and, according to this model, paradise, the region of the righteous, is located at the mythical ends of the earth, far beyond the reach of mere mortals (Greek Apocalypse of Ezra). Texts adopting Greco-Roman models of the cosmos and/or astral images of the afterlife customarily locate paradise somewhere in the heavenly realms. Naturally, texts with a single-heaven cosmography simply locate paradise in heaven (e.g., 1 Enoch 1–36, 37, 69; 4 Ezra; Dead Sea Scrolls). Texts with multiple-heaven cosmographies exhibit some variety on the location of this place for the righteous. For example, 2 Cor. 12, 2 Enoch, and the Apocalypse of Paul locate paradise in the third heaven (cf. Apocalypse of Sedrach). Baruch saw this place in the fourth heaven (3 Baruch 10). It was also common to locate the ultimate abode of the righteous in the highest of all the heavenly realms (Ascension of Isaiah, Gnostic Apocalypse of Paul), thereby stressing the nearness to God that the faithful would enjoy eternally. But why the image of a garden? While the vision of a verdant, luxurious garden appeals to the senses, this imagery harkens back to the Garden of Eden not because of its refreshing environment but because this was the place of which God, upon completing and beholding his work, noted "behold, it is very good." All humans know that our realm is certainly not "very good"; in fact, it can be down right hostile. The longing for a postmortem place in a verdant garden, be it on earth or in heaven, is a longing to return to this "very good" mythical place, the place where humans existed before evil, pain, and suffering were introduced into our existence.

The Beings of Heaven

The topic of the emergence and development of the myths about angels in the Greco-Roman period is a topic itself worthy of an extended monograph, so the following remarks are intended as a summary. As one might expect, early Jewish and Christian texts often mention the presence of angels in the heavenly realms. These beings bring God's word to humans and bear human prayers to God. Holy angels fight against the wicked and for the righteous, while wicked angels oppose the righteous. The images of angels evolved out of earlier Israelite religiosity. The gods of the nations, gods that were regarded as Yahweh's equals in the early stages of Israelite religion, were eventually downgraded in the later stages of biblical religion to the status of subordinate divine beings. These heavenly beings were subsequently further downgraded to beings created by Yahweh to serve him in running the universe. As was the custom of the gods in Homeric epics, heavenly beings appear now and then in the Hebrew Bible to help or hinder human beings, even taking on the physical form of humans (e.g., Gen. 16:7–12, 18; Dan. 10–12). When some ancient Jews came to adopt the Greek ideas about the immortality of the soul and its desire to return to the highest celestial realms after death, they, too, believed that the soul of the dead ascended heavenward after death. In Greek and Persian thought souls had to shed their physicality and all their infirmities as they ascended. Angels, loyal as they are to God, were charged in Jewish thought with protecting the divine realm from unworthy souls. They also were responsible for inflicting appropriate punishments on human souls in return for their wicked deeds. After death, an angel escorted one's soul to the place of one's eternal abode, be it good or bad. The dead encountered angelic opposition during the course of their postmortem journey, and if they were not quite worthy, their destiny was a place of punishment. The just or worthy souls, on the other hand, had supportive angelic guides who assisted them in the course of their ascent and helped them reach their permanent residence in the heavenly realm. The idea of "purgatory" or "purgation," the idea that because of their sins people would suffer punishments in intermediate heavens until they were cleansed from their sins and then would be fit to ascend farther, begins in this era (2 Macc. 12:39–45), but it would be later Christian theologians who would develop this theme into an integral part of Christian theology.

The Divine Presence: Heaven as a Palace

Since God is a holy being, he must be attended by holy beings. In many ways the divine presence or abode is much like a temple, a theme that harkens back to biblical images of the Jerusalem Temple.[5] These motifs from the ancient temple cultus reoccur in later Jewish literature as well. The ancient model of God being attended by other gods was radically changed in the evolution of Jewish ideas about the divine. What began as the Israelite god Yahweh functioning as an equal member and then the leader of a council of gods became Yahweh as the undisputed creator and master of all other gods.[6] Eventually, this idea was further refined to the point that there were no other gods at all or that the other "divine beings" (i.e., angels) were simply created by Yahweh to serve him. As Himmelfarb has shown, the angels as well as the objects and activities in heaven can be construed as part of a great celestial temple. This is only part of the picture and perhaps not the central metaphor for the divine dwelling.

As I hope I have shown in the preceding chapters, both in the biblical and in the later sources heaven and the divine dwelling are imagined principally in the terms of a royal court. One phrase aptly describes the early Jewish and Christian view of God as king: "Lord of all, king on the exalted throne, you who rule the world" (Test. Moses 4:2). This image of God as king continues throughout the entire history of Jewish liturgy, in which God is consistently addressed with the phrase "Blessed are you, O God, *King* of the universe!" (ברוך אתה יהוה מלך העולם). When the ancients imagined the heavenly realm, they transposed the highest form of human government to the heavenly realm. Thus, by analogy heaven was a royal court with all its furnishings, court officials, and protocols.[7] How did these authors become so intimately familiar with the royal throne room? Surely not all these people had visited this august place. It seems likely that people who had been summoned before the king, those who worked as royal attendants, or those who had regular cause to appear before the king recounted their experiences to their peers, adding of course a touch of hyperbole. Not everyone appeared before the king, but everyone knew of his power and had at least some hint at the opulence in which he lived. The unrivaled power and opulence enjoyed by the king, no matter how much at times it was resented, left most people awestruck. Since the rise of kingship in the ancient Near East, the gods, the divine rulers of the cosmos, came to be imagined in forms analogous to these exalted human rulers. Just as the kings had their official attendants who knew the details of courtly protocol, so the gods had both heavenly (angels) and earthly (priests) servants who attended them and who stood between them and their subjects. Moreover, the kings typically provided public monumental depictions of the throne room, and the purpose of such monuments was to impress the king's subjects with his power and splendor. Descriptions of throne rooms can be found in classical literature as well. The descriptions of the palaces of Alcinous the king of the Achaeans in *Odyssey* 7.78–132 and that of Menelaus of Lacedaemon in *Odyssey* 4.43–81 resemble the descriptions of the palaces of God in the ascent apocalypses in many respects. The most prominent image of God, therefore, is that of a king enthroned in all his splendor. He is fittingly identified as "the king of heaven" (Dan. 4:37).

The Afterlife: Heaven as the Home of the Righteous

Many Jews modified or abandoned the traditional (i.e., biblical) views of the afterlife in favor of Hellenistic images during the course of the Second Temple period. According to the Hebrew Bible, when people died they descended to the netherworld. Although a few passages in the Hebrew Bible may suggest the beginnings of belief in the segregation of the dead into groups, in general death was simply neutral: their state was neither good nor bad, and they received neither reward nor punishment.[8] In the biblical period Israelite religious behavior was largely determined by family, clan or national associations. In the Greco-Roman periods Jews had additional options and potentially even wider associations through the increasingly popular civic and personal religions.[9] Hellenization, the process of adopting Greek-like culture, occurred differently in different places, among different people, in different classes, in both political and economic spheres, as well as in religious and intellectual spheres. By adopting and adapting some Hellenistic ways while yet remaining true to their ancestral traditions, the Jews of the Greco-Roman period expressed their many and varied ideas of Judaism in new forms that addressed the issues of the new era.[10] The idea of immortality developed in Judaism during the Second Temple Period in part as an answer to the difficult questions of theodicy: "why do the wicked prosper and the righteous suffer, especially at the hands of the wicked?" Personal immortality provided the oppressed with a potential solution. Whatever problems they may experience in this passing life will be remedied in the next when the righteous are vindicated and the wicked punished. Thus, there began to appear a belief in a vast divide between groups of people in the after-life: one's postmortem fate was determined on the basis of one's behavior.[11] The wicked would be sent to punishment (either in the netherworld or in a region of one of the heavens), while the righteous would be rewarded with a place among the immortals. The famous Jewish historian Josephus described the belief in the immortality of the soul among the Jewish sectarians known as the Essenes.

> For it is a fixed belief of theirs that the body is corruptible and its constituent matter impermanent, but that the soul is immortal and imperishable. Ema-nating from the finest ether, these souls become entangled, as it were, in the prison-house of the body, to which they are dragged down by a sort of natu-ral spell; but when once they are released from the bonds of the flesh, then, as though liberated from a long servitude, they rejoice and are borne aloft. Sharing the belief of the sons of Greece, they maintain that for virtuous souls there is reserved an abode beyond the ocean, a place which is not oppressed by rain or snow or heat, but is refreshed by the ever gentle breath of the west wind coming in from the ocean; while they regulate base souls to a murky and tempestuous dungeon, big with never-ending punishments. The Greeks, I imagine, had the same conception when they set apart the isles of the blessed for their brave men, whom they call heroes and demi-gods, and the region of the impious for the souls of the wicked down in Hades, where, as their mythologists tell, persons such as Sisyphus, Tantalus, Ixion and Tityus, are undergoing punishment. Their aim was first to establish the doctrine of the immortality of the soul, and secondly to promote virtue and to deter from vice; for the good are made better in their lifetime by the hope of a reward after death, and the passions of the wicked are restrained by the fear that, even though they escape detection while alive, they will undergo never-ending punishment after their decease. Such are the theological views of the Essenes concerning the soul, whereby they irresistibly attract all who have once tasted their philosophy. (*Jewish War* 2.154–58)[12]

The Essenes held one of the views common among Greeks—that the righ-teous had a luxurious place at the ends of the earth awaiting them after death. This was a belief common in Greece as early as the Homeric Age. Other groups had somewhat different expectations of a this-worldly afterlife. According to the Testament of Levi 18:10–11, a messianic priest will come in the eschaton to lead the righteous back to the Garden of Eden, restoring humans to their original paradisical abode on earth and giving them access to the fruit of the Tree of Life. Neither during his ascent nor during the angelic explanation of the things located in the various heavens did Levi see the righteous dwelling in any of the heavenly spheres. For this text the eternal dwelling place of the righteous is located on the terrestrial plane: the righteous apparently do not dwell in heaven with God and his angelic retinue. Likewise, the New Testament Book of Revelation has the righteous enjoying a renewed heaven and earth. Life for the righteous is lived on the restored earth in the New Jerusalem which has come down from heaven (Rev. 20–21).

Many Jewish authors located the postmortem realm of the righteous in the heavenly realms. Such a Jewish belief is expressed for the first time in Daniel 12:2–3, a text dating to ca. 165 BCE.

> Many of those who sleep in the dust of the earth will awake, some to eternal life, others to reproaches and everlasting disgust. But the wise will shine like the brilliant expanse of the sky, and those who lead many to righteousness will be like the stars for ever and ever.

This appears to mean that the righteous will shine like the starry host of heaven; that is, they will become stars or angelic beings.[13] This statement is clearly influenced by Hellenistic ideas of astral immortality and is the only passage in the Hebrew Bible/Old Testament that imagines a celestial afterlife for the righteous. In the late second or early first century BCE, Jason of Cyrene wrote a five-volume history of the Jews, a work that has been preserved only partially in an abridgment know as 2 Maccabees. In this work one reads of the "Seven Brothers and their Mother" who willingly submitted to martyrdom instead of committing religious sacrilege. Some of their comments to their persecutors illustrate that by this time some Jews expected to be rewarded in the afterlife for their piety as suggested in Daniel 12.[14]

> You wretch, you remove us from this present life, but the King of the universe will raise us who have died for his laws up to an everlasting life. (7:9)
> I received these (hands) from Heaven and for his laws I despise them, and from him I hope to receive them again. (7:11; cf. 14:46)
>> It is preferable to be put to death by men and to maintain hope in God of being resurrected by him. For you, however, there will be no resurrection to life. (7:14)
>> The Creator of the universe . . . will give back to you both breath and life by his mercy since you now give up yourselves for the sake of his laws. (7:23)

In the end the soul of the righteous makes its way to the heavenly realms. Many of the statements from Jewish authors sound as if they came right out of the mouths of Greek authors.

> When the decisive decree has gone forth from the Most High that a man shall die, as the soul leaves the body to return again to him who gave it, first of all it adores the glory of the Most High. (4 Ezra 7:78)
>> The thoughts of mortals are worthless, and our designs are likely to fail. A perishable body weighs down the soul, and this earthy tent weighs down the thoughtful mind. (Wisd. of Sol. 9:14–15)

The underlying belief is that the body has a corrupting influence on the soul. The soul originated in the heavenly realms and after death wishes to return to its pure, ethereal, preincarnate state. Writing to Christians and echoing this Jewish belief, the apostle Paul claims that before the faithful can join their resurrected Lord, "this perishable body must be clothed with the imperishable and the mortal body with the immortal" (1 Cor. 15:53). Philo, a thoroughly Hellenized Jew to be sure, in describing the nature of the human soul notes that it has a natural affinity with the heavenly realm of the divine because the soul is that part of humankind that is created in God's image (Genesis 1:26–27).

> After all the rest, as I have said, Moses tells us that man was created after the image of God and after His likeness (Gen. i. 26). Right well does he say this, for nothing earth-born is more like God than man. Let no one represent the likeness as one to a bodily form; for neither is God in human form, nor is the human body God-like. No, it is in respect of the Mind, the sovereign element of the soul, that the word "image" is used; for after the pattern of a single Mind, even the Mind of the Universe as an archetype, the mind in each of those who successively came into being was moulded [*sic*]. It is in a fashion a god to him who carries and enshrines it as an object of reverence; for the human mind evidently occupies a position in men precisely answering to that which the great Ruler occupies in all the world. It is invisible while itself seeing all things, and while comprehending the substances of others, it is as to its own substance unperceived; and while it opens by arts and sciences roads branching in many directions, all of them great highways, it comes through land and sea investigating what either element contains. Again, when on soaring wing it has contemplated the atmosphere and all its phases, it is borne yet higher to the ether and the circuit of heaven, and is whirled round with the dances of planets and fixed stars, in accordance with the laws of perfect music, following that love of wisdom which guides its steps. And so, carrying its gaze beyond the confines of all substance discernible by sense, it comes to a point at which it reaches out after the intelligible world, and on descrying in that world sights of surpassing loveliness, even the patterns and the originals of the things of sense which it saw here, it is seized by a sober intoxication, like those filled with Corybantic frenzy, and is inspired, possessed by a longing far other than theirs and a nobler desire. Wafted by this to the topmost arch of the things perceptible to mind, it seems to be on its way to the Great King Himself; but, amid its longing to see Him, pure and untempered rays of concentrated light stream forth like a torrent, so that by its gleams the eye of the understanding is dazzled. (*On the Creation of the World* 69–71)[15]

The expectation of postmortem heavenly ascent is succinctly stated in the admittedly late Greek Apocalypse of Ezra 6–7 where, in a debate between Ezra and God about what happens at death, God ends the discussion by saying: "Therefore, fear not death. For that which is from me, the soul, departs for heaven. That which is from the earth, the body, departs for the earth from which it was taken" (Gk. Apoc. Ezra 7:3). In fact, the point of every ascent account is that the righteous have the hope of heavenly ascent after death or in the eschaton. The seer's ascent to heaven foreshadows what the righteous can expect.

But not all Jews adopted these new ideas of resurrection and celestial immortality. The book of ben Sira (Ecclesiasticus), a text roughly contemporary with the book of Daniel, claims that the dead forever remain in the netherworld:

> Give, take, and enjoy yourself for in Hades one cannot seek pleasure. All flesh becomes old like a garment, for the decree from of old is "you must surely die!" Like the green leaves on a flourishing tree that sheds some and grows others, so are the generations of flesh and blood: one dies and another is born. Everything decays and comes to an end, and the one who made it will pass away with it. (ben Sira 14:16–17; cf. 41:10, 46:19–20, 49:14)

Texts such as this evidence beliefs that depend on the biblical ideas of what happens to a person at death. The old biblical images of life, death, and afterlife continued to influence the way some Jews thought about their world. This naturally created an intellectual crisis for some: how would they imagine themselves, their destiny, and their universe? As this study has tried to suggest, some remained resolute in their commitment to preserving many aspects of the old (obsolete?) biblical traditions; others abandoned these traditions altogether; and still others created a remarkable new synthesis. What is certain is that the Greco-Roman world opened the Jewish communities to new ways of imagining themselves and their world and of articulating their religion.

Sectarian Visions of Who's In and Who's Out

Much like many modern fundamentalistic groups, some ancient groups thought that they had a monopoly on heaven. They firmly believed that they alone held the keys to the gates of heaven and that unless a person followed their manner of life and agreed with their religious beliefs, there was no possibility of entering heaven. Several individuals used their visions of the heavenly realm to substantiate the authority of their teachings. While some authors claimed authority on the basis of their conformity to authoritative texts or traditions (i.e., "thus it is written"), and rabbinical figures claimed authority on the basis of another acknowledged authority (i.e., "thus rabbi so-and-so said"), the people who claim to have ascended to heaven assert that the authority of their teachings rests on God alone, a God whose heavenly abode they had personally visited! Their claim to have ascended to heaven is virtually unassailable. The many features that these heavenly travelogues share (gates, angels, places for the reward of the righteous and the punishment of the wicked, repositories for the meteorological elements, etc.) show that there was a stock of motifs that these authors drew on for their accounts. Each author, to be sure, crafted his or her document from such stock items, expanding or elaborating as they saw fit, and thus the individuality of these texts arises from their focus on different topics or themes.[16] For example, the Testament of Levi is interested in showing why Levi is a priest; 1 Enoch 72–82, the Astronomical Book, focuses on astronomy since it enables one to identify the correct calendar whereby the festival dates are determined; and 3 Baruch demonstrates that God punishes sinners and attends to the prayers of the righteous. Heaven, the realm of the Divine, the realm of permanence and purity, the place whither the faithful hoped one day to ascend, provided the organizing structure of life. In contrast to this world of pain and unrelenting atrophy, heaven was the realm where the truly worthy would one day find relief. Each of the heavenly tourists who 'returned' to tell of their adventures hoped to inspire their readers to live a life that would please God, and each of them had his or her own ideas of just what kind of behavior and belief the Divine expected of people. On the one hand, the ideology of 3 Baruch is rather universalist—Jew and non-Jew alike can qualify based on virtuous living. Other groups had decidedly more restrictive views on who could "get into heaven."

The early Christian community created an image of heaven as an exclusive club. The Gospel of Matthew claims that Jesus said that entry into the "kingdom of heaven" is difficult, especially for some elites (Matt. 5:20; 7:21; 18:3; 19:23). Much of the Christian faith is based on the claim that Jesus was divine and came to earth only to die and then rise from the dead and ascend back into heaven to retake his place next to God (Mark 16:19; John 3:13; Acts 7:55; 1 Thess. 1:10; Heb. 9:24; 1 Pet. 3:22). Moreover, in its most exclusivist expression, some early Christians thought that only those who believe in Jesus as the Messiah are the ones who shall be favored with a heavenly afterlife: "There is salvation in no one else, for there is no other name under heaven given among mortals by which we must be saved" (Acts 4:12). Many early Christians thought, and this has been the basis of much of Christianity's self-understanding through the ages, that their true identity is defined not by their nationality or their life and work on earth, but by their heavenly citizenship: "Our citizenship is in heaven, and it is from there that we are awaiting a Savior, the Lord Jesus Christ" (Phil. 3:20). The Christian expectation is that Jesus will descend once again from heaven in a company of angels (2 Thess. 1:7) to rescue them from this tumultuous world.

> This we tell you by the word of the Lord: we who are still living when the Lord comes will by no means precede those who have died. For the Lord himself, with a command, an archangel's call, and the sound of God's trumpet, will descend from heaven, and the dead Christians will rise first. Then we who are still alive will be caught up in the clouds together with them to meet the Lord in the air. Thus we will be with the Lord forever. (1 Thess. 4:15–17)

The closing line of this passage—"Thus we will be with the Lord forever"— is telling. It is this hope that drives Christianity which is for the most part heavenly oriented. While it is fitting for followers of Christ to serve humanity during the course of their lives, the ultimate goal of life is to receive a heavenly reward from Christ. This orientation gives meaning to a world that seems otherwise meaningless. It creates a guide for life. It provides a goal.

Christians, however, were not the only and certainly not the first religious group to imagine themselves as God's favored people, favored because they were living as God intended people to live. In fact, this was a foundational motif in most all Greco-Roman mystery religions. The people of the Qumran settlement, the people of the Dead Sea Scrolls, likewise imagined themselves as God's elect.[17] The Qumran sectarians who were part of the Essene movement thought that they were God's favored people because of their extreme religious devotion and their adherence to the correct calendar.[18] Under the guidance of their divinely inspired leader, the "Teacher of Righteousness," and those who followed him, this group developed a sectarian view of their world and the future.[19] The Qumran sectarians believed that this "Teacher" was sent by God to teach them the correct interpretation of the Bible and of events in their days.

> God saw their works for they sought Him with a whole heart, so God raised up for them a Teacher of Righteousness to guide them in the way of His heart. (CD I,12–13)
>
> God told Habakkuk to write down that which will happen to the last generation. But about the end of time he did not inform him. And regarding what He said: "*so that he may read it quickly*" (Hab. 2:2), this refers to the Teacher of Righteousness to whom God made known all the mysteries of His servants the prophets. (1QpHab VII,1–5)
>
> "*The righteous will live by his faith in him*" (Hab. 2:4b): this refers to all those who obey the Torah in the House of Judah whom God will rescue from the House of Judgment because of their suffering and their faith in the Teacher of Righteousness. (1QpHab VIII,1–3)

In their opinion, they were the righteous ones who alone were favored by God; all others, Jew and non-Jew alike, were the wicked. The people of Qumran were God's chosen ones:

> To those whom God has chosen He has given them [i.e., wisdom and knowledge] as an eternal possession, and has caused them to inherit the lot of the Holy Ones. He has joined their assembly to the Sons of Heaven [i.e., angels] to be a Council of the Community and a foundation of the Building of Holiness for an eternal Plantation throughout all ages to come. (1QS XI,7–9)
>
> Then the Priests bless all those of God's lot who walk perfectly in all of His ways, saying "May He bless you with every good thing and may He guard you from every evil thing. May He enlighten your heart with insight for living. May He graciously endow you with the knowledge of eternal things, and lift up His gracious countenance upon you for everlasting peace." Then the Levites curse all those of Belial's lot. They shall respond and say, "Cursed

are you for all your wicked, guilty deeds. May God give you terror by all those who vengefully retaliate and may He punish your offspring with destruction by those who mete out recompense. Cursed are you without mercy according to your dark deeds. You are sentenced to eternal flames.... Then all those entering into the Covenant shall respond and say after them, "Amen, amen." (1QS II,1–18)

Other fragmentary texts from the Dead Sea Scrolls echo similar themes:

Afterwards they shall damn Belial [Satan] and all his guilty lot. They shall answer and say, cursed be Belial in his hostile plan, and damned in his guilty service. Cursed be all the spirits of his lot in their wicked plan, and damned in their unclean, impure thoughts. For they are the lot of darkness and their appointment is for eternal destruction. Amen, amen. . . . Cursed be the wicked in all his wicked plans and damned be all the people of Belial in all the sin of their positions. (4Q286)[20]

. . . for guilt in the Community with the Counsel of his people, to wallow in people's sin, and for great judgments and terrible diseases in the flesh. By God's mighty deeds and according to their wickedness by their impurity, He delivers the people of heaven and earth to a wicked community until the end. According to God's compassion, by His goodness and the wonder of His glory, He brought some of the people of the world near . . . to be reckoned with Him in the Community of the divine beings, for a Congregation of Holiness in service for eternal life and in lot with His Holy Ones . . . each one according to his lot which He cast for him . . . for eternal life. (4Q181)

In addition to their elevated estimation of themselves, it appears that the people of Qumran also believed that people could ascend to heaven during this life and return to tell about it, much like the ascent apocalypses. The author of the fragmentary text 4Q491 seems to suggest that he had been ushered into the heavenly realm.

He established His truth from of old, and the mysteries of His cunning in eve[ry . . .] strength [. . .] and the society of the oppressed as an eternal congregation [. . .] perfect of [. . .] eternal, a mighty throne in the congregation of the gods. None of the ancient kings shall sit on it, and their nobles [shall] not [. . . there are no]ne comparable [to me in] my glory, no one shall be exalted besides me; none shall associate with me. For I dwelt in [. . .] in the heavens, and there is no one [. . .]. I am reckoned with the gods and my abode is in the holy congregation. [My] desi[re] is not according to the flesh, and everything precious to me is in the glory [of] the holy [habit]tation. [Wh]om have I considered contemptible? Who is comparable to me in my glory? Who of those who sail the seas shall return telling [of] my [equa]l? Who shall [experience] troubles like me? And who is like me [in bearing] evil? I have not been taught, but no teaching compares [with my teaching]. Who then shall attack me when [I] ope[n my mouth]? Who can endure the utterance of my lips? Who shall arraign me and compare with my judgment [. . . Fo]r I am reck[oned] with the gods, [and] my glory with *that of* the sons of the King.[21]

This text appears to be the ravings of one of the inspired leaders of the Qumran community.[22] It shows that at Qumran there was the belief that humans could join the heavenly ranks. Surely most expected this in the afterlife, but some truly exceptional people could aspire to it while still alive. In fact, the people of Qumran customarily referred to themselves as the "people (literally, children) of heaven" (בני השמים), a title clearly patterned after the biblical phrase "people (children) of Israel" (בני ישראל), but here denoting that their association was not principally with a piece of land or a particular people but with the heavenly realm and the heavenly beings (בני אלהים). As in the ascent apocalypses, those who claimed to have ascended into the heavenly realms—much less claiming to be one of the highest beings in that realm as this author does—stand before their compatriots as "holy people" to be sure. This person was likely one of the inspired leaders of the community and imagined himself, and perhaps even his followers imagined him, to be divine or at least divinely inspired.[23]

The people of Qumran appear to have been rather elitist—the blessed future was theirs alone, while a future damnation awaited all others. The idea of a heavenly reward for the righteous and the punishment of everyone else was a theme inherited and not created by Christianity. This radical polarization stems from an attempt to justify and fortify sectarian beliefs. A group's self-image becomes remarkably stronger when the members come to believe that membership in their group secures divine merit. Heaven, as it were, is on their side. Such exclusivist claims to heaven would come to dominate subsequent images of heaven, especially in Christian circles.

Summary and Conclusion

The texts and traditions discussed in this and preceding chapters show that early Jewish and Christian cosmic speculation developed out of the dynamic interaction between ancient Near Eastern and Hellenistic models of the cosmos. These various texts attest different schemas for the structure and appearance of the cosmos. Several authors knew of seven heavens (Philo of Alexandria, Testament of Levi, Testament of Hezekiah, Ascension of Isaiah, Apocalypse of Paul, 2 Enoch [A], Apocalypse of Abraham). Many seem to assume that there is only one heaven (1 Enoch, 4 Ezra, Testament of Abraham, Greek Apocalypse of Ezra, Vision of Ezra). Fewer texts mention three heavens (2 Corinthians, Apocalypse of Sedrach; cf. Life of Adam and Eve). Two texts identified ten heavens (2 Enoch [J], Gnostic Apocalypse of Paul). The five-heaven schema was found in 3 Baruch and perhaps in the Apocalypse of Zephaniah. All this indicates that there was no one schema that completely dominated early Jewish and Christian speculations on the overall structure of the cosmos. The seven heavens of these early Jewish and Christian texts are clearly not the same as the seven spheres of the Hellenistic astronomers[24] since they are not, strictly speaking, planetary spheres. Rather, the Hellenistic astronomical model that came to be popularly known as the "Ptolemaic model," in which the individual heavens are planetary spheres—the model that would become the dominant image of the cosmos until Copernicus and was the basis for the cosmic structure in Dante's *Divine Comedy*—was either only partially understood by these early Jewish and Christian authors or it was purposefully modified for other purposes. These authors were not interested in science but in theology. They sought to promote their versions of orthodox belief and practice and were more interested in being associated with religious leaders such as Moses or Jesus of Nazareth, not astronomers such as Ptolemy or Aristarchus of Samos.

Why was there no consensus regarding the structure of the heavenly realm in early Judaism and Christianity? The answer seems to be twofold. First, it is clear that the ancient Near Eastern images of the cosmos had a formative influence on biblical images of the cosmos, images that the various early Jewish and Christian communities inherited from the Hebrew Bible/Old Testament. Eventually, these traditional images came into contact with Greco-Roman astronomy. A conflict developed as people reacted to the changing size and shape of the cosmos. Some Jews and later Christians adopted the Greek system of multiple heavens without difficulty, and the apparent plurality of the Hebrew word for heaven, שמים, no doubt justified this choice. Others tried to adapt the Greek model to the one they had inherited from the Bible. Still others repudiated the new Greek model because it opposed the religious traditions they had come to regard as authoritative. A late example, *mutatis mutandis*, of this "fundamentalist" approach is the Egyptian Monk Cosmas, also known as Cosmas Indicopleustes, that is, Cosmas the "Indian Navigator."[25] This mid-sixth century CE Christian traveler and apologist vehemently denounced as heretical any view of the cosmos other than the flat earth in a geocentric universe precisely because that was the view taught in the Bible! Clearly in Cosmas's case religious beliefs have overruled any scientific data. Such an attitude may explain why some of the Jewish and Christian texts surveyed above rejected the more "modern" images of the cosmos in favor of the "obsolete," biblically inspired models.

Second, while most early Jews and Christians adopted a multiple-heaven cosmography, the total number and the individual characteristics of these heavens differ significantly from author to author. Depending on an author's religious beliefs or "scientific" data, the structure of the celestial realm was either a single- or multiple-layered heaven. These authors then creatively filled out their picture of the heavenly realm with whatever items fit their literary or theological goals. In other words, each author followed his or her own imagination when it came to the details. This being the case, to examine the cosmographic structure or contents of a text and compare it with another to determine the relative dating of the two is somewhat misdirected. To assume a relatively simple evolution from simple to complex in these matters is unsound because the descriptions of the heavens in early Jewish and Christian texts are highly idiosyncratic. There does not seem to be any strict or programmatic development in the depictions of the heavenly realm during this period. Many of the elements in these depictions have roots in ancient Babylonian cosmic speculation, but the overall multiple-heaven schema itself derives from Greek models of the universe.

In the course of the Second Temple Period Jews, and eventually Christians, began to describe the universe in new terms. The model of the universe inherited form the Hebrew Bible and the Ancient Near East of a flat earth completely surrounded by water with a heavenly realm of the gods arching above from horizon to horizon became obsolete. In the past the heavenly realm was for gods only. It was the place where all events on earth were determined by the gods, and their decisions were irrevocable. The gulf between the gods and humans could not have been greater. The evolution of Jewish cosmography in the course of the Second Temple Period followed developments in Hellenistic astronomy. Rather than there being a single flat heaven suspended above a flat earth, Hellenistic astronomers began to image the cosmos in terms of several concentric spheres surrounding the earth. The earth was the center of the universe, and everything revolved around it. The divine resided in the farthest heavenly realms, far beyond human sight or imagination.

It would be a mistake to think that this widening gap suggests that for these people God was becoming further removed from humans. God was no further removed from humans than before, and certainly no less concerned with humans affairs. The very fact that people believed that some fortunate individuals were able to ascend into the heavenly realm and return to tell about it suggests that God is indeed accessible, at least to some. Eventually the idea developed that, although an exceptional seer might bridge the gap and ascend to heaven to encounter God during his or her life, all the righteous can expect to spend an eternity with God in the heavenly realms.[26] This image of the heavenly afterlife, too, was a remarkable innovation. The biblical materials, like their ancient Near Eastern counterparts, imagined a morally neutral afterlife in the netherworld. As they interacted with Persian and Hellenistic models of the afterlife, Jews began to redefine how they imagined the "world-to-come." Now the faithful could expect to join the Divine in the heavenly realm, a thought that would have shocked the ancient Israelites. This redefinition of the afterlife in terms of Hellenistic images of the immortality of the soul spawned an insatiable quest to describe the heavenly realms, and this quest continues to this day in many spiritual communities. Much of this focus on heaven and the rewards or pleasures that await the faithful is driven by the goal of promoting orthodoxy or orthopraxy, correct religious belief or religious behavior. In this regard, a comment by Josephus cited above in his description of the Essenes and their images of the afterlife is most apropos: "for the good are made better in their lifetime by the hope of a reward after death, and the passions of the wicked are restrained by the fear that, even though they escape detection while alive, they will undergo never-ending punishment after their decease."[27] Many people's visions of heaven were prompted by a desire to prove that God favors one group exclusively, their group. True, these visions inspire hope for the members of the favored group, but they also create a dangerous sense of superiority over outsiders by dehumanizing or demonizing them. Sadly, for many, as vast as it is according to some descriptions, heaven is not big enough to include those whose religious beliefs differ even slightly from their own.

LATER DEVELOPMENTS IN JEWISH, CHRISTIAN, AND ISLAMIC IMAGES

Is there a heaven? Oh yeah, its the place where dreams come true.

Field of Dreams, Universal Studios, 1988

The preceding review of the texts and traditions that describe the heavenly realm ends with sources that can in some way be dated to at least the second century CE. Obviously, heavenly speculation did not end at this point. Jewish, Christian, and Islamic authors continued to develop images of the heavenly realm. The following is a very brief overview of these speculations in order to show how some of the themes discussed in previous chapters developed in subsequent Jewish, Christian, and Islamic communities. This topic has been the focus of several successful books. A most helpful sketch of the images of heaven from ancient to modern times can be found in Colleen McDannell and Bernhard Lang, *Heaven: A History* (New Haven, Conn.: Yale University Press, 1988). The analyses by McDannell and Lang are somewhat superficial since their survey covers several millennia. Nonetheless, their book fills an important role as a synthesis of the literary and artistic images of heaven in western thought. More recently Jeffrey Burton Russell's *A History of Heaven: The Singing Silence* (Princeton, N.J.: Princeton University Press, 1997) provides an insightful study of the topic focusing on Christian materials.

Jewish Traditions

'Olam Ha-Ba'— *"the world-to-come"*

Unlike Christianity, Judaism for the most part did not use the image of heaven to encourage ethical behavior. Judaism in most all its varieties has been more

this-worldly oriented. Such an orientation began already in the Bible. Deuteronomy 30:14 states that the guiding principles of life, Torah, are not se-
creted away in heaven but are freely available to all. Later generations would
receive guidance through the interpretations of the Bible and other authoritative documents by their authoritative teachers, the Rabbis. The this-worldly
focus of much of Judaism did not completely exclude speculation on esoteric
topics; it did, however, largely marginalize such endeavors. One of the earliest
rabbinic legal codes, the Mishnah, hints at the rabbis' hesitance to encourage
esoteric speculations: "Whoever contemplates four things, it would have been
better for him if he had not come into the world—that which is above, that
which is beneath, that which was before time, and that which will be hereafter" (Mishnah, *Hagiga* 2:1). Although the third century CE editors of the
Mishnah and their successors seem to resist esoteric speculations, they did not
completely oppose speculation on such related topics as resurrection and afterlife (Mishnah *Sanhedrin* 10:1). Furthermore, the rabbis actually produced texts
that speculate on the heavenly realm and even the appearance of the divine.

In the biblical period most Israelites and Judeans imagined that God was to
be encountered in the temple. This belief was rocked when the Babylonians
destroyed the temple in 586 BCE, but this disaster was ameliorated when the
temple was restored with Persian assistance in 520–515 BCE. The temple then
resumed its place as the Jewish nexus between earth and heaven until its destruction by the Romans in 70 CE, when the synagogue began to emerge as
the community's central institution where the Jewish community could encounter God corporately: "Wherever ten people congregate in the synagogue,
the divine presence (the Shekinah) is with them, as Scripture says, 'God stands
in the congregation of God'" (Ps. 82:1; *Mekhilta*, 11:47–49; Lauterbach, 2.287).
God is, however, far removed from humanity: "See how high the Holy One,
Blessed be He, is above this world. Nonetheless, when a person enters a synagogue, stands behind a column, and prays quietly, the Holy One, Blessed be
He, still hears his prayer, as Scripture says, 'Hannah was speaking in her heart,
only her lips moved, and her voice was not heard' [1 Sam. 1:13]. Nonetheless, the Holy One, Blessed be He, heard her prayer" (Jerusalem Talmud
Berakot 9:1).

Some people sought an encounter with the Divine apart from or in addition to the synagogue, which was a place for communal study and prayer. The
most extensive collections of speculations on the realm of the divine are known
as *hekhalot* and *merkavah* literature. The hekhalot texts describe the seven
hekhalot, "palaces," in the divine realm. These texts recount the fictive "journeys" of a great sage—typically rabbis Akiba or Ishmael—through seven heavenly palaces. The *merkavah* literature, on the other hand, uses the image of God's
merkavah, "chariot," to imagine the divine presence. These texts describe how
great sages of the past allegedly entered into the divine presence.

Rabbi Ishmael said: When I ascended to the height to behold the vision of
the chariot, I entered six palaces, one inside the other, and when I reached
the door of the seventh palace I paused in prayer before the Holy One, blessed

be he; I looked up and said: "Lord of the Universe, grant, I beseech you, that the merit of Aaron, son of Amram, lover of peace and pursuer of peace, who received on Mount Sinai the crown of priesthood in the presence of your glory, may avail for me now, so that Prince Qaspi'el, and the angels with him, may not prevail over me and cast me from heaven." At once the Holy One, blessed be he, summoned to my aid his servant, the angel Metatron, Prince of the Divine Presence. He flew out to meet me with great alacrity, to save me from their power. He grasped me with his hand before their eyes and said to me, "Come in peace into the presence of the high and exalted King to behold the likeness of the chariot." Then I entered the seventh palace and he led me to the camp of the Shekinah and presented me before the glory so that I might behold the chariot.[1]

This brief quotation recounts how Rabbi Ishmael achieved his goal of seeing the divine chariot and heavenly palaces as well as his success at avoiding the danger of angelic opposition during his ascent. By reading these mystical texts the reader learns how the great sages "ascended" to the Divine presence. Such a trip is a daunting undertaking to be sure because heaven is not a place for just any human; rather, it is a place of absolute holiness and only the worthy can be admitted. Moreover, the holiness of the place is safeguarded by angels who oppose humans during their ascent. The holiness of the divine presence was apparent already on earth through the biblical descriptions of the activities of the priests serving in the Jerusalem Temple. All the priestly rituals recounted in the Bible were designed to protect the divine presence in the temple from defilement or impurity brought on by humans.[2] How much more important was it to protect the sanctity of heaven! Humans are impure—they even smell, according to some texts—and are unfit to be in the heavenly realm. The angels who resist and even assault people as they ascend are attempting to prevent the unfit from entering the divine realm.[3] In order to prepare to ascend safely, therefore, one must perform several purifying rituals and memorize secret passwords to be used along the way.[4] The importance of knowing secret passwords and performing appropriate rituals to guide one safely through the other realm was a motif popular in Egypt as early as the third millennium BCE. The other realms—netherworldly and heavenly—are the provenance of the gods who protect their territory jealously, and for humans to enter or pass through successfully, they need to know when, where, and how to use these secret passwords and rituals. The hekhalot and merkavah literatures provide just this kind of information necessary for a successful ascent to the divine. According to the hekhalot texts, the heavenly realm contains seven palaces placed one inside the other, with God residing in the innermost palace. The awe-inspiring experiences of the ascending sage as he passes through each marvelous palace and encounters the angelic retinue of God along the way surely reflect actual court etiquette of how one approaches the emperor, or at least how these rabbinic scholars imagined one did.[5] Here, however, the king is none other than God, the "King of kings."[6]

Actually, there is an ongoing scholarly debate about the exact purpose of these Jewish ascent texts. On the one hand, these texts may evidence the early practice of mystical ascent by mainstream rabbinic sages.[7] That is to say, the rabbis actually did attempt to enter an altered state wherein they might mystically encounter the Divine in the heavenly realms. If this is the case, then they would seem to be the latter-day practitioners of the kinds of ascents narrated in the texts discussed earlier in chapters 5 through 7. On the other hand, these texts might also be the product of disenfranchised commoners revolting intellectually and religiously against the rabbinic elite. These common folk believed that these incantations might provide them with a shortcut to the esoteric wisdom necessary for an encounter with the divine, a type of wisdom that in the rabbinic tradition comes only from arduous study of religious laws and traditions over a lifetime. These texts thus stem from the religiosity of people trying to find a way to organize their world and connect with God apart from the classical rabbinic modes. God can be encountered not just through Torah contemplation and Torah mastery, but through a mystical encounter.[8] Such an end-run around the rabbinic modes of spirituality was probably a major motivating factor in the efforts by some rabbis to regulate this kind of piety.

Another body of Jewish mystical speculations on the divine presence is known as the *Shi'ur Qomah*, "the measurement of the (divine) body." This material is much like that found in the merkavah and hekhalot texts and was also transmitted in the names of rabbis such as Akiba, Ishmael, and Nathan. *Shi'ur Qomah* focuses on the names and measurements of God's physical features as he sits on his heavenly throne. The following is only a brief section of this long and often tedious text.

> Rabbi Ishmael says, "What is the measure of the body of the Holy One, Blessed be he, who lives and exists forever?" "May his name be blessed for ever and ever. The soles of his feet fill the entire universe, as Scripture says, 'the heavens are my throne and the earth my footstool' (Isa. 66:1). The height of his soles is 30,000,000 parasangs; its name is Parmesiyah. From the bottom of his feet to ankles is 10,000,500 parasangs. The name of his right ankle is Atarqam and the left is Ava Targam. From his ankles to his knees is 190,000,000 parasangs; its name is Qenangi. The name of the right calf is Qangi and the left is Mehariah. From his knees to his thighs is 120,000,000 parasangs. The name of his right knee is Stamnegatz and the left is Pedangas. The name of the right thigh Vihmai and the left is Partemai. From his thighs to his neck is 240,000,000 parasangs. His neck is 130,000,000 parasangs tall. The name of his neck is Semghu Vihteratz. The circumference of his head is 10,000,033 and a third parasangs . . . its name is Atar Huriyah Vaatasiyah. His beard is 11,500 parasangs; its name is Hadarqamsiah. The appearance of the face and the appearance of the cheeks are spirit-like and in the form of a soul. No human can recognize it. His body is like Tarshish. His splendor sparkles awesomely within the darkness. Cloud and fog surround him . . . His tongue reaches from one end of the universe to the other, as Scripture says, 'he declares his words to Jacob' (Ps. 137:19). The width of his forehead is 130,000,800. The

name of the width of his forehead is Istagyahu. . . . But he told me the calculation of the parasangs, how much is their measurements: a parasang is four
mils; a mil is 10,000 cubits; a cubit is three spans, and His span fills the entire
universe, as Scripture says, 'who measured out the waters in the hollow of his
hand, and gauged the skies with his span' (Isa 40:12). . . . The entire measurement is 100,000,000,000 parasangs tall and 10,000,000,000 parasangs wide."
(*Sepher HaQomah* 51–85, 104–8, 117–19)[9]

While the utter physicality of this description scandalizes modern readers,
the dimensions are surely not meant as actual physical measurements of the
divine being. These sages are not trying to limit the divine to three-dimen-
sional measurements; rather, the fantastic numbers point to the awesome greatness of God. Why would someone devote what must have been countless hours
to learning this mystical material? The texts of the *Shi'ur Qomah* literature answer this question directly: "All who know this secret are certain to enter the
world-to-come. The Holy One, Blessed be He, will rescue him from every
evil thing—all kinds of sorcery, the evil eye, the evil inclination, evil thoughts,
all kinds of destroyers, all kinds of damagers, poverty, and evil plans" (*Sepher
HaQomah* 24–27).[10] "Whoever knows this measurement of his Creator and
the glory of the Holy One, Blessed be he, is secured in this world and in the
world-to-come. He lives long in this world, and he lives long and well in the
world-to-come. He does good in this world and in the world-to-come. Rabbi
Ishmael said, 'I and Rabbi Aqiba guarantee this, that in this world such a one
has a good life and in the world-to-come a good name, but only if he recites
this as a Mishnah every day'" (*Sepher HaQomah* 121–27).[11] The appeal of this
kind of literature is obvious: it promises to safeguard a person both in this world
and the next. It offers security in an otherwise terribly insecure world.

Judaism has typically identified the postmortem fate of humanity as *'Olam
Ha-Ba'*, "the world-to-come." Where it is and what it looks like are themes
touched on throughout the course of Jewish history. One's admission into the
world-to-come is based on living an honest, ethical, and moral life, and this is
open to Jew and non-Jew alike. The Mishnah hinted at how one ought to
prepare for this realm: "Rabbi Jacob said, 'this world is like a foyer to the world-
to-come; prepare yourself in the foyer so that you may enter into the banquet hall.' He also said, 'better is one hour of repentance and good deeds in
this world than an entire life of the world-to-come; and better is one hour
of bliss in the world-to-come than the entire life of this world'" (Mishnah,
Avot 4:16–17).

Interestingly enough, as was discussed in previous chapters, biblical, early
Jewish, and rabbinic sources all associate God with astronomical symbols. Several
Byzantine-era synagogues in Israel have splendid mosaic floors with zodiac
symbols—Beth Alpha, Hammat Tiberias, Husifa, Na'aran, Susita, Sepphoris,
and Ein Gedi—and it seems that these were not simply decorations without
significance to the worshippers.[12] The iconography of these Jewish houses of
study, worship, and prayer suggests that these Jews expressed their Judaism with
symbols derived ultimately from Hellenistic astral religion. That is to say, their

Judaism was expressed in the terms common to broader Greco-Roman and Byzantine culture.[13] As the zodiacs on the floors of these synagogues attest, the astrology and astronomical interests that had been part of Jewish culture since biblical times continued among at least some Jews. The Babylonian Talmud, the principle Jewish legal code, itself presents two conflicting attitudes toward astrology among two third-century rabbis (Babylonian Talmud, *Shabbat* 156a). That such a debate even took place indicates that the issue was still up for discussion, even among these traditionalist leaders.

Rabbinic literature was codified in a post-Ptolemy world and presents a plethora of possibilities regarding the number of heavens, demonstrating that the sages could not reach a consensus on the matter.[14] The rabbinic sages carefully examined biblical words and phrases used for the heavenly realm and were able to create several models, as, for example, the Midrash to the book of Psalms indicates: "Our rabbi said, there are two firmaments for it is said 'to the one riding the ancient highest heavens' (שְׁמֵי קדם שְׁמֵי; Ps 68:34). Our masters said there are three for it is said 'heaven and the heaven of heavens' (וּשְׁמֵי הַשָּׁמַיִם הַשָּׁמַיִם; 1 Kgs 8:27). And Rabbi Eleazar says there are seven: *vîlôn* (וילון), *rāqîaʿ* (רקיע), *šehāqîm* (שחקים), *zevul* (זבל), *māʿôn* (מעון), *mākôn* (מכון), and *ʿărāvôt* (ערבות), and the glory of the Holy One, Blessed be He, is in the *ʿărāvôt . . .*" (Midrash Psalms 114:2).[15] Thus, rabbinic speculation concluded that there may be two,[16] three,[17] seven,[18] eight,[19] ten,[20] or even more than 955 heavens.[21] Jewish tradition, then, has imagined heaven, the world-to-come, in myriad forms and motifs, and as on many other topics of speculative theology, Judaism has always tolerated a wide variety of speculations regarding the realm of the divine and the postmortem fate of humanity.

Christian Traditions

"To Be with the Lord Forever"

Heavenly speculation has always been a significant, even a central, aspect of Christian theology. The New Testament has at least two visions of the eternal state of the righteous. The writings ascribed to the Apostle Paul suggest that in the eschaton all the righteous will ascend into the heavenly realms and enter their eternal residences:

> This we tell you by the word of the Lord. We who are still alive when the Lord comes will by no means precede those who have died. The Lord himself will descend from heaven with a loud call, with the sound of the archangel and God's trumpet, and the dead Christians will rise first. Afterwards, we who are still alive will be caught-up with them in the clouds to meet the Lord in the air. Thus we will be with the Lord forever. Encourage one another with these words. (1 Thess. 4:15–18)

"Encourage one another" indeed! This text holds out hope for all Christians, living or dead, to be united with Christ in heaven, and it is this hope that was intended to inspire fidelity to Christian teachings no matter what distractions or opposition may arise. The final book of the New Testament, the Book of Revelation, ends with a somewhat different description of the eternal blessed state of the righteous Christians (Rev. 20–22). Rather than the righteous ascending into heaven at the end of time, God will bring heaven to earth, creating a new heaven and a new earth for the righteous. The focal point of the new earth is the "New Jerusalem that comes down from heaven" (Rev. 21:2, 10). God will reinhabit the temple on earth, and once again the Divine will reside with the righteous. So, rather than transport the righteous into the heavenly realm to be with God, the author of the Book of Revelation suggests that God will renew the entire cosmos and make the earth an Edenic paradise once again. The Christian hope of being ever with God will be realized not in heaven but on the "new earth."

The Church leaders largely adopted the seven-heaven Ptolemaic model of the universe that came to dominate both astrological and theological speculations on the heavenly realms in the Roman world. After the Christianization of the Roman Empire under Constantine in the fourth century CE, the now "Christian" state tried unsuccessfully to control or limit astrology. What the state could not achieve by its political powers, the church achieved through its theological power. The church branded astrology a heresy that was contrary to Christian teaching and then began to persecute all astrologers.[22] The fourth century Apostolic Constitutions (5:12) unequivocally condemned astrology along with a host of other forms of divination. The Church leaders' opposition to astrology stems from the fear that this form of divination could offer a rival to their claim to divine authority and truth; this potentially rival claim to divine inspiration and authority had to be removed.

Christian interest in the heavenly realms continued and reached a climax in Dante's *Divine Comedy*: its speculations in "Paradisio" were thoroughly shaped by Ptolemaic astronomy with its seven concentric spheres encircling the earth. Each of Dante's spheres contained a celestial body, as in astronomical science, but each also contained certain religious features such as angels, places of punishment, and so forth. Dante had thus successfully fused the stereotypical religious interests and features with correct astronomy. The early Jewish and Christian texts discussed in the preceding chapters often used a seven- or multiple-heaven schema, but they did not seem to understand the models completely, and they certainly did not locate the celestial bodies in the appropriate spheres. By the time of Dante, this inadequate understanding of Greco-Roman astronomy among religious writers had been remedied. The great poet's descriptions of ascending through the heavens hand-in-hand with his beloved Beatrice have inspired the spiritual imagination of generations.[23] Following the pattern found in earlier Jewish and Christian ascent texts, Dante described his encounters with various saints as he ascended through each of the heavenly spheres. He indicated his personal bias by allocating the positions of highest respect in the heavenly realms to the contemplative monastics, and chief among them is St. Bernard of Clairvaux who escorted Dante into the Divine presence. In this part of the *Divine Comedy*, therefore, Dante suggested that God has the highest regard for those who follow the religious beliefs and behaviors of the monastics, thereby encouraging people who are likewise seeking divine approval to follow the monastics' mode of spirituality. Dante's description of the heavenly realm beyond the planetary spheres has influenced almost all Western images of heaven: it is a vast place of inestimable beauty where time ceases and where the righteous are enveloped in the love of God.

The popularity of the theme of the mystical ascent to heaven continued among medieval Christians.[24] For the most part they continued the motif of heaven as the reward of the righteous Christian in contradistinction to the tortures of hell that awaited all others.[25] Heavenly ascents were attributed to Constantine,[26] Augustine, St. Drythelm, Gregory the Great, and St. Owen, to name just a few.[27] Accounts of such ascents and "near death" experiences of traveling upward toward a bright light continue even today to inspire people to believe that there is a life beyond this realm.[28] Heaven was and remains in most Christian thought the final goal of life, and since each community develops its own ideas about how one could reach this goal, the accounts of what is required for admission differ from community to community.

Islamic Traditions

al-Akhira—*"the hereafter"*

Not surprisingly, the heavenly realm is a focal point of Islamic spirituality much as it is in Judaism and Christianity.[29] The Quran, betraying its authors' adoption of the Ptolemaic model, states that the heavenly realm consists of seven spheres (17:44; 65:12; 78:12). The prophet Muhammad is believed to have ascended into the heavenly realm, and the traditions about this ascent (Mir'āj) assimilated to other traditions about Muhammad's miraculous night journey from Mecca to Jerusalem on his winged-horse Buraq.[30] Once in Jerusalem, Muhammad ascended into heaven from the place now commemorated by the Dome of the Rock. These stories serve to legitimate Muhammad as Allah's designated prophet. Islam, then, inherited ideas of multiple heavens and of heavenly ascent as a means to authorize religious claims.

> One whom I have no reason to doubt told me on the authority of Abu Sa'id al-Khuduri: I heard the Messenger [i.e., Muhammad] say, "After the completion of my business in Jerusalem (on the occasion of the Night Journey) a ladder was brought to me finer than any I have ever seen. It was that to which the dying man looks when death approaches. My companion mounted it with me until we came to one of the gates of heaven called the Gate of the Watchers. An angel called Isma'il was in charge of it, and under his command were twelve thousand angels, each of them having (another) twelve thousand under his command." As he told the story the Messenger used to say, "and none knows the armies of God but He" (Quran 74:31). "When Gabriel brought me in, Isma'il asked who I was, and when he was told that I was Muhammad, he asked if I had been given a mission, and on being assured I had, he wished

me well." . . . Then I was taken up to the second heaven and there were the two maternal cousins, Jesus, Son of Mary, and John, son of Zakariah. Then to the third heaven and there was a man whose face was as the moon at full. This was my brother Joseph, son of Jacob. Then to the fourth heaven and there was a man called Idris [i.e., Enoch], "and We have exalted him to a lofty place" (Quran 19:56–57). Then to the fifth heaven and there was a man with white hair and a long beard; never before have I seen a more handsome man than he. This was the beloved among his people, Aaron, son of Imran. Then to the sixth heaven and there was a dark man with a hooked nose like the Shanu'a.[31] This was Moses, son of Imran. Then to the seventh heaven and there was a man sitting on a throne at the gate of the immortal mansions. Every day seventy thousand angels went in, not to come back until the Resurrection Day. Never have I seen a man more like myself. This was my father Abraham."[32]

As is readily apparent, this text builds on the traditions about heavenly ascents and the appearance of the heavenly realms traced in the preceding chapters.[33] The Prophet was accompanied by a guiding angel as he ascended, and prior to entering the heavenly realm he was stopped by another angel whose job was to protect the divine realm from unwanted or unqualified visitors. In the heavens Muhammad met several notable religious figures (Enoch, Abraham, Aaron, Moses, and Jesus) whose presence in the heavenly realm shows that only the truly righteous belong there. The high point of the experience was seeing Abraham as he sat at the gate leading into the place where the righteous live in their mansions. This narrative follows precisely the format and themes of the earlier Greek, Roman, Jewish, Christian, and Persian ascent texts. For those who accept Muhammad's teachings, the traditions about his heavenly ascent justify his claims to being God's appointed prophet and also give his teachings divine authority. Muhammad, like Enoch, Paul, Jesus, and many other notables, was given a tour of the heavenly realm, a realm where only the deserving will be admitted after death. And what will make one deserving of such a postmortem honor? Fidelity to the precepts of Islam, as explained by Muhammad, Allah's prophet.

Muhammad was not the last Muslim to have visions of the heavenly realm. These visions come via dreams in which the dreamer either encounters a deceased person or experiences a heavenly ascent.[34] The dreams involving a deceased family member, friend, or Muslim notable typically recount how a Muslim dreams of an encounter with a deceased individual who regales his still-living colleague with stories about the appearance of heaven and what happens there. These dreams customarily focus on instructions that guide the righteous Muslim in proper conduct and on the rewards that await the pious in heaven. Likewise, the ascent accounts describe the appearances of the next world in vivid detail. Pious Muslims learn that luxurious palaces, verdant gardens, magnificent feasts, and all manner of unending pleasure await them as rewards for their fidelity to the ways of Islam. A feature that is striking to non-Muslim minds, although it is certainly not the central tenet of Muslim heavenly speculation, is that of the *hur*, the chaste maidens of paradise.[35] These indescribably gorgeous, virginal female beings exist in paradise to attend to the pious Muslim male's every physical and sexual desire.

> A palace in Paradise is made from a pearl; within it are 70 courts of red ruby, in every court 70 houses of green emerald, in every house 70 bedrooms and in every bedroom 70 sleeping mats from every color, and on every mat a woman; in every house 70 tables, on every table 70 different types of food, in every house 70 slaves and concubines giving the believer strength to make the rounds in one meal.[36]

According to Islamic thought, at death people will be judged on the basis of their behavior, again much like Judaism and Christianity.[37]

> In this surely is a sign for him who fears the torment of the Hereafter, the day when mankind will be assembled together, which will be a day when all things would become evident. We are deferring it only for a time ordained. The day it comes no soul will dare say a word but by His leave, and some will be wretched and some will be blessed. And those who are doomed will be in Hell; for them there will be sighing and sobbing, where they will dwell so long as heaven and earth endure, unless your Lord will otherwise. Verily, your Lord does as He wills. Those who are blessed will be in Paradise, where they will dwell so long as heaven and earth survive, unless your Lord will otherwise: this will be a gift uninterrupted. (Quran 11:103–8)
> God has promised men and women who believe gardens with streams of running water where they will abide forever, and beautiful mansions in the Garden of Eden, and the blessings of God above all. That will be happiness supreme. (Quran 9:72)[38]

The Quran could not say it any more clearly: the blessed, that is the obedient followers of Islam, can expect a paradisical afterlife in beautiful mansions, while the wicked are doomed to torment in Hell. Holding out such a hope of post-mortem happiness in heaven surely provides adequate motivation to inspire people to follow the religious precepts that they think will earn them uninter-rupted happiness.

Closing Remarks

Images of heaven continue to be popular even in this postmodern world. We live after the day when the first Soviet cosmonaut reported back to his comrades that after circling the earth and looking as far and wide as possible he did not see God or any heavenly palaces. We live in a time when astronomers and astro-physicists tell us about the vastness, even limitlessness, of space. We now know that what we may perceive as faint stars in the clear night sky are actually galaxies as vast as ours but billions of light years away. In Stephen Hawking's words,

We now know that our galaxy is only one of some hundred thousand million that can be seen using modern telescopes, each galaxy itself containing some hundred thousand millions stars. . . . We live in a galaxy that is about one hundred thousand light-years across and is slowing rotating; the stars in its spiral arms orbit around its center about once every several hundred million years. Our sun is just an ordinary, average-sized, yellow star, near the inner edge of one of the spiral arms. We have certainly come a long way since Aristotle and Ptolemy, when we thought that the earth was the center of the universe.[39]

We have developed from the geocentric cosmologies of Ptolemy and his forebearers, through the heliocentric cosmology of Copernicus and Galileo, to the modern picture in which the earth is a medium-sized planet orbiting around an average star in the outer suburbs of an ordinary spiral galaxy, which is itself only one of about a million million galaxies in the observable universe.[40]

Such reminders of how infinitely small we are give us pause. On the one hand, Vincent van Gogh has forever captured the awe of the night sky in his painting La Nuit Etoilée, "The Starry Night," painted in Saint-Rémy, France in mid-June 1889. This painting contrasts the robust vitality of the starry night with the sleepy calm of the village below. The heavens overwhelm the darkened village and suggest that the realm of real importance is not the village, or its central but small church, but the heavenly realm with its Milky Way, vibrant stars, and spiral galaxies. In van Gogh's painting, the heavenly horizon is pierced by a cypress tree and the church's steeple. While the steeple reaches only feebly above the horizon, the tree boldly reaches high into the sky. The artist seems to suggest by this that the natural sciences (i.e., meditation on nature) are more capable of penetrating the deeper secrets of the cosmos than theology: the church's images of the heavens barely scratch the surface of the mysterious realm overhead. The painting leaves the observer experiencing the curious mixture of awe and solace: awe at the vigor and mystery of the cosmos, and solace because the village and its inhabitants remain serene in the midst of the cosmos exploding with activity. Vincent van Gogh's image, then, is at once scientific and religious, imparting a sense of comfort.[41] On the other hand, thoughtful contemplation of the incomprehensible enormity and complexity of the cosmos can also lead the modern mind to a sense of alienation, and in this vein, as Nietzsche has so pointedly noted, the universe seems to have become "colder."

We have killed him [i.e., God]—you and I! We all are his murderers! But how have we done this? How have we been able to drink up the sea? Who gave us the sponge with which we erased the entire horizon? What did we do when we cut earth loose from its sun? Now where does it move? Where in fact do we move? Away from all suns? Are we not forever falling? Backward, sideways, forward, in all directions? Is there any 'above' or "below" anymore? Are we not wandering as through an endless void? Are we not haunted by the empty space. Has it not become colder?[42]

This "Nietzschean" existential despair in the face of dizzying changes in our perceptions of ourselves and the cosmos is not the only option. The image of the heavenly realm where the Divine resides and which has an unfaltering permanence and regularity has given meaning to human lives throughout history. The images we create of our cosmic neighborhood in part give meaning and structure to life; thus, trying to comprehend one's position in the cosmos is not simply a scientific endeavor, it is an existential struggle to know oneself and one's place in the cosmos. Today, fundamentalist Christian preachers of all kinds cajole people into accepting their particular dogma with promises of heavenly bliss. Middle Eastern Islamic fundamentalist clerics promise heavenly rewards for people who die as martyrs in the service of Islam. The issue is so popular that the cover story of the March 24, 1997 issue of Time magazine was "Does Heaven Exist?" and the article reported that an overwhelming majority of Americans still believe in the existence of heaven. This is, of course, not surprising since images of heaven continue to influence humans from all cultures and religions. As we have seen, the realm "up there" continues to strike humans with sometimes overwhelming awe, be it the single heaven above the azure sky of the ancient Near Eastern peoples, the multiple heavens of Greco-Roman astronomy, or our modern limitless and ever-expanding cosmos. Since the dawn of human history people have looked to the heavens for hope amid their at times seemingly chaotic and meaningless world. We humans still find no better image of stability than the heavenly realms where the celestial bodies travel in unfaltering, always reliable patterns and where almost all the world's religions locate the Divine Being. The crucial question remains: will the images people construct of the heavenly realm be used for good or evil, for inclusion or exclusion, to inspire hope or fear? Heaven knows.

NOTES

Preface

1. Robert Eisler, *Weltenmantel und Himmelszelt: Religionsgeschichtliche Untersuchungen zur Urgeschichte des antiken Weltbildes*, 2 vols. (Munich: C. H. Beck, 1910) traces the variety in how different cultures portray the celestial realm.

2. "Die Himmelsreise der Seele," *Archiv für Religionswissenschaft* 4 (1901): 234–49.

3. *Die himmlische Welt im Urchristentum und Spätjudentum*, WUNT 2 (Tübingen: Verlag J. C. B. Mohr/Paul Siebeck, 1951).

4. *Heaven: A History* (New Haven: Yale University Press, 1988).

5. *Ascent to Heaven in Jewish and Christian Apocalypses* (New York/Oxford: Oxford University Press, 1993).

6. *A History of Heaven: The Singing Silence* (Princeton, NJ: Princeton University Press, 1997).

7. *Figures du ciel: de l'harmonie des sphères à la conquête spatial* (Seuil: Bibliothèque nationale de France, 1998).

8. See Peter C. Chemery, "Sky: Myths and Symbolism," *The Encyclopedia of Religion*, ed. Mircea Eliade, 16 vols. (New York: Macmillan Publishing Company, 1987) 13.345–53.

Chapter 1

1. For readable and readily available syntheses, see William G. Dever, *Recent Archaeological Discoveries and Biblical Research* (Seattle, Wash.: University of Washington

Press, 1990); Amihai Mazar, *Archaeology of the Land of the Bible, 10,000–563 B.C.E.: An Introduction*, ABRL (New York: Doubleday, 1990); Mark S. Smith, *The Early History of God* (San Francisco: Harper and Row, 1990); and Victor H. Matthews and Donald C. Benjamin, *The Social World of Ancient Israel, 1250–587 BCE* (Peabody, Mass.: Hendrickson Publishers, 1993).

2. Note the avidly positivist Christian evolutionary perspective of W. F. Albright, *From Stone Age to Christianity: Monotheism and the Historical Process* (Baltimore, Md.: Johns Hopkins University Press, 1940).

3. For concise overviews of Egyptian history, see William W. Hallo and William Kelly Simpson, *The Ancient Near East: A History* (New York: Harcourt Brace Jovanovich, 1971), 185–298; and Sabatino Moscati, *The Face of the Ancient Orient: A Panorama of the Near Eastern Civilizations in Pre-Classical Times* (Chicago: Quadrangle Books, 1960), 97–150.

4. On the stability of the Egyptian worldview in the New Kingdom and its continuity with earlier ideas, see B. G. Trigger, B. J. Kemp, D. O'Connor, and A. B. Lloyd, *Ancient Egypt: A Social History* (Cambridge: Cambridge University Press, 1983), 188–202.

5. On this see Henri Frankfort, *Ancient Egyptian Religion: An Interpretation* (New York: Harper & Row, 1961), 3–22; cf. C. J. Bleeker, "The Religion of Ancient Egypt," *Historia Religionum: Handbook for the History of Religions*, vol. 1, *Religions of the Past*, ed. C. Jouco Bleeker and Geo Widengren (Leiden: E. J. Brill, 1969), 40–114.

6. John A. Wilson, "Egypt," *The Intellectual Adventure of Ancient Man: An Essay on Speculative Thought in the Ancient Near East*, ed. H. Frankfort et al. (Chicago: University of Chicago Press, 1946), 33.

7. For Egyptian cosmology, see Siegfried Morenz, *Ägyptische Religion*, Die Religionen der Menschheit 8 (Stuttgart: Kohlhammer Verlag, 1960), 180–83; and Hermann Grapow, *Die Bildlichen Ausdrücke des Aegyptischen von Denken und Dichten Einer Altorientalsichen Sprache* (Leipzig: J. C. Hinrichssche Buchhandlung, 1924), 22–37.

8. See Morenz, *Ägyptische Religion*, 192–223, A. J. Spencer, *Death in Ancient Egypt* (New York: Penguin Books, 1982), and Leonard H. Lesko, "Death and the Afterlife in Ancient Egyptian Thought," *Civilizations of the Ancient Near East*, 4 vols., ed. Jack M. Sasson (New York: Charles Scribner's Sons, 1995), 3.1763–74, for thorough treatments of Egyptian views of death and the afterlife. The Egyptian funerary texts are summarized in Hermann Kees, *Totenglauben und Jenseitsvorstellungen der Alten Ägypter*, 2d ed. (Berlin: Akademie Verlag, 1956), 8–12, and E. A. Wallis Budge, *The Egyptian Heaven and Hell*, 3 vols. (London: Kegan Paul, Trench, Trübner & Co., 1906; reprint, 3 vols. in 1, Mineola, N.Y.: Dover Publications, Inc., 1996), 3.vii–xiv, 1–26.

9. See Kees, *Totenglauben und Jenseitsvorstellungen*, 67–97. Recent research in the layout of the Great Pyramids of Geza suggests that the so-called "air shafts" radiating out from the burial chambers in the pyramids were oriented toward the stellar constellation Orion; see Robert G. Bauval and Adrian Gilbert, *The Orion Mystery: Unlocking the Secrets of the Pyramids* (London: Heinemann, 1994), Edwin C. Krupp, "Egyptian Astronomy: A Tale of Temples, Tradition, and Tombs," *Archaeoastronomy and the Roots of Science*, American Association for the Advancement of Science 71, ed. E. C. Krupp (Boulder, Colo.: Westview Press, 1984) 289–320, and Steven C. Haack, "The Astronomical Orientation of the Egyptian Pyramids," *Archaeoastronomy* 7 (1984), 119–25. Such astronomical explanations of the pyramids' layout, however, have not been universally accepted; see John A. R. Legon, "The Orion Correlation and Air-Shaft Theories," *Discussion in Egyptology* 33 (1995): 45–56, who concludes that "the design of these shafts was determined by considerations of geometry, symmetry, and the desire for a coher-

ent dimensional design, and can have had nothing to do with the conjectured astronomical alignments" (55).

10. Raymond O. Faulkner, *The Ancient Egyptian Pyramid Texts*, 2 vols. (Oxford: Oxford University Press, 1969), 1.117, §361; cf. Kurt Sethe, *Übersetzung und Kommentar zu den Altägyptischen Pyramidentexten*, 6 vols. (Glückstadt: J. J. Augustin, 1935–62), 3.120–21.

11. Faulkner, *Pyramid Texts*, 1.123–24, §373. The "Imperishable Stars" are also called the "northern gods the Imperishable Stars" (Faulkner, *Pyramid Texts*, 1.147, §441; cf. 1.169, §481), and are the northern circumpolar stars that seem never to set.

12. Faulkner, *Pyramid Texts*, 1.135–36, §412. The phrase "doors are opened ... doors are thrown open" is common in the Pyramid Texts, cf. §§536, 553, 563, 666A, 667A, 670.

13. Faulkner, *Pyramid Texts*, 1.58, §245; cf. 1.60, §248. On the "Lone Star," see R. O. Faulkner, "The King and the Star Religion in the Pyramid Texts," *JNES* 25:3 (1966): 153–61, who has collected the texts that associate the pharaoh with the stars.

14. On this "personification" of heaven, see Ioan P. Culianu, "Sky: The Heavens as Hierophany," *The Encyclopedia of Religion*, 16 vols., ed. Mircea Eliade (New York: Macmillan, 1987), 13.344.

15. For this period see William C. Hayes, "The Middle Kingdom in Egypt," *Cambridge Ancient History*, 3d ed., vol. 1, pt. 2: *Early History of the Middle East*, ed. I. E. S. Edwards, C. J. Gadd, and N. G. L. Hammond (Cambridge: Cambridge University Press, 1971), 518–23.

16. The goal of these religious texts is stated plainly in the following words from the Book of the Dead in the Papyrus of Ani: "If this chapter be known [by the deceased] upon earth, [or if it be done] in writing upon [his] coffin, he shall come forth by day in all the forms which he is pleased [to take], and he shall enter in to [his] place and shall not be driven back" (Book of the Dead §72; Budge, *Book of the Dead*, 2.242). A similar theme appears in the Book of Tuat which describes the journey of the sun through the netherworld; see Budge, *Egyptian Heaven and Hell*, 1.146, 162, 215, 240, 258; cf. 2.26, 36, 38–39.

17. For motifs shared by Egyptian and biblical cosmologies see James K. Hoffmeier, "Some Thoughts on Genesis 1 & 2 and Egyptian Cosmology," *JANES* 15 (1983): 45–46. The Egyptian iconographic materials depicting the sky are treated by Wolfhart Westendorf, *Altägyptische Darstellungen des Sonnenlaufes auf der abschüssigen Himmelsbahn*, Münchner Ägyptologische Studien 10 (Berlin: Bruno Hessling, 1966). See also Othmar Keel, *The Symbolism of the Biblical World: Ancient and Near Eastern Iconography and the Book of Psalms*, trans. Timothy J. Hallett (New York: Seabury Press, 1978), 22–56, and more summarily by Izak Cornelius, "The Visual Representation of the World in the Ancient Near East and the Hebrew Bible," *JNWSL* 20:2 (1994): 196–98.

18. See R. A. Parker, "Ancient Egyptian Astronomy," *The Place of Astronomy in the Ancient World*, ed. F. R. Hodson (London: Oxford University Press, 1974), 43–65; Bartel L. van der Waerden, *Science Awakening II: The Birth of Astronomy* (Leiden/New York: Noordhoff International Publishing/Oxford University Press, 1974), 8–45; and G. J. Toomer, "Mathematics and Astronomy," *The Legacy of Egypt*, ed. J. R. Harris (Oxford: Clarendon, 1971), 45–54.

19. See Henri Frankfort, *Kingship and the Gods: A Study of Ancient Near Eastern Religion as the Integration of Society* (Chicago: University of Chicago Press, 1948), 36–40.

20. See Richard H. Wilkinson, "The Horus Names and the Form and Significance of the Serekh in the Royal Egyptians Inscriptions," *Journal of the Society for the Study of Egyptian Antiquities* XV:3 (1987): 98–104, and Wilkinson, *Symbol and Magic in*

Egyptian Art (New York: Thames and Hudson, 1994), 134. I am greatly indebted to my colleague Richard Wilkinson for his help with the Egyptian materials. Any misrepresentations or inaccuracies are, of course, my responsibility.

21. See Alexandre Piankoff, *The Shrines of Tut-Ankh-Amon*, Bollingen Series 40:2, Egyptian Religious Texts and Representations (New York: Pantheon Books, 1955), 26–37; Erik Hornung, *Der Ägyptische Mythos von der Himmelskuh: Eine Ätiologie des Unvollkommenen*, OBO 46 (Göttingen: Vandenhoeck & Ruprecht, 1982), 81–87, 96–101; and Westendorf, *Altägyptische Darstellungen des Sonnenlaufes*, 10–12. For parallels between Egyptian and biblical creation accounts of the separation of earth and sky, see Viktor Notter, *Biblischer Schöpfungsbericht und ägyptische Schöpfungsmythen*, Stuttgarter Bibelstudien 68 (Stuttgart: Verlag Katholisches Bibelwerk, 1974), 70–90.

22. "Nut became (a cow), and the majesty of Re was on her back. Men were (astonished when) . . . they saw him on the back of the cow" (Piankoff, *Shrines of Tut-Ankh-Amon*, 29).

23. She is also named Mehurt; see Hornung, *Himmelskuh*, and Rudolf Anthes, "Mythology in Ancient Egypt," *Mythologies of the Ancient World*, ed. S. N. Kramer (New York: Doubleday, 1961), 16–22.

24. Figure 1.1 reproduced from James H. Breasted, *A History of Egypt: From Earliest Times to the Persian Conquest*, 2d ed. (New York: Charles Scribner's Sons, 1924), 54–55, figure 30 is from the tomb of Seti I (ca. 1309–1291) in Thebes, but it also appears on the walls of several other tombs dating between 1350 and 1100 BCE. Cf. Charles Maystre, "Le Livre de la Vache du Ciel dans les tombeaux de la Vallée des Rois," *BIFAO* 40 (1941): 53–55; Piankoff, *Shrines of Tut-Ankh-Amon*, facing 27, plates 56–57; and Anthes, "Mythology," 16–17.

25. Inscription of Queen Hatshepsut (18th Dynasty); James H. Breasted, *Ancient Records of Egypt: Historical Documents from the Earliest Times to the Persian Conquest*, 5 vols. (Chicago: University of Chicago Press, 1906–7), 2.§318.

26. Inscription of Harmhab (19th Dynasty); Breasted, *Ancient Records*, 3.§16.

27. Coffin Texts §335; R. O. Faulkner, *The Ancient Egyptian Coffin Texts*, 3 vols. (Warminster, England: Aris & Phillips, 1973–78), 1.260; cf. Book of the Dead 17:75–76 (Budge, *Book of the Dead*, 98–99).

28. In addition to the Pyramid Texts, Coffin Texts, and the Book of the Dead, see Budge, *Egyptian Heaven and Hell*, Breasted, *Development*, pp. 49–69; and Frankfort, *Ancient Egyptian Religion*, 88–123.

29. Book of the Dead §15 (Budge, *Book of the Dead*, 1.64).

30. Budge, *Egyptian Heaven and Hell*, 1.191, cf. 1.264–65.

31. See Westendorf, *Altägyptische Darstellungen des Sonnenlaufes*, 63–66, figs. 51–53. Figure 1.2 is from a New Kingdom coffin now in the Louvre; here reproduced from Breasted, *History*, 55, fig. 31. Compare E. A. Wallis Budge, *The Greenfield Papyrus in the British Museum* (London: British Museum, 1912), 79–81, pls. 105–7, and *ANET*, 183, pl. 542.

32. Inscription from the tomb of Tutankhamon; see Piankoff, *Shrines of Tut-Ankh-Amon*, 97.

33. Coffin Text §77; Faulkner, *Coffin Texts*, 1.81; cf. Piankoff, *Shrines of Tut-Ankh-Amon*, 35–36. On Shu as the one who separated the sky from the earth, see H. te Velde, "The Theme of Separation of Heaven and Earth in Egyptian Mythology," *Studia Aegyptica* 3 (1977): 161–70; and compare the discussion of Egyptian ideas about the creation of the earth and sky in Susanne Bickel, *La cosmogonie égyptienne*, OBO 134 (Fribourg: Editions Universitaires, 1994), 176–98. The idea that sky and earth were originally united and only later separated into two realms is common to many ancient

cultures; see Peter C. Chemery, "Sky: Myths and Symbolism," *Encyclopedia of Religion*, 13.348–50.

34. From a relief of the reign of Thutmose III; see Breasted, *Ancient Records of Egypt*, 2.§285.

35. Faulkner, *Pyramid Texts*, 1.182, §1101.

36. Figure 1.3 reprinted from Keel, *Symbolism*, 36, figure 32.

37. See Henri Frankfort, *The Cenotaph of Seti I at Abydos*, 2 vols. (London: Egypt Exploration Society, 1933), 1.27, 72–75, 2. pl. LXXXI; Frankfort, *Ancient Egyptian Religion*, fig. 10; and Keel, *Symbolism*, 31–33.

38. Figure 1.4 drawn by Theodore W. Burgh after photo in Hermann Kees, *Der Götterglaube im altern Ägypten*, 3d ed. (Berlin: Akademie Verlag, 1977), tafel IIIb. Figure 1.5 reprinted from Keel, *Symbolism*, 38, figure 33. Cf. Westendorf, *Altägyptische Darstellungen des Sonnenlaufes*, taflen 26–27, abb. 51, 53.

39. Frankfort, *Cenotaph of Seti I*, 1.83. Cf. "The Book of Gates" in Budge, *Egyptian Heaven and Hell*, 2.258, where the gods pulling the boat of Re in the netherworld say to him as he nears the end of the journey: "The ways of the hidden place are open to thee, and [the portals] which are in the earth are unfolded for thee, the SOUL which Nut loveth, and we will guide thy wings to the mountain. Hail! Enter thou into the East, and make thou thy passage from between the thighs of thy mother."

40. See Otto Neugebauer, *The Exact Sciences in Antiquity*, 2d ed. (New York: Harper Torchbooks, 1962), 80–89.

41. Budge, *Book of the Dead*, 2.234 [69:5–6].

42. See Budge, *Egyptian Heaven and Hell*, 2.53.

43. Figure 1.6 reprinted from Keel, *Symbolism*, 34, figure 30.

44. See Edward Brovarski, "The Doors of Heaven," *Or* 46 (1977): 107–10; cf. Westendorf, *Altägyptische Darstellungen des Sonnenlaufes*, 14–21, figs. 3–13; and Keel, *Symbolism*, 24–28, figs. 10–21.

45. Coffin Text §474; Faulkner, *Coffin Texts*, 2.114. For lexical information see "*pt*" in Adolf Erman and Herman Grapow, *Wörterbuch der ägyptischen Sprache*, 5 vols. (Leipzig: J. C. Hinrichssche Buchhandlung, 1926–31), 1.490–92, and Sir Alan Gardiner, *Egyptian Grammar*, 3d ed. (London: Oxford University Press, 1964), 485.

46. Hymn to Aton from the period of Amenhotep IV (Akhenaton, 1380–1362); *ANET*, 370–71.

47. From a hymn to Ra prefixed to the Book of the Dead; Budge, *Book of the Dead*, 1.13.

48. Coffin Text §74; Faulkner, *Coffin Texts*, 1.70.

49. Coffin Text §761; Faulkner, *Coffin Texts*, 1.293.

50. Figure 1.7 reprinted from Frankfort, *Kingship and the Gods*, figure 17; figure 1.8 reprinted from Keel, *Symbolism*, 27, figure 20.

51. See Wilkinson, *Symbol and Magic*, 133–34, 138–39, figs. 86–87.

52. These cosmic pillars have parallels elsewhere in the ancient Near East. See Luis I. J. Stadelmann, *The Hebrew Conception of the World: A Philological and Literary Study*, AnBib 39 (Rome: Pontifical Biblical Institute, 1970), 1–36, 45. In Babylonia the horizon is the "foundation of heaven," *išid šami* (P. Jensen, *Die Kosmologie der Babylonier: Studien und Materialien* [Strassburg: Karl J. Trübner, 1890], 9). Note also the "pillars of heaven" in Job 26:11.

53. From a victory hymn of Thutmose III (1490–1436); *ANET*, 374.

54. Budge, *Book of the Dead*, 2.102.

55. From the inscriptions of Ramses II at Luxor; Breasted, *Ancient Records of Egypt*, 3.§480.

56. Breasted, *Ancient Records of Egypt*, 2.§601.

57. Breasted, *Ancient Records of Egypt*, 2.§889; cf. 3.§§406, 545. The idea that the magnificent pillars in the colonnaded halls of the Egyptian temples are like those that support the heavens is reflected in some texts. Regarding the pillars in the Luxor Temple, Amenhotep III says: "its towers reach heaven, and mingle with the stars" (Breasted, *Ancient Records of Egypt*, 2.§886); and regarding the Soleb Temple he declares, "its pylons reach heaven, and the flagstaves, the stars of heaven" (Breasted, *Ancient Records of Egypt*, 2.§894).

58. Coffin Text §160; Faulkner, *Coffin Texts*, 1.138; cf. *ANET*, 12; Book of the Dead §108 (Budge, *Book of the Dead*, 2.315). "Bakhu" refers to the mountains east of the Nile.

59. Figures 1.9–1.11 reprinted from Keel, *Symbolism*, 24, figure 15; and 26, figures 17–18.

60. Figures 1.12–1.13 drawn by Theodore W. Burgh after photos in Evelyn Rossiter, *Le Livre des Morts: Papyrus égyptiens (1420–1100 av.J.C.)* (Geneve: Productions Liber SA, 1984), 26, 80–81. On the apes as the ideal worshippers of the sun, see H. te Velde, "Some Remarks on the Mysterious Language of the Baboons," *Funerary Symbols and Religion: Essays Dedicated to Professor M. S. H. G. Heerma van Voss*, ed. J. H. Kamstra, H. Milde, and K. Wagtendonk (Kampen, The Netherlands: J. H. Kok, 1988), 129–37. Apes also open the doors in the west when the sun descends into the netherworld; see Budge, *Egyptian Heaven and Hell*, 1.19.

61. See Budge, *Egyptian Heaven and Hell*. On the gates through which one must pass in the netherworld, see J. Zandee, *Death as an Enemy*, Studies in the History of Religions (Leiden: E. J. Brill, 1960), 112–25.

62. The Book of Am-Tuat (Budge, *Egyptian Heaven and Hell*, 1.248–55, 2.94–95, 234–35) graphically describes the fate of the unjust. The confusion about the ultimate fate of humans in Egyptian funerary texts comes about because these texts incorporate disparate traditions about the hereafter. Basically, however, one goes to the netherworld or to the celestial realm. For how the two traditions are incorporated into the Book of Two Ways, see Leonard H. Lesko, "Some Observations on the Composition of the Book of Two Ways," *JAOS* 91 (1971): 30–43.

63. Budge, *Egyptian Heaven and Hell*, 3.65.

64. Budge, *Egyptian Heaven and Hell*, 3.67.

65. See Frankfort, *Ancient Egyptian Religion*, 88–123, Budge, *Egyptian Heaven and Hell*, 3.64–74, and Dieter Mueller, "An Early Egyptian Guide to the Hereafter," *Journal of Egyptian Archaeology* 58 (1972): 99–125. Note also Coffin Texts §§404–405, and Faulkner, *Coffin Texts*, 2.48–57.

66. Faulkner, *Pyramid Texts*, 1.40, §213.

67. See Faulkner, *Pyramid Texts*, 1.17–41.

68. On the doors of the sun god Re, see Coffin Text §696; Faulkner, *Coffin Texts*, 2.261; and Faulkner, *Pyramid Texts*, 1.59, §246. For the ascent of the stars in the east to begin their nightly journeys, see Coffin Text §722 and Faulkner, *Coffin Texts*, 274. The iconography is treated by Brovarski, "Doors of Heaven," 107–10.

69. Coffin Text §159; Faulkner, *Coffin Texts*, 1.137–38; *ANET*, 33. Cf. Book of the Dead §109, §149 (Budge, *Book of the Dead*, 318, 486).

70. Figure 1.14 from Keel, *Symbolism*, 24, figs. 10–12.

71. See Zandee, *Death as an Enemy*, 118–21.

72. Faulkner, *Pyramid Texts*, 1.104–5, §325, cf. 1.167, 227, §§479, 572; for a clearly celestial Field of Rushes, see 1.154, §461; and for an apparently terrestrial one see 1.185–86, §510. Note that the location where the deceased was to "bathe" prior to ascending

to the celestial realm is sometimes also in the netherworld: "O King, you are the son of a great one; bathe in the lake of the Netherworld and take your seat in the Field of Rushes."

73. Budge, *Book of the Dead*, 2.138, 139.

74. Coffin Text §44; Faulkner, *Coffin Texts*, 1.35.

75. Coffin Text §492; Faulkner, *Coffin Texts*, 2.134.

76. Faulkner, *Pyramid Texts*, 281, §667A; cf. Wilkinson, *Symbol and Magic*, 23–27.

77. Faulkner, *Pyramid Texts*, 1.275, §665. Figure 1.15 drawn by Theodore W. Burgh after photo in Rossiter, *Le Livre des Morts*, 11, 49. Figure 1.16 from Budge, *Book of the Dead*, 2.295.

78. Book of the Dead §78 (Budge, *Book of the Dead*, 2.250–58).

79. An old Hittite (modern Turkey) myth mentions a ladder or staircase with nine steps that leads up to the heavenly realm; see Harry A. Hoffner, Jr., *Hittite Myths*, SBLWAW 2 (Atlanta: Scholars Press, 1990), 32.

80. Faulkner, *Pyramid Texts*, 1.166, §478.

81. Faulkner, *Pyramid Texts*, 1.93, §304.

82. Book of the Dead §110 (Budge, *Book of the Dead*, 2.327).

83. Coffin Text §159; Faulkner, *Coffin Texts*, 1.137–38; *ANET*, 33. Cf. Coffin Text §161; Faulkner, *Coffin Texts*, 1.139–40.

84. Coffin Text §581; Faulkner, *Coffin Texts*, 2.184–85.

85. Coffin Text §190; Faulkner, *Coffin Texts*, 1.158.

86. See Frankfort, *Ancient Egyptian Religion*, 109–14.

87. Faulkner, *Pyramid Texts*, 1.191. On whether this is located in the east of heaven or the north, see Kees, *Totenglauben und Jenseitsvorstellungen*, 88–89.

88. Coffin Text §293; Faulkner, *Coffin Texts*, 1.218. It may be that these celestial waters are related to the theme that the just were "washed in the Lake of Perfection" (Book of the Dead §172; Budge, *Book of the Dead*, 3.586). This is a purification rite that the just underwent after being tried by Osiris in the netherworld but prior to taking their place in the Field of Rushes or among the starry host.

89. From Hymn to Ra, Budge, *Book of the Dead*, 1.71–72; cf. Book of the Dead §98–99.

90. Budge, *Book of the Dead*, 1.77–78.

91. Pyramid Text §419; Faulkner, *Pyramid Texts*, 1.138.

92. Inscription of Thutmose II (18th Dynasty); Breasted, *Ancient Records of Egypt*, 2.§118.

93. Book of the Dead §79 (Budge, *Book of the Dead*, 2.260).

94. Pyramid Text §210; Faulkner, *Pyramid Texts*, 1.39.

95. Book of the Dead §136a (Budge, *Book of the Dead*, 3.409).

96. Book of the Dead §72 (Budge, *Book of the Dead*, 2.242).

97. Coffin Text §227; Faulkner, *Coffin Texts*, 1.179–80.

98. Faulkner, *Pyramid Texts*, §355, 671, 674, 675; cf. Morenz, *Ägyptische Religion*, 214–15, and Kees, *Totenglauben und Jenseitsvorstellungen*, 92–94.

99. See Pyramid Text §485, Faulkner, *Pyramid Texts*, 1.172; Book of the Dead §106, 136a, 172 (Budge, *Book of the Dead*, 2.313, 3.410, 3.586).

Chapter 2

1. A. Leo Oppenheim, *Ancient Mesopotamia: Portrait of a Dead Civilization* (Chicago: University of Chicago Press, 1964), 172. Oppenheim's statement has its critics, how-

ever. H. W. F. Saggs, *The Encounter with the Divine in Mesopotamia and Israel* (London/ Atlantic Highlands, N.J.: Athlone Press/Humanities Press, 1978), challenges Oppenheim's contention, while Thorkild Jacobsen in his book *The Treasures of Darkness: A History of Mesopotamian Religion* (New Haven: Yale University Press, 1976) actually writes a history of Mesopotamian religions!

2. For general survey of Mesopotamian religions, in addition to the sources cited in note 1, see W. H. Ph. Römer, "The Religion of Ancient Mesopotamia," *Historia Religionum: Handbook for the History of Religions*, vol. 1, *Religions of the Past*, ed. C. Jouco Bleeker and Geo Widengren (Leiden: E. J. Brill, 1969), 115–94.

3. S. N. Kramer, *History Begins at Sumer* (Garden City, N.Y.: Doubleday and Company, 1959).

4. Joan Oates, *Babylon* (London: Thames and Hudson Ltd., 1979), 15–22. S. N. Kramer estimates that over 95 percent of Sumerian texts are economic in character; see *Sumerian Mythology: A Study of Spiritual and Literary Achievement in the Third Millennium B.C.*, rev. ed. (Westport, Conn.: Greenwood Press, 1972), 10.

5. On Sumerian religion in general see Thorkild Jacobsen, "Formative Tendencies in Sumerian Religion," *The Bible and the Ancient Near East: Essays in Honor of William Foxwell Albright*, ed. G. Ernest Wright (Garden City, N.Y.: Doubleday and Company, 1961) 267–78. For the basic features of Sumerian cosmology, see Kramer, *History Begins at Sumer*, 119–56, and Kramer, *Sumerian Mythology*, 37–41, 73–75.

6. Edward Chiera, *Sumerian Religious Texts*, Babylonian Publications 1 (Upland, Penn.: Crozer Theological Seminary, 1924), 27. Cf. P. Jensen, *Die Kosmologie der Babylonier: Studien und Materialien* (Strasbourg: Karl J. Trübner, 1890), 4–5.

7. Note the opening lines of the myth "Creation of the Pickax": "Enlil . . . took care to separate heaven and earth." Cf. Kramer, *Sumerian Mythology*, 37–40, 51–53. In ancient Greek thought Atlas held heaven above the earth (Hesiod, *Theogony*, 519–22, 746–48), while in ancient Egypt the god Shu performed this task.

8. Jacobsen, *Treasures of Darkness*, 77–84, and Kramer, *The Sumerians: Their History, Culture, and Character* (Chicago: University of Chicago Press, 1963), 114–15. Jacobsen, *Treasures of Darkness*, notes that in Mesopotamia images of the gods reflect the nature of human society at any given time. In the fourth millennium, before the rise of urban centers, the gods were imagined as providers for these pastoralists. With the rise of cities in the third millennium, the image of the gods evolved to that of great kings comparable to the rulers of the cities. Finally, with the rise of personal religion in the second millennium, the gods were imagined as parents who cared for the individual worshipper.

9. See Åke W. Sjöberg and E. Bergmann, *The Collection of the Sumerian Temple Hymns*, Texts from Cuneiform Sources 3 (Locust Valley, N.Y.: J. J. Augustin Publisher, 1969), 50.

10. Figure 2.1 from P. R. S. Moorey, *Ur "Of the Chaldees": A Revised and Updated Edition of Sir Leonard Woolley's Excavations at Ur* (Ithaca, N.Y.: Cornell University Press, 1982), 48; cf. Ernst Heinrich, *Die Tempel und Heiligtümer in Alten Mesopotamien: Typologie, Morphologie und Geschichte*, Denkmäler Antiker Architektur 14 (Berlin: Walter de Gruyter, 1982), fig. 226; cf. 142–44, 154–55, and fig. 224. On early Mesopotamian temples in general, see Richard Zettler, *The Ur III Temple of Inanna at Nippur: The Operation and Organization of Urban Religious Institutions in Mesopotamia in the Late Third Millennium BC*, Berliner Beiträge zum Vorderen Orient 11 (Berlin: Dietrich Reimer Verlag, 1992), and J. N. Postgate, *Early Mesopotamia: Society and Economy at the Dawn of History* (New York: Routledge, 1994), 109–36. There was a seven-storied tower at Borsippa, but these seven levels reflect not seven celestial

"spheres" but simply the seven planets (with sun and moon replacing the planets Neptune and Uranus that were discovered only in modern times); see Jensen, *Kosmologie*, 12.

11. Noted in the Sumerian account of the flood, *ANET*, 43, lines 88–90.

12. Quoted from Kramer, *The Sumerians*, 120–21; cf. *ANET*, 573–76.

13. Sjöberg and Bergmann, *Sumerian Temple Hymns*, 17.

14. Sjöberg and Bergmann, *Sumerian Temple Hymns*, 29. Similar phraseology appears in other temple hymns, see ibid., pp. 32, 34, 35.

15. Kramer, *The Sumerians*, 113, cf. *History Begins at Sumer*, 120.

16. Kramer, *The Sumerians*, 120; cf. *ANET*, 584.

17. See Harriet Crawford, *Sumer and the Sumerians* (Cambridge: Cambridge University Press, 1991) 103–23.

18. See S. N. Kramer, "The Death of Gilgamesh," *BASOR* 94 (1944): 2–12.

19. W. G. Lambert, "The Theology of Death," *Death in Mesopotamia: Papers Read at the XXVIe Rencontre assyriologique internationale*, Copenhagen Studies in Assyriology 8, ed. Bendt Alster (Copenhagen: Akademisk Forlag, 1980), 55.

20. S. N. Kramer, "Death and Nether World According to the Sumerian Literary Texts," *Iraq* 22 (1960): 66.

21. "Man and His God," *ANET*, 589–91; cf. Kramer, *The Sumerians*, 126–32.

22. S. N. Kramer, "The Death of Ur-Nammu and his Descent to the Netherworld," *JCS* 21 (1967): 104–22.

23. The myth of "Enki and Ninhursag" quoted from Bendt Alster, "Dilmun, Bahrain, and the Alleged Paradise in Sumerian Myth and Literature," *Dilmun: New Studies in the Archaeology and Early History of Bahrain*, ed. Daniel T. Potts, Berliner Beiträge zum Vorderen Orient 2 (Berlin: Dietrich Reimer Verlag, 1983), 63; cf. *ANET*, 38, lines 1–64. On this myth note also Stephen Langdon, *Sumerian Epic of Paradise, The Flood and the Fall of Man*, University Museum Publications of the Babylonian Section, 10:1 (Philadelphia: University Museum, 1915), 8–12, 69–87; S. N. Kramer and John Maier, *Myths of Enki, The Crafty God* (New York: Oxford University Press, 1989), 23–24; and Kramer, *Sumerian Mythology*, 54–59.

24. See *ANET*, 38, lines 32–64.

25. On the location of "Dilmun" to the east of Mesopotamia, see S. N. Kramer, "Dilmun, The Land of the Living," *BASOR* 96 (1944): 18–28. The place of the sunrise is near the "cedar mountain" in later texts; see Wolfgang Heimpel, "The Sun at Night and the Doors of Heaven in Babylonian Texts," *JCS* 38 (1986): 144–45. According to the Sumerian myth "Gilgamesh and the Land of the Living," the Land of the Living is also the "cedar land"; see S. N. Kramer, "Gilgamesh and the Land of the Living," *JCS* 1 (1947): 8–9.

26. See P. B. Cornwall, "On the Location of Dilmun," *BASOR* 103 (1946): 3–11, and "Two Letters from Dilmun," *JCS* 6 (1952): 137–38, 141–42; cf. Alster, "Dilmun, Bahrain, and the Alleged Paradise," 52–60. As Cornwall suggests, "Land of the Living," 4, the fact that Dilmun is said to be "the place where the sun rises" strongly indicates a location east of Mesopotamia. Nonetheless, since the Persian Gulf is termed "the sea of the rising sun" (see Daniel D. Luckenbill, *Ancient Records of Assyria and Babylonia*, 2 vols. [Chicago: University of Chicago Press, 1927] 2.§§41, 70, 92, 185), the identification with the island of Bahrain is more likely correct; cf. Wayne Horowitz, *Mesopotamian Cosmic Geography*, Mesopotamian Civilizations 8 (Winona Lake, Ind.: Eisenbrauns, 1998), 104–5, 328–29.

27. Cf. "Gilgamesh in the Land of the Living," *ANET*, 47–50; and S. N. Kramer, "Gilgamesh and the Land of the Living," 3–46.

28. See S. N. Kramer, "Mythology of Sumer and Akkad," *Mythologies of the Ancient World*, ed. S. N. Kramer (Garden City, N.Y.: Doubleday and Company, 1961) 95–119; cf. Wayne Horowitz, "The Babylonian Map of the World," *Iraq* 50 (1988): 161. The Sumerian account of the Flood reports: "Ziusudra, the king, Prostrated himself before Anu (and) Enlil. *Anu (and) Enlil cherished* Ziusudra, Life like (that of) a god they give him, Breath eternal like (that of) a god they *bring down* for him. Then, Ziusudra the king, The *preserver of the name of vegetation (and)* of the seed of mankind, In the land *of crossing*, the land of Dilmun, the place where the sun rises, they caused to dwell" (*ANET*, 44).

29. Kramer, *The Sumerians*, 148–49.

30. See S. N. Kramer, "Inanna's Descent to the Nether World," *RA* 34:3 (1937): 93–134; *Sumerian Mythology*, 83–96; and "'Inanna's Descent to the Nether World' Continued and Revised," *JCS* 5 (1951): 1–17.

31. *ANET*, 53, lines 34–36, 40–42; cf. *ANET*, 55, lines 170–81.

32. For Mesopotamian views of death see Jean Bottéro, "La mythologie de la mort en Mésopotamie ancienne," *Death in Mesopotamia* (ed. Alster), 25–52.

33. See Horowitz, *Mesopotamian Cosmic Geography*, 166–68 for texts; cf. Kramer, *The Sumerians*, 137–40.

34. Horowitz, *Mesopotamian Cosmic Geography*, 167.

35. Wolfram von Soden, *The Ancient Orient: An Introduction to the Study of the Ancient Near East*, trans. Donald G. Schley (Grand Rapids, Mich.: William B. Eerdmans, 1994), 157, n. 19.

36. See Hugo Radau, *Sumerian Hymns and Prayers to God Nin-Ib from the Temple Library of Nippur*, The Babylonian Expedition of the University of Pennsylvania, Series A: Cuneiform Texts 29:1, ed. H. V. Hilprecht (Philadelphia: University of Pennsylvania, 1911), 32–37.

37. S. N. Kramer, "New Literary Catalogue from Ur," *RA* 55 (1961): 172, lines 49–50.

38. Kramer, "Gilgamesh and the Land of the Living," 11, line 28.

39. Kramer, "Death of Ur-Nammu," 118, line 82.

40. Kramer, "Gilgamesh and the Land of the Living," 21, line 150.

41. For a convenient survey of Mesopotamian history, see William W. Hallo and William Kelly Simpson, *The Ancient Near East: A History* (New York: Harcourt Brace Jovanovich, 1971), 3–183; or A. Kirk Grayson, "Mesopotamia, History of (Assyria and Babylonia)," *The Anchor Bible Dictionary*, 6 vols., ed. David Noel Freedman (New York: Doubleday, 1992), 4.732–77.

42. See Peter Machinist, "On Self-Consciousness in Mesopotamia," *The Origins and Diversity of Axial Age Civilizations*, ed. S. N. Eisenstadt, SUNY Series in Near Eastern Studies (Albany, NY: SUNY Press, 1986), 183–202.

43. Although dated, see the survey in Morris Jastrow, *The Religion of Babylonia and Assyria*, Handbooks on the History of Religions 2 (Boston: Ginn & Company, 1898), 253–93, 328–406. For the incantation series *Maqlû*, see Tzvi Abusch, "Mesopotamian Anti-Witchcraft Literature: Texts and Studies. Part I, The Nature of *Maqlû*: Its Character, Divisions and Calendrical Setting," *JNES* 33 (1974): 251–62, and Abusch, "Some Reflections on Mesopotamian Witchcraft," *Religion and Politics in the Ancient Near East*, ed. Adele Berlin (Bethesda, Md.: University Press of Maryland, 1996), 21–33.

44. See Jacobsen, *Treasures of Darkness*, 178–80, and W. G. Lambert, "The Cosmology of Sumer and Babylon," *Ancient Cosmologies*, ed. Carmen Blacker and Michael Loewe (London: George Allen and Unwin Ltd., 1975), 55–58.

45. This line represents a belief that rain falls from a vast celestial body of water; cf. Jensen, *Kosmologie*, 5, 344.

46. See also MUL.APIN I.1.36–37: "... the constellations that pass through the northernmost gates belong to the path of Enlil, those that pass through the central gates belong to the path of Anu, and those that pass through the southernmost gates belong to the path of Ea" (Hermann Hunger and David Pingree, *MUL.APIN: An Astronomical Compendium in Cuneiform*, AfO 24 [Horn, Austria: Ferdinand Berger & Sönne Gesellschaft, 1989], 139).

47. Enûma Elish, iv.135–v.23; quoted from *ANET*, 67–68.

48. General surveys of ancient Near Eastern views of the world can be found in Lambert, "Cosmology of Sumer and Babylon," and Horowitz, *Mesopotamian Cosmic Geography*. The tripartite structure of the universe is evident also in the iconographical material. A *kudurru* or boundary stone from the twelfth century BCE appears to reflect this tripartite schema. The top register depicts the realm of the gods, the middle the earthly realm of humans, and the third the netherworld. See Othmar Keel, *The Symbolism of the Biblical World: Ancient Near Eastern Iconography and the Book of Psalms*, trans. Timothy J. Hallet (New York: Seabury Press, 1977), 46–47; and Izak Cornelius, "The Visual Representation of the World in the Ancient Near East and the Hebrew Bible," *JNWSL* 20:2 (1994): 198–200.

49. See Jensen, *Kosmologie*, 6–9; for additional terms see Horowitz, *Mesopotamian Cosmic Geography*, 223–42.

50. *CAD*, B, 344–45.

51. *CAD*, Š, 339–48.

52. *CAD*, I, 240, and E, 79; cf. *CAD*, Š, 343–46.

53. See Heimpel, "Sun at Night and Doors of Heaven," 146–50, and Jean Bottéro, "Les morts et l'au-delà dans les rituels en accadien contre l'action des 'revenants'," *ZA* (1983): 201–3.

54. For texts see Heimpel, "Sun at Night and Doors of Heaven," 132–40; cf. *CAD*, Š, 344; and note Tzvi Abusch, "The Socio-Religious Framework of the Babylonian Witchcraft Ceremony Maqlû: Some Observations on the Introductory Section of the Text, Part II," *Solving Riddles and Untying Knots: Biblical, Epigraphic, and Semitic Studies in Honor of Jonas C. Greenfield*, ed. Ziony Zevit, Seymour Gitin, and Michael Sokoloff (Winona Lake, Ind.: Eisenbrauns, 1995), 476–77, 486–87.

55. See Heimpel, "Sun at Night and Doors of Heaven," 143–46.

56. Figure 2.2 (Akkadian Period Cylinder seal [2350–2150], BM 89110) from Henri Frankfort, *Cylinder Seals: A Documentary Essay on the Art and Religion of the Ancient Near East* (London: Macmillan, 1939), plate XVIIIa; cf. Keel, *Symbolism*, 23, fig. 9. Note also Othmar Keel and Christoph Uehlinger, *Altorientalische Miniaturkunst* (Mainz am Rhein: Verlag Philipp von Zabern, 1990) 36, fig. 30; and Martin Metzger, *Königsthron und Gottesthron. Thronformen und Throndarstellungen in Ägypten und im Vorderen Orient in dritten und zweiten Jahrtausand vor Christus und deren Bedeutung für das Verständnis von Aussagen über den Thron im Alten Testament*, AOAT 15,1–2 (Kevelaer/Neukirchen-Vluyn: Butzon and Bercker/Neukirchener Verlag, 1985), 2.128, plate 63. Figure 2.3 from Urs Winter, *Frau und Göttin: Exegetische und ikonographische Studien zum weiblichen Gottesbild im alten Testament und dessen Umwelt*, OBO 53 (Göttingen/Freiburg: Vandenhoeck & Ruprecht/Universitätsverlag Freiburg, 1983), 183; cf. Frankfort, *Cylinder Seals*, plate XIXa.

57. Quoted from Heimpel, "Sun at Night and Doors of Heaven," 143.

58. Quoted from Frankfort, *Cylinder Seals*, 98.

59. Cf. AO 8196 iv. 20–22 (AfO 19, pl. XXXIII). For the text of *KAR* 307 see Erich Ebeling, *Tod und Leben Nach den Vorstellungen der Babyloner* (Berlin: Walter de Gruyter and Co., 1931), 1.28–37. For a thorough treatment of this text see Horowitz, *Mesopotamian Cosmic Geography*, 1–19, and "Two Notes on Etana's Flight to Heaven," *Or* 59 (1990): 515–17. Note also Alasdair Livingstone, *Mystical and Mythological Explanatory Works of Assyrian and Babylonian Scholars* (Oxford: Clarendon Press, 1986), 79–91.

60. Cf. Enûma Elish, vi.42.

61. Enûma Elish, v.1–8, says that Marduk arranged the stars in heaven.

62. Or "he did not identify rebellion."

63. *KAR* 307.30–38 obverse.

64. Benno Landsberger, "Über Farben im Sumerisch-akkadischen," *JCS* 21 (1967): 154–55, doubts that these materials can be reliably identified.

65. Erica Reiner and David Pingree, *ENUMA ANU ENLIL, Tablets 50–51*, Bibliotheca Mesopotamica 2:2, Babylonian Planetary Omens 2 (Malibu, Calif.: Undena Publications, 1981), 19. Although he is dealing with the various colors of the eight spheres encircling the earth, note that Plato (*Republic* 10) speculates on the color of these celestial realms.

66. The Akkadian phrase is *ina muḫḫi*, but contrast *ina libbi* for how the Igigi, the spirits of mankind, Ea, and the Anunakki dwell in their heavens, i.e., on and above the surface. See Wolfram von Soden, *Grundriss der Akkadischen Grammatik*, Analecta Orientalia 33/47 (Rome: Pontificium Institutum Biblicum, 1969), §115.

67. Note Enûma Elish v. 1–7:

> He (Marduk) constructed their stations for the great gods,
> Fixing their astral likenesses as constellations.
> He determined the year by designating the zones:
> He set up three constellations for each of the twelve months.
> After defining the days of the year [by means] of (heavenly) bands,
> That none might transgress or fall short.

According to the "Astrolabes" and the *MUL.APIN* texts (see below), each of the three paths has a set of three stars for each of the twelve months, providing a total of thirty-six stars. These astronomical texts describe the seasonal movements of each of these stars within their respective paths and calculate their heliacal risings throughout the year. For texts and translations see Hunger and Pingree, *MUL.APIN*. See also Horowitz, *Mesopotamian Cosmic Geography*, 151–92.

68. See *luludānītu* in *CAD*, L.243–44.

69. Note Gilgamesh Epic, xi.113–14, where the gods respond to the Deluge by fleeing to the "heaven of Anu." This assumes that the "heaven of Anu" was as far as possible removed from the realm of the deluge. Cf. Shupru, VIII.78, "On this day let the Great Gods who reside in the heaven of Anu rel[ease you and ab]solve you in their assembly," quoted from Erica Reiner, *Shupru: A Collection of Sumerian and Akkadian Incantations*, AfO Beiheft 11 (Osnabrück: Biblio Verlag, 1970), 243. Enûma Elish, vi.37–44, 69, mentions the gods, Igigi and Anunakki, who reside in this heaven. Note that none of these texts actually specifies the three-heaven structure itself, so we cannot say for certain that each of these texts likewise ascribes to a tripartite heavenly structure.

70. Margaret Huxley, "The Shape of the Cosmos According to Cuneiform Sources," *JRAS* 3:7:2 (1997): 189–98, has proposed that *KAR* 307 and other cuneiform texts suggest that the ancient Mesopotamians imagined the cosmos to be spherical. Moreover, according to Huxley's reading of *KAR* 307, this text describes not the stony heavenly floors but stony heavenly ceilings. That is to say, the jasper heaven separates earth's

atmosphere from the lower heaven, the *saggilmut* heaven separates the lower heaven from the upper heaven, and the *luludanitu* heaven forms the outer boundary of the cosmos (note Huxley, p. 197, fig. 3). The idea of three heavens may also appear in Ugarit. The name *prgl.ṣqrn* in *KTU* 1.41:50 may refer to divinities and has been rendered by one scholar as "Pirigalu of the Third Heaven"; see Johannes C. de Moor, "Ugaritic Lexicographical Notes I," *UF* 18 (1986): 255–61 and de Moor, *Anthology of Religious Texts from Ugarit*, Nisaba: Religious Texts Translation Series 16 (Leiden: E. J. Brill, 1987), 165.

71. Leonard W. King, *Babylonian Boundary-Stones and Memorial-Tablets in the British Museum* (London: British Museum, 1912), 120–27, plates XCVIII–CII. See also Metzger, *Königsthron und Gottesthron*, 1.226–30, 2.210, plate 100A; cf. *ANEP*, 529.

72. Figure 2.4 from King, *Babylonian Boundary-Stones*, plate XCVIII; cf. Tryggve N. D. Mettinger, "YHWH SABAOTH—The Heavenly King on the Cherubim Throne," *Studies in the Period of David and Solomon and Other Essays*, ed. Tomoo Ishida (Tokyo: Yamakawa-Shuppansha, 1982), 120.

73. For other representations of the heavenly ocean see David Neiman, "The Supercaelian Sea," *JNES* 28 (1969): 243–49; Mettinger, "YHWH SABAOTH," 131–34; G. W. Ahlström, "Heaven and Earth—At Hazor and Arad," *Religious Syncretism in Antiquity*, ed. Birger A. Pearson (Missoula, Mont.: Scholars Press, 1975), 67–83; and M. Metzger, "Himmelische und irdische Wohnstatt Jahwes," *UF* 2 (1970): 139–58.

74. For general introductions, see Ulla Koch-Westenholz, *Mesopotamian Astrology: An Introduction to Babylonian and Assyrian Celestial Divination* (Copenhagen: Museum Tusculanum Press, 1995); Bartel L. van der Waerden, *Science Awakening II: The Birth of Astronomy* (Leiden/New York: Noordhoff International Publishing/Oxford University Press, 1974), 46–126; Francesca Rochberg-Halton, "Astrology in the Ancient Near East," *ABD*, 4.504–7, Rochberg-Halton, "Astronomy and Calendars in Ancient Mesopotamia," *Civilizations of the Ancient Near East*, ed. Jack M. Sasson, 4 vols. (New York: Charles Scribner's Sons, 1995), 3.1925–40; and Tamsyn Barton, *Ancient Astrology* (New York: Routledge Press, 1994), 9–31.

75. A. Leo Oppenheim, "A Babylonian Diviner's Manual," *JNES* 33:2 (1974): 204.

76. See A. Sachs, "Babylonian Horoscopes," *JCS* 6 (1952): 51, 53; cf. Francesca Rochberg-Halton, "New Evidence for the History of Astronomy," *JNES* 43:2 (1984): 115–40, and Rochberg-Halton, "Babylonian Horoscopes and their Sources," *Or* 58 (1989): 102–23.

77. Ioan P. Culianu, "Astrology," *Encyclopedia of Religion*, 1.473–74.

78. See A. J. Sachs, "La naissance de l'astrologie horoscopique en Babylonie," *Archeologia* 15 (Mars–Avril 1967): 12–19.

79. Mathematical astronomy is discussed in Otto E. Neugebauer, *The Exact Sciences in Antiquity*, 2d ed. (New York: Harper Torchbooks, 1962), 97–144. "Nonmathematical" may be a better term than "observational" because not all of these texts are based on or record celestial observations. For these Babylonian "non-mathematical" texts, see A. Sachs, "Babylonian Observational Astronomy," *The Place of Astronomy in the Ancient World*, ed. F. R. Hudson (London: Oxford University Press, 1974), 43–50. For texts see Ernst F. Weidner, *Handbuch der babylonischen Astronomie*, Assyriologische Bibliothek 23 (Leipzig: J. C. Hinrichssche, 1915); A. Sachs, "A Classification of the Babylonian Astronomical Tablets of the Seleucid Period," *JCS* 2 (1950): 271–90; and T. G. Pinches, J. N. Strassmaier, and A. J. Sachs, *Late Babylonian Astronomical and Related Texts* (Providence: Brown University Press, 1955).

80. Alternatively, it has been suggested that these are three bands above only the eastern horizon where the celestial bodies rise. See Reiner and Pingree, *ENUMA ANU ENLIL, Tablets 50–51,* 7–18. But compare Johannes Koch, *Neue Untersuchungen zur*

Topographie des babylonischen Fixsternhimmels (Wiesbaden: Otto Harrassowitz, 1989), 14–22, and the critique of Koch by Heinz Neumann, "Anmerkungen zu Johannes Koch, Neue Untersuchungen sur Topographie des babylonischen Fixsternhimmels," *AfO* 38–39 (1991–92): 111.

81. A. Sachs, "Sirius Dates in Babylonian Astronomical Texts of the Seleucid Period," *JCS* 6 (1952): 105. Van der Waerden, "Babylonian Astronomy, II," 16–18, suggests that some of the observations recorded in one *MUL.APIN* text may come from as early as 1400 BCE, and that the tradition of recording celestial observations that became part of *MUL.APIN* goes back as far as 1700 BCE. Ernst F. Weidner, "Ein babylonisches Kompendium der Himmelskunde," *American Journal of Semitic Languages and Literatures* 40 (1924): 207–8, maintains that these observations originated as early as the third millennium BCE!

82. Hunger and Pingree, *MUL.APIN*; cf. Weidner, "Ein babylonisches Kompendium," 186–208. Note also, Matthias Albani, *Astronomie und Schöpfungsglaube: Untersuchungen zum Astronomishen Henochbuch*, WMANT 68 (Neukirchen-Vluyn: Neukirchener Verlag, 1994), 173–272.

83. Translation from Horowitz, *Mesopotamian Cosmic Geography*, 254; cf. Bartel L. van der Waerden, "History of the Zodiac," *AfO* 16 (1952–53): 221.

84. Ernst F. Weidner, "Die astrologische Serie *Enûma Anu Enlil* (mit 8 Tafeln)," *AfO* 14:3–4 (1941–44): 172–95; idem., "Die astrologische Serie *Enûma Anu Enlil* (Fortsetzung mit 4 Tafeln)," *AfO* 14:5–6 (1941–44): 308–18; idem, "Die astrologische Serie *Enûma Anu Enlil* (mit 5 Tafeln)," *AfO* 17 (1954–56): 71–89; idem, "Die astrologische Serie *Enûma Anu Enlil*," *AfO* 22 (1968–69): 65–75. Cf. Wilfred H. van Soldt, *Solar Omens of Enuma Anu Enlil: Tablets 23 (24)–29 (30)* (Istanbul: Nederlands Historisch-Archaeologisch Instituut, 1995); and Erica Reiner and David Pingree, *ENUMA ANU ENLIL Tablet 63: The Venus Tablet of Ammiṣaduqa*, ed. Giorgio Buccellati, Bibliotheca Mesopotamica 2:1, Babylonian Planetary Omens 1 (Malibu, Calif.: Undena Publications, 1975). For texts in translation, see R. Campbell Thompson, *The Reports of the Magicians and Astrologers of Nineveh and Babylon in the British Museum*, 2 vols. (London: Luzac and Co., 1900), vol. 2; and Hermann Hunger, *Astrological Reports to Assyrian Kings*, State Archives of Assyria 8 (Helsinki: Helsinki University Press, 1992).

85. My translation based on text in Reiner and Pingree, *Venus Tablet of Ammiṣaduqa*, 29.

86. Reiner and Pingree, *Venus Tablet of Ammiṣaduqa*, 61.

87. Reiner and Pingree, *ENUMA ANU ENLIL, Tablets 50–51*, 41.

88. See Jensen, *Kosmologie*, 95–144, and Morris Jastrow, *Die Religion Babyloniens und Assyriens*, 2 vols. (Giessen: Alfred Töpelmann, 1912) 2.415–705, for details on Mesopotamian observations of the movements of the sun, the moon, and the five planets. This section of Jastrow, *Religion Babyloniens und Assyriens*, is a revised and vastly expanded German edition of Jastrow, *Religion of Babylonia and Assyria*, 356–73.

89. See F. Rochberg-Halton, "New Evidence for the History of Astrology," *JNES* 43:2 (1984): 115, 123.

90. Vitruvius, *De architectura* 9.6.2, ed. and trans. F. Granger, 2 vols., LCL (Cambridge: Harvard University Press, 1934) 2.245, 247.

91. See van der Waerden, *Science Awakening II*, 96–100.

92. See Sachs, "Classification of the Babylonian Astronomical Tables," 285–86.

93. Ibid., 277–85.

94. Cuneiform horoscope for the date 3 June 235 BCE, quoted from A. Sachs, "Babylonian Horoscopes," *JCS* 6 (1952): 60. Although this is a Hellenistic era text, it reflects Babylonian horoscopic practices as least back to the fifth century BCE.

95. So Otto Neugebauer, *A History of Ancient Mathematical Astronomy* (New York/Berlin: Springer-Verlag, 1975), 5.

96. Cf. ibid., 309–22; and Horowitz, *Mesopotamian Cosmic Geography*, 208–20.

97. Jensen, *Kosmologie*, 11–12; and contrast Alfred Jeremias, *Die Babylonisch-Assyrischen Verstellungen vom Leben nach dem Tode* (Leipzig: J. C. Hinrichssche Buchhandlung, 1887), 60.

98. For the general features of Mesopotamian ideas of the afterlife, see Jo Ann Scurlock, "Death and the Afterlife in Ancient Mesopotamian Thought," *Civilizations of the Ancient Near East*, ed. Jack M. Sasson, 3.1883–93; and Manfred Hutter, *Altorientalische Vorstellungen von der Unterwelt: Literar- und religionsgeschichtliche Überlegungen zu "Nergal und Ereškigal,"* OBO 63 (Göttingen: Vandenhoeck and Ruprecht, 1985), 116–65. The Hittites, neighbors of the Mesopotamians in Anatolia (modern Turkey), had a similar outlook on the afterlife. The Hittites, however, appear to have thought that their kings had access to an afterlife in heaven with the gods, as the words from a ritual for a deceased king indicate: "You have summoned me [the king] to the spirits of the dead. I have presented myself to you, O Sungod of Heaven, my lord. Now admit me to my divine destiny among the gods of heaven, and release me from the midst of the spirits of the dead!" Quoted from Volkert Haas, "Death and the Afterlife in Hittite Thought," *Civilizations of the Ancient Near East*, ed. Jack M. Sasson, 3.2023.

99. Jeffrey H. Tigay, *The Evolution of the Gilgamesh Epic* (Philadelphia: University of Pennsylvania Press, 1982).

100. *ANET*, 107.

101. See Michael Fishbane, *Biblical Interpretation in Ancient Israel* (Oxford: Clarendon Press/New York: Oxford University Press, 1985), 443–57.

102. A. Leo Oppenheim, *The Interpretation of Dreams in the Ancient Near East, with a Translation of an Assyrian Dream-Book*, TAPS 46:3 (Philadelphia: American Philosophical Society, 1956) 258, 282.

103. Oppenheim, *Interpretation of Dreams*, 258, 287.

104. Note Sigmund Freud, *The Interpretation of Dreams*, trans. A. A. Brill (New York: Random House, 1950), 170–71.

105. Tzvi Abusch, "Mesopotamian Anti-Witchcraft Literature," 251–62. Note also Abusch, "Ascent to the Stars in a Mesopotamian Ritual: Social Metaphor and Religious Experience," *Death, Ecstasy, and Other Worldly Journeys*, ed. John J. Collins and Michael Fishbane (Albany: SUNY Press, 1995), 15–39.

106. Abusch, "Socio-Religious Framework," 467–94.

107. The ancient Near Eastern gods typically convene in a divine assembly or council; see E. Theodore Mullen, Jr., *The Divine Council in Canaanite and Early Hebrew Literature*, HSM 24 (Atlanta: Scholars Press, 1980), and Lowell K. Handy, *Among the Host of Heaven: The Syro-Palestinian Pantheon as Bureaucracy* (Winona Lake, Ind.: Eisenbrauns, 1994).

108. Abusch proposes such alternatives as well; see "Socio-Religious Framework," 478, n. 25, 479, and p. 488: "The speaker is on earth but he is also in the heavens. In some sense, his vision is like Isaiah's vision of God, a vision that is both terrestrial and heavenly. . . ." Just such an image is represented on the Nabuapaliddina tablet (figure 2.4) discussed above.

109. See W. G. Lambert, "Enmeduranki and Related Matters," *JCS* 21 (1967): 126–38, James VanderKam, *Enoch and the Growth of an Apocalyptic Tradition*, CBQMS 16 (Washington, DC: Catholic Biblical Association, 1984) 33–38, and VanderKam, *Enoch: A Man for All Generations*, Studies on Personalities of the Old Testament (Columbia, S.C.: University of South Carolina Press, 1995), 6–14.

110. Quoted from Lambert, "Enmeduranki," 132.

111. Rykle Borger, "Die Beschwörungsserie *bīt mēseri* und die Himmelfahrt Henochs," *JNES* 33 (1974): 183–96.

112. For English translation see *ANET*, 101–3, and Stephanie Dalley, *Myths From Mesopotamia* (Oxford: Oxford University Press, 1989), 184–88.

113. On Adapa's wisdom see Peter Machinist and Hayim Tadmor, "Heavenly Wisdom," *The Tablet and the Scroll: Near Eastern Studies in Honor of William W. Hallo*, ed. Mark E. Cohen, Daniel C. Snell, and David B. Weisberg (Bethesda, Md.: CDL Press, 1993) 146–51.

114. From Dalley, *Myths from Mesopotamia*, 186. Note that the gate of heaven is guarded by heavenly beings, a theme that will reappear commonly in early Jewish and Christian ascent texts.

115. Dalley, *Myths from Mesopotamia*, 187.

116. As John D. Evers has noted, *Myth and Narrative: Structure and Meaning in Some Ancient Near Eastern Texts*, AOAT 241 (Kevelaer/Neukirchen-Vluyn: Butzon and Bercker/Neukirchener Verlag, 1995), 23–32, the offer of eternal life was limited to Adapa alone and was not a universal offer to all humans. For the contrary view see Speiser, "Adapa," *ANET*, 101; Alexander Heidel, *The Babylonian Genesis*, 2d. ed. (Chicago: University of Chicago Press, 1951), 124; S. N. Kramer, "Mythology of Sumer and Akkad," 125; and H. W. F. Saggs, *The Greatness That Was Babylon* (London: Sidgwick and Jackson, 1962), 407.

117. Erica Reiner, "The Etiological Myth of the Seven Sages," *Or* 30 (1961): 1–11, finds another reference to the myth of Adapa ascending to heaven in another text. Her thesis was challenged on the basis of additional texts by Borger who showed that Reiner was wrong to supply the name "Adapa" at the beginning of the line mentioning the ascent to heaven. The copies of the text he uncovered have the name Utuabzu: "*Utuabzu, der zum Himmel emporgestiegen ist.*" This is the Utuabzu mentioned above who was no normal human being, but the last of the seven antediluvian sages. Borger claims, therefore, that the later Jewish tradition of Enoch (the seventh generation after Creation) ascending into heaven stems from this antediluvian figure: "*Das Mythologem von der Himmelfahrt Henochs stammt jedoch von Enmedurankis Ratgeber, dem sebienten vorsint-flutlichen Weisen names Utuabzu her!*" (Borger, "Himmelfahrt Henochs," 193).

118. S. Langdon, *The Legend of Etana and the Eagle* (Paris: Librairie Orientaliste Paul Geuthner, 1932); J. V. Kinnier-Wilson, *The Legend of Etana* (Warminster, UK: Aris & Phillips Ltd., 1985); *ANET*, 114–17; and Dalley, *Myths From Mesopotamia*, 189–202.

119. Thorkild Jacobsen, *The Sumerian King List*, Assyriological Studies 11 (Chicago: University of Chicago Press, 1939).

120. The text as it is presented here is a compilation from middle-Assyrian and neo-Assyrian versions found in Horowitz, *Mesopotamian Cosmic Geography*, 43–66, and Kinnier-Wilson, *Etana*.

121. For the "Heaven of Anu" in other texts see Gilgamesh Epic xi. 114, Nergal and Ereshkigal iv.25 (*ANET*, 510) and the texts cited in Horowitz, "Two Notes on Etana's Flight to Heaven," 516, n. 7.

122. The same phrase, "the gate of Anu, Enlil, and Ea," appears in the Sumerian Myth of "Nergal and Ereshkigal" (see *ANET*, 510, 511). In this text, the god ascends to this gate via "the long stairway of heaven"; see Alan R. Millard, "The Celestial Ladder and the Gate of Heaven (Genesis xxviii.12, 17)," *ExpTim* 78 (1966–67): 86–87.

123. Contra Langdon, *Etana and the Eagle*, 3–5.

124. On the gates for the celestial bodies, see Jensen, *Kosmologie*, 9; Horowitz, *Mesopotamian Cosmic Geography*, 266–67; Heimpel, "Sun at Night and the Doors of

Heaven," 127–51; and O. Neugebauer, "Notes on Ethiopic Astronomy," *Or* 33 (1964): 49–71.

125. Figure 2.5 by Theodore Burgh after Frankfort, *Cylinder Seals*, 138–39, plate XXIVh.

126. Lambert, "Cosmology of Sumer and Babylon," 57–59, suggests that the Enûma Elish also exhibits a multiple heaven schema.

127. Cf. *CAD*, Š, 345; Lambert, "Cosmology of Sumer and Babylon," 61–62; and Margaret Huxley, "Shape of the Cosmos," 189–98.

128. Ludlul Bel Nemeqi II.46–47, quoted from W. G. Lambert, *Babylonian Wisdom Literature* (Oxford: Clarendon Press, 1960), 41; cf. Dialogue of a Pessimist 83, 149.

129. Gilgamesh Epic, III.iv.5–8, quoted from Dalley, *Myths from Mesopotamia*, 144.

130. See H. Ringgren, "The Religion of Ancient Syria," *Historia Religionum: Handbook for the History of Religions*, vol. 1, *Religions of the Past*, ed. C. Jouco Bleeker and Geo Widengren (Leiden: E. J. Brill, 1969) 195–222. For the Phoenician pantheon see Edward Lipínski, *Dieux et déesses de l'univers phénicien et punic*, Studia Phenicia 14, Orientalia Lovaniensia Analecta 64 (Leuven: Peeters, 1995).

131. For general outlines of Ugaritic religion see André Caquot and Maurice Sznycer, *Ugaritic Religion*, Iconography of Religions 15.8 (Leiden: E. J. Brill, 1980), 1–21.

132. On the difficulty of identifying the referents of the term "Canaanite," see Lester L. Grabbe, "'Canaanite': Some Methodological Observations in Relation to Biblical Study," *Ugarit and the Bible: Proceedings of the International Symposium on Ugarit and the Bible—Manchester, September 1992*, ed. George J. Brooke, Adrian H. W. Curtis, and John F. Healey (Münster: Ugarit-Verlag, 1994), 113–22, and Anson F. Rainey, "Who is a Canaanite? A Review of the Textual Evidence," *BASOR* 304 (1996): 1–16.

133. *KTU* 1.2.21–22, 30–32; cf. Michael David Coogan, *Stories from Ancient Canaan* (Philadelphia: Westminster Press, 1978), 86, 87.

134. Cf. Mullen, *Divine Council*, 274–80; Saul M. Olyan, *A Thousand Thousands Served Him: Exegesis and the Naming of Angels in Ancient Judaism*, Texte und Studien zum antiken Judentum 36 (Tübingen: J.C.B. Mohr, 1993).

135. *KTU* 1.7, VI:34–48, quoted from Coogan, *Stories from Ancient Canaan* 37. Cf. *ANET*, 151; John F. Healey, "The Immortality of the King: Ugarit and the Psalms," *Or* 53 (1984): 245–48; and Paolo Xella, "Death and the Afterlife in Canaanite and Hebrew Thought," *Civilizations of the Ancient Near East*, ed. Jack M. Sasson, 3.2063.

136. Baruch Margalit, "Death and Dying in the Ugaritic Epics," *Death in Mesopotamia*, ed. Bendt Alster, 253.

137. For Ugaritic views of the realm of the dead see Michael C. Astour, "The Nether World and Its Denizens at Ugarit," *Death in Mesopotamia*, ed. Bendt Alster, 227–38.

138. Healey, "Immortality of the King," 245–54; Klaas Spronk, *Beatific Afterlife in Ancient Israel and in the Ancient Near East* (Neukirchen-Vluyn: Neukirchener Verlag/ Kevelaer: Butzon and Bercker, 1986); de Moor, *Anthology of Religious Texts from Ugarit*, 169, n. 8, 262.

139. See Karel van der Toorn, "Funerary Rituals and Beatific Afterlife in Ugaritic Texts and the Bible," *Bibliotheca Orientalis* 48 (1991): 40–66; and Mark S. Smith and Elizabeth M. Bloch-Smith, "Death and Afterlife in Ugarit and Israel," *JAOS* 108:2 (1988): 277–84.

140. Theodore J. Lewis, *Cults of the Dead in Ancient Israel and Ugarit*, HSM 39 (Atlanta: Scholars Press, 1989), concludes that although there was a vibrant cult of the dead at Ugarit, this did not involve the "deification" of deceased kings. See also Brian B. Schmidt, *Israel's Beneficent Dead: Ancestor Cult and Necromancy in Israelite Reli-*

gion and Tradition, Forschungen zum Alten Testament 11 (Tübingen: J. C. B. Mohr [Paul Siebeck], 1994), 47–122.

141. "Panammu Inscription," lines 15–18a; *KAI*, 1.39, 2.215, 219–20; cf. John C. L. Gibson, *Textbook of Syrian Semitic Inscriptions*, 3 vols. (Oxford: Clarendon Press, 1971–82), 2.66–67.

142. Michael C. Astour, "The Nether World and Its Denizens at Ugarit," *Death in Mesopotamia*, ed. Alster, 228. For an indication of early Phoenician belief in resurrection see Aharon Kempinski, "From Death to Resurrection: The Early Evidence," *BARev* 21:5 (September/October 1995): 56–65, 82.

143. *KAI*, 1.3, 2.19–23; Gibson, *Textbook*, 107; *ANET*, 662.

Chapter 3

1. Although the literature on this is vast, for concise presentations of the issues see Richard E. Friedman, *Who Wrote the Bible?* (New York: Summit Books, 1987), and Morton Smith, *Palestinian Parties and Politics That Shaped the Old Testament* (New York: Columbia University Press, 1971).

2. Gen. 1:1, 2:4; Ex. 20:11; Isa. 45:12; Neh. 9:6; Ps. 8:4, 33:6, 146:6; Prov. 3:19. See also Cornelius Houtman, *Der Himmel im Alten Testament: Israels Weltbild und Weltanschauung*, Oudtestamentische Studiën 30 (Leiden: E. J. Brill, 1993), 85–116.

3. See Mark S. Smith, *The Early History of God: Yahweh and the Other Deities in Ancient Israel* (San Francisco: Harper & Row, 1990), 7–12; Patrick D. Miller, Jr., "El, the Creator of the Earth," *BASOR* 239 (1980): 43–46; and Johannes C. de Moor, *The Rise of Yahwism: The Roots of Israelite Monotheism*, BETL 91 (Leuven, Belgium: Leuven University Press, 1990), 69, 229, 252–55.

4. The same combination appears in Ugaritic texts: see *Ras Shamra Parallels*, ed. Loren R. Fisher and Stan Rummel, AnOr 49–51 (Rome: Pontifical Biblical Institute, 1972–81), 1.126, 356; 2.411–15; 3.487. Marjo Christina Annette Korpel, *A Rift in the Clouds: Ugaritic and Hebrew Descriptions of the Divine*, UBL 8 (Münster: Ugarit-Verlag, 1990), 560–77, presents many facets of Israel's cosmology within their Canaanite context. See also Houtman, *Der Himmel*, 26–84.

5. W. G. Lambert and A. R. Millard, *Atra-Hasis: The Babylonian Story of the Flood* (Oxford: Clarendon Press, 1969), 43, i.1–18.

6. On the development of the aniconic tradition in ancient Israel see Tryggve N. D. Mettinger, *No Graven Image?: Israelite Aniconism in Its Ancient Near Eastern Context*, ConBOT 42 (Stockholm: Almqvist & Wiksell International, 1995).

7. For additional philological data see Luis I. J. Stadelmann, *The Hebrew Conception of the World: A Philological and Literary Study*, AnBib 9 (Rome: Pontifical Biblical Institute, 1970), 37–39, and Houtman, *Der Himmel*, 5–20.

8. Apart from the standard lexica, note "šmym" in J. Hoftijzer and K. Jongeling, *Dictionary of the North-West Semitic Inscriptions*, 2 vols., Handbuch der Orientalistik 21.1–2 (Leiden: E. J. Brill, 1995), 1160–62. For this and other terms for celestial phenomena, see Wilhelm Eilers, "Stern-Planet-Regenbogen: Zur Nomenklatur der orientalischen Himmelskunde," *Der Orient in der Forschung: Festschrift für Otto Spies zum 5. April 1966*, ed. Wilhelm Hoenerbach (Wiesbaden: Otto Harrassowitz, 1967), 92–146.

9. GKC, §§88, 124b; cf. Paul Joüon, *A Grammar of Biblical Hebrew*, 2 vols., trans. and rev. T. Muraoka, Subsidia Biblica 14.I–II (Rome: Pontifical Biblical Institute, 1993), §91f; Bernard Alfrink, "L'expression 'šamain or šᵉmei Haššmaim' dans l'Ancien Testa-

ment," *Mélanges Eugène Tisserant*, ed. Eugène Tisserant, Studie Testi 231 (Vatican City: Biblioteca Apostolica Vaticana, 1964), 1–7; and Houtman, *Der Himmel*, 5–20.

10. P. Ildefonse de Vuippens, *La paradis terrestre au troisième ciel: Exposé historique d'une conception chrétienne des premiers siècles* (Fribourg: Librairie de l'oeuvre de S.-Paul, 1925), 79–80.

11. Hans Bauer and Pontus Leander, *Historische Grammatik der hebräischen Sprache des Alten Testaments, I* (Hildesheim: Georg Olms Verlagsbuchhandlung, 1962), 621. Note Ps. 148:4: "praise Yahweh, O vast sky, and water that is above the sky." This is precisely how some rabbinic texts explain the origin of the term; cf. שָׁם מִים, "there is water there" (Re'uyot Yehezqel, *BM*, 2.131). Note also that in Akkadian the homonym *šamû* (*šamum*) means "rain"; *CAD*, Š, 349–50; von Soden, *AHW*, 1161.

12. Cited in the explanatory list of gods in Inamgišuranki, *CT* 25, 50:17. I owe thanks to Joel H. Hunt for this reference.

13. GKC, 133i; *HALAT*, 4.1444. Cf. ben Sira 16:18.

14. Othmar Keel, *The Symbolism of the Biblical World: Ancient Near Eastern Iconography and the Book of Psalms*, trans. Timothy J. Hallet (New York: Seabury Press, 1977), 34: "The psalms are also aware of a plural number of heavens (e.g., Ps.. 148:4)." Cf. Paul Volz, *Die Biblischen Altertümer* (Calw and Stuttgart: Verlag der Vereinsbuchhandlung, 1914), 434: "Über dem Gewölbe bauen sich die verschiedenen Himmel auf; im äussersten hat Gott sienen Palast, Ps.. 148:4, Mi 1:2." Stadelmann, *Hebrew Conception*, 41–42, 51, follows B. Meissner, *Babylonien und Assyrien* (Heidelberg: Carl Winters Universitäts-buchhandlung, 1925), 2.107–8 in imagining a seven-storied heaven in ancient Near Eastern thought.

15. The Vav conjunction functions in an explicative sense. Note Deut. 10:14, 1 Kings 8:27; 2 Chr. 2:5; and Neh. 9:6. Cf. Houtman, *Der Himmel*, chapter 8.

16. Note also the phrase בֵּין הַשָּׁמַיִם (הָאָרֶץ) וּבֵין הָאָרֶץ (הַשָּׁמַיִם) (2 Sam. 18:9, Ezek. 8:3, Zech. 5:9, and 1 Chr. 21:16), which means "mid-air."

17. See James K. Hoffmeier, "Some Thoughts on Genesis 1 & 2 and Egyptian Cosmology," *JANES* 15 (1983): 45–46.

18. 2 Sam. 22:10; Isa. 40:22, 42:5, 44:24, 45:12, 51:13, 16; Jer. 10:12 = 51:15; Zech. 12:1; Ps. 104:2; Job 9:8. Cf. Stadelmann, *Hebrew Conception*, 51–52, and Houtman, *Der Himmel*, 210–22. Note that the Egyptian sun god Ra is praised for having done the same: "Thou didst stretch out the heavens wherein thy two eyes might travel"; E. A. Wallis Budge, *The Book of the Dead: An English Translation of the Chapters, Hymns, Etc., of the Theban Recension, with an Introduction, Notes, Etc.*, 2d ed., 3 vols. (Routledge & Kegan Paul Ltd., 1960), 2.87.

19. Gen. 12:8, 26:25, 33:19, 35:21; Ex. 33:7; Judges 4:11; 2 Sam. 6:17=1 Chr. 16:1; Jer. 10:20; 2 Chr. 1:4.

20. Norman C. Habel, "'He Who Stretches Out the Heavens'," *CBQ* 34 (1972): 430.

21. Another term found once in the Hebrew Bible for vast sky is אֲגֻדָּה (*'ăgudāh*): "Yahweh . . . who builds his upper chambers in the heavens, and founds his vault (אֲגֻדָּה *'ăgudāh*) upon the earth; who calls for the waters of the sea, and pours them out upon the surface of the earth—Yahweh is his name" (Amos 9:6).

22. Cf. Ex. 24:9–10. Regarding the platform on which the throne sits, Othmar Keel, *Jahwe-Visionen und Siegelkunst: Eine neue Deutung der Majestätsschilderungen in Jes 6, Ez 1 und Sach 4*, Stuttgarter Bibelstudien 84–85 (Stuttgart: Verlag Katholisches Bibelwerk, 1977), 255, notes that "Die Platte bezeichnet ja die Grenze zwischen der unzugänglichen

heiligen Sphäre Gottes und dem Bereich der Schöpfung." For comparative iconography see Keel, *Jahwe-Visionen*, figures 108–15.

23. Philip R. Davies, *In Search of Ancient Israel* (Sheffield: JSOT Press, 1992). While I do not follow Davies's approach to the history of Ancient Israel—see the critique by William G. Dever, "'Will the Real Israel Please Stand Up?' Archaeology and Israelite Historiography: Part 1," *BASOR* 297 (1995): 67–69—nonetheless, I think Davies' terminology provides a useful distinction between the different portrayals of Israelite history and religion available from the diverse sources.

24. Cf. Gen. 8:2; Deut. 11:11; Isa. 55:10; Jer. 10:13, 51:16; Ps. 135:7; Job 38:22; ben Sira 43:14.

25. Precipitation comes from the celestial ocean via windows (ארבות), doors (דלתות), or water channels (פלג); cf. Isa. 24:18, 60:8; Hos. 13:3; Job 26:27–28, 38:25–27; and Houtman, *Der Himmel*, 120–26.

26. Enuma Elish iv.128–41 from *ANET*, 67.

27. See Peter C. Chemery, "Sky: Myths and Symbolism," *The Encyclopedia of Religion*, ed. Mircea Eliade, 15 vols. (New York: Macmillan Publishing Company, 1987), 13.350–53.

28. Stadelmann, *Hebrew Conception*, 92, expresses a common misconception of ancient Israelite religion when he claims that the worship of celestial bodies ". . . was introduced into Palestine with the Assyrian invasions of that country, beginning with Shalmaneser III (858–824 B.C.), and reached its climax during the reign of the Judean kings, Manasseh (ca. 687–642 B.C.) and Amon (ca. 642–640 B.C.), who were vassals of the Assyrians." It seems more likely that this was a common ancient Near Eastern religious phenomenon and was a natural part of Israelite religion. Statements such as Stadelmann's reflect more the bias of the Deuteronomistic editors of the Hebrew Bible than the actual religious milieu of ancient Israel. See also Silvia Schroer, *In Israel Gab Es Bilder: Nachrichten von darstellender Kunst im alten Testament*, OBO 74 (Göttingen/Freiburg: Vandenhoeck and Ruprecht/Universitätsverlag Freiburg, 1987), 257–300; and E. Walter Maunder, *The Astronomy of the Bible: An Elementary Commentary on the Astronomical References of Holy Scripture* (New York: Mitchell Kennedy, 1908), 213–42.

29. Cf. Ex. 20:4, Deut. 4:17, 17:3; 2 Kings 17:16, 21:3–5, 23:5; Jer. 8:2, 19:13, 44:17–19; Ezek. 8:16; Am. 5:26; and Zeph. 1:5. Job 31:26–28 refers to "kissing the hand" as part of a gesture involved in worshipping the moon.

30. See David Noel Freedman, "Early Israelite Poetry and Historical Reconstructions," *Symposia: Celebrating the Seventy-Fifth Anniversary of the Founding of the American Schools of Oriental Research (1900–1975)*, ed. Frank Moore Cross (Cambridge, Mass.: American Schools of Oriental Research, 1979), 85–96.

31. This is, therefore, an example of a biblical text that retains traces of the Canaanite, polytheistic milieu of early Israel; cf. Niels Peter Lemche, "The Development of the Israelite Religion in the Light of Recent Studies on the Early History of Israel," *Congress Volume: Leiden 1989*, ed. J. A. Emerton, VTSup 43 (Leiden: E. J. Brill, 1991), 97–115.

32. Note also Isa. 13:10 where the term כְּסִיל seems to refer generally to constellations; cf. Stadelmann, *Hebrew Conception*, 94–95.

33. Tallay Ornan, "The Mesopotamian Influence on West Semitic Inscribed Seals: A Preference for the Depiction of Mortals," *Studies in the Iconography of Northwest Semitic Seals: Proceedings of a symposium held in Fribourg on April 17–20, 1991*, ed. Benjamin Sass and Christoph Uehlinger, OBO 125 (Göttingen: Vandenhoeck and Ruprecht, 1993), 52–73, notes (64 n. 17) that depictions of the Pleiades on West Semitic seals are rare, although they are common in Mesopotamia. Depictions of the Pleiades can be found

in Pierre Bordreuil, "Le répertoire iconographique des sceaux araméens inscrits et son évolution," in Sass and Uehlinger, eds., *Iconography of Northwest Semitic Seals*, 74–100, figs. 6 (p. 77, cf. pp. 78–79 [9th BCE]), 7 (p. 81, cf. pp. 79–80 [8th BCE]), 34 (p. 93, cf. pp. 94–95 [7th BCE]). Note also Eric Gubel, "Iconography of Inscribed Phoenician Glyptic," in Sass and Uehlinger, eds., *Iconography of Northwest Semitic Seals*, 101–29, fig. 32 (p. 117, cf. 118, 126); and Othmar Keel and Christoph Uehlinger, *Altorientalische Miniaturkunst* (Mainz am Rhein: Verlag Philipp von Zabern, 1990), who provide several examples of neo-Assyrian Pleiades; see tafel II and figs. 52 (p. 46), 49 (p. 44), 13 (p. 24). For second millennium examples see Donald M. Matthews, *Principles of Composition in Near Eastern Glyptic of the Later Second Millennium* B.C., OBO 8 (Göttingen: Vandenhoeck and Ruprecht, 1990), illustrations 491, 500, 533, 538, 570, 615; and Claude Doumet, *Sceaux et cylindres orientaux: la collection Chiha* (OBO 9; Göttingen: Vandenhoeck and Ruprecht, 1992), 82, fig. 152.

34. עַיִשׁ (*'ayiš*) here and in Job 38:32 seems to refer to a constellation or star (Ursa Major?), but which one is not certain; cf. Stadelmann, *Hebrew Conception*, 95–96.

35. This may be cognate to the Akkadian *kayyamānu*, "Saturn."

36. Interestingly, Francis I. Andersen and David Noel Freedman, *Amos*, AB 24A (New York: Doubleday, 1989), 533, note regarding the astral aspects mentioned here: "Because the gods in question are most probably Assyro-Babylonian astral deities, they are probably a feature of contemporary worship in Israel, already infected by influences from that quarter. . . . If Israelites ever worshiped this planet (i.e., Saturn), it was most likely a practice lately borrowed from Assyria." The worship of celestial bodies was certainly not "lately borrowed" by the Israelites but an ancient practice. And it was certainly no infection in the minds of its practitioners.

37. See Schroer, *In Israel Gab Es Bilder*, 267–72. Curiously, and apparently display-ing either a misunderstanding of this text or a deliberate attempt to subvert the refer-ence to "other" gods, the Damascus Document (VII.13–20), known from both the Qumran Scrolls and the Cairo Geniza fragments, reinterprets this passage as a promise of deliverance instead of a threat of exile.

38. Ex. 20:4; Deut. 4:19, 5:8, 17:3; 2 Kings 17:16, 21:3–5 (=2 Chr. 33:3–5); Isa. 47:13; Jer. 7:18, 10:2, 19:13, 44:15–25; Zeph. 1:5. Stadelmann is incorrect to conclude from the meager evidence in the Hebrew Bible that ". . . it would seem that astronomy was never grasped or pursued as a science in ancient Israel" (Stadelmann, *Hebrew Con-ception*, 96).

39. Gen. 1:16; Ps. 136:4–9, 147:4; Job 38:12–15; Neh. 9:6. Note also 1 Kings 8:12, where the Septuagint text (now after 8:53) adds the following: ". . . ἥλιον ἐγνώρισεν ἐν οὐρανῷ κύριος (the Lord manifested the sun in the sky)."

40. Judg. 5:20; Isa. 13:10, 45:12; Jer. 31:35; Ps. 8:4; Job 9:7–9, 38:31–33.

41. Cf. Stadelmann, *Hebrew Conception*, 61–96; and A Leo. Oppenheim, *Ancient Mesopotamia: Portrait of a Dead Civilization* (Chicago: University of Chicago Press, 1964), 224–25, 307–10.

42. Josh. 10:12–13; Isa. 38:8; Hab. 3:10–11; Job 9:7, 22:12, 38:7, 12.

43. The Babylonian "Shamash Hymn" praises the sun god Shamash with terminol-ogy and motifs that could easily be used in praise of Yahweh; see W. G. Lambert, *Babylonian Wisdom Literature* (Oxford: Clarendon Press, 1960), 127–38. P. E. Dion, "YHWH as Storm-God and Sun-God: The Double Legacy of Egypt and Canaan as Reflected in Psalm 104," *ZAW* 103:1 (1991): 64, suggests that solar worship was a for-eign element that the Israelites "assimilated" into Yahwism. Again, I submit that this was an integral part of Yahwism from the beginning that was eventually written-out by later Deuteronomistic officials and biblical editors. Cf. Othmar Keel and Christoph

Uehlinger, "Jahwe und die Sonnengottheit von Jerusalem," *Ein Gott allein? JHVH-Verehrung und biblischer Monotheismus im Kontext der israelitischen und altorientalischen Religionsgeschichte*, ed. Walter Dietrich and Martin A. Klopfenstein (Freiburg: Universitätsverlag Freiburg, 1994), 269–306.

44. Figure 3.1 from Yigael Yadin, *Hazor I* (Jerusalem: Magnes Press/Hebrew University), 87–90, plate XXIX, 2. Cf. Amnon Ben-Tor, "Hazor," *The New Encyclopedia of Archaeological Excavations in the Holy Land*, ed. Ephraim Stern, Ayelet Levinzon-Gilboa, and Joseph Aviram, 4 vols. (Jerusalem: Israel Exploration Society & Carta/New York: Simon & Schuster, 1993), 2.596; and Othmar Keel and Christoph Uehlinger, *Göttinnen, Götter und Gottessymbole: Neue Erkenntnisse zur Religionsgeschichte Kanaans und Israels aufgrund bislang unerschlossener ikonographischer*, Quaestiones Disputatae 134 (Freiburg: Herder, 1992), 58.

45. Figure 3.2 after Schroer, *In Israel Gab Es Bilder*, frontispiece. For discussion of this cult stand see J. Glen Taylor, *Yahweh and the Sun: Biblical and Archaeological Evidence for Sun Worship in Ancient Israel*, JSOTSup 111 (Sheffield: Academic Press, 1993); Smith, *Early History of God*, 115–24; idem, "The Near Eastern Background of Solar Language for Yahweh," *JBL* 109:1 (1990) 29–39; and Susan Ackerman, *Under Every Green Tree: Popular Religion in Sixth-Century Judah*, HSM 46 (Atlanta: Scholars Press, 1992), 79–99. Hans-Peter Stähli, *Solare Elemente im Jahweglauben des Alten Testaments*, OBO 66 (Göttingen: Vandenhoeck und Ruprecht, 1985), traces the development of solar aspects of Yahwism as a means to explain the solar imagery found in several Byzantine-era synagogues. Cf. Frans du T. Laubscher, "Epiphany and Sun Mythology in Zechariah 14," *JNWSL* 20:1 (1994): 125–38; and Matthias Albani, *Astronomie und Schöpfungsglaube: Untersuchungen zum Astronomishen Henochbuch*, WMANT 68 (Neukirchen-Vluyn: Neukirchener Verlag, 1994), 311–13.

46. On Jer. 2:27 and misdirected prostrations see Ziony Zevit, "Proclamations to the Fruitful Tree and the Spiritualization of Androgyny," *Echoes of Many Texts: Reflections on Jewish and Christian Traditions—Essays in Honor of Lou H. Silberman*, ed. William G. Dever and J. Edward Wright, BJS 313 (Atlanta: Scholars Press, 1997), 43–50.

47. Cf. Deut. 4:19, 17:3; 2 Kings 17:3, 21:3, 5, 22:19; Isa. 34:4, 40:26, 45:12; Jer. 8:2, 19:13, 33:22; Zeph. 1:5; Neh. 9:6; 2 Chr. 18:18, 33:3, 5.

48. See Tryggve N. D. Mettinger, "YHWH SABAOTH—The Heavenly King on the Cherubim Throne," *Studies in the Period of David and Solomon and Other Essays*, ed. Tomoo Ishida (Tokyo: Yamakawa-Shuppansha, 1982), 109–38. Ex. 15:11; 1 Kings 17:1, 18:15, 22:19; 2 Kings 3:14, 5:16; Isa. 6:2; Jer. 23:18, 22; Zech. 3:4, 4:14, 6:5 all use the image of standing before God in the sense of being in the presence of the celestial assembly.

49. See Taylor, *Yahweh and the Sun*, 99–107.

50. See Frank Moore Cross Jr., *Canaanite Myth and Hebrew Epic: Essays in the History of the Religion of Israel* (Cambridge, Mass.: Harvard University Press, 1973), 69–71; cf. J. P. Ross, "Jahweh ṣeba'ôṯ in Samuel and Psalms," *VT* 17:1 (1967): 76–92; and C. L. Seow, *Myth, Drama, and the Politics of David's Dance*, HSM 44 (Atlanta: Scholars Press, 1989), 11–54, 77–78.

51. For example see Gen. 21:17; Judg. 13:3; Zech. 1:9–14; Ps. 35:5–6.

52. Gen. 6:2,4; Deut. 32:8; Ps. 29:1, 89:7; Job 1:6, 2:1, 38:7.

53. These concepts are treated in Volkmar Hirth, *Gottes Boten im Alten Testament: die alttestamentliche Mal'ak Vorstellung unter besonderer Berucksichtigung des Mal'ak Yahweh Problem*, Theologische Arbeiten 32 (Berlin: Evangelisch Verlagsanstalt, 1975). Note also D. N. Freedman, B. E. Willoughby, H. Ringgren, and H.-J. Fabry, "*mal'ak*," *TDOT*, ed. G. Johannes Botterweck, Helmer Ringgren, et al. (Grand Rapids, Mich.: W. B.

Eerdmans, 1986–), 8.308–25; and Carol A. Newsome, "Angels, Old Testament," *ABD*, 1.248–53.

54. The text is part of the Yahwistic sources and likely originated sometime in the tenth century BCE; see Cross, *Canaanite Myth*, 45–46.

55. Cornelius Houtman, "What Did Jacob See in His Dream at Bethel?" *VT* 27:3 (1977): 337–38 notes that some have suggested that the term "ladder" should be understood in connection with the Mesopotamian ziggurats and the stairways leading to their summits. Alan R. Millard, "The Celestial Ladder and the Gate of Heaven (Genesis xxviii. 12 and 17)," *ExpTim* 78 (1966–67): 86–87, observes that the "ladder" may be parallel to the "long staircase of heaven" mentioned in the myth of Nergal and Ereshkigal whose summit is at the gate of Anu, Enlil, and Ea. J. Gwyn Griffiths, "The Celestial Ladder and the Gate of Heaven (Genesis xxviii, 12 and 17)," *ExpTim* 76 (1964–65): 229–30, suggests that the ladder finds it parallel in the Egyptian Pyramid Texts that speak of the deceased pharaoh ascending the ladder in order to take his place in the celestial circuit. Either way, this Israelite motif has analogs in other ancient Near Eastern cultures.

56. The cognate in Akkadian, *simmiltu*, is used to designate the stairway leading up to a temple; see *CAD*, S, p. 274.

57. "Where pre-exilic and exilic biblical texts suggest a divine realm populated by thousands of unnamed angels praising God and serving him in war and in judgment, the materials of ancient and medieval Judaism present a very different picture: The angelic host is beyond counting, named and articulated in detail" (Saul M. Olyan, *A Thousand Thousands Served Him: Exegesis and the Naming of Angels in Ancient Judaism*, Texte und Studien zum Antiken Judentum 36 [Tübingen: J. C. B. Mohr {Paul Siebeck}, 1993] 2).

58. On the increased individuality of the angels in later texts see Olyan, *A Thousand Thousands Served Him*; and Michael Mach, *Entwicklungsstadien des jüdischen Engelglaubens in vorrabbinischer Zeit*, Texte und Studien zum Antiken Judentum 34 (Tübingen: J. C. B. Mohr, 1992).

59. See John J. Collins, *The Apocalyptic Vision of the Book of Daniel*, HSM 16 (Missoula, Mont.: Scholars Press, 1977), 101–4.

60. See Olyan, *A Thousand Thousands Served Him*, 31–69.

61. Baruch Halpern, *The Emergence of Israel in Canaan*, SBLMS 29 (Chico, CA: Scholars Press, 1983), 246, emphasis added. Cf. Lester L. Grabbe, "'Canaanite': Some Methodological Observations in Relation to Biblical Study," *Ugarit and the Bible: Proceedings of the International Symposium on Ugarit and the Bible, Manchester, September 1992*, ed. George J. Brooke, Adrian H. W. Curtis, and John F. Healey (Münster: Ugarit-Verlag, 1994), 119; and Anson F. Rainey, "Who is a Canaanite? A Review of the Textual Evidence," *BASOR* 304 (1996): 1–16.

62. See Cross, *Canaanite Myth*, 1–75; Smith, *Early History of God*; de Moor, *Rise of Yahwism*, 223–60. Note also the essays in Diana Vikander Edelman, ed., *The Triumph of Elohim: From Yahwisms to Judaisms* (Kampen: Kok Pharos/Grand Rapids: Eerdmans, 1995), and those in Dietrich and Klopfenstein, *Ein Gott allein*.

63. See Smith, *Early History of God*; William G. Dever, "Religion and Cult in Ancient Israel: Social and Economic Implications," *Scienze dell'antichità: Storia Archeologia Antropologia* 3–4 (1989–1990): 175–80; de Moor, *Rise of Yahwism*, and Rainer Albertz, *A History of Israelite Religion in the Old Testament Period*, 2 vols. (Louisville, Ky.: Westminster/John Knox, 1994) 1.76–79, 95–99, 198–231.

64. See Ziony Zevit, "Three Ways to Look at the Ten Plagues," *BibRev* 6:3 (June 1990): 16–23, 42.

65. An Iron Age I cultic site in the central part of Israel has yielded a bronze statuette of a bull (figure 3.3). The bull was either the symbol of the gods El, Baal, and

Yahweh, or it was the animal on whose back they rode. Either way, one cannot say for certain which god this bull represented at this Canaanite or early Israelite site. See Amihai Mazar, "The 'Bull Site': An Iron Age I Open Cult Place," *BASOR* 247 (1982): 27–42; Schroer, *In Israel Gab Es Bilder*, 81–104.

66. Cf. Isa. 44:6–20; 1 Chr. 17:20. The theme continued in later Jewish literature; note Wisdom 13:1–5: "For all people who were ignorant of God were foolish by nature; and they were unable from the good things that are seen to know the one who exists, nor did they recognize the artisan while paying heed to his works; but they supposed that either fire or wind or swift air, or the circle of the stars, or turbulent water, or the luminaries of heaven were the gods that rule the world. If through delight in the beauty of these things people assumed them to be gods, let them know how much better than these is their Lord, for the author of beauty created them. And if people were amazed at their power and working, let them perceive from them how much more powerful is the one who formed them. For from the greatness and beauty of created things comes a corresponding perception of their Creator."

67. Cf. Psalms 29:1; 82:6–7; 86:8; 89:6–9; 95:3; 96:4; 97:9. See also C. J. Labuschagne, *The Incomparability of Yahweh in the Old Testament* (Leiden: E. J. Brill, 1966).

68. See Susan Ackerman, "'And the Women Knead Dough': The Worship of the Queen of Heaven in Sixth-Century Judah," *Gender and Difference in Ancient Israel*, ed. Peggy L. Day (Minneapolis: Fortress, 1989), 109–24. The issue is summarized in Philip J. King, *Jeremiah: An Archaeological Companion* (Louisville, Ky.: Westminster/John Knox Press, 1993) 102–9.

69. See Beth Alpert Nakhai, "Religion in Canaan and Israel: An Archaeological Perspective" (Ph.D. diss., University of Arizona, 1993), 284–324, and "What's a Bamah? How Sacred Space Functioned in Ancient Israel," *BARev* 20:3 (May/June 1994): 18–29, 77–79.

70. Figure 3.4 from Alain Chambon and Henri de Contenson, *Tel el-Far'ah I: L'Age du Fer* (Paris: Editions Recherche sur les civilisations, 1984), plate 66.

71. The term was coined by Smith, *Palestinian Parties and Politics*, 29. Bernhard Lang, "Life After Death in the Prophetic Promise," *Congress Volume: Jerusalem 1986*, ed. J. A. Emerton, VTSup 40 (Leiden: E. J. Brill, 1988), 145–56, notes that these ruthlessly monotheistic beliefs disrupted Israelite religion, cutting people off from the private, family, mortuary, and other gods.

72. See Smith, *Palestinian Parties and Politics*, 41–45.

73. The phrase is that of George Foot Moore, *Judaism in the First Centuries of the Christian Era*, 2 vols. (Cambridge: Harvard University Press, 1927; Reprint, New York: Schocken Books, 1971), 1.3, and I use it knowing that there is no such thing as "norminative" Judaism until much later in Jewish history. In this regard, note Smith, *Palestinian Parties and Politics*, 99–125.

74. See Elizabeth Ann Remington Willett, "Women and Household Shrines in Ancient Israel" (Ph.D. diss., University of Arizona, 1999).

75. See Michael David Coogan, *West Semitic Personal Names in the Murashû Documents*, HSM 7 (Missoula, Mont.: Scholars Press, 1976), 122–26; *idem*, "Patterns in Jewish Personal Names in the Babylonian Diaspora," *JSJ* 4:2 (1973): 183–91; and Ran Zadok, *The Jews in Babylonia During the Chaldean and Achaemenian Periods According to the Babylonian Sources* (Haifa, Israel: University of Haifa, 1979), 78–89.

76. See Michael H. Silverman, *Religious Values in the Jewish Proper Names at Elephantine*, AOAT 217 (Kevelaer: Butzon and Bercker/Neukirchen-Vluyn: Neukirchener Verlag, 1985); and Bezalel Porten, "The Religion of the Jews of Elephantine in Light of the Hermopolis Papyri," *JNES* 28 (1969): 116–21.

77. Karel van der Toorn, "Anat-Yahu, Some Other Deities, and the Jews of El-ephantine," *Numen* 39 (1992): 80–101, notes that the goddess Anat-Yahu mentioned at Elephantine has Aramean origins and was introduced to Israel (i.e., the Northern King-dom) in the eighth century BCE. She thus became an Israelite goddess and eventually moved to Egypt along with the Israelites who fled there after the destruction of the Northern Kingdom in 722. For Elephantine texts see Bezalel Porten, *The Elephantine Papyri in English*, Documenta et monumenta Orientalis antiqui 22 (Leiden: E. J. Brill, 1996).

78. *Ugaritica V*, ed. Jean Nougayrol, Emmanuel Laroche, Claude Virolleaud, and Claude F. A. Schaeffer (Paris: Imprimerie Nationale, 1968), 2.2b–3a. Cf. E. Theodore Mullen Jr., *The Divine Council in Canaanite and Early Hebrew Literature*, HSM 24 (Chico, Calif.: Scholars Press, 1980) 120–28.

79. Albertz, *History of Israelite Religion*, 1.193–95.

80. The literature on this topic is vast, but see the following: Tilde Binger, *Asherah: The Goddess in the Texts from Ugarit, Israel and the Old Testament*, JSOTSup 232 (Sheffield: Sheffield Academic Press, 1997); Othmar Keel and Christoph Uehlinger, *Gods, God-desses, and Images of Gods in Ancient Israel*, trans. Allan W. Mahnke (Philadelphia: For-tress Press, 1997); William G. Dever, "Asherah, Consort of Yahweh? New Evidence from Kuntillet 'Ajrud," *BASOR* 255 (1984): 21–37; Ziony Zevit, "The Khirbet el-Qôm Inscription Mentioning a Goddess," *BASOR* 255 (1984): 39–47; John Day, "Ashera in the Hebrew Bible and Northwest Semitic Literature," *JBL* 105 (1986): 385–408; Judith M. Hadley, "Some Drawings and Inscriptions on Two Pithoi from Kuntillet 'Ajrud," *VT* 37 (1987): 180–213 and Hadley "The Khirbet el-Qôm Inscription," *VT* 37 (1987): 60–62; Saul M. Olyan, "Some Observations Concerning the Identity of the Queen of Heaven," *UF* 19 (1987): 286–300, and Olyan *Asherah and the Cult of Yahweh in Israel*, SBLMS 34 (Atlanta: Scholars Press, 1988); Klaus Koch, "Aschera als Himmel-skönigin in Jerusalem," *UF* 20 (1988) 97–120; Ackerman, *Under Every Green Tree*; and Manfried Dietrich and Oswald Loretz, *"Jahwe und seine Aschera": Anthropomorphes Kultbild in Mesopotamien, Ugarit und Israel: Das biblische Bilderverbot*, UBL 9 (Münster: Ugarit-Verlag, 1992).

81. In addition to the studies in the preceding note, the iconography of ancient Near Eastern goddesses and the accompanying ideology are treated in detail by Urs Winter, *Frau und Göttin: Exegetische und ikonographische Studien zum weiblichen Gottesbild im alten Testament und dessen Umwelt*, OBO 53 (Göttingen/Freiburg: Vandenhoeck & Ruprecht/ Universitätsverlag Freiburg, 1983).

82. Figures 3.5–3.6 from Winter, *Frau und Göttin*, figures 30, 33; cf. 409.

83. Figure 3.7a–b from Winter, *Frau und Göttin*, figure 63.

84. Figure 3.8–3.9 from Winter, *Frau und Göttin*, figures 41–42; cf. 504 (Ishtar).

85. Figure 3.10 from Ze'ev Meshel, "Kuntillet 'Ajrud—An Israelite Site from the Monarchical Period on the Sinai Boarder," *Qadmoniot* 9 (1976): 118–24 [Hebrew], and "Did Yahweh Have a Consort?" *BARev* 5:2 (1979): 24–36. Cf. Winter, *Frau und Göttin*, figures 514, 502 (Ishtar), and Schroer, *In Israel gab es Bilder*, figure 63 (Ishtar).

86. See Cross, *Canaanite Myth*; Conrad E. L'Heureux, *Rank Among the Canaanite Gods: El, Ba'al, and the Repha'im* (Missoula, Mont.: Scholars Press, 1979); Mullen, *Divine Council*; de Moor, *Rise of Yahwism*; and Lowell K. Handy, *Among the Host of Heaven: The Syro-Palestinian Pantheon as Bureaucracy* (Winona Lake, Ind.: Eisenbrauns, 1994).

87. The bibliography on this motif is considerable, but note especially Marc Brettler, *God is King: Understanding an Israelite Metaphor*, JSOTSup 76 (Sheffield: JSOT Press, 1989); M. Tsevat, "God and the Gods in Assembly," *HUCA* 40 (1969): 123–37; Korpel, *Rift in the Clouds*, 281–86; Christoph Uehlinger, "Audienz in der Götterwelt: Anthropo-

morphismus und Soziomorphismus in der Ikonographie eines altsyrischen Zylinder-siegels," *UF* 24 (1992): 339–59; and J. C. L. Gibson, "The Kingship of Yahweh against its Canaanite Background," *Ugarit and the Bible*, ed. George J. Brooke et al., 101–12.

88. The setting and some details here find parallels in the lives of the prophets Isaiah and Jeremiah who had encounters with kings. See Hedwige Rouillard, "Royauté céleste et royauté terrestre en I R 22," *Le trône de Dieu*, ed. Marc Philonenko, WUNT 69 (Tübingen: J. C. B. Mohr [Paul Siebeck], 1993) 100–107.

89. On the term '*satan*,' its meaning in the biblical period, and its subsequent evolution see Peggy L. Day, *An Adversary in Heaven: Sātān in the Hebrew Bible*, HSM 43 (Atlanta: Scholars Press, 1988); Elaine H. Pagels, *The Origin of Satan* (New York: Random House, 1995); and Jeffrey Burton Russell, *Satan: The Early Christian Tradition* (Ithaca, N.Y.: Cornell University Press, 1981).

90. Figure 3.11 from C. F.-A. Schaeffer, "Les Fouilles de Ras Shamra-Ugarit, Huitième campagne," *Syria* 18 (1937): 129, plate XVII; cf. Nicolas Wyatt, "The Stela of the Seated God from Ugarit," *UF* 15 (1983) 271–77.

91. See Mitchell Dahood, *Psalms II: 50–100*, AB 17 (New York: Doubleday, 1968), 268–71; and Hans-Joachim Kraus, *Psalmen*, 2 vols., BKAT 15 (Neukirchen: Neukirchener Verlag, 1961), 2.569–74.

92. Deut. 4:39, 26:15; 1 Kings 8:23, 30–49; 2 Chr. 7:14, 30:27; Isa. 63:15, 66:1; Neh. 9:13, 27–28; Ps. 11:4, 14:2, 20:7, 33:13, 53:3, 57:4, 76:9, 80:15, 102:20, 103:19, 115:3, 123:1; Lam. 3:41, 50; Dan 2:28.

93. Ps. 57:6,12, 108:6, 113:4; Job 11:8, 22:12.

94. 1 Kings 22:19; Ps. 103:21, 148:2.

95. אל השמים, *'el haššāmayim* (Ps. 136:26); more commonly אלהי השמים, *'ĕlohê haššāmayim* (Gen. 24:3, 7; Jonah 1:9; Ezra 1:2; Neh. 1:4, 5, 2:4, 20; 2 Chr. 36:23); or its Aramaic form אלה שמיא, *'ĕlāh šĕmayyā'* (Dan. 2:18,19, 37, 44; Ezra 5:11,12; 6:9, 10; 7:12, 21, 23; cf. Jer. 10:11).

96. בעל שמם or בעל שמין. Note for example *KAI* 202, A 3, 11, 12, 13, B 23; 244, 1, 3; 245, 1; 246, 2; 247, 3; 248, 7; 259, 3; 266, 2. See Smith, *Early History of God*, 42–44. The phrase "abomination which causes desolation" (שקץ משמם) in Daniel 11:31 and 12:11 is clearly a derogatory theological rendering of the name Baal Shamayim (בעל שמים); cf. Michael Fishbane, *Biblical Interpretation in Ancient Israel* (Oxford: Clarendon Press/New York: Oxford University Press, 1985), 71–72.

97. See Albert Vincent, *La religion des judéo-araméens d'Éléphantine* (Paris: Librairie Orientaliste Paul Geuthner, 1937), 116–43.

98. Ibid., 93–103.

99. 1 Macc. 3:18–19, 50; 4:10, 24, 40, 55; 12:15; 16:3; 2 Macc 7:11. Cf. Houtman, *Der Himmel*, 74–76.

100. Other common terms are בית (*bayit*, "house"); מקום (*māqôm*, "place"); מכון (*mākôn*, "residence"); and מעון (*mā'ôn*, "dwelling place").

101. Mic. 1:2; Hab. 2:20; Ps. 11:4, 18:7 (2 Sam. 22:7); cf. Ps. 36:9 where it is paired with בית (*bayit*, "house").

102. *CAD* E, 52–61.

103. Deut. 12:5, 11, 21; 14:23–24; 16:2, 6; 26:2; 1 Kgs. 8:29 (2 Chr. 6:20); Neh. 1:9.

104. Cf. Isa. 26:21; Mic. 1:3. Menahem Haran, "The Divine Presence in the Israelite Cult and the Cultic Institutions," *Bib* 50 (1969): 259, observes that the Deuteronomists typically use the verb שכן, "dwell, pitch a tent," for God's dwelling in the earthly temple, but use the verb ישב, "sit," for his residing in the heavenly palace.

105. See Menahem Haran, "Temple and Community in Ancient Israel," *Temple in Society*, ed. Michael V. Fox (Winona Lake, Ind.: Eisenbrauns, 1988) 18: "Just as every temporal king, and indeed any man, has his own domicile, so the divine king, in whose shadow the community finds protection, has a residence of his own. And in this dwelling place, just as in every luxurious house, the master of the residence is provided with all his "needs": bread set on the table, incense for smell, lamps for light, meat-, grain-, and drink-offerings presented on the outer altar—the altar which in the fossilized cultic language is still referred to as "the Lord's table" (Ezek. 44:16; Mal. 1:7). In this dwelling place, moreover, the master of the residence has his own servants, the priests, who care for his necessities and keep the house in order—just as any reigning monarch has in his palace servants and retinue surrounding him constantly and performing his orders."

106. The priestly dimensions of early Jewish descriptions of the divine presence are well documented by Martha Himmelfarb, *Ascent to Heaven in Jewish and Christian Apocalypses* (New York/Oxford: Oxford University Press, 1993).

107. See Oppenheim, *Ancient Mesopotamia*, 186–93.

108. William W. Hallo, "Sumerian Religion," *kinattūtu ša dārâti: Raphael Kutscher Memorial Volume*, ed. A. F. Rainey (Tel Aviv: Tel Aviv University Institute of Archaeology, 1993), 18. Cf. Hallo, "Texts, Statues and the Cult of the Divine King," VTSup 40 (1988): 54–66, and A. Leo Oppenheim, "The Significance of the Temple in the Ancient Near East II: The Mesopotamian Temple," *BA* 7 (1944): 58–59.

109. Hans Küng, *Eternal Life? Life After Death as a Medical, Philosophical, and Theological Problem* (Garden City, N.Y.: Doubleday & Co., 1984) 197–99.

110. The layout of palaces in the biblical period in Syria-Palestine is discussed by David Ussishkin, "King Solomon's Palaces," *BA* 36:3 (1973): 78–105; William G. Dever, "Palaces and Temples in Canaan and Ancient Israel," *Civilizations of the Ancient Near East*, 4 vols., ed. J. M. Sasson (New York: Charles Scribner's Sons, 1995), 1.605–14; and Dever, "Palace," *ABD* 5.56–58. Martin Metzger, *Königsthron und Gottesthron. Thronformen und Throndarstellungen in Ägypten und im Vorderen Orient in dritten und zweiten Jahrtausend vor Christus und deren Bedeutung für das Verständnis von Aussagen über den Thron im Alten Testament*, AOAT 15, 1–2 (Kevelaer/Neukirchen-Vluyn: Butzon und Bercker/Neukirchener Verlag, 1985) 2.174, tafel 86, shows the throne room at Mari, and the throne is set on a platform raised above the floor about three feet.

111. Figure 3.12 from Ussishkin, "King Solomon's Palaces," 87, fig. 5.

112. See Volkmar Fritz, "Temple Architecture: What Can Archaeology Tell Us about Solomon's Temple?" *BARev* 13:4 (July-August 1987): 38–49 (reprinted in *Essential Papers on Israel and the Ancient Near East*, ed. Frederick E. Greenspahn [New York: New York University Press, 1991] 116–28); and Keel and Uehlinger, *Göttinnen, Götter und Gottessymbole*, 189–96. Figures 3.13 after Fritz, "Temple Architecture," 41; figure 3.14 by Leen Ritmeyer.

113. Keel, *Jahwe-Visionen*, 15–45. For the relationship of the ark and the cherubim see Menahem Haran, "The Ark and the Cherubim," *Eretz-Israel* 5 (*Mazar Volume*), ed. Michael Avi-Yonah, et al. (Jerusalem: Israel Exploration Society, 1958), 83–90 [Hebrew]; English translation in *IEJ* 9 (1959): 30–38, 89–94; cf. Elizabeth Bloch-Smith, "'Who Is the King of Glory?' Solomon's Temple and Its Symbolism," *Scripture and Other Artifacts: Essays on the Bible and Archaeology in Honor of Philip J. King*, ed. Michael D. Coogan, J. Cheryl Exum, and Lawrence E. Stager (Louisville, Ky.: Westminster/John Knox Press, 1994), 18–31.

114. For details on the iconography see Keel, *Jahwe-Visionen*, 46–124.

115. For details on the iconography see Keel, *Jahwe-Visionen*, 125–273.

116. Figure 3.15 from sarcophagus of King Hiram of Byblos by A. H. Detweiler in W. F. Albright, "What Were the Cherubim," *BA* 1:1 (Feb. 1938): 1–3. Figure 3.16 from Megiddo ivories in *ANEP*, 332. Cf. Keel, *Jahwe-Visionen* 80, 152–58; Metzger, *Königsthron und Gottesthron*, 1.260–71, 2.236, tafel 113.

117. Figure 3.17 from Keel, *Jahwe-Visionen*, 260, fig. 10.

118. See *HALOT*, 2.764.

119. Keel, *Jahwe-Visionen*, 255–60.

120. For the iconography of Yahweh seated on a cherubim throne and its ancient Near Eastern parallels, see Keel, *Jahwe-Visionen*, 15–45; Metzger, *Königsthron und Gottesthron*, 2.236–48, plates 113–18; and Schroer, *In Israel Gab Es Bilder*, 78–81.

121. A. T. Olmstead, *History of the Persian Empire* (Chicago: University of Chicago Press, 1948), 162–84.

122. See Margaret Cool Root, *The King and Kingship in Achaemenid Art*, Acta Iranica 19 (Leiden: E. J. Brill, 1979), and Pierre Briant, *Histoire de L'Empire Perse: De Cyrus à Alexandre* (Paris: Librairie Arthème Fayard, 1996) 230–35. For illustration compare Root, *King and Kingship*, fig. 11.

123. Root, *King and Kingship*, 234.

124. See Root, *King and Kingship*, 284.

125. See Briant, *Histoire de L'Empire Perse*, 177–235.

126. For a description of the Persian court's personnel and court protocol see Briant, *Histoire de L'Empire Perse*, 266–366, and W. W. How and J. Wells, *A Commentary on Herodotus* (Oxford: Clarendon Press, 1928) 1.104.

127. See Briant, *Histoire de L'Empire Perse*, 326–27.

128. Martin Metzger, "Himmlische und irdische Wohnstatt Jahwes," *UF* 2 (1970): 144: "Das Heiligtum ist der Ort, an dem der Unterscheid zwischen Himmel und Erde, zwischen 'Diesseits' und 'Jenseits' aufgehoben ist." Cf. Metzger, *Königsthron und Gottesthron*, 1.229–30, *idem*, "Jahwe, der Kerubenthroner, die von Keruben flankierte Palmette und Sphingenthrone aus dem Libanon," *"Wer ist wie du, Herr, unter den Göttern?" Studien zur Theologie und Religionsgeschichte Israels für Otto Kaiser zum 70. Geburtstag*, ed. Ingo Kottsieper, Jürgen van Oorschot, Diethard Römheld, and Harald Martin Wahl (Göttingen: Vandenhoeck & Ruprecht, 1994), 75–90. Note also Mettinger, "YHWH SABAOTH," 119–21, and *ANEP*, 178, fig. 529. Menahem Haran, *Temples and Temple Service in Ancient Israel: An Inquiry into the Character of Cult Phenomena and the Historical Setting of the Priestly School* (Oxford: Clarendon Press, 1978), 246–59, acknowledges the iconographical or ideological connections, but doubts the idea that the god actually or in any real sense can be thought to "dwell" on the earthly throne (p. 257). Figure 2.4 is taken from Leonard W. King, *Babylonian Boundary-Stones and Memorial-Tablets in the British Museum* (London: British Museum, 1912), plate XCVIII.

129. See "*pt*" in Adolf Erman and Herman Grapow, *Wörterbuch der ägyptischen Sprache*, 5 vols. (Leipzig: J. C. Hinrichssche Buchhandlung, 1926–31), 1.491. Note that the fifth century BCE Phoenician inscriptions of Eshmunazar (*KAI* 14, 16, 17) and Bodashtart (*KAI* 15), respectively, refer to Astarte's sacred area in Tyre as שמם אדרם and שמם רמם, "lofty heaven"; cf. John C. L. Gibson, *Textbook of Syrian Semitic Inscriptions* (Oxford: Clarendon Press, 1971–82), 3.108–9, 112.

130. Victor Hurowitz, *I Have Built You an Exalted House: Temple Building in the Light of Mesopotamian and Northwest Semitic Writings*, JSOTSup 115, JSOT/ASOR Monograph Series 5 (Sheffield: Sheffield Academic Press, 1992), 285–300, observes that although in its present form the prayer of 1 Kgs. 8 is Deuteronomistic, the editors may have been

drawing on literary themes and motifs common to dedicatory prayers for newly constructed temples in the ancient Near East.

131. 1 Kings 8:32, 34, 36, 39, 43, 45, 49.

132. Note William Schniedewind, *Society and the Promise to David* (New York/Oxford: Oxford University Press, 1999), chapters 3–4.

133. See especially the textual and iconographic materials assembled in Metzger, *Königsthron und Gottesthron*, and note the many parallels presented by Roland de Vaux, "Les chérubins et l'arche d'alliance, les sphinx gardiens et les trônes divins dans l'ancien Orient," *Bible et Orient* (Paris: Éditions du Cerf, 1967), 231–59, plates II-VII. Note also F. Briquel-Chatonnet, *Les relations entre les cités de la côte phénicienne et les royaumes d'Israël et de Juda*, Studia Phoenicia XII, Orientalia Lovaniensia Analecta 46 (Leuven: Peeters, 1992), 360–62; and Mettinger, "YHWH SABAOTH," 113–19.

134. See Dieter Kolbe, *Die Reliefprogramme religiösmythologischen Charakters in den neuassyrischen Palästen: die Figurentypen, ihre Benennung und Bedeutung* (Frankfort am Main: Peter Lang, 1981), 1–14; and A. Green, "Mischwesen, B" *Reallexikon der Assyriologie und Vorderasiatischen Archäologie* 8:3–4 (1994) 255.

135. Figure 3:19 from *ANEP* 212, fig. 646.

136. Keel, *Jahwe-Visionen*, demonstrates how Yahweh's throne is depicted as winged beings (cherubim) and how it fits within ancient Near Eastern iconographic depictions of royal and divine thrones. Cf. Houtman, *Der Himmel*, 318–68.

137. See David Halperin, *The Merkavah in Rabbinic Literature* (New Haven, Conn.: American Oriental Society, 1980), and *Faces of the Chariot: Early Jewish Responses to Ezekiel's Vision* (Tübingen: J. C. B. Mohr [Paul Siebeck], 1988).

138. According to the hymn in 2 Sam. 22:11 (parallel in Ps. 18:11), when Yahweh comes from his heavenly palace, he mounts a cherub: "He mounted a cherub and flew; he appeared on the wings of the wind." Texts such as this provide a literary explanation of why Yahweh's throne was fashioned after the likeness of these mysterious beasts.

139. See Paolo Xella, "Death and the Afterlife in Canaanite and Hebrew Thought," *Civilizations of the Ancient Near East*, ed. J. M. Sasson, 3.2059–70; and William W. Hallo, "Disturbing the Dead," *Minḥah lᵉNaḥum: Biblical and Other Studies Presented to Nahum M. Sarna in Honour of his 70th Birthday*, ed. Marc Brettler and Michael Fishbane, JSOTSup 154 (Sheffield: Sheffield Academic Press, 1993), 183–92.

140. Other designations for this realm include אבדון (*'ăbaddôn*, "destruction"), קבר (*qeber*, "grave"), or בור (*bôr*, "pit"). Interestingly, שחת (*šaḥat*) can be read as if it comes from the root שוח (*šûaḥ*, "pit") or שחת (*šaḥat*, "destruction").

141. See Elizabeth Bloch-Smith, *Judahite Burial Practices and Beliefs about the Dead*, JSOTSup 123, JSOT/ASOR Monograph Series 7 (Sheffield: JSOT Press, 1992). Cf. Bloch-Smith, "The Cult of the Dead in Judah: Interpreting the Material Remains," *JBL* 111:2 (1992): 213–24; Brian B. Schmidt, *Israel's Beneficent Dead: Ancestor Cult and Necromancy in Ancient Israelite Religion and Tradition*, Forschungen zum Alten Testament 11 (Tübingen: J. C. B. Mohr [Paul Siebeck] 1994); and Ron Tappy, "Did the Dead Ever Die in Biblical Judah?" *BASOR* 298 (1995): 59–68.

142. See Michael Kleiner, *Saul in En-Dor, Wahrsagung order Totenbeschwörung?: Eine synchrone und diachrone Untersuchung zu 1 Sam. 28*, Erfurter Theologische Studien 66 (Leipzig: Benno, 1995).

143. See Bloch-Smith, *Judahite Burial Practices*, 130–32, 146–51.

144. Schmidt, *Israel's Beneficent Dead*, 241–45, 275, maintains that necromancy was a late, foreign import. Theodore J. Lewis, *Cults of the Dead in Ancient Israel and Ugarit*, HSM 39 (Atlanta: Scholars Press, 1989), finds that there was a vibrant cult of the dead

in Israel—as in the surrounding cultures—but that the Deuteronomistic, Yahweh-alone movement opposed this practice.

145. Mark S. Smith and Elizabeth M. Bloch-Smith, "Death and Afterlife in Ugarit and Israel," *JAOS* 108:2 (1988): 284.

146. Emile Puech, *La croyance des esseniens en la vie future—immortalite, resurrection, vie eternelle: histoire d'une croyance dans le judaisme ancien*, 2 vols. Etudes bibliques 21–22 (Paris: J. Gabalda, 1993), 1.55–73, thinks that these verses are some of the earliest examples of an early Jewish belief in resurrection. This is, however, a motif of national restoration and not of personal life after death; cf. George W. E. Nickelsburg, Jr., *Resurrection, Immortality, and Eternal Life in Intertestamental Judaism*, HTS 26 (Cambridge: Harvard University Press, 1972), 17–18.

147. On this theme see Lang, "Life After Death,"; *idem*, "Afterlife: Ancient Israel's Changing Vision of the World Beyond," *BibRev* 4:2 (1988): 12–23; Daniel I. Block, "Beyond the Grave: Ezekiel's Vision of Death and Afterlife," *BBR* 2 (1992): 113–41; Samuel E. Loewenstamm, "The Death of the Upright and the World to Come," *From Babylon to Canaan: Studies in the Bible and its Oriental Background* (Jerusalem: Magnes Press/Hebrew University, 1992), 28–31; and Gerhard F. Hasel, "Resurrection in the Theology of Old Testament Apocalyptic," *ZAW* 92 (1980): 267–84. Cf. John J. Collins, *Daniel: A Commentary on the Book of Daniel*, Hermeneia (Minneapolis: Fortress Press, 1993), 394–98.

148. See Klaas Spronk, *Beatific Afterlife in Ancient Israel and in the Ancient Near East* (Neukirchen-Vluyn: Neukirchener Verlag/Kevelaer: Butzon and Bercker, 1986), 315–16, 327–28, 334–40.

149. Note Michael Fishbane, *Text and Texture: Close Readings of Selected Biblical Texts* (New York: Schocken Books, 1979), 34–38.

150. See also Karel van der Toorn, "Funerary Rituals and Beatific Afterlife in Ugaritic Texts and the Bible," *BO* 48 (1991): 66.

151. See C. L. Seow, "Linguistic Evidence and the Dating of Qohelet," *JBL* 115:4 (1996): 643–66.

152. For a detailed discussion of the pertinent issues see Collins, *Daniel*, 1–71.

153. Houtman, *Der Himmel*, 282–317.

154. Figure 3.20 from Sarna, *Understanding Genesis: The Heritage of Biblical Israel* (New York: Schocken Books, 1966), 5.

155. A depiction that has many features in common with Sarna's but which is a bit more animated is that offered by F. E. Deist, "Genesis 1:1–2:4a: World View and World Picture," *Scriptura* 22 (1987): 1–17; presented also in Izak Cornelius, "The Visual Representation of the World in the Ancient Near East and the Hebrew Bible," *JNWSL* 20:2 (1994): 211.

156. Figure 3.21 by Alexandra Schober, in T. Schwegler, *Probleme der biblischen Urgeschichte* (Munich: 1960), plate 1.

157. Figure 3:22 from Victor H. Matthews and Don C. Benjamin *Old Testament Parallels: Laws and Stories from the Ancient Near East* (Mahwah, N.J.: Paulist Press, 1991), 22, fig. 10.

158. Figure 3.23 from Keel and Uehlinger, *Altorientalische Miniaturkunst*, 15, fig. 6; cf. "Das sogenannte altorientalische Weltbild," *Bibel und Kirche* 40:4 (1985): 160–61, fig. 1. For other depictions see Keel, *Symbolism*, 56–57 figs. 56, 57.

159. King, *Babylonian Boundary-Stones*, plate XCVIII.

160. These themes have been highlighted by James L. Crenshaw, *Prophetic Conflict: Its Effect Upon Israelite Religion*, BZAW 124 (Berlin: de Gruyter, 1971).

161. Kuntillet 'Ajrud pithos 1; see Ze'ev Meshel, "Kuntillet 'Ajrud—An Israelite Site from the Monarchical Period on the Sinai Border," *Qadmoniot* 9 (1976): 118–24 [Hebrew], and "Did Yahweh Have a Consort?" *BARev* 5:2 (1979): 24–36.

162. Ibid.

163. Khirbet el-Qom inscription; see William G. Dever, "Iron Age Epigraphic Material from the Area of Khirbet el-Kôm," *HUCA* 40–41 (1969–70): 139–204.

164. The literature on the inscriptions and drawings from Kuntillet 'Ajrud and the goddess figurines continues to grow; see the studies cited in the preceding notes and in note 80.

165. See my forthcoming article "Wither Elijah? The 'Ascent' of Elijah in Biblical and Extrabiblical Traditions."

166. See Alan Bernstein, *The Formation of Hell: Death and Retribution in the Ancient and Early Christian Worlds* (Ithaca, N.Y.: Cornell University Press, 1993).

Chapter 4

1. S. N. Eisenstadt, "The Axial Age Breakthroughs—Their Characteristics and Origins," *The Origins and Diversity of Axial Age Civilizations*, ed. S. N. Eisenstadt, SUNY Series in Near Eastern Studies (Albany, N.Y.: SUNY Press, 1986), 1–39. For Second Temple Period Judaism see Michael E. Stone, "Eschatology, Remythologization, and Cosmic Aporia," ibid., 241–51; and F. E. Peters, *The Harvest of Hellenism: A History of the Near East from Alexander the Great to the Triumph of Christianity* (New York: Simon and Schuster, 1970).

2. For an excellent introduction to astronomy see John D. Fix, *Astronomy: Journey to the Cosmic Frontier* (St. Louis: Mosby-Year Book, Inc., 1995). For surveys of the early history of Greek astronomy see J. L. E. Dreyer, *A History of Astronomy from Thales to Kepler*, 2d ed. (New York: Dover Publications Inc., 1953); Sir Thomas L. Heath, *Aristarchus of Samos: The Ancient Copernicus* (Oxford: Clarendon Press, 1913; reprint, New York: Dover Publications, Inc., 1981); and Heath, *Greek Astronomy* (London: J. M. Dent & Sons, Ltd., 1932; reprint, Dover Publications, 1991).

3. Otto Neugebauer, *The Exact Sciences in Antiquity*, 2d ed. (New York: Harper Torchbooks, 1962), 145–90, traces the relationships between the Near East and Greece. See also Neugebauer, "Exact Science in Antiquity," *Studies in Civilization* (Philadelphia: University of Pennsylvania Press, 1941), 22–31. Walter Burkert, *The Orientalizing Revolution: Near Eastern Influence on Greek Culture in the Early Archaic Age*, Revealing Antiquity 5 (Cambridge: Harvard University Press, 1992), 5–7, 16–18.

4. See Bartel L. van der Waerden, *Science Awakening II: The Birth of Astronomy* (Leiden/New York: Noordhoff International Publishing/Oxford University Press, 1974), 530–33.

5. Neugebauer, *Exact Sciences in Antiquity*, 4.

6. Homer, *Iliad*, xiv.246, xviii.607, and xxi.194; *Odyssey*, x.467–xii.6 and xxiv.1; Hesiod, *Works and Days*, 168–75.

7. On the Pythagoreans see Dreyer, *Astronomy from Thales to Kepler*, 35–52.

8. This idea was reintroduced by Johannes Kepler (ca. 1610 CE) after his discovery of his "Third Law of Planetary Motion," the so-called Harmonic Law. Kepler even attempted to identify actual musical notes for these sounds; see Fred Hoyle, *Astronomy* (Garden City, N.Y.: Doubleday & Co., 1962), 119. I thank my colleague Raymond E. White for bringing this to my attention.

9. See André-Jean Festugière, *Personal Religion among the Greeks* (Berkeley: University of California Press, 1954), 42–52, and Ioan P. Culianu, *Psychanodia I: A Survey of the Evidence Concerning the Ascension of the Soul* (Leiden: E. J. Brill, 1983).

10. The English term "planet" comes from the Greek term designating the celestial bodies that do not move in harmony with the fixed stars—πλανήτης (*planētēs*), "wanderer."

11. Dreyer, *Astronomy from Thales to Kepler*, 44–45, notes that there was confusion already in antiquity about the sequence of the planets. Nonetheless, in antiquity the order earth, moon, sun, Venus, Mercury, Mars, Jupiter, Saturn came to dominate. By distance the order from the earth is moon, Mercury, Venus, Sun, Mars, Jupiter, and Saturn. Uranus, Neptune, and Pluto, the "outer planets," were discovered in the eighteenth, nineteenth, and twentieth centuries, respectively.

12. See *Republic* 10 and *Timaeus* 38 c–e. For Plato's astronomy see Dreyer, *Astronomy from Thales to Kepler*, 51–86.

13. For details see Heath, *Aristarchus of Samos*, 190–212.

14. For details see Dreyer, *Astronomy from Thales to Kepler*, 87–107.

15. Aristotle, *On the Heavens*, trans. W. K. C. Guthrie LCL (Cambridge: Harvard University Press, 1945).

16. For details see Dreyer, *Astronomy from Thales to Kepler*, 108–22.

17. See *Metaphysics*, Λ. 8,1073 b 38–1074 a 15.

18. *On the Heavens* I.3 (270b, 22).

19. *Meterologica* I.3, 340b.

20. Just a few weeks before his death in 1543, Nicolaus Copernicus published his *De Revolutionibus Orbium Coelestium* in which he outlined his heliocentric cosmography. On the Copernican theory see Thomas S. Kuhn, *The Copernican Revolution: Planetary Astronomy in the Development of Western Thought* (Cambridge: Harvard University Press, 1957), and Shmuel Sambursky, "Copernicus in the Perspective of Our Generation," *Proceedings of the Israel Academy of Sciences and Humanities, Volume 5 (1971–1976)* (Jerusalem: The Israel Academy of Sciences and Humanities, 1976) 297–312.

21. See Otto Neugebauer, *A History of Ancient Mathematical Astronomy*, 3 vols. (New York/Heidelberg/Berlin: Springer-Verlag, 1975), 2.675–705.

22. Archimedes, *Psammites*, 1; translation based on Greek text in Charles Mugler, *Archimède*, 4 vols. (Paris: Les Belles Lettres, 1971), 2.135. Cf. Health, *Greek Astronomy*, 106.

23. Figure 4.2 from Othmar Keel, *The Symbolism of the Biblical World: Ancient Near Eastern Iconography and the Book of Psalms*, trans. Timothy J. Hallet (New York: Seabury Press, 1977), 34, fig. 30.

24. B. G., Trigger et al., eds., *Ancient Egypt: A Social History* (Cambridge: Cambridge University Press, 1983), 195.

25. Keel, *Symbolism*, 34–35, seems to think that each Nut and the figure of Geb enclose stars in different realms. I would suggest, however, that the stars are outside of the images. That is, they are not enclosed in any of the realms but are in the background and beyond the different realms depicted by the figures of the gods.

26. For other models of the universe according to classical Greek thought see David Furley, *The Greek Cosmologists*, 2 vols. (Cambridge: Cambridge University Press, 1987), and Neugebauer, *Ancient Mathematical Astronomy*, 2.675–705.

27. See Neugebauer, *Exact Sciences in Antiquity*, 191–207, and Dreyer, *Astronomy from Thales to Kepler*, 191–206, for detailed accounts of Ptolemaic astronomy.

28. Ptolemy, *Claudii Ptolemaei opera quae extant omnia*, vol. 2: *Opera astronomica minora*, ed. J. L. Heiberg (Leipzig: Teubner, 1907), 141. He eventually expanded this system

to forty-one spheres. For a thorough examination of Ptolemy's work see Neugebauer, *Ancient Mathematical Astronomy*, 2.834–941.

29. Cicero, *De Re Publica, De Legibus*, trans. Clinton Walker Keyes, LCL 213 (Cambridge: Harvard University Press, 1959), 269–71.

30. Cf. Cicero's *De Natura Deorum* 2.20, §§52–53 and *De Divinatione* 2.43, §91.

31. See Michael J. Crowe, *Theories of the World from Antiquity to the Copernican Revolution* (New York: Dover Publications, Inc., 1990) 32–44, and Dreyer, *Astronomy from Thales to Kepler*, 149–70.

32. This has been noted by Kuhn, *Copernican Revolution*, 59–77.

33. The title of this book was originally μαθηματική σύνταξις (*mathēmatikē suntaxis*, "the mathematical compilation"). It was later known as the μεγίστη σύνταξις (*megistē suntaxis*, "the greatest compilation"), and ultimately became known in medieval Arabic scholastic circles as simply "Al-majisti" ("the great work"), and from this it became known in the English world as the "Almagest."

34. Epigram of Ptolemy; translation by Robert Bridges quoted in Festugière, *Personal Religion Among the Greeks*, 118.

35. For general surveys see A. T. Olmstead, *History of the Persian Empire* (Chicago: University of Chicago Press, 1948), and Edwin M. Yamauchi, *Persia and the Bible* (Grand Rapids, Mich.: Baker Book House, 1990).

36. For issues see Eric M. Meyers, "Second Temple Studies in the Light of Recent Archaeology: Part I: The Persian and Hellenistic Periods," *Currents in Research: Biblical Studies* 2 (1994): 25–42. The artifactual evidence in Palestine from this period is presented by Ephraim Stern, *Material Culture of the Land of the Bible in the Persian Period 538–332 BC* (Warminster: Aris and Phillips, 1982).

37. In this regard see the articles by Elias Bickerman and Martin Hengel conveniently reprinted in *Emerging Judaism: Studies on the Fourth & Third Centuries B.C.E.*, ed. Michael E. Stone and David Satran (Minneapolis: Fortress Press, 1989) 9–45 and 147–66. Also note Dominique Auscher, "Les relations entre la Grèce et la Palestine avant la conquête d'Alexandre," *VT* 17:1 (1967): 8–30, and Meyers, "Second Temple Studies."

38. The texts are presented in Otto Neugebauer, *Astronomical Cuneiform Texts: Babylonian Ephemerides of the Seleucid Period for the Motion of the Sun, the Moon, and the Planets*, 3 vols. (Princeton: Institute for Advanced Study/London: Lund Humphries, 1955).

39. See A. Sachs, "Babylonian Horoscopes," *JCS* 6 (1952): 49–75.

40. See Ioan P. Culianu, "Astrology," *The Encyclopedia of Religion*, 16 vols., ed. Mircea Eliade (New York: Macmillan, 1987) 1.472–75, and Francesca Rochberg-Halton, "Astronomy and Calendars in Ancient Mesopotamia," *Civilizations of the Ancient Near East*, 4 vols., ed. Jack M. Sasson (New York: Charles Scribner's Sons, 1995), 3.1932–33.

41. See Waerden, *Science Awakening II*, 93–94, and Cumont, *L'Egypte des astrologues* (Bruxelles: Fondation egyptologique, 1937).

42. Waerden, *Science Awakening II*, 95, identifies the following features of Persian period astronomy/astrology: (1) Systematic, dated and recorded observations of eclipses and lunar and planetary phenomena. (2) Calculation of Periods. (3) Prediction of eclipses. (4) Division of the zodiac into 12 signs of 30° each. (5) Rise of horoscope astrology. (6) Development of mathematical astronomy.

43. Mary Boyce, *A History of Zoroastrianism*, 3 vols. (Leiden: E. J. Brill, 1975–91), 2.233. Cf. Yasna 46, 51; Vendidad VII 52. Wilhelm Bousset suggested that the idea of the soul's journey began with such a Persian myth ("Die Himmelsreise der Seele," *Archiv für Religionswissenschaft* 4 [1901]: 142–44).

44. Ioan P. Culianu, "Ascension," *Encyclopedia of Religion*, ed. Eliade (New York: Macmillan, 1987), 1.439.

45. Quoted in Waerden, *Science Awakening II*, 148.

46. F. H. Cramer, *Astrology in Roman Law and Politics* (Philadelphia: American Philosophical Society, 1954), 58.

47. On dating see Richard Janko, *Homer, Hesiod, and the Hymns* (Cambridge: Cambridge University Press, 1982).

48. Quoted from Herodotus, *The Persian Wars*, trans. George Rawlinson (New York: Random House, 1942), 144.

49. *Odyssey* 1.22–95; *Theogony* 60, 883. The Homeric epics *Iliad* and *Odyssey* and Hesiod's *Theogony* were likely written in the eighth century BCE; the Homeric *Hymn to Demeter* in the eighth or seventh century BCE.

50. Ovid *Meta* 1.175–176; *Ars Amat* 3.119.

51. *Iliad* 3.276, 19.258; *Odyssey* books 10 and 12; *Theogony* 622, 246; *Hymn to Demeter* 1–37, 375–85.

52. For texts see Otto Neugebauer and H. B. van Hoesen, *Greek Horoscopes* (Philadephia: American Philosophical Society, 1959).

53. See Francesca Rochberg-Halton, "New Evidence for the History of Astrology," *JNES* 43:2 (1984): 116–17.

54. Waerden, *Science Awakening II*, 127–204, focuses solely on Iran as the source for the origin of astral religions in the Near East and Mediterranean basin, but this seems a bit one-sided.

55. Figure 4.6 from *Études Mithriaques: Actes de Congrès IV*, Acta Iranica 17 (Leiden: E. J. Brill, 1978), plate XXI, fig. 9.

56. Compare Franz Cumont, *Astrology and Religion among the Greeks and Romans* (New York: Dover Publications, 1960), and *Mithraic Studies: Proceedings of the International Congress of Mithraic Studies, University of Manchester 1971*, ed. John R. Hinnells (Manchester: Manchester University Press/Totowa, N.J.: Rowman and Littlefield, 1975).

57. David Ulansey, *Origins of Mythraic Mysteries: Cosmology and Salvation in the Ancient World* (New York: Oxford, 1989).

58. *PGM* IV.476–829; English translation in *The Greek Magical Papyri in Translation, Including the Demotic Spells*, ed. Hans Dieter Betz (Chicago: University of Chicago Press, 1985), 48–54.

59. Betz, *Greek Magical Papyri*, 48.

60. See Michael A. Williams, *Rethinking "Gnosticism": An Argument for Dismantling a Dubious Category* (Princeton: Princeton University Press, 1996).

61. See Kurt Rudolph, *Gnosis: The Nature and History of Gnosticism*, trans. Robert McLachan Wilson (San Francisco: Harper & Row, 1987), 171–204.

62. Apuleius, *Metamorphoses*, 11.21.

63. See Franz Cumont, *Afterlife in Roman Paganism* (New Haven: Yale University Press, 1922; reprint New York: Dover Books, 1959), 91–109, and Martin Hengel, *Judaism and Hellenism: Studies in Their Encounter in Palestine During the Early Hellenistic Period*, 2 vols. (Philadelphia: Fortress Press, 1974), 1.196–202. In this regard note Daniel 12:2–3: "Many of those that sleep in the dust of the earth will awake, some to everlasting life, and some to taunts and everlasting abhorrence. The wise will shine like the brightness of the sky; and those who lead the many to righteousness will be like the stars for ever and ever." This second century biblical text is the first Jewish text to mention explicitly the idea of resurrection and the righteous joining the celestial realms. A later and possibly Jewish epitaph from Corycos, Cilicia in modern-day Turkey also contains

this theme: "Do not despair. No one is immortal except the One who has ordered this to happen, who has placed us in the sphere of the planets" (*CII* 788).

64. All quotes from the Odyssey are taken from Homer, *The Odyssey*, 2 vols., trans. A. T. Murray, rev. George E. Dimock, LCL (Cambridge: Harvard University Press, 1995). On the theme of Hades in Homeric thought see Alan E. Bernstein, *The Formation of Hell: Death and Retribution in the Ancient and Early Christian Worlds* (Ithaca, N.Y.: Cornell University Press, 1993), 23–33.

65. Cf. *Iliad* 23.69–70; *Odyssey* 11.71–78. For a general survey of some issues of afterlife in the period, see Charles Penglase, "Some Concepts of Afterlife in Mesopotamia and Greece," *The Archaeology of Death in the Ancient Near East*, ed. Stuart Campbell and Anthony Green, Oxbow Monographs 15 (Oxford: Oxbow Books, 1995), 209–20.

66. *Odyssey* 24.204. Cf. 10.175, 564; 11.64–65; 12.21; 15.348–50; 20.207–8; 24.24,1–18, 264; *Iliad* 7.131; 17.855–57; 23.19–23, 179. There seems to be a contradiction here, but perhaps the island Odysseus visits is simply the "intersection" between Hades and earth. Odysseus reached this island at night and then dug a pit and performed a ritual intended to initiate the "descent."

67. Bernstein, *Formation of Hell*, 33.

68. See especially *Iliad* 11 and 24. Note the touchingly sad account of Odysseus' attempt to embrace his mother in Hades as his arms pass through her as if she were a ghost (11.204–24).

69. Regarding Greek myths about these realms, see Paul Capelle, "Elysium und die Inseln der Seligen," *Archiv für Religionswissenschaft* 25/26 (1927/28): 245–64/17–40; Helen F. North, "Death and Afterlife in Greek Tragedy and Plato," *Death and Afterlife: Perspectives of World Religions*, ed. Hiroshi Obayashi (New York: Greenwood Press, 1992), 49–64; and Culianu, *Psychanodia I*. The first century CE Jewish historian Josephus attributes to the Essenes a belief that after death the virtuous souls go to "an abode beyond the ocean, a place not oppressed by rain, snow, or heat, but refreshed by a gentle west wind from the ocean. . . . It seems to me that the Greeks had the same conception when they set apart the Isles of the Blessed for their brave men whom they call heroes and demigods" (*War*, 2.155).

70. See Lewis Richard Farnell, *Greek Hero Cults and Ideas of Immortality* (Oxford: Clarendon Press, 1921; reprint 1970), and Martin P. Nilsson, *A History of Greek Religion*, 2d ed., trans. F. J. Fielden (Oxford: Clarendon Press, 1949).

71. Quoted from *Pindar*, 2 vols., ed. and trans. William H. Race, LCL 56, 485; (Cambridge: Harvard University Press, 1997), 1.69–71.

72. See Plato, *Phaedo*, 85E–86D; 91C–95A; 115C–D; and 246E–249D; and Bousset, "Himmelsreise der Seele."

73. Book 10, 614A–621D.

74. Cicero, *De Re Publica, De Legibus* (tr. Keyes) 265, 279, 283. The Roman poet Vergil (70–19 BCE) describes ancient Greek beliefs about netherworldly punishments that purify a soul so that it might be reincarnated into a physical body; see *Aeneid* book 6.

75. *Epigrammata graeca ex lapidibus conlecta*, ed. Georgius Kaibel (Berlin: Reimer, 1878), 2.

76. *CPJ* 1510 (3.157).

77. E. A. Wallis Budge, *The Book of the Dead: An English Translation of the Chapters, Hymns, Etc., of the Theban Recension, with an Introduction, Notes, Etc.*, 2d ed., 3 vols. in 1 (London: Routledge & Kegan Paul Ltd., 1960), 1.lvii.

78. See the dated but still relevant essays reprinted in Stone and Satran, *Emerging Judaism*.

79. See now John M. G. Barclay, *Jews in the Mediterranean Diaspora: From Alexander to Trajan (323 BCE–117 CE)* (Edinburgh: T&T Clark, 1996).

80. See Morton Smith, *Palestinian Parties and Politics That Shaped the Old Testament* (New York: Columbia University Press, 1971), 57–81, 227–37, now reprinted in Stone and Satran, *Emerging Judaism*, 103–28. For the archaeological evidence for Persian and Greek influence in this period see Stern, *Material Culture*, and Charles E. Carter, "A Social and Demographic Study of Post-Exilic Judah," (Ph.D. diss., Duke University, 1991).

81. John Strange, "Hellenism in Archaeology," *In the Last Days: On Jewish and Christian Apocalyptic and its Period*, ed. Knud Jeppesen, Kirsten Nielsen and Bent Rosendal (Esbjerg, Denmark: Aarhus University Press, 1994), 175–80, suggests that based on the archaeological evidence of cultural continuity, the "Hellenistic Period" is better understood as lasting from Alexander to the Abbasids, roughly 300 BCE to 750 CE. Also in this regard see Meyers, "Second Temple Studies," 30, and Hans-Peter Kuhnen, *Palästina in griechisch-römischer Zeit*, Handbuch der Archäologie, Vorderasien 2.2 (München: C. H. Beck'sche Verlagsbuchhandlung, 1990), 43–69.

82. See Inge Nielsen, "The Hellenistic Palaces of the Jewish Kings," *In the Last Days*, 181–84, and Nielsen, *Hellenistic Palaces: Tradition and Renewal* (Esbjerg, Denmark: Aarhus University Press, 1994).

83. Saul Lieberman, *Greek in Jewish Palestine: Studies in the Life and Manners of Jewish Palestine in the II–IV Centuries C.E.* (New York: Jewish Theological Seminary of America, 1942), 21; cf. Elias J. Bickerman, "The Historical Foundations of Postbiblical Judaism," *The Jews: Their History, Culture, and Religion*, 2 vols., ed. Louis Finkelstein, 3d ed. (New York: Jewish Publication Society of America, 1960), 1.93–94.

84. This has been detailed by Saul Lieberman in several important publications: *Greek in Jewish Palestine*; *Hellenism in Jewish Palestine: Studies in the Literary Transmission, Beliefs and Manners of Palestine in the I Century B.C.E.–IV Century C.E.* (New York: Jewish Theological Seminary of America, 1950); and "How Much Greek in Jewish Palestine?" *Biblical and Other Studies*, ed. Alexander Altman, Philip W. Lown Institute of Advanced Judaic Studies: Studies and Texts 1 (Cambridge, Mass.: Harvard University Press, 1963), 123–41.

Chapter 5

1. Hans Bietenhard, *Die himmlische Welt im Urchristentum und Spätjudentum*, WUNT 2 (Tübingen: Verlag J. C. B. Mohr/Paul Siebeck, 1951); Alan F. Segal, "Heavenly Ascent in Hellenistic Judaism, Early Christianity and their Environment," *ANRW* II:23:2 (1980): 1333–94; James D. Tabor, *Things Unutterable: Paul's Ascent to Paradise in Its Greco-Roman, Judaic, and Early Christian Contexts* (Lanham, Md.: University Press of America, 1986); and Martha Himmelfarb, *Ascent to Heaven in Jewish and Christian Apocalypses* (New York/ Oxford: Oxford University Press, 1993). Note also Gerhard Lohfink, *Die Himmelfahrt Jesu: Untersuchungen zu den Himmelfahrts und Erhöhungstexten bei Lukas*, SANT 26 (Kösel: Verlag München, 1971), 51–74; and Adela Yarbro Collins, "The Seven Heavens in Jewish and Christian Apocalypses," *Death, Ecstasy, and Other Worldly Journeys*, ed. John J. Collins and Michael Fishbane (Albany: SUNY Press, 1995), 59–93.

2. On this issue see, Robert A. Kraft, "The Multiform Jewish Heritage of Early Christianity," *Christianity, Judaism and Other Greco-Roman Cults*, ed. Jacob Neusner (Leiden: E. J. Brill, 1975), 184–87.

3. For introductory issues see "1 Enoch," *The Apocryphal Old Testament*, ed. H. F. D. Sparks (Oxford: Clarendon Press, 1984), 169–84; E. Isaac, "1 (Ethiopic Apoca-

lypse of) Enoch," *OTP*, 1.5–12; and Michael E. Stone, "Apocalyptic Literature," *Jewish Writings of the Second Temple Period*, ed. Michael E. Stone, CRIANT, II:2 (Assen/ Philadelphia: Van Gorcum/Fortress Press, 1984), 395–406. For a thorough treatment of the textual base for this pseudepigraphon see M. A. Knibb, *The Ethiopic Book of Enoch: A New Edition in the Light of the Aramaic Dead Sea Fragments*, 2 vols. (Oxford: Clarendon Press, 1978), 2.1–52.

4. In 1:4 the Ethiopic text reads: ". . . and God will appear in the strength of his power from heaven." The Greek version, however, reads ". . . from the heaven of the heavens" (see Matthew Black, *Apocalypsis Henochi Graece*, PVTG 13 [Leiden: E. J. Brill, 1970], 19). This is not an indication of plural heavens but a phrase inspired by the biblical phrase שְׁמֵי הַשָּׁמַיִם, i.e., "vast heaven."

5. On the complex relationships between the traditions embedded here see the discussion between Paul D. Hanson, "Rebellion in Heaven, Azazel, and Euhemeristic Heroes in 1 Enoch 6–11," *JBL* 96:2 (1977): 195–233, and George W. E. Nickelsburg, "Apocalyptic and Myth in 1 Enoch 6–11," *JBL* 96:3 (1977): 383–405. This discussion is critiqued by John J. Collins, "Methodological Issues in the Study of I Enoch: Reflections on the Articles of P. D. Hanson and G. W. E. Nickelsburg," *Society of Biblical Literature 1978 Seminar Papers*, 2 vols., ed. Paul J. Achtemeier (Missoula, Mont.: Scholars Press, 1978), 1.315–22, and Divorah Dimant, "1 Enoch 6–11: A Methodological Perspective," ibid., 1.323–39.

6. According to Larson, in the several Greek manuscripts of 1 Enoch the Aramaic plural form is rendered by the Greek plural form, οὐρανοί, only four times and by the singular form, οὐρανός, 52 times; see Erik W. Larson, "The Translation of Enoch: From Aramaic into Greek" (Ph.D. diss., New York University, 1995), 270–71. The singular form is standard Greek usage while the plural is "translation Greek," i.e., inspired by biblical idiom.

7. Cf. 1 Enoch 13:10; 14:3–5; 15:2–10; 16:2–3.

8. On the nature of the divine response to the Watchers' pleas, see Jonathan Paige Sisson, "Intercession and the Denial of Peace in 1 Enoch 12–16," *Hebrew Annual Review* 11, ed. Reuben Ahroni (Columbus: Ohio State University, 1987), 371–86.

9. David J. Halperin, *The Faces of the Chariot: Early Jewish Responses to Ezekiel's Vision* (Tübingen: J.C.B. Mohr/Paul Siebeck, 1988), 81–82, notes the cultic ideology here: Enoch has become the heavenly High Priest mediating in the Holy of Holies on behalf of sinning beings, much like the Israelite High Priest on the Day of Atonement. As in the ideology of the Temple, God alone resides in the Holy of Holies. The angelic beings Enoch saw are like the priests who cannot enter the Holy of Holies but who stand and sing outside. As the narrative develops, there is an implication that Enoch is greater than the angels who were already there singing praises to God because he is addressed individually and is brought near to God. Martha Himmelfarb, "From Prophecy to Apocalypse: The Book of Watchers and Tours of Heaven," *Jewish Spirituality: From the Bible Through the Middle Ages*, World Spirituality: An Encyclopedic History of the Religious Quest, vol. 13 (New York: Crossroad, 1986), 149–53, and *Ascent to Heaven*, 14–23, also notes that in this text the divine presence is located in a heavenly temple.

10. Was this account patterned after ancient Near Eastern models (see Pierre Grelot, "La géographie mythique d'Hénoch et ses sources orientales," *RB* 65 [1958]: 33–69; Rykle Borger, "Die Beschwörungsserie *bīt mēseri* und die Himmelfahrt Henochs," *JNES* 33 [1974]: 183–96; and J. T. Milik, *The Books of Enoch: Aramaic Fragments of Qumran Cave 4* [Oxford: Clarendon Press, 1976], 29–31, 37–38)? Or was it patterned after Greek models (see R. H. Charles, *The Book of Enoch* [Oxford: Clarendon Press, 1912], 38, and George W. E. Nickelsburg, *Jewish Literature Between the Bible and the*

Mishnah [Philadelphia: Fortress Press, 1981], 54, 66, n. 27)? Rather than decide in favor of one over the other, it may be that this motif had become common property of both civilizations long before the time this text was written. That such may indeed be the case is made plausible by the many parallels between the Homeric and Enochic geographies delineated by Grelot, "La géographie mythique d'Hénoch," 50, cf. 53–54, 63–64.

11. Gilgamesh traveled to a mountain where heaven and earth meet, Epic of Gilgamesh ix.2.1–5. See H. Lundin Jansen, *Die Henochgestalt: Eine Vergleichende Religionsgeschichtliche Untersuchung* (Oslo: I Kommisjon Hos Jacob Dybwad, 1939), 73.

12. The items described in 18:1–5 customarily appear in a tour through the celestial realms and do not, properly speaking, belong on the earthly plane. Either the author is simply listing serially items that apocalyptic seers typically encounter on their ascents without noticing that these things are customarily located in the heavenly realms, or in the cosmography of this author these items are actually found at the mythic ends of the earth.

13. Pillars of heaven appear in Job 26:11. The four winds of heaven appear in Zech. 2:10, 6:5; Dan 8:8, 11:4. Note that these are all late biblical texts.

14. On the connection of prevailing winds on earth and the movements of the celestial bodies, see F. Rochberg-Halton, "New Evidence for the History of Astrology," *JNES* 43:2 (1984): 118–23, 127–29.

15. See Charles, "I Enoch" *APOT*, 2.68, 199, 201; and Isaac, "1 Enoch," *OTP*, 1.22, 24.

16. Nickelsburg, *Jewish Literature*, 54–55, views these as a collection of supplementary traditions about Enoch's travels. Even if these are supplementary traditions, they have been integrated into a coherent account of a journey to the farthest reaches of the earth.

17. These demonstrative explanations of the things encountered by the seers in their otherworldly tours are explained thoroughly by Martha Himmelfarb, *Tours of Hell: An Apocalyptic Form in Jewish and Christian Literature* (Philadelphia: Fortress Press, 1983), 41–67. On the exegesis of dreams in general see Michael Fishbane, *Biblical Interpretation in Ancient Israel* (Oxford: Clarendon/New York: Oxford University Press, 1985), 443–524.

18. On the technique of "repetitive resumption" see Shemaryahu Talmon, "The Presentation of Synchroneity and Simultaneity in Biblical Narrative," *Studies in Hebrew Narrative Art Through the Ages*, ed. Joseph Heinemann and S. Werses, Scripta Hierosolymitana 27 (Jerusalem: Magnes Press, 1978) 9–26.

19. See George W. E. Nickelsburg, Jr., *Resurrection, Immortality, and Eternal Life in Intertestamental Judaism*, HTS 26 (Cambridge: Harvard University Press, 1972), 134–37.

20. The place of holding until judgment is located at the mythical ends of the earth and not in the underworld as is otherwise common in biblical tradition. Grelot, "La géographie mythique d'Hénoch," 41, notes that although the biblical materials do not describe the path one takes to arrive at the entrance to Sheol, this Enochic passage may preserve some otherwise unknown ancient Hebrew tradition on this matter (cf. Isa. 38:10).

21. This journey to the east corresponds to his previous journey to the west (Grelot, "La géographie mythique d'Hénoch," 42). J. T. Milik, "Hénoch au pays des aromates," *RB* 65 (1958): 70–77, provides a botanical identification of the plants mentioned in the account of the journey, and attempts to demonstrate that this narrative depicts a journey along the trade routes from Israel to India. Moshe Gil, "Enoch in the Land of Eternal Life," *Tarbiz* 38:4 (1969): 322–37 [Hebrew], using the same botanical information

concluded that this is not a journey to the eastern land of spices, but is a metaphorical journey in which the plants symbolize Enoch's passage into the realm of eternal life. According to Gil, (p. 331), all these plants are native to Syria-Palestine, so there is no need to locate them in India or other eastern regions. Moreover, according to Gil, these plants were used traditionally in connection with the burying of the dead. As a result, the journey and the plants depict a symbolic journey into the realm of eternal life, the journey all humans take at death (pp. 333–35). Gil's intriguing thesis has not, in my opinion, successfully disproven Milik's interpretation. The journey to the east to acquire some kind of superhuman knowledge has a long history in ancient Near Eastern mythology beginning at least with the Epic of Gilgamesh. Moreover, two independent but complimentary studies, P. Grelot, "La legend d'Henoch dans les Apocryphes et dans la Bible: origin et signification," *RSR* 46 (1958): 5–26, and Jansen, *Die Henochgestalt*, have clearly demonstrated that the depiction of the figure of Enoch in 1 Enoch is based on ancient Near Eastern models; cf. Helge S. Kvanvig, *Roots of Apocalyptic: The Mesopotamian Background of the Enoch Figure and of the Son of Man*, WMANT 61 (Neukirchen-Vluyn: Neukirchener Verlag, 1988). Milik's idea about the journey into the land of fragrances and spices fits with this overall model and explains the evidence better than Gil's symbolic interpretation.

22. Ethiopic reads "north," but the Aramaic reads "northeast" (see Milik, "Hénoch au Pays des Aromates," 71, and Knibb, *Ethiopic Book of Enoch*, 2.120–21).

23. Both Milik, "Hénoch au Pays des Aromates," 72, 75–76, and Grelot, "La géographie mythique d'Hénoch," 42–43 translate "Erythrean Sea."

24. The darkness is mentioned only in the Aramaic fragment (see Milik, "Hénoch au Pays des Aromates," 71). Grelot, "La géographie mythique d'Hénoch," 43, following Milik, "Hénoch au Pays des Aromates," 76, thinks the Ethiopic "Zotiel" is a corruption of Greek ζόφος or ζοφώδης. This term appears in Classical Greek usage for the "nether darkness" or the dark region of the world customarily located in the west, though in the north according to Strabo, 10.2.12. See ζόφος in Henry George Liddell and Robert Scott, eds., *A Greek-English Lexicon, with a Supplement*, rev. ed. by Henry Stuart Jones (Oxford: Clarendon Press, 1968), 756–57.

25. As Grelot has pointed out, "La géographie mythique d'Hénoch," 43–44, the author of this portion of the Enochic corpus has either creatively exegeted Gen. 2–3 by identifying two Edenic locales, one in the extreme northwest where the divine being resides and one in the extreme northeast, or he has depended on a then-current interpretation of the mythic geography of Genesis 2–3. In this regard the biblical text is understood to mean that there was once one Edenic region in the northeast, but after the "Fall" God moved his residence to the northwest and along with it the Tree of Life. The traditions about the northern, mountainous residence of God common to many Syro-Palestinian religions fits with this conception. The eastern "garden" was still accessible and here the antediluvian heroes learned their secrets. The western "garden" was where Enoch resided following his ascension (cf. 1 Enoch 70–71).

26. Knibb, *Ethiopic Book of Enoch*, 2.124–25.

27. See chapter 4 and note Homer, *Odyssey* x.467–xii.6 and xxiv.1; Hesiod, *Works and Days* 168–75; and Herodotus, *Persian Wars*, iv.36.

28. *On the Heavens*. For an excellent account of the development of ancient geography, see E. H. Bunbury, *A History of Ancient Geography: Among the Greeks and Romans from the Earliest Ages Till the Fall of the Roman Empire*, 2 vols. (London: John Murray, 1979).

29. Strabo, *Geography*, ii,2.

30. Strabo, *Geography*, i.7, ii.5; Pliny, *Natural History*, ii.108.

31. J. T. Milik, the original editor of the 1 Enoch material, claimed that at Qumran there was what amounted to an "Enochic Pentateuch." In this Enochic Pentateuch, however, there were no Parables of Enoch (also known as the "Book of the Similitudes"), which Milik considered a Christian composition from the third century CE (Milik, *Books of Enoch*, 92–96). Few have followed Milik in this, preferring to date the "Parables" to the first century CE at the latest. The definitive refutation of Milik's thesis is that by Jonas C. Greenfield and Michael E. Stone, "The Enochic Pentateuch and the Date of the Similitudes," *HTR* 70:1–2 (1977): 51–65, who identify this as a Jewish text from the first century BCE. David W. Suter, *Tradition and Composition in the Parables of Enoch*, SBLDS 47 (Missoula, Mont.: Scholars Press, 1979), dates the Similitudes between the mid-first century BCE and the latter part of the first century CE. See also Jonas C. Greenfield, "Prolegomena," in Hugo Odeberg, *3 Enoch or the Hebrew Book of Enoch*, rev. ed. (New York: KTAV Publishing House, 1973), xi–xlii; and Michael A. Knibb, "The Date of the Parables of Enoch: A Critical Review," *NTS* 25 (1979): 345–59, who claims that they were written by a Jew shortly after the Jewish revolt against Rome in 66–73 CE. Compare also Ephraim Isaac, "The Oldest Ethiopic Manuscript (K-)* of the Book of Enoch and Recent Studies of the Aramaic Fragments of Qumran Cave 4," *"Working With No Data": Semitic and Egyptian Studies Presented to Thomas O. Lambdin*, ed. David M. Golomb (Winona Lake, Ind.: Eisenbrauns, 1987), 204–6.

32. See Suter, *Tradition and Composition*, 1–33. An example of the older source-critical approach of separating a text into its allegedly original units can be found in Beer, "Das Buch Henoch," *APAT*, 2.227–28, and Charles, *Book of Enoch*, 64–65.

33. On the beasts around the throne see Halperin, *Faces of the Chariot*, 38–48, 115–29.

34. Some scholars assume that Noah was the recipient of this vision; see 1 Enoch 60:8, Charles, *Book of Enoch*, 112, and Knibb, *Ethiopic Book of Enoch*, 2.142. However, 1 Enoch 68:1 makes it clear that this section contains material that Noah learned from Enoch before the Flood: "And after this my great-grandfather Enoch gave me the explanation of all the secrets in a book and the parables which had been given to him; and he put them together for me in the words of the Book of the Parables."

35. According to Grelot, "La Géographie mythique d'Hénoch," 44, the location of Behemoth is best placed to the north of the place in the northwest identified as the region of the righteous where God resides and where Enoch ascended (chapters 70–71). The mythic monsters of the sea (Yamm) and the desert (Mot) are an ancient pair attested in the late second millennium BCE texts of Ugarit where they are the enemies of Baal; see Andrée Herdner, *Corpus des tablettes en cunéiformes alphabétiques découvertes à Ras Shamra-Ugarit*, 2 vols., MRS 10 (Paris: Imprimerie Nationale, 1963), 1–6. These mythic creatures were subdued by Yahweh according to ancient Israelite mythology (Isa. 43:16–21; Deut. 32:7–14). An account of the subsequent development of the Leviathan-Behemoth theme in Jewish tradition is provided by Jefim Schirmann, "The Battle Between Behemoth and Leviathan According to an Ancient Hebrew *Piyyut*," *Proceedings of the Israel Academy of Sciences and Humanities; Volume 4, 1969–1970* (Jerusalem: The Israel Academy of Sciences and Humanities, 1971), 327–69.

36. On the various locations of "the garden" in this book see 18:6, 32:2–3, 70:2–4 and 77:3. See also Charles, *Book of Enoch*, 59.

37. As Michael E. Stone has demonstrated, "Lists of Revealed Things in the Apocalyptic Literature," *Magnalia Dei: The Mighty Acts of God, Essays on the Bible and Archaeology in Memory of G. Ernest Wright*, ed. Frank Moore Cross, Werner E. Lemke and Patrick D. Miller, Jr. (Garden City, N.Y.: Doubleday & Company, Inc., 1976), 414–52, these lists demonstrate a central interest in cosmological speculation among the early

Jewish apocalypticists. Regarding their location and function within the apocalypse, Stone notes that "these lists occur as summaries of information revealed to the seers. Such lists are to be found either as the high point of visionary experiences or as summaries of the subject matter revealed in the context of later recapitulation of visionary experiences" (p. 435).

38. The several Qumran manuscripts of the Astronomical Book indicate that the text type represented in the Ethiopic version is an abbreviated form of text type represented in the Qumran Aramaic fragments. For this see J. T. Milik, "Hénoch au Pays des Aromates." Whether the Ethiopic translation depends primarily upon the Greek or upon the Aramaic with some recourse to the Greek is debated. For dependence on the Greek see H. F. D. Sparks, "1 Enoch," *AOT* 175–76, and Stone, "Apocalypses," 405. For the view that the Ethiopic translator(s) depended primarily on the Aramaic with some recourse to the Greek see E. Ullendorf, "An Aramaic 'Vorlage' of the Ethiopic Text of Enoch," *Atti del Convegno Internazionale di Studi Etiopici* (Rome: Academia Nazionale dei Lincei, 1960), 259–67, reprinted in Ullendorf, *Ethiopia and the Bible*, Schweich Lectures, 1967 (London: Oxford, 1968), 61–62, and Knibb, *Ethiopic Book of Enoch*, 2.37–46. For the text of the fragments and accompanying translations, see Milik, *The Books of Enoch*, 274–97.

39. That Enoch was believed to have received this type of knowledge is apparent from Jubilees 4:17: "And he was the first among men that are born on earth who learnt writing and knowledge and wisdom and who wrote down the signs of heaven according to the order of their months in a book, that men might know the seasons of the years according to the order of their separate months" (quoted from R. H. Charles, "The Book of Jubilees," *APOT*, 2.18). For additional information on the antiquity of the traditions about Enoch's cosmological knowledge, see Milik, *Books of Enoch*, 8–10; James C. VanderKam, *Enoch: A Man for All Generations*, Studies on Personalities of the Old Testament (Columbia, S.C.: University of South Carolina Press, 1995); and Christfried Böttrich, "Astrologie in der Henochtradition," *ZAW* 109:2 (1997): 222–45.

40. Milik, *The Books of Enoch*, 273–74, and Michael E. Stone, "The Book of Enoch and Judaism in the Third Century BCE," *CBQ* 40 (1978): 479–92.

41. This is in contrast to Martin Hengel's "pietistic" groups—see his *Judaism and Hellenism: Studies in Their Encounter in Palestine During the Early Hellenistic Period* (Philadelphia: Fortress Press, 1974), 1.175–218—and to Paul Hanson's "heirocratic" groups—see his *The Dawn of Apocalyptic* (Philadelphia: Fortress Press, 1975).

42. Text in Menahem Stern, *Greek and Latin Authors on Jews and Judaism: Edited with Introductions, Translations and Commentary*, 3 vols. (Jerusalem: Israel Academy of Sciences and Humanities, 1974–84), 1.10.

43. See Jonas C. Greenfield and Michael E. Stone, "The Books of Enoch and the Traditions of Enoch," *Numen* 26 (1979): 89–103.

44. See Bartel L. van der Waerden, *Science Awakening II: The Birth of Astronomy* (Leiden/New York: Noordhoff International Publishing/Oxford University Press, 1974), 80–86, 205–49.

45. Compare *2 Enoch* 1–15 and 3 Apoc. Bar 6. The sun being drawn across the sky in a chariot is a motif with deep roots in Israelite religion. One image of Yahweh is as the sun, and like the sun gods of the neighboring cultures, some Israelites imaged their god as the sun riding in a chariot. See J. Glen Taylor, *Yahweh and the Sun: Biblical and Archaeological Evidence for Sun Worship in Ancient Israel*, JSOTSup 111 (Sheffield: Sheffield Academic Press, 1993), and Matthias Albani, *Astronomie und Schöpfungsglaube: Untersuchungen zum Astronomischen Henochbuch*, WMANT 68 (Neukirchen-Vluyn: Neukirchener Verlag, 1994), 155–56.

46. The belief that the celestial bodies passed through "gates" in order to enter into the visible sky began with the ancient Babylonians; see Wolfgang Heimpel, "The Sun at Night and the Doors of Heaven in Babylonian Texts," *JCS* 38:2 (1986): 127–51. For additional speculation on the names and sizes of the sun, see 1 Enoch 78:1–5. CD X.14–17 states that cessation of work on Friday evening begins when the sun reaches a distance equivalent to its diameter above the "gate." It seems likely that the text is referring to some such celestial gates. Cf. Matthias Albani and Uwe Glessmer, "Un instrument de mesures astronomiques à Qumrân," *RB* 104:1 (1997): 108–11.

47. The calendar of 1 Enoch 72–82, based on the reckoning of the movements of the sun, begins at the spring equinox when the hours of daylight begin to outnumber the hours of darkness. The calculations of the intensity of the sun's light and the length of the day in this section are the closest early Jewish attempts to imitate the vast body of Greek mathematical astronomy; see Otto Neugebauer, *A History of Ancient Mathematical Astronomy* (New York/Heidelberg/Berlin: Springer–Verlag, 1975). In general the material here parallels, but is technically inferior to, the calculations in the Mesopotamian "Astrolabes" and *MUL.APIN* texts; see Hermann Hunger and David Pingree, *MUL.APIN: An Astronomical Compendium in Cuneiform*, AfO 24 (Horn, Austria: Verlag Ferdinand Berger & Söhne Gesellschaft, 1989), and Francesca Rochberg-Halton, "Astronomy and Calendars in Ancient Mesopotamia," *Civilizations of the Ancient Near East*, 4 vols., ed. Jack M. Sasson (New York: Charles Scribner's Sons, 1995), 3.1925–40.

48. Aristotle, *Meteorologics*, ii.1.16, noted that there were earlier meteorologists who held views similar to this. This was also the view of the Greek astronomer Anaximenes (ca. 585–526); see J. L. E. Dreyer, *A History of Astronomy from Thales to Kepler*, 2d ed. (New York: Dover Publications Inc., 1953), 16, and Sir Thomas L. Heath, *Aristarchus of Samos: The Ancient Copernicus* (Oxford: Clarendon Press, 1913; reprint, New York: Dover Publications, Inc., 1981), 40–41.

49. For the fragmentary Aramaic texts of 4QEn[ast] describing the movements of the moon, see Milik, *The Books of Enoch*, 278–84. The calculations here are again modeled on, but inferior to, older Mesopotamian lunar observations and calculations to be found in the series Enûma Anu Enlil and are certainly inferior to Greek computations; see B. L. van der Waerden, "Babylonian Astronomy, III: The Earliest Astronomical Computations," *JNES* 10 (1951): 20–34, and F. N. H. Al-Rawi and A. R. George, "Enuma Anu Enlil XIV and Other Early Astronomical Tables," *AfO* 38–39 (1991–92): 52–73. Similar descriptions of the phases of the moon are found among the Qumran Scrolls; note especially 4Q317.

50. See Otto Neugebauer, "Notes on Ethiopic Astronomy," *Or* 33 (1964): 59–60.

51. Michael E. Stone, "Enoch, Aramaic Levi and Sectarian Origins," *JSJ* 19:2 (1988): 159–70, has noted that this book provides insight into its author's interest in earlier Mesopotamian astronomical models that had become obsolete in the Greco-Roman world. Note also Otto O. Neugebauer, *The "Astronomical" Chapters of the Ethiopic Book of Enoch (72–82)*, Royal Danish Academy of Sciences and Letters, Mathematics-Physics Series 40/10 (Copenhagen: Munksgaard, 1981). Neugebauer, based on his considerable knowledge of ancient mathematics and astronomy, also concludes that this material is likely more indebted to earlier Babylonian speculations than to later Hellenistic or Persian influences (p. 4). Neugebauer claims that one cannot specify, however, the exact time period when the speculations of 1 Enoch 72–82 were likely to have been recorded. He notes that many of the traditions represented here had a long life in the ancient world; they even survived the development of more advanced methods (p. 12). See also Uwe Glessmer, "Das astronomische Henoch-Buch als Studienobjekt," *Biblische*

Notizen 36 (1987): 69–129, and Glessmer, "Horizontal Measuring in the Babylonian Astronomical Compendium Mul.Apin and in the Astronomical Book of 1 En.," *Henoch* 18 (1996): 259–82.

52. Examples of contemporary but much more precise astronomical calculations can be found in Otto Neugebauer, *Astronomical Cuneiform Texts: Babylonian Ephemerides of the Seleucid Period for the Motion of the Sun, the Moon, and the Planets,* 3 vols. (London/ Princeton: Lund Humphries/Institute for Advanced Study, 1955), vol. 2. See also Uwe Glessmer, "Horizontal Measuring."

53. This follows the accepted definition of an apocalypse provided by John J. Collins and the Apocalypse Group of the SBL Genres Project in *Apocalypse: The Morphology of a Genre,* Semeia 14 (Missoula, Mont.: Scholars Press, 1979), 9: "'*Apocalypse' is a genre of revelatory literature with a narrative framework, in which a revelation is mediated by an otherworldly being to a human recipient, disclosing a transcendent reality which is both temporal, insofar as it envisages eschatological salvation, and spatial insofar as it involves another, supernatural world.*"

54. Shemaryahu Talmon, "The 'Dead Sea Scrolls' or 'The Community of the Renewed Covenant'?" *Echoes of Many Texts: Reflections on Jewish and Christian Traditions—Essays in Honor of Lou H. Silberman,* ed. William G. Dever and J. Edward Wright, BJS 313 (Atlanta: Scholars Press, 1997), 129–45.

55. In general see Lawrence H. Schiffman, *Reclaiming the Dead Sea Scrolls: The History of Judaism, the Background of Christianity, the Lost Library of Qumran* (Philadelphia: Jewish Publication Society, 1994), and James C. VanderKam, *The Dead Sea Scrolls Today* (Grand Rapids, Mich.: Eerdmans, 1994).

56. Devorah Dimant, "Men as Angels: The Self-Image of the Qumran Community," *Religion and Politics in the Ancient Near East,* ed. Adele Berlin (Bethesda, Md.: University Press of Maryland, 1996) 93–103.

57. See Jonas Greenfield and Michael Sokoloff, "Astrological Omens in Jewish Palestinian Aramaic" *JNES* 48:3 (1989): 210–14 and *idem,* "An Astrological Text from Qumran (4Q318) and Reflections on some Zodiacal Names," *RevQ* 16 (1995): 507–25. Cf. James H. Charlesworth, "The Jewish Interest in Astrology during the Hellenistic and Roman Period," *ANRW* II, 20.2 (1987) 926–50; Lester J. Ness, "Astrology and Judaism in Late Antiquity," Ph.D. diss., Miami University (Ohio), 1990; and Albani, *Astronomie und Schöpfungsglaube,* 83–87, 123–29.

58. Albani and Glessmer, "Un instrument de mesures astronomiques," 88–115, regard it as a type of sundial; cf. Albani, Glessmer and Gerd Grasshoff, "An Instrument for Determining the Hours of the Day and the Seasons (Sundial)," *A Day at Qumran: The Dead Sea Sect and Its Scrolls,* ed. Adolfo Roitman (Jerusalem: Israel Museum, 1997), 20–22; and Emanuel Tov et al., *The Dead Sea Scrolls on Microfiche: A Comprehensive Facsimile Edition of the Texts from the Judean Desert* (Leiden: E. J. Brill, 1993), "Companion Volume," 89.

59. Research on the Qumran calendrical texts and system is vast, but note especially Shemaryahu Talmon, "The Calendar Reckoning of the Sect from the Judaean Desert," *Aspects of the Dead Sea Scrolls,* ed. Chaim Rabin and Yigael Yadin, Scripta Hierosolymitana 4 (Jerusalem: Magnes Press/Hebrew University, 1965), 162–99.

60. Lawrence H. Schiffman, "4QMysteries[a]: A Preliminary Edition and Translation," *Solving Riddles and Untying Knots: Biblical, Epigraphic, and Semitic Studies in Honor of Jonas C. Greenfield,* ed. Ziony Zevit, Seymour Gitin, and Michael Sokoloff (Winona Lake, Ind.: Eisenbrauns, 1995), 227.

61. As Schiffman notes, "4QMysteries[a]," 228, the scribe mistakenly wrote עד here, perhaps dittography from בעד.

62. Note Liddell and Scott, *Greek-English Lexicon*, 1273. Note also Hans Bietenhard, "Heaven, Ascend, Above—οὐρανός," *NIDNTT*, 2.191. For plural Greek forms see 2 Macc. 15:23; 3 Macc. 2:2; Wisd 9:10; and Tobit 8:5.

63. Note Helmut Traub, "Septuagint and Judaism," *TDNT* 5.509–11.

64. For text see Marc Philonenko, *Joseph et Aséneth: Introduction, texts critique, traduction et notes*, Studia Postbiblica 13 (Leiden: E. J. Brill, 1968).

65. On the role of conversion in this text see Randall D. Chesnutt, *From Death to Life: Conversion in Joseph and Aseneth*, JSPSup 16 (Sheffield: Sheffield Academic Press, 1995).

66. This term is the typical LXX term to render רקיע, "firmament" (Gen. 1). Greek text of Joseph and Aseneth from C. Burchard, "Ein vorläufiger griechischer Text von Joseph und Asenet," *Dielheimer Blätter zum Alten Testament* 14 (1979): 2–53 and printed in Albert-Marie Denis, *Concordance grecque des pseudepigraphes d'Ancien Testament* (Leiden: E. J. Brill, 1987) 851–59.

67. Liddell and Scott, *Greek-English Lexicon*, 1910.

68. Two versions (Syriac and Armenian) locate this in different heavens. The Syriac version reads the "third" heaven, while the Armenian reads "second" heaven; see C. Burchard, "Joseph and Aseneth," *OTP* 2.239, n. 22s.

69. On this see Nickelsburg, *Resurrection, Immortality, and Eternal Life*, 138–40.

70. Michael E. Stone, *Fourth Ezra: A Commentary on the Book of Fourth Ezra*, Hermeneia (Minneapolis: Fortress, 1990), 219–20, 238–46, and Stone, "A New Edition and Translation of the *Questions of Ezra*," *Solving Riddles and Untying Knots*, ed. Zevit et al., 294.

71. See Hans Lewy, *Chaldean Oracles and Theurgy: Mysticism Magic and Platonism in the Later Roman Empire*, new ed., ed. Michel Tardieu (Paris: Études Augustiniennes, 1978), 413–25.

72. Hermann Cremer, *Biblico-Theological Lexicon of New Testament Greek*, trans. William Urwick (Edinburgh: T. & T. Clark, 1895; Reprint 1977) 465.

73. Matt 5:3//Luke 6:20; Matt 13:11//Mark 4:11//Luke 8:10; Matt 13:31//Mark 4:30//Luke 13:18. Cf. Gerhard Schneider, "'Im Himmel—auf Erden,' eine Perspektive matthäischer Theologie," *Studien zum Matthäusevangelium: Festschrift für Wilhelm Pesch*, ed. Ludger Schenke (Stuttgart: Verlag Katholisches Bibelwerk, 1988), 283–97; and Kari Syreeni, "Between Heaven and Earth: On the Structure of Matthew's Symbolic Universe," *JSNT* 40 (1990): 3–13.

74. For modern trends in research on this apocalypse see Frederick J. Murphy, "The Book of Revelation," *Currents in Research: Biblical Studies* 2 (1994): 181–225.

75. David E. Aune, "The Influence of Roman Imperial Court Ceremonial on the Revelation of John," *BibRev* 28 (1983): 5–26.

76. A recent commentary on the book of Revelation—Bruce J. Malina, *On the Genre and Message of Revelation: Star Visions and Sky Journeys* (Peabody, Mass.: Hendrickson, 1995)—reads the entire book as astral prophecy based on astronomical observations.

77. See Albert-Marie Denis, *Introduction aux pseudépigraphes grecs d'Ancien Testament*, SVTP 1 (Leiden: E. J. Brill, 1970), 91–92, and Stone, "Greek Apocalypse of Ezra," *OTP*, 1.563.

78. See Stone, "Greek Apocalypse of Ezra," *OTP*, 1.563, 571, n. i.

79. For texts and descriptions see Himmelfarb, *Tours of Hell*. Note that punishments are meted out in the heavenly realms also in Quest. Ezra, Apoc. Sedr., Test. Levi, 2 Enoch, and Gn. Apoc. Paul.

80. Greek text in *Apocalypsis Esdrae, Apocalypsis Sedrach, Visio Beati Esdrae*, ed. Otto Wahl, PVTG 4 (Leiden: E. J. Brill, 1977), 25–34.

81. It could be argued that Ezra is not in heaven at this point but back on earth, for the text does not state explicitly that Ezra is still in heaven. My reconstruction of Ezra's movements is based on the current state of the text. The text is composed of several sources and the juxtaposition of these sources does not produce a coherent narrative. Given this, one could argue that the text in its current form has simply left Ezra in heaven at 5:19 and switched to a new source at 5:20 that has Ezra moving to the east on the surface of earth and visiting "Paradise" on this plane. The well-known tradition of Paradise being on the earthly plane would lie behind such an explanation of these difficult passages. That a paradise was thought to be located in the heavenly realm is attested in LAE 25–29, 37:3–5; Apoc. Mos. 1:1–2, 29:5, 37:3–5, 40:1; Test. Abr. 11:1–4; Apoc. Sedr., 9:1, and 16:5–7.

Chapter 6

1. Quotation from Michael A. Knibb, *The Ethiopic Book of Enoch: A New Edition in the Light of the Aramaic Dead Sea Fragments*, 2 vols. (Oxford: Oxford University Press, 1978), 2.166.

2. Ibid. 166–67.

3. See James H. Charlesworth, "Treatise of Shem," *OTP*, 1.473–86.

4. Quotation from Charlesworth, "Treatise of Shem," *OTP*, 1.477.

5. Cf. Michael Wise, Martin Abegg, Jr., and Edward Cook, *The Dead Sea Scrolls: A New Translation* (New York: HarperCollins, 1996) 245.

6. Charlesworth, "Treatise of Shem," *OTP*, 1.477.

7. See M. de Jonge, "The Testament of Levi and 'Aramaic Levi'," *RevQ* 13 (1988): 367–70, and Robert A. Kugler, *From Patriarch to Priest: The Levi-Priestly Tradition from "Aramaic Levi" to "Testament of Levi,"* Early Judaism and Its Literature 9 (Atlanta: Scholars Press, 1996).

8. Robert A. Kraft, "Christian Transmission of Greek Jewish Scriptures: A Methodological Probe," *Paganisme, Judaïsme, Christianisme: Influences et affrontements dans le monde antique, Mélanges offerts à Marcel Simon*, ed. André Benoit, Marc Philonenko, and Cyrille Vogel (Paris: Éditions E. De Boccard, 1978), 207–26, addresses the methodological issues in determining whether a document was originally Jewish or Christian.

9. See John J. Collins, "Testaments," *Jewish Writings of the Second Temple Period*, ed. Michael E. Stone, CRIANT, II:2 (Philadelphia/Assen: Fortress Press/Van Gorcum, 1984), 342–43.

10. The various texts are published in Michael E. Stone and Jonas C. Greenfield, "Aramaic Levi Documents," *Qumran Cave 4, XVII: Parabiblical Texts, Part 3*, ed. G. Brooks et al., DJD XXII (Oxford: Clarendon Press, 1996) 1–72. Cf. R. H. Charles, *The Greek Versions of the Testaments of the Twelve Patriarchs, Edited from Nine MSS. together with the Variants of the Armenian and Slavonic Versions and Some Hebrew Fragments* (Oxford: Clarendon Press, 1908; reprint, Hildesheim: Georg Olms Verlagsbuchhandlung, 1960) 245–56; J. T. Milik, "Le Testament de Lévi en araméen," *RB* 62 (1955): 398–406; Milik, *The Books of Enoch: Aramaic Fragments of Qumran Cave 4* (Oxford: Clarendon Press, 1976) 23–25; D. Barthélemy and J. T. Milik, *Qumran Cave 1*, DJD I (Oxford: Oxford University Press, 1955), 87–91; and Kugler *Patriarch to Priest*, 61–138. A translation of the various fragments by Jonas C. Greenfield and Michael E. Stone appears as "Appendix III: The Aramaic and Greek Fragments of a Levi Document," *The Testaments of the Twelve Patriarchs: A Commentary*, ed. H. W. Hollander and M. de Jonge, SVTP 8 (Leiden: E. J. Brill, 1985), 457–69.

11. See M. de Jonge, *The Testaments of the Twelve Patriarchs: A Study of Their Text, Composition and Origin*, 2d ed. (Assen: Van Gorcum, 1975), 39–42, 129–31; Jonas C. Greenfield and Michael E. Stone, "Remarks on the Aramaic Testament of Levi from the Geniza," *RB* 86 (1979): 227–29; and Hollander and de Jonge, *Commentary*, 17–24, 130.

12. Note also James C. VanderKam, "The Scrolls, the Apocrypha, and the Pseudepigrapha," *Hebrew Studies* 34 (1993): 45; and Kugler, *Patriarch to Priest*, 171–74.

13. Various opinions on the date of this text are summarized in Kugler, *Patriarch to Priest*, 131–38.

14. "Die Textüberlieferung der Testamente der zwölf Patriarchen," *ZNW* 63 (1972): 24–44; reprinted in *Studies on the Testaments of the Twelve Patriarchs: Text and Interpretation*, ed. M. de Jonge, SVTP 3 (Leiden: E. J. Brill, 1975), 45–62.

15. Charles, *Greek Versions of the Testaments of the Twelve Patriarchs*; and Charles, "The Testaments of the Twelve Patriarchs," *APOT*, 2.304–6.

16. This is assumed also by Hans Bietenhard, *Die himmlische Welt im Urchristentum und Spätjudentum*, WUNT 2 (Tübingen: Verlag J. C. B. Mohr/Paul Siebeck, 1951), 3–4, and H. C. Kee, "Testaments of the Twelve Patriarchs," *OTP*, 1.788 n. d.

17. The prayer induces the vision. On induction techniques see Daniel Merkur, "The Visionary Practices of the Jewish Apocalyptists," *The Psychoanalytic Study of Society*, vol. 14, ed. L. Bryce Boyer and Simon A. Grolnick (Hillsdale, N.J.: The Analytic Press, 1989), 119–48, and "Prophetic Initiation in Israel and Judah," *The Psychoanalytic Study of Society*, vol. 12, ed. L. Bryce Boyer and Simon A. Grolnick (Hillsdale, N.J.: The Analytic Press, 1988) 37–67. Probably the most thorough and balanced review of this issue is that of Martha Himmelfarb, "The Practice of Ascent in the Ancient Mediterranean World," *Death, Ecstasy, and Other Worldly Journeys*, ed. John J. Collins and Michael Fishbane (Albany: SUNY Press, 1995), 123–37. Himmelfarb notes that what is commonly taken to be techniques intending to induce a vision or ascent are actually practices that make the seer worthy to ascend or receive the vision. The initiative for these events depends not on the seer but on God who grants them to worthy people.

18. Neither Charles nor de Jonge et al. included this section in their editions and translations. The Greek text of "e" can be found in *The Testaments of the Twelve Patriarchs: A Critical Edition of the Greek Text*, ed. M. de Jonge, H. W. Hollander, H. J. de Jonge, and Th. Korteweg, PVTG 1.2 (Leiden: E. J. Brill, 1978), 25, and is translated by Greenfield and Stone, "Aramaic and Greek Fragments," 458–60.

19. On this prayer see Jonas C. Greenfield and Michael E. Stone, "Two Notes on the Aramaic Levi Document," *Of Scribes and Scrolls: Studies on the Hebrew Bible, Intertestamental Judaism, and Christian Origins Presented to John Strugnell on the Occasion of his Sixtieth Birthday*, ed. Harold W. Attridge, John J. Collins, and Thomas H. Tobin, College Theology Society Resources in Religion 5 (Lanham, Md.: University Press of America, 1990), 153–58.

20. Compare the words of the request in ALD and Gk. Test. Levi manuscript "e" verse 17—εἰσάκουσον δὲ καὶ τῆς φωνῆς τοῦ παιδός σου Λευὶ γενέσθαι σοι ἐγγύς, with Gk. Test. Levi 2:9b–10a—ὅτε ἀνελθῇς ἐκεῖ ὅτι σὺ ἐγγὺς κυρίου στήσῃ. The latter passage is virtually a literal fulfillment of the request in the former.

21. 4QTLevi[a] I:12–13. The text is in Stone and Greenfield, "Aramaic Levi Documents," 28; cf. Milik, "Le Testament de Lévi en araméen," 400–401.

22. See de Jonge, "Testament of Levi and 'Aramaic Levi'," 368–69.

23. This statement refers to the celestial waters that produce the rains. The idea derives from simple observation and from the cosmology of Gen. 1:6–8; cf. Ps. 148:4; 1 Enoch 54:8; Jub. 2:4; Test. Abr 8:3(B), 3 Apoc. Bar 2:1; and 2 Enoch 3:3(J), 4:2(A).

24. On the origin and development of the angelic class "thrones," see Saul M. Olyan, *A Thousand Thousands Served Him: Exegesis and the Naming of Angels in Ancient Judaism*, Texte und Studien zum Antiken Judentum 36 (Tübingen: J. C. B. Mohr [Paul Siebeck], 1993) 61–66.

25. Michael E. Stone, "Abel-Meholah," *Encyclopedia Judaica*, 16 vols. (Jerusalem: Keter Publishing House Ltd., 1971), 2.62, suggests that Abel-Maoul is a corruption of Abel-Meholah, a mountain in central Palestine. The text of the ALD here has the name "Abel-Main" (cf. 1 Kings 15:26; 2 Chr. 16:4), a mountain in the extreme north of Palestine. See also Milik, "Le Testament de Lévi en araméen," 403–5. George W. E. Nickelsburg, "Enoch, Levi, and Peter: Recipients of Revelation in Upper Galilee," *JBL* 100 (1981): 575–600, notes that several visions are said to have occurred in this region, and he identifies the mountain as Mt. Hermon.

26. See also Mary Dean-Otting, *Heavenly Journeys: A Study of the Motif in Hellenistic Jewish Literature*, Judentum und Umwelt 8 (Frankfort am Main/Bern/New York: Peter Lang, 1984) 87, for a possible reconstruction of the stages in Levi's ascent.

27. As Bietenhard notes, *Die himmlische Welt*, 4, the textual difficulties have confused the structure here. According to the two Greek recensions of the text at this point, the great sea is located either in the first heaven or between the first and second heavens. This motif of the sea suspended in the first heaven occurs also in Re'uyot Yehezqel (*BM*, 2:131). The idea developed from Gen. 1:7–8: "And God made the atmosphere and separated between the water which is under the atmosphere and the water which is above the atmosphere. And it was so. And God called the atmosphere sky. And there was evening and there was morning, the second day." As Re'uyot Yehezqel indicates, some explained the term שמים (*šamayim*), sky, as deriving from or meaning שם מים (*šam mayim*), "there is water there."

28. Compare 1 Enoch 14, 41:1–9, 44:1, 59:1–3, 60:11–22; 2 Enoch 5:1–6:1.

29. A similar dissonance between a vision and its angelic interpretation occurs in 4 Ezra 13, the "Son of Man" vision. On this see Michael E. Stone, "The Concept of the Messiah in IV Ezra," *Religions in Antiquity: Essays in Memory of Erwin Ramsdell Goodenough*, ed. Jacob Neusner (Leiden: E. J. Brill, 1968), 295–312, and Stone, *Fourth Ezra: A Commentary on the Book of Fourth Ezra*, Hermenia (Minneapolis: Augsburg Fortress, 1990), 396–400.

30. Such ethical exhortations are characteristic of the testaments. See Walter Harrelson, "The Significance of 'Last Words' for Intertestamental Ethics," *Essays in Old Testament Ethics*, ed. James T. Crenshaw and J. T. Willis (New York: KTAV, 1974), 203–13. Cf. Hollander and de Jonge, *Commentary*, 36–38.

31. There is, however, another way to read this form of the text based on how one reads and translates the initial words of 3:5 and 8. The ἐν τῷ μετ᾽ αὐτῶν of the "α" family may be read as ἐν τῷ μετ᾽ αὐτόν, that is, "in the one next to it," meaning the one below. This is the reading adopted by Charles, "The Testaments of the Twelve Patriarchs," *APOT*, 2.306. This does not seem to be the best translation, however. Had the author intended the next lower heaven, he had a precise phrase to indicate exactly this, namely ἐν τῷ ὑποκάτω. The author used this phrase in 3:7 to indicate "in the heaven below it," and the sense is immediately clear. Moreover, if one follows Charles, the result is not three heavens but four: the first is at 3:8, the second at 3:7, the third at 3:5, and the fourth, "the highest," at 3:4. It seems better to translate the opening phrase of 3:5 and 3:8 as "in the heaven with him/them." The result is a three-heaven cosmography.

32. οἱ δὲ εἰς τὸν τέταρτον ἐπάνω τούτων ἅγιοί εἰσιν (*Critical Edition*, 27). Cf. Charles, "The Testaments of the Twelve Patriarchs," *APOT*, 2.305; Kee, "Testaments of the Twelve Patriarchs," *OTP*, 1.789; and Dean-Otting, *Heavenly Journeys*, 87.

33. *Commentary*, 136.

34. Although the parallels they cite explicitly describe heaven as "holy," *Commentary*, 138, this does not mean that Gk. Test. Levi 3:3 does the same. The context is determinative, and here the context is concerned with the content or inhabitants of the heavens.

35. At 3:5 and 3:8 there is a problem regarding the preposition μετά and the case of the object it governs. If μετά governs the accusative αὐτόν as in the edition of de Jonge, then the thrones, authorities, and angels of praise are in the next lower heaven, the fifth (Liddell and Scott, *Greek-English Lexicon*, 1109; cf. Dean-Otting, *Heavenly Journeys*, 87). Otherwise, the variant reading with μετά governing the genitive αὐτῶν would indicate that these heavenly beings are located "with" the angels of sixth heaven (Liddell and Scott, *Greek-English Lexicon*, 1108d-9a). If this is the case, then the angel's comments in 3:4–6 describe the seventh (if the "highest of all" in 3:4 is the seventh) and 3:7–8 describe the sixth. The narrative skips the fifth heaven, while 2:7–3:3 describes heavens one through four and 3:4–8 describes heavens seven and six.

36. As Gk. Test. Levi 8 and the Aramaic Levi fragments suggest, Levi was appointed both priest and warrior. See P. Grelot, "Notes sur le Testament Araméen de Levi," *RB* 63 (1956): 393–97.

37. This is detailed in Martha Himmelfarb, *Ascent to Heaven in Jewish and Christian Apocalypses* (New York/Oxford: Oxford University Press, 1993).

38. See Charles, "The Testaments of the Twelve Patriarchs," *APOT*, 2.304; Bietenhard, *Die himmlische Welt*, 3–4; and Kee, "Testaments of the Twelve Patriarchs," *OTP*, 1.788–89. Adela Yarbro Collins, "The Seven Heavens in Jewish and Christian Apocalypses," *Death, Ecstasy, and Other Worldly Journeys*, ed. Collins and Fishbane, 62–66, relates the three-heaven schema to the three heavenly levels mentioned in the Mesopotamian text *KAR* 307 (see pp. 43–45 above). A. Y. Collins connects several three-heaven models with this Mesopotamian model, but given the cultural and chronological separation between all these texts, I doubt that any such Mesopotamian connection exists.

39. J. W. Hunkin, "The Testaments of the Twelve Patriarchs," *JTS* 16 (1915): 80–97, and de Jonge, "Die Textüberlieferung der Testamente der zwölf Patriarchen," 45–62.

40. Note also James H. Charlesworth, *The Old Testament Pseudepigrapha and the New Testament* (Cambridge: Cambridge University Press, 1985), 65.

41. See Andrew T. Lincoln, *Paradise Now and Not Yet: Studies in the Role of the Heavenly Dimension in Paul's Thought with Special Reference to His Eschatology*, SNTSMS 43 (Cambridge: Cambridge University Press, 1981), 71–73.

42. Bousset, "Himmelsreise der Seele," 143, maintains that "third heaven" and "Paradise" are two different stages in the ascent. Paradise in located in the third heaven also in Apoc. Mos. 37:5 and 2 Enoch 8:1. On the early Christian traditions locating "Paradise" in the third heaven see P. Ildefonse de Vuippens, *La paradis terrestre au troisième ciel: Exposé historique d'une conception chrétienne des premiers siècles* (Fribourg/Paris: Librairie de l-oeuvre de S.-Paul/Librairie Saint-François d'Assise, 1925), 134–37, 144.

43. Quoted from M. A. Knibb, "Martyrdom and Ascension of Isaiah," *OTP* 2.164–65.

44. See Merkur, "Visionary Practices," and David Halperin, "Heavenly Ascension in Ancient Judaism: The Nature of the Experience," *Society of Biblical Literature 1987 Seminar Papers*, ed. Kent Harold Richards (Atlanta: Scholars Press, 1987), 218–32.

45. This issue is treated well in Lincoln, *Paradise Now and Not Yet*, 77–84; note also Bientenhard, *Die himmlische Welt*, 166.

46. Note also Friedrich Blass and Albert Debrunner, *A Greek Grammar of the New Testament and Other Early Christian Literature*, trans. and rev. Robert W. Funk (Chicago: University of Chicago Press, 1961), §141.

47. *Philo IV*, trans. F. H. Colson and G. H. Whitaker, LCL 261 (Cambridge: Harvard University Press, 1932), 393, 395.

48. *Philo II*, trans. F. H. Colson and G. H. Whitaker, LCL 227 (Cambridge: Harvard University Press, 1929), 21, 23.

49. *Philo, Supplement I: Questions and Answers on Genesis*, trans. Ralph Marcus, LCL 380 (Cambridge: Harvard University Press, 1953), 352.

50. *Philo IV*, 425.

51. See Martin Hengel, *The "Hellenization" of Judaea in the First Century after Christ* (Philadelphia: Trinity Press International, 1989).

52. For introductory issues see M. R. James, *The Testament of Abraham*, Texts and Studies 2:2, ed. J. Armitage Robinson (Cambridge: Cambridge University Press, 1892), 1–76. George W. E. Nickelsburg, Jr., "Structure and Message in the Testament of Abraham," *Studies on the Testament of Abraham*, ed. George W. E. Nickelsburg, Jr., SBLSCS 6 (Missoula, Mont.: Scholars Press, 1976), 85–93, refers to it as "a non-testament."

53. Test. Abr. 9:5–6A; translation based on Greek text in Michael E. Stone, *The Testament of Abraham: The Greek Recensions*, SBLTT 2, Pseudepigrapha Series 2 (Missoula, Mont.: Society of Biblical Literature, 1972), 20, 22.

54. The standard critical edition of this text is Francis Schmidt, *Le Testament grec d'Abraham* (Tübingen: J. C. B. Mohr/Paul Siebeck, 1986). Following Stone, *Testament of Abraham*, and E. P. Sanders, "Testament of Abraham," *OTP*, 1.871–902, I designate the long recension "A" and the short recension "B."

55. Test. Abr. 9:8A. The parallel for this in recension B 8:2–3 reads: "and the Lord replied to Michael, 'Go and take Abraham up in the body and show him everything, and whatever he says to you, do it for him because he is my friend.' So Michael went forth and took Abraham up in the body on a cloud, and he brought him to the river Okeanus."

56. On ether and the ethereal realm, see Mary B. Hesse, "Models in Physics," *British Journal for the Philosophy of Science*, 4 (1958): 198–214.

57. God's words to Michael were, "lead Abraham up to the first gate of heaven" (ἀνάγαγε δὲ τὸν Ἀβραὰμ ἐν τῇ πρώτῃ πύλῃ τοῦ οὐρανοῦ). But the account of the event says that Michael "led Abraham to the east, to the first gate of heaven" (ἤνεγε τὸν Ἀβραὰμ ἐπὶ τὴν ἀνατολὴν ἐν τῇ πύλῃ τῇ πρώτῃ τοῦ οὐρανοῦ). See Schmidt, *Testament*, 128–29, for the textual issues.

58. This image parallels the idea in Apoc. Zeph. where Mt. Seir is the crossroad or intersection between heaven, earth, and Hades. There is a place, according to these traditions, at the mythic ends of the earth where one's fate is decided, and after the fateful decision has been made, sinners proceed to the region of punishment while the righteous go to the region of reward. This image seems also to lie behind the "wide and narrow gates" referred to by Jesus (Mt. 7:13–14). Note also the Gn. Apoc. Paul 22:2–10.

59. On the traditions about Abel as judge and martyr, see M. Delcor, "De l'origine de quelques traditions contenues dans le Testament d'Abraham," *Proceedings of the Fifth World Congress of Jewish Studies, The Hebrew University Mount Scopus-Givat Ram; Jerusalem, 3–11 August 1969* (Jerusalem: World Union of Jewish Studies, 1969), 192–200.

60. Compare 9:8A and 15:12A with 8:3B and 12:1B.

61. Quoted from Plato, *The Republic*, trans. Paul Shorey, 2 vols., LCL (Cambridge: Harvard University Press, 1937), 2.493.

62. In recension A 20:14 "the garden" (Paradise) is the place for the final disposition of the righteous.

63. Several theological differences between the two versions of the Testament of Abraham are highlighted by Anitra Bingham Kolenkow, "The Genre Testament and the Testament of Abraham," *Studies on the Testament of Abraham*, ed. Nickelsburg, 149 n. 1.

64. The manuscripts of this apocalypse were transmitted in a confused state. This problem was resolved by Georg Steindorf in *Die Apokalypse des Elias: Eine unbekannte Apokalypse und Bruchstücke der Sophonias-Apokalypse*, TU 17.3 (Leipzig: J. C. Hinrichssche Buchhandlung, 1899). For an English translation and introduction see O. S. Wintermute, "Apocalypse of Zephaniah," *OTP*, 1.497–515, or K. H. Kuhn, "The Apocalypse of Zephaniah and an Anonymous Apocalypse," *AOT*, 919–25.

65. This phrase reminds one of the statement in the Gnostic Apocalypse of Paul where it is said of God's throne that it was "brighter than the sun by seven times" (Gn. Apoc. Paul 22:29–30; see *The Nag Hammadi Library*, 3d rev. ed., ed. James M. Robinson [San Francisco: Harper & Row Publishers, 1988], 259).

66. Translation based on text in Albert-Marie Denis, *Fragmenta Pseudepigraphorum Quae Supersunt Graeca*, PVTG 13 (Leiden: E. J. Brill, 1970), 129.

67. Compare Gk. Test. Levi 2:5; 5:2; Test. Abr. 11:1–4(A), 8:3(B).

68. "Seir" here likely derives from Judges 5:4–5, one of the oldest hymns in the Bible; see David Noel Freedman, "'Who is Like Thee Among the Gods?' The Religion of Early Israel," *Ancient Israelite Religion*, ed. Patrick D. Miller, Paul D. Hanson, and S. Dean McBride (Philadelphia: Fortress Press, 1987), 316–36. Seir may refer to the Sinai region and perhaps Mt. Sinai and the events that transpired there. The author of the Apocalypse of Zephaniah, however, was unaware of the transformations in ancient Israelite mythology that took traditions about Mt. Seir in Edom and transferred them to the developing complex of traditions about Mt. Sinai and Yahweh. On the various holy mountain traditions among Israel and its neighbors, see Richard J. Clifford, *The Cosmic Mountain in Canaan and the Old Testament*, HSM 4 (Cambridge: Harvard University Press, 1972).

69. A change into heavenly garments typically accompanies an ascent or transition into the heavenly realm. Cf. 1 Enoch 62:15–16, 71:1, 90:31; 2 Enoch 22:8–10; 3 Enoch (Sepher Hekhalot) 12:1–2, 18:22; Apoc. Abr. 13:14; Apoc. Pet. 13; Asc. Isa. 8:14; 9:2, 9, 17–18, 24–26; Pirqe R. El. 33 (Friedlander, 245); *Alphabet of Rabbi Aqiba*, Kaph (*BHM*, 3.33–34). See also Martha Himmelfarb, "From Prophecy to Apocalypse: The Book of the Watchers and Tours of Heaven," *Jewish Spirituality: From the Bible Through the Middle Ages*, ed. Arthur Green (New York: Crossroad, 1986), 152, and Himmelfarb, *Tours of Hell: An Apocalyptic Form in Early Jewish and Christian Literature* (Philadelphia: Fortress Press, 1988), 156–57; and John Strugnell, "The Angelic Liturgy at Qumran—4QSerek Šîrôt 'Olat Haššabbat," VTSup 7 (1960), 340.

70. This is noted also by Himmelfarb, *Ascent to Heaven*, 32. I would not, however, follow Himmelfarb (p. 51) in concluding that the single heaven cosmography of the Coptic text suggests an earlier date. One cannot use cosmography, i.e., single versus multiple heavens, to determine a text's date.

71. This has been noted also by Himmelfarb, *Ascent to Heaven*, 58–59.

72. The Martyrdom of Isaiah is likely a Jewish work composed in the second century BCE; see M. A. Knibb, "Martyrdom and Ascension of Isaiah," *OTP*, 2.143, 146–47, 149 and Charlesworth, *PMR*, 125–26.

73. The so-called "Testament of Hezekiah" and the Ascension of Isaiah are generally regarded as Christian compositions of the first or second century CE; see Knibb,

"Martyrdom and Ascension," 143, 147–48, and Charlesworth, *PMR*, 125–26, 149–50. A. Y. Collins, "Seven Heavens," 77, notes that the Ascension of Isaiah is probably the oldest Christian text to make use of the seven-heaven schema.

74. On the psychic nature of the experience note David Halperin, *The Faces of the Chariot: Early Jewish Responses to Ezekiel's Vision* (Tübingen: J. C. B. Mohr [Paul Siebeck], 1988), 66 who observes how this is a "vivid and realistic-sounding account of a shamanistic trance."

> The visionary loses consciousness, though his eyes remain wide and staring; his soul seems to leave his inert body and travel through distant realms; only when he comes to himself again can he tell his audience what he has seen. . . . I know of nothing in the Jewish apocalyptic literature that is comparable, in that it gives a circumstantial account of a trance which creates the impression that the author experienced or witnessed something of the kind.

Halperin cites the Acts of Thomas 5–8 and Hekalot Rabbati (*BM*, 1.91–98) as exhibiting similar psychic energy. Contrary to Halperin's skepticism about the reality of these experiences (pp. 67–69), regarding them as arising primarily from a driving exegetical interest, I would maintain that these often reflect the real psychic experiences of the authors of these pseudonymous works. Halperin demonstrates, conclusively in my opinion, that there was an exegetical interest behind these texts. But can it not be that the people who were involved in this exegetical scrutiny of the traditions might also have so thoroughly ingrained these beliefs in their consciousness that their alternate state experiences (visions/dreams) were based on their reconfigurations of the traditional materials? That is to say, they saw in their visions exactly what they had taught themselves to see. For more on this topic especially as it relates to apocalyptic materials, see Daniel Merkur, "The Visionary Practices." On the possibility that an apocalypse mirrors the actual psychological state of the author, see Stone, *Fourth Ezra*, 21–33.

75. This text is expanding a tradition reflected in Hebrews 4:14 that says that Jesus passed through the heavens on his way to earth: "Having, therefore, a great high priest who has passed through the heavens, Jesus the son of God, let us hold firmly to the confession." On Jesus in the seventh heaven as found in fragments of this text see Denis, *Fragmenta Pseudepigraphorum*, 105.

76. Theodore Silverstein, *Visio Sancti Pauli: The History of the Apocalypse in Latin Together with Nine Texts* (London: Christophers, 1935), offers a complete treatment of the manuscript evidence for this text. An English translation can be found in Hugo Duensing and Aurelio de Santos Otero, "Apocalypse of Paul," *New Testament Apocrypha*, rev. ed., ed. Edgar Hennecke, Wilhelm Sneemelcher, and R. McL. Wilson, 2 vols. (Cambridge/Louisville, Ky.: James Clarke/Westminster/John Knox Press, 1991–92), 2.712–48. Note also R. Casey, "The Apocalypse of Paul," *JTS* 34 (1933): 1–32, and Himmelfarb, *Tours of Hell*, 18–19.

77. "Apocalypse of Paul," 719.

78. For the Latin text see M. R. James, *Apocrypha Anecdota*, Texts and Studies 2:3, ed. J. Armitage Robinson (Cambridge: Cambridge University Press, 1893), 1–42.

79. On the theme of angelic opposition to human ascent into the heavenly realm see Peter Schäfer, *Rivalität zwischen Engeln und Menschen*, Studia Judaica (Berlin: Walter de Gruyter, 1975), and Joseph P. Schultz, "Angelic Opposition to the Ascension of Moses and the Revelation of the Law," *JQR* 61 (1970–71): 282–307. In order to ascend safely there are a multitude of rituals one must perform; see Michael D. Swartz, "'Like Ministering Angels': Ritual and Purity in Early Jewish Mysticism and Magic," *AJSRev* 19:2 (1994): 135–67.

80. This event takes place at Mt. Seir according to Apoc. Zeph., and at the river Okeanus (8:3B) or at the gate of the first heaven (11–15A) according to Test. Abr.

81. Cf. Silverstein, *Visio Sancti Pauli*, 136, 149, 153, 156, 205, 209.

82. The theme of Lake Acherusia and the Isles of the Blessed has a long history in Greek thought and appears frequently in early Jewish and Greek thought. Compare, for example, Homer, *Odyssey* iv.561–69; Hesiod, *Works and Days* 167–73; Apoc. Sedr. 2, 9; Apoc. Mos. 37; 3 Apoc. Bar 10:2; Apoc. Pet. 14; Sib. Or. 2:234–39.

83. These include the Virgin Mary (§46); Abraham, Isaac, Jacob and the 12 Patriarchs (§47); Moses (§48); Isaiah, Jeremiah, and Ezekiel (§49); Noah (§50); Elijah and Elisha, Enoch, Zechariah and John the Baptist, Cain, and Adam (§51).

84. For a translation of this text see George W. MacRae and William R. Murdock, "The Apocalypse of Paul," *The Nag Hammadi Library*, 256–59.

85. This idea is found also in the "Hermetic Corpus," a collection of materials attributed pseudepigraphically to the Hellenistic-Egyptian god Hermes Trismégiste. In the tractate "Poimandres" we read of a soul passing through the spheres on its way to God after death:

> And thus one finally starts upward through the composite framework, handing over in the first heavenly sphere the agencies of growth and waning away; in the second, the means of evil action—a craft henceforth inactive; in the third, the deception of desire—henceforth inactive; in the fourth, eminence associated with rule—henceforth free from avarice; in the fifth, impious arrogance and the rashness of recklessness; in the sixth, evil pretexts for wealth; in the seventh heavenly sphere, plotting falsehood. And next, stripped of the composite framework's effects and having only one's very own power, one comes to the nature of the eighth heaven and along with the existents lifts up praise unto the parent. And those who are present rejoice together at one's advent. So having assimilated to those who are also there, one hears also certain powers that exist superior to the nature of the eighth heaven lifting up praise unto god with a kind of sweet voice. And next, in an orderly manner they ascend to the parent and personally hand themselves over to become powers, and by becoming powers they come to be within god. Such is the good end of those who possess acquaintance: to become god.

Poimandres 26, quoted from Bentley Layton, *The Gnostic Scriptures* (Garden City, N.Y.: Doubleday and Co. 1987), 457–58; cf. Bousset, "Himmelsreise," 267.

86. For other traces of the eight-heaven cosmography, see Apocryphon of John 11:4; Epiphanius, *Against Heresies*, 1.5.2; 40.2.3; 26.10.1–4; and Hypostasis of the Archons 95:13–96:3.

87. The (First) Apocalypse of James 26:13–18, translation in *The Nag Hammadi Library*, 263.

88. See Iraneaus, *Against Heresies*, 1.24.3.

89. For general descriptions see Kurt Rudolph, *Gnosis: The Nature and History of Gnosticism* (San Francisco: Harper and Row Publishers, 1987) 67–70; and Michael A. Williams, *Rethinking "Gnosticism": An Argument for Dismantling a Dubious Category* (Princeton: Princeton University Press, 1996).

90. See J. Edward Wright, "Baruch: His Evolution from Loyal Scribe to Apocalyptic Seer," *Biblical Figures Outside the Bible*, ed. Michael E. Stone and Theodore Bergren (Philadelphia: Trinity Press International, 1998), 264–89, and Wright, *From Scribe to Seer: Baruch ben Neriah in History and Tradition*, Studies on Personalities of the Old Testament (Columbia, S.C.: Univeristy of South Carolina Press) forthcoming. The most

recent and thorough treatment of this long-neglected apocalypse is Daniel C. Harlow, *The Greek Apocalypse of Baruch (3 Baruch) in Hellenistic Judaism and Early Christianity*, SVTP 12 (Leiden: E. J. Brill, 1996).

91. Among the translators note the following: W. Hage, "Die griechische Baruch-Apokalypse," *JSHRZ*, 5:1, p. 18; Victor Ryssel, "Die Griechische Baruchapokalypse," *APAT*, 2.447; H. Maldwyn Hughes, "The Greek Apocalypse of Baruch," *APOT*, 2.527; and A. W. Argyle, "The Greek Apocalypse of Baruch," *AOT*, 897.

92. James, *Apoc. Anec.*, li.

93. Albert-Marie Denis, *Introduction aux pseudépigraphes grecs d'Ancient Testament* (Leiden: E. J. Brill, 1970), 79, 82; and Jean Riaud, "Apocalypse grecque de Baruch," *La Bible: Écrits intertestamentaires*, ed. André Dupont-Sommer, Marc Philonenko, et al. (Paris: Gallimard, 1987), 1150 n. 2, also warn against the hasty conclusion that Origen is referring to the text now known by the title "3 Baruch."

94. Cf. Pirqe R. El. 3, 6 (Friedlander, 16–17, 39); 1 Enoch 17:1–18:5, 33:1; Test. Abr. (B) 8:3; Josephus, *War* 2.155; Apoc. Paul 21, 31; Hist. Rech. 2:3–7; 3:2–4; St. John of Damascus, *On the Orthodox Faith* 2:9; John Chrysostom, *Homilies on the Epistle to the Romans* 25:3; and Augustine, *De Civitate Dei* 12:12. This belief is behind the tenth-century story of "St. Brendan's Voyage," according to which the saint, who lived ca. 486–578, undertook a seven-year voyage to reach the land of the blessed; see *Visions of Heaven and Hell Before Dante*, ed. Eileen Gardiner (New York: Italica Press, 1989), 81–127. Not all Greeks accepted the idea of the all-encircling sea, however, as Herodotus points out in *History* iv.36.

95. Asc. Isa 7:18, 28; 3 Enoch 22C; b. Hag. 13a; Masseket Hekalot 4 (*BHM*, 2.43); Re'uyot Yehezq'el (*BM*, 2.131; ed. Gruenwald, 121). Note also Louis Ginzberg, *Legends of the Jews*, trans. Henrieta Szold, 7 vols. (Philadelphia: The Jewish Publication Society of America, 1909–38) 5.10–11 n. 22 and 5.19 nn. 20–21.

96. On the difficulty in knowing about the future or the heavenly realm see 4 Ezra 4:1–12; 5:36–40; and Apoc. Sedr. 8:4–10. This tradition can be traced back to Job 38 and the questions put to Job by God. Note in this regard Michael E. Stone, "Lists of Revealed Things in Apocalyptic Literature," *Magnalia Dei: The Mighty Acts of God*, ed. F. M. Cross, W. E. Lemke, and P. D. Miller, Jr. (Garden City, N.Y.: Doubleday, 1976) 414–52. On the other hand, there are texts where precisely this kind of unknowable information is the focus of attention—ascent texts and 1 Enoch 72–82, The Astronomical Book, come immediately to mind.

97. The question "who are these?" and the answer "these are . . ." follows a long-standing technique of dream interpretation whereby the dreamer states what he or she has seen, and the interpreter responds by saying "these are . . ." On this type of dream exegesis see Michael Fishbane, *Biblical Interpretation in Ancient Israel* (Oxford: Clarendon Press/New York: Oxford University Press, 1985), 443–57, and Himmelfarb, *Tours of Hell*, 41–67.

98. John J. Collins, *The Apocalyptic Imagination* (New York: Crossroad, 1984), 200, notes that the builders of the tower represent the Babylonians who presumably find their counterpart in the Romans and who are punished not for destroying Jerusalem but for imposing hard labor on pregnant women and for attempting to discover the nature of the heavens.

99. It is somewhat unclear whether the beast resides in the third heaven and has direct, daily access to the ocean, or whether it resides on earth and was only seen by Baruch from the third heaven. If this beast is somehow related to the *ouroborus*, the serpent with its tail in its mouth that encircles the world, as James thinks (*Apoc. Anec.*, lx–lxi), then a more fitting place to have encountered such a beast would have been at the first stop on Baruch's journey at the ends of the earth where the ocean that no one could

cross was located (2:1). On the *ouroborus*, see Jeffrey Burton Russell, *The Devil: Perceptions of Evil From Antiquity to Primitive Christianity* (Ithaca: Cornell University Press, 1977), 39, 68–69.

100. The Slavonic text compares the size of the serpent's belly with Hades (5:3), while the Greek identifies the belly as Hades itself (5:3). On the identification of the serpent and Hades see also Ulrich Fischer, *Eschatologie und Jenseitserwartung im hellenistischen Diasporajudentum* (Berlin/New York: Walter de Gruyter, 1978), 80–82.

101. According to 2 Enoch 11–17 and Sepher Harazim IV, the sun travels in the fourth heaven.

102. The immense size of the bird is also mentioned in 2 Enoch 12:2. James, in his characteristically thorough manner, has drawn attention to several texts that reflect traditions identical or at least similar to these about the sun and this bird; see James, "Notes on Apocrypha," *JTS* 16 (1915): 410–13. What James regards as the rather direct dependence of the later texts on 3 Baruch, I prefer to view as their mutual dependence on common traditions.

103. The traditions about this mythical beast have been elaborated by R. van den Broek, *The Myth of the Phoenix*, trans. I. Seeger (Leiden: E. J. Brill, 1972), and J. Hubaux and M. Leroy, *Le mythe du phénix dans les littératures grecque et latione* (Paris: Liège, 1939).

104. The sun's crown is mentioned in 2 Enoch 14:2–3; Pirqe R. El. 6 (Friedlander, 40); and Num. Rab. 12:4. Andersen, "2 Enoch," *OTP*, 1.126 n. 14f, traces the image to the iconography of the Greek god Helios.

105. Cf. Pirqe R. El. 6 (Friedlander, 40); 1 Enoch 72:4–5; and 2 Enoch 11–12.

106. Quoted from F. I. Andersen, "2 Enoch," *OTP*, 1.126.

107. 3 Apoc. Bar. 8:4–5; cf. Gk. Test. Levi 3:2; 2 Enoch 14:2–3; Apoc. Abr. 10 [A]; and Apoc. Paul §4–5.

108. This translation is based on the text published by K. H. Kuhn, "A Coptic Jeremiah Apocryphon," *Le Muséon* 83:1–2 (1970): 95–136, and *Le Muséon* 83:3–4 (1970): 291–350.

109. On the rivalry between the sun and the moon and the punishment of the moon see also b. Hul. 60b; b. Shebu. 9a; Gen. Rab. 86 (6:3); Pirqe R. El. 6 (Friedlander, 31); and Tg. Ps.-Jon. to Gen. 1:16.

110. James, *Apoc. Anec.*, lxvii–lxix; Hughes, "Gk. Apoc. Bar.," 539 n. X. 2; Gaylord, "3 Baruch," 673 n. 10 b; and Fischer, *Eschatologie und Jenseitserwartung*, 77–78.

111. See especially Homer, *Odyssey*, iv.561–69; Plato, *Phaidon*, 113A; and Hesiod, *Works and Days*, 167–73. This same theme is found also in the Sib. Or., 2:313–38 and Hist. Rech. 3–16.

112. For a striking, albeit late, example of just such a heavenly geography see the painting by Fra Angelico entitled "The Last Judgment." This painting is reproduced in Colleen McDannell and Bernhard Lang, *Heaven: A History* (New Haven: Yale University Press, 1988), 129. In this painting some of the saints are represented standing in the fields outside of the heavenly gates, while others are walking through the gates into the holy area, and still others are standing within the gates.

113. On the angels as intercessors note Job 33:23–24; 1 Enoch 9:3, 15:2, 39:4–5, 47:2, 99:3, 104:1; and LAE (Greek rec. = Apoc. Mos.) 27–29. Note also 1 Enoch 9:1–3 in Matthew Black, *Apocalypsis Henochi Graece*, PVTG 3 (Leiden: E. J. Brill, 1970), 23, where Michael, Ouriel, Raphael, and Gabriel are called the four angels who bear petitions to God on behalf of men. In Test. Abr. 9:2–3 Michael is said to carry the prayers of humans to God. Note that Uriel is the angel of repentance who conducts prayers to God in Apoc. Adam. Gabriel is noted for interceding and praying on behalf of those

who dwell upon the earth and supplicating in the name of the Lord of the Spirits in 1 Enoch 40:6, 9. The regular prayer of the angels, specifically Michael, is mentioned also in Test. Abr. 4:4–6 (B).

114. Quoted from S. E. Robinson, "The Testament of Adam," *OTP*, 1.993.

115. Gaylord, "3 Baruch," 657; James, *Apoc. Anec.*, li; Hughes, "Gk. Apoc. Bar.," 527; Hage, "griechische Baruch-Apokalypse," 18; Ryssel, "Griechische Baruchapokalypse," 446–47; and Collins, *Apocalyptic Imagination*, 199. Note also Stone, "Apocalyptic Literature," 410–11, and Denis, *Introduction*, 79.

116. This element is lacking in the account of the entry into the fourth heaven. The text recounting the entry into the third heaven also lacks this vocabulary (4:2), but this absence is due to textual corruption, and the remaining text does presuppose such a journey.

117. Harlow, *Apocalypse of Baruch*, 36 proposes that the descriptions of their movements "presume" that Baruch and his angelic guide entered this heaven. Harlow's careful observations are indeed helpful, but I remained unconvinced on this point. Baruch and his angel never enter through the gates.

118. Note the critique of this model by Harlow, *Apocalypse of Baruch*, 41–50.

119. Picard, *Apoc. Bar. Gr.*, 77, and "Observations," 94 n. 2; Harlow, *Apocalypse of Baruch*, 34–76.

120. On oil as the fruit of the "tree of life," see LAE 36:1–2, 40:1–3; Apoc. Mos. 9:3, 28:1–4. For the motif of this oil as a symbol for eternal life, see Esther C. Quinn, *The Quest of Seth for the Oil of Life* (Chicago: The University of Chicago Press, 1962).

121. For introductions and translations see A. Vaillant, *Le Livre des Secrets d'Hénoch: texte slave et traduction française* (Paris: Institut d'etudes slaves, 1952); G. Nathanael Bonwetsch, *Die Bücher der Geheimnisse Henochs: Das Sogenannte Slavische Henochbuch*, Texts und Untersuchungen zur Geschichte der Altchristlichen Literatur 44.2 ed. A. von Harnack and Carl Schmidt (Leipzig: J. C. Hinrichssche Buchhandlung, 1922); and F. I. Anderson, "2 (Slavonic Apocalypse of) Enoch," *OTP*, 1.91–221. All quotations here are from Andersen's translation. Christfried Böttrich, "Recent Studies in the *Slavonic Book of Enoch*," *JSP* 9 (1991): 35–42, provides an update on more recent developments in the study of this text.

122. Nathaniel Schmidt, "The Two Recensions of Slavonic Enoch," *JAOS* 41 (1921): 310–12, demonstrates that these two recensions are based on two different Greek recensions. Additionally, he has "no doubt" that the shorter Greek recension was the earliest and was a translation of an original Hebrew or Aramaic text written before 70 CE in Palestine. The longer Greek recension, in his opinion, is an expansion of the shorter Greek recension done sometime before the fifth century CE. Böttrich, "Recent Studies," 40, notes: "With the manuscripts and the means available, it has been possible to show that the shorter recension of the text is the result of reworking and cutting in the Slavonic sphere." The use of such late, i.e., medieval, manuscripts for evidence of early Jewish or Christian thought is a problem frequently encountered in the study of Jewish and Christian apocryphal and pseudepigraphic literature. As Michael Stone has pointed out, however, it is entirely possible that a tenth century or later translation (say Armenian or Slavonic) of an early Greek text may preserve a better text than an earlier manuscript in Greek depending on how they fare during the process of transmission and translation. See Stone, "Methodological Issues in the Study of the Text of the Apocrypha and Pseudepigrapha," *Proceedings of the Fifth World Congress of Jewish Studies: The Hebrew University, Mount Scopus— Givat Ram, Jerusalem, 3–11 August 1969* (Jerusalem: World Union of Jewish Studies, 1969), 211–17.

123. "2 Enoch," 97. Compare Vaillant, *Le livre des secrets d'Hénoch*, viii–x, and Gershom Scholem, *Ursprung und Anfänge der Kabbala* (Berlin: W. de Gruyter, 1962), 64 n. 37.

124. The account of the onset of this vision seems to reflect some possible induction technique. On the use of such induction techniques utilized by Jewish mystics see Gershom G. Scholem, *Major Trends in Jewish Mysticism*, 3d ed. (New York: Schocken Books, 1954; reprint, New York: Schocken Books, 1961), 49–54. That early apocalyptists fit within this mystic tradition has been demonstrated by Daniel Merkur, "Visionary Practices," and "Prophetic Initiation." Additional examples of various forms of withdrawal used by early Jewish and Christian mystics to induce visions are catalogued in Violet MacDermot, *The Cult of the Seer in the Ancient Middle East* (Berkeley, Calif.: University of California Press, 1971), 26–48.

125. On the nature of astronomical speculation in Old Church Slavonic literature see W. F. Ryan, "Astronomy in Church Slavonic: Linguistic Aspects of Cultural Transmission," *The Formation of the Slavonic Literary Languages*, ed. Gerald Stone and Dean Worth, UCLA Slavic Studies 11 (Columbus, Ohio: Slavica Publishers, Inc., 1985), 53–60, and Ryan, "Curious Star Names in Slavonic Literature," *Russian Linguistics* 1 (1974): 139–50.

126. The shorter "A" recension notes that at this point Enoch also learned about the courses of the stars. Although the governors of the stars appear in this heaven, the stars themselves are located in the fourth heaven (2 Enoch 11–17), and the several angelic beings who study the movements of the celestial bodies are located in the sixth heaven (2 Enoch 19:2).

127. On the various locations of "Paradise" in the Enochic corpus, see Andersen, "2 Enoch," 114–15, n. 8b, and Pierre Grelot, "La geographie mythique d'Henoch et ses sources orientales," *RB* 65 (1958): 33–69.

128. The phrase in 2 Enoch 12:1 is "phoenixes and khalkedras," but this seems to be hendiadys. The plural "phoenixes" is surely wrong; see Andersen, "2 Enoch," 122, n. 12c.

129. According to 1 Enoch 75, the moon uses the same six gates as the sun in the east and the west. Andersen's supposition (p. 128, n. 16b) is that this problem arises from a confusion with the twelve gates mentioned for the winds in 1 Enoch 76. It may be, however, that the author distinguishes twelve gates on either horizon for the moon to use in its annual north–south migrations across the horizon so that it does not use the same six gates both on its northward and its southward journeys. Neugebauer, "Notes on Ethiopic Astronomy," *Or* 33 (1964) 61, suggests that the author simply ". . . invented 12 gates each in the east and in the west and assigned to them, rather arbitrarily, numbers of days, e.g., 30, 31, 35, 22, etc., but such that the total again came to 364 days."

130. The divine throne is in the seventh heaven according to the shorter "A" recension. It appears from this passage that the longer recension does not represent the original form of the text. Why would the seer report to have seen God in the tenth heaven if he was standing in the seventh? This confusion is resolved if the narrative in the longer "J" recension is secondary. This difficulty indicates that the editors of the "J" recension adapted the shorter "A" recension to fit a ten-heaven schema, and the remaining incongruity indicates that their revision was somewhat inelegant.

131. It is not completely clear, however, whether these angels are standing on ten steps in the tenth or the seventh heaven. Most likely they are standing in the seventh heaven and directing their praises to God in the tenth. This vision is deeply influenced by temple or priestly traditions about the appearance of the divine presence.

132. There is some confusion in this text regarding the location of the stellar bodies. Their governors appear in the first heaven (4:2); the sun and moon are in the fourth heaven (11–17); and the zodiacs are in the eighth and ninth heavens (21:5–6; cf. 30:5–6). The "A" recension does not mention the zodiacs at all, an omission that may indicate that the editors of this recension objected to this astrological idea.

133. On this see Erwin R. Goodenough, *Jewish Symbols in the Greco-Roman Period*, 12 vols. (New York: Bollingen Foundation, 1964) 8.166–218; Lee I. Levine, *Ancient Synagogues Revealed* (Jerusalem: Israel Exploration Society, 1981); *Sacred Realm: The Emergence of the Synagogue in the Ancient World*, ed. Steven Fine (New York: Yeshiva University Press/Oxford University Press, 1996); and Joseph Naveh and Shaul Shaked, *Magic Spells and Formulae: Aramaic Incantations of Late Antiquity* (Jerusalem: Magnes Press, 1993), Geniza 10.

134. Or two periods of thirty days and thirty nights according to 68:1–2; see also Andersen, "2 Enoch," 141, n. 23d. Compare 4 Ezra 14:37–50, and Stone, *Fourth Ezra*, 437–42.

135. Compare chapters 40–48 where Enoch recounts to his "children" all that he had learned. For additional traditions about the knowledge and wisdom Enoch revealed to his generation before ascending into heaven, see "The Life of Enoch," *BHM*, 4.129–32.

136. The "A" recension lacks the account of the seven circles, thereby maintaining a consistent cosmography of seven heavens. The longer "J" recension is complex in several ways. First, it has a cosmography of ten heavens in chapters 1–21. Second, in chapters 22–73 it sets forth a cosmography with earth surrounded by seven concentric circles in each of which travels a star or planet. Whether the number of heavens is seven or ten, the cosmography of 2 Enoch 1–21 is based on a geocentric view of the universe with the layers of the several heavens superimposed above the earth. 2 Enoch 22–71, on the other hand, clearly depends on a form of the Ptolemaic model of the universe. The unusual feature here is that the stars reside in the several circles above the earth. In most Greek astronomy the stars were located beyond the seven spheres of the planets at the boundary beyond which the "infinite" universe began. On this see David Furley, *The Greek Cosmologists*, 2 vols. (Cambridge: Cambridge University Press, 1987), 136, and Hans Lewy, *Chaldean Oracles and Theurgy: Mysticism Magic and Platonism in the Later Roman Empire*, new ed., ed. Michel Tardieu (Paris: Études Augustiniennes, 1978), 413.

137. Notice how this idea of each of these seven stars having its own path within its own heaven contrasts with the portrayal in 4:1–2 of the stars and their angelic commanders in the first heaven.

138. For the Hebrew names of the planets see b. Shabb. 156a and Robert R. Stieglitz, "The Hebrew Names of the Seven Planets," *JNES* 40:2 (1981): 135–37.

139. For an introduction and translation see R. Rubinkiewicz and H. G. Lunt, "Apocalypse of Abraham," *OTP*, 1.681–705. Note also G. H. Box, *The Apocalypse of Abraham* (London: SPCK, 1918); and Emil Turdeanu, "L'Apocalypse d'Abraham en slave," *JSJ* 3 (1972): 153–80. An insightful interpretation of this text is offered by Ryszard Rubinkiewicz, "La vision de l'histoire dans l'Apocalypse d'Abraham," *ANRW*, II:19:1 (1979): 137–51. Whether this text was composed by a Christian or Jew cannot be determined definitively. Arie Rubinstein, "Hebraisms in the Slavonic 'Apocalypse of Abraham,'" *JJS* 4 (1953): 108–15, and "Hebraisms in the 'Apocalypse of Abraham,'" *JJS* 5:3 (1954): 132–35, argues that it was written in Hebrew by a Jew. The evidence he marshals, however, is not convincing. The features he regards as clear evidence for a Hebrew original could also be reasonably explained as a Koine Greek composition

influenced by biblical idiom. This objection does not, however, negate the possibility that the work was originally composed by a Jew.

140. See 12:10, 15:2–4. Enoch and Sedrach ascended to heaven on the wings of angels (2 Enoch 3:1; Apoc. Sedr. 2: 5). The theme also reminds one of Etana's flight into the heavenly realm on the back of an eagle; see pp. 45–47 above.

141. For Greek text see M. R. James, "Apocalypse of Sedrach," *Apocrypha Anecdota*, Texts and Studies, 2:3, ed. J. Armitage Robinson (Cambridge: Cambridge University Press, 1893) 130–37. For the identity of "Sedrach," see James, "Apocalypse of Sedrach," 127–29, and Michael E. Stone, "An Armenian Tradition Relating to the Death of the Three Companions of Daniel," *Muséon* 86 (1973): 111–23. See also S. Agourides, "Apocalypse of Sedrach," *OTP*, 1.605–13. Agourides concludes that "it may be fairly stated that the sermon on love is a product of Byzantine Christianity and that the apocalypse itself originated in Jewish circles" (*OTP*, 1.607).

142. "Apocalypse of Sedrach," *OTP* 1.610.

Chapter 7

1. This feature has been noted by E. R. Dodds, *The Greeks and the Irrational* (Berkeley: University of California Press, 1959), 179.

2. See Michael E. Stone, "Lists of Revealed Things in Apocalyptic Literature," *Magnalia Dei: The Mighty Acts of God*, ed. F. M. Cross, W. E. Lemke, and P. D. Miller, Jr. (Garden City, N.Y.: Doubleday, 1976), 414–52; and Martha Himmelfarb, *Ascent to Heaven in Jewish and Christian Apocalypses* (New York/Oxford: Oxford University Press, 1993), 72–94.

3. For additional early Christian sources see P. Ildefonse de Vuippens, *La paradis terrestre au troisième ciel: Exposé historique d'une conception chrétienne des premiers siècles* (Fribourg: Librairie de l'oeuvre de S.-Paul, 1925), 52–96.

4. In this regard see Izak Cornelius, "Paradise Motifs in the 'Eschatology' of the Minor Prophets and the Iconography of the Ancient Near East: The Concepts of Fertility, Water, Trees, and 'Tierfrieden' and Gen. 2–3," *JNWSL* XIV (1988): 41–42; Hans Bietenhard and Colin Brown, "Paradise," *NIDNTT*, 2.760–64; K. Galling, "Paradeisos," *Paulys Realencyclopädie der Classischen Altertumswissenschaft*, ed. Georg Wissowa et al. (Stuttgart: Alfred Druckenmüller, 1949), 18:3, 1131–34; Edwin M. Yamauchi, *Persia and the Bible* (Grand Rapids, Mich.: Baker Book House, 1990) 332–34; and J. B. Frey, "La Vie de l'au-delà dans les Conceptions Juives au Temps de Jésus-Christ," *Bib* 13 (1932): 129–68.

5. This has been well documented by Himmelfarb in *Ascent to Heaven*. Devorah Dimant, "Jerusalem and the Temple according to the Animal Apocalypse (1 Enoch 85–90) in the Light of the Ideology of the Dead Sea Sect," *Shnaton*/שנתון 5–6 (1981–82): 177–93, notes that the people of Qumran imagined the eschatological Jerusalem as a "Temple-city." The city has no temple because it is itself a temple or holy place. This is similar to the note at the end of the New Testament Book of Revelation that there is no temple in the eschatological New Jerusalem (Rev. 21:22).

6. The most influential treatments of this theme are Albrecht Alt, "The God of the Fathers," *Essays on Old Testament History and Religion*, trans. R. A. Wilson (Garden City, N.Y.: Doubleday, 1967), 1–100; William F. Albright, *Yahweh and the Gods of Canaan: An Historical Analysis of Two Conflicting Faiths* (Garden City, N.Y.: Doubleday, 1968); Frank Moore Cross, *Canaanite Myth and Hebrew Epic: Essays in the History of the Religion of Israel* (Cambridge: Harvard University Press, 1973); Mark S. Smith, *The Early History*

of God: Yahweh and the Other Deities in Ancient Israel (San Francisco: Harper & Row, 1990); and Othmar Keel and Christoph Uehlinger, *Gods, Goddesses, and Images of God in Ancient Israel*, trans. Allan W. Mahnke (Philadelphia: Fortress Press, 1997).

7. See for example Zech. 3; Jub. 17:15–18:16 (much like Job 1); Gk. Test. Levi 5:1–3; Asc. Mos. 10:3; and Wisd. Sol. 18:15. David E. Aune, "The Influence of Roman Imperial Court Ceremonial on the Revelation of John," *BibRev* 28 (1983): 5–26, suggests that the depiction of the divine throne room in the Book of Revelation is based on the structure and ceremony of the Roman imperial court.

8. On this see Alan Bernstein, *The Formation of Hell: Death and Retribution in the Ancient and Early Christian Worlds* (Ithaca, N.Y.: Cornell University Press, 1993), 133–77.

9. See André-Jean Festugière, *Personal Religion among the Greeks* (Berkeley: University of California Press, 1954), 40–41.

10. On this see Martin Hengel, *Jews, Greeks and Barbarians* (Philadelphia: Fortress Press, 1980), and John J. Collins, *Between Athens and Jerusalem: Jewish Identity in the Hellenistic Diaspora* (New York: Crossroad, 1983).

11. See Bernstein, *Formation of Hell*, 179–247.

12. Josephus II, trans. H. St. J. Thackeray, LCL 203 (Cambridge: Harvard University Press, 1927), 381, 383. A similar description of these Essene beliefs appears in Hippolytus of Rome (*Refutation of All Heresies*, 9.27), who may be depending on Josephus; for text and translation see *The Essenes According to the Classical Sources*, ed. Geza Vermes and Martin D. Goodman, Oxford Centre Textbooks 1 (Sheffield: Sheffield Academic Press, 1989), 72–73.

13. For a treatment of the issue of the emergence of the idea of resurrection and astral immortality see John J. Collins, "Cosmos and Salvation: Jewish Wisdom and Apocalyptic in the Hellenistic Age," *HR* 17 (1977), 121–42, and Collins, *Daniel: A Commentary on the Book of Daniel*, Hermenia (Minneapolis: Fortress Press, 1993), 393–98.

14. Cf. George W. E., Nickelsburg, Jr., *Resurrection, Immortality, and Eternal Life in Intertestamental Judaism*, HTS 26 (Cambridge: Harvard University Press, 1972), 93–111.

15. *Philo I*, trans. F. H. Colson and G. H. Whitaker, LCL 226 (Cambridge: Harvard University Press, 1929), 55, 57.

16. The structure and purpose of the various ascent accounts are treated insightfully by Himmelfarb, *Ascent to Heaven*.

17. For general introductions to the study of Qumran and the Dead Sea Scrolls note especially *Understanding the Dead Sea Scrolls*, ed. Hershel Shanks (New York: Random House, 1992); Lawrence H. Schiffman, *Reclaiming the Dead Sea Scrolls: The History of Judaism, the Background of Christianity, the Lost Library of Qumran* (Philadelphia: Jewish Publication Society, 1994); and James C. VanderKam, *The Dead Sea Scrolls Today* (Grand Rapids, Mich.: Eerdmans, 1994).

18. The literature on the calendar at Qumran is vast; see especially Shemaryahu Talmon, "The Calendar Reckoning of the Sect from the Judaean Desert," *Aspects of the Dead Sea Scrolls*, ed. Chaim Rabin and Yigael Yadin, Scripta Hierosolymitana 4 (Jerusalem: Magnes Press/Hebrew University, 1965), 162–99; Talmon, *The World of Qumran from Within* (Jerusalem: Magnes Press, 1989), 147–85; and James C. Vander-Kam, "Calendrical Texts and the Origins of the Dead Sea Scroll Community," *Methods of Investigation of the Dead Sea Scrolls and the Khirbet Qumran Site*, ed. Michael O. Wise et al., Annals of the New York Academy of Sciences 722 (New York: New York Academy of Sciences, 1994), 371–88.

19. The translation "Legitimate Teacher" aptly captures the sectarians' view of their leader; see Shemaryahu Talmon, "The 'Dead Sea Scrolls' or the 'Community of the

Renewed Covenant'?" *The Echoes of Many Texts: Reflections on Jewish and Christian Traditions*, ed. William G. Dever and J. Edward Wright, BJS 313 (Atlanta: Scholars Press, 1997), 129–45.

20. Fragment 7, column II. Compare Geza Vermes, *The Dead Sea Scrolls in English*, rev. 4th ed. (New York: Penguin Books, 1995), 185.

21. Manuscript C, fragment 11, column 1, 10–18; text in Maurice Baillet, *Qumrân Grotte 4,III (4Q482–4Q520)*, DJD 7 (Oxford: Clarendon Press, 1982) §491. I have here quoted the fine translation of this enigmatic text from Michael Wise, Martin Abegg, Jr., and Edward Cook, *The Dead Sea Scrolls: A New Translation* (New York: HarperCollins, 1996), 171.

22. Morton Smith, "Ascent to the Heavens and Deification in 4QM^a," *Archaeology and the History in the Dead Sea Scrolls: The New York University Conference in Memory of Yigael Yadin*, ed. Lawrence H. Schiffman, JSPSup 8, JSOT/ASOR Monographs 2 (Sheffield: Sheffield Academic Press, 1990), 181–88; and Smith, "Two Ascended to Heaven—Jesus and the Author of 4Q491," *Jesus and the Dead Sea Scrolls*, ed. James H. Charlesworth, ABRL (New York: Doubleday, 1992), 290–301. Some identify the archangel Michael as the subject of this passage; see Baillet, *Qumrân Grotte 4*, 26–29; and Vermes, *Dead Sea Scrolls*, 147.

23. This is also noted by John J. Collins, "A Throne in the Heavens: Apotheosis in Pre-Christian Judaism," *Death, Ecstasy, and Other Worldly Journeys*, ed. John J. Collins and Michael Fishbane (Albany: SUNY Press, 1995), 41–58, and Collins, *The Scepter and the Star: The Messiahs of the Dead Sea Scrolls and Other Ancient Literature*, ABRL (New York: Doubleday, 1995), 136–53.

24. Adela Yarbro Collins, "The Seven Heavens in Jewish and Christian Apocalypses," *Death, Ecstasy, and Other Worldly Journeys*, ed. Collins and Fishbane, 57–93, finds the source of this enumeration in ancient Mesopotamian astronomical lore or symbolism; I am inclined to find it in Greco-Roman astronomy.

25. Text and translation in Cosmas Indicopleustès, *Topography Chrétienne*, ed. Wanda Wolska-Conus, SC 141, 159, 197 (Paris: Les Éditions du Cerf, 1968, 1970, 1973); cf. *The Christian Topography of Cosmas, An Egyptian Monk*, edited by J. W. McCrindle (New York: Burt Franklin, 1967).

26. In this regard see Himmelfarb, "Revelation and Rapture: The Transformation of the Visionary in the Ascent Apocalypses," *Mysteries and Revelations: Apocalyptic Studies since the Uppsala Colloquium*, ed. John J. Collins and James H. Charlesworth, JSPSup 9 (Sheffield: Sheffield Academic Press, 1991), 70–90.

27. *Jewish War* 2.156–57 (trans. Thackeray, p. 383).

Chapter 8

1. Translation from Peter Alexander, "3 (Hebrew Apocalypse of) Enoch," OTP 1.255–56. The title "3 Enoch" is misleading as this text is better known as *Sepher Hekhalot*, "Book of Palaces."

2. The priestly rituals and ideology are carefully detailed in Jacob Milgrom, *Leviticus 1–16: A New Translation with Introduction and Commentary*, AB 3 (New York: Doubleday, 1991).

3. On the theme of angelic opposition to human ascent into the heavenly realm see Peter Schäfer, *Rivalität zwischen Engeln und Menschen*, Studia Judaica (Berlin: Walter de Gruyter, 1975), and Joseph P. Schultz, "Angelic Opposition to the Ascension of Moses and the Revelation of the Law," *JQR* 61 (1970–71): 282–307.

4. See Michael D. Swartz, "'Like Ministering Angels': Ritual and Purity in Early Jewish Mysticism and Magic," *AJSRev* 19:2 (1994): 135–67, and Swartz, "Book and Tradition in Hekhalot and Magical Literatures," *Journal of Jewish Thought and Philosophy* 3:2 (1994): 189–229.

5. See Philip S. Alexander, "The Family of Caesar and the Family of God: The Image of the Emperor in the Heikhalot Literature," *Images of Empire*, ed. Loveday Alexander, JSOTSup 122 (Sheffield: JSOT Press, 1991), 276–97.

6. The motif of God as king has been prominent throughout the history of Jewish theology since the Bible. See Marc Brettler, *God is King: Understanding an Israelite Metaphor*, JSOTSup 76 (Sheffield: JSOT Press, 1989); Anna Maria Schwemer, "Irdischer und himmlischer König. Beobachtungen zur sogenannten David-Apokalypse in Hekhalot Rabbati §§122–126," *Königsherrschaft Gottes und himmlischer Kult im Judentum, Urchristentum und in der hellenistischen Welt*, ed. Martin Hengel and Anna Maria Schwemer, WUNT 55 (Tübingen: J. C. B. Mohr [Paul Siebeck], 1991), 309–59; and Beate Ego, "Der Diener im Palast des himmlischen Königs. Zur Interpretation einer priesterlichen Tradition im rabbinischen Judentum," *Königsherrschaft Gottes und himmlischer Kult*, 361–84.

7. The classic expression of this approach was by Gershom Scholem: see his *Major Trends in Jewish Mysticism*, 3d ed. (New York: Shocken Books, 1954; reprinted New York: Shocken Books, 1961), and *Jewish Gnosticism, Merkavah Mysticism, and Talmudic Tradition*, 2d ed. (New York: Jewish Theological Seminary of America, 1965).

8. See Peter Schäfer, *The Hidden and Manifest God: Some Major Themes in Early Jewish Mysticism*, SUNY Series in Judaica: Hermeneutics, Mysticism, and Religion (Albany, N.Y.: SUNY Press, 1992); David Halperin, *The Faces of the Chariot: Early Jewish Responses to Ezekiel's Vision* (Tübingen: J. C. B. Mohr [Paul Siebeck], 1988); and Swartz, "Book and Tradition."

9. Translation based on the Hebrew text in Martin Samuel Cohen, *The Shiʿur Qomah: Texts and Recensions* (Tübingen: J. C. B. Mohr [Paul Siebeck], 1985) 136–43, 147–48, 150.

10. See Cohen, *Shiʿur Qomah*, 129, 133.

11. See Cohen, *Shiʿur Qomah*, 150, 152.

12. On the solar aspects of ancient Yahwism see Hans-Peter Stähli, *Solare Elemente im Jahweglauben des Alten Testaments*, OBO 66 (Göttingen: Vandenhoeck und Ruprecht, 1985), who presents the solar images in earlier Israelite religion as a background to understanding the synagogue iconography.

13. On this issue see Erwin R. Goodenough, *Jewish Symbols in the Greco-Roman Period*, 12 vols. (New York: Bollingen Foundation, 1964) 8.166–218; Lee I. Levine, *Ancient Synagogues Revealed* (Jerusalem: Israel Exploration Society, 1981); and *Sacred Realm: The Emergence of the Synagogue in the Ancient World*, ed. Steven Fine (New York: Yeshiva University Press/Oxford University Press, 1996).

14. See Gad ben-ami Sarfatti, "Talmudic Cosmography," *Tarbitz* 35:2 (1965): 144–46 [Hebrew].

15. Cf. Abot R. Nat. 37; Sefer Razi'el 341–43 (Cohen, *Shiʿur Qomah*, 112).

16. b. Hag. 12b; Deut Rab. 2.

17. Midr. Ps. 114:2 (ed. Buber, 236a).

18. Sepher Hekalot (3 Enoch) 17:1–3; 18:1–2; b. Hag. 11b–16a; b. Shabb. 156a; Pirqe R. El. 19, 154b; Masseket Hekalot 4, 5 (*BHM*, 2.42); Re'uyot Ezekiel (*BM*, 2.129–30); Midr. Konen (BHM, 2.53); S. Rab. deBereshit (BM, 1.29); Songs Rab. 5; Baraita deMaaseh Bereshit (ed. Séd, A 72–123, 296–369; B 60–112, 263–304); Gen Rab. 6; Pesiq. R. 5; Midr. Ps. 92:2; Sefer Razi'el 343 (Cohen, *Shiʿur Qomah*, 112).

19. b. Hag. 13a.

20. Num Rab. 14 (on Num 7:78); cf. 2 Enoch (long "J" recension).

21. Sepher Hekalot (3 Enoch) A48:1; Masseket Hekalot 7 (*BHM*, 2.45). The number 955 is likely based on the gematria for the phrase "the highest of the heavens" (שמי העליונים השמים), and suggests the absolute remoteness or greatness of God.

22. See Tamsyn Barton, *Ancient Astrology*, Sciences of Antiquity (New York: Routledge Press, 1994), 64–85.

23. For an insightful treatment of Dante's *Paradisio*, see Jeffrey Burton Russell, *A History of Heaven: The Singing Silence* (Princeton: Princeton University Press, 1997), 165–85.

24. Medieval notions of heavenly ascent and journeys to the mystical reaches of the earth are described quite thoroughly in Claude Carozzi, *Le voyage de l'âme dans l'au-delà d'après la littérature latine (Xᵉ-XIIIᵉ siècle)*, Collection de l'École Française de Rome 189 (Rome: École Française de Rome, 1994). The depictions of the heavenly realm in medieval Christian iconography are treated in André Grabar, "L'Iconographie du Ciel dans l'art chrétien de l'Antiquité et du haut Moyen Age," *Cahiers archeologiques*, 30 (1982): 3–24, and Grabar, *Christian Iconography: A Study of its Origin* (Princeton: Princeton University Press, 1968).

25. This theme is treated in Bernard McGinn, *Visions of the End: Apocalyptic Traditions in the Middle Ages* (New York: Columbia University Press, 1979).

26. See, for example, Lieselotte Kötzsche-Breitenbruch, "Zur Darstellung der Himmelfahrt Constantins des Grossen," *Jenseitsvorstellung in Antike und Christentum*, ed. Alfred Stuiber, Jahrbuch für Antike und Christentum 9 (Münster: Aschendorff Verlag, 1982), 215–24.

27. For texts and issues see *Visions of Heaven and Hell Before Dante*, ed. Eileen Gardiner (New York: Italica Press, 1989).

28. On near-death experiences see Carol Zaleski, *Otherworldly Journeys: Accounts of Near-Death Experience in Medieval and Modern Times* (New York/Oxford: Oxford University Press, 1987) and Zaleski, *The Life of the World to Come: Near-Death Experience and Christian Hope* (New York/Oxford: Oxford University Press, 1996).

29. See E. Johimowicz, "Islam," *Ancient Cosmologies*, ed. Carmen Blacker and Michael Loewe (London: George Allen and Unwin Ltd., 1975), 143–71. I thank David Cook for introducing me to the fascinating world of Islamic traditions of heaven, hell, and other apocalyptic themes.

30. The origin and development of the themes in the tradition about Muhammad's ascent to heaven are traced by Herbert Busse, "Jerusalem in the Story of Muhammad's Night Journey and Ascension," *Jerusalem Studies in Arabic and Islam* 14 (1991): 1–40; cf. F. E. Peters, *A Reader on Classical Islam* (Princeton: Princeton University Press, 1994), 64–67.

31. The Shanu'a is a south Arabian tribe possibly related to the Ethiopians.

32. Peters, *Reader on Classical Islam*, 168–69.

33. In this respect note also David Halperin, "Hekhalot and Mir'āj: Observations on the Heavenly Journey in Judaism and Islam," *Death, Ecstasy, and Other Worldly Journeys*, ed. John J. Collins and Michael Fishbane (Albany: SUNY Press, 1995), 265–88.

34. See Leah Kinberg, "Interaction Between This World and the Afterworld in Early Islamic Tradition," *Oriens* 29–30 (1986): 285–308; and Jane I. Smith and Yvonne Y. Haddad, *The Islamic Understanding of Death and Resurrection* (Albany: SUNY Press, 1981), 31–61.

35. See Smith and Haddad, *Islamic Understanding*, 164–68.

36. al-Haythami, *Majma 'al-zawa'id*, X, p. 420. Translation courtesy of David Cook. Cf. Kinberg, "Interaction," 298–301.

37. See William C. Chittick, "Eschatology," *Islamic Spirituality: Foundations*, ed. Seyyed Hossein Nasr, World Spirituality: An Encyclopedic History of the Religious Quest 19 (New York: Crossroad, 1991) 378–409.

38. Quotations from Peters, *Reader on Classical Islam*, 409, 410.

39. Stephen W. Hawking, *A Brief History of Time: From the Big Bang to Black Holes* (New York: Bantam Books, 1988), 37.

40. Ibid., 126.

41. On van Gogh as an astronomer and theologian see Charles A. Whitney, "The Skies of Vincent van Gogh," *Art History* 9 (1986): 351–62, and Albert Boime, "Van Gogh's *Starry Night*: A History of Matter and a Matter of History," *Arts Magazine* 59:4 (December 1984): 86–103.

42. Friedrich Nietzsche, "Die frühliche Wissenschaft," 125; my translation from *Nietzsche Werke*, vol. 5, part 2, ed. Giorgio Colli and Mazzimo Montinari (Berlin: Walter de Gruyter, 1973), 159.

BIBLIOGRAPHY

Aaboe, A. "Scientific Astronomy in Antiquity." In *The Place of Astronomy in the Ancient World*, edited by F. R. Hudson, 21–42. London: Oxford University Press, 1974.

Abusch, Tzvi. "Ascent to the Stars in a Mesopotamian Ritual: Social Metaphor and Religious Experience." In *Death, Ecstasy, and Other Worldly Journeys*, edited by John J. Collins and Michael Fishbane, 15–39. Albany, N.Y.: SUNY Press, 1995.

———— "Mesopotamian Anti-Witchcraft Literature: Texts and Studies. Part I, The Nature of *Maqlû*: Its Character, Divisions and Calendrical Setting." *JNES* 33 (1974): 251–62.

———— "The Socio-Religious Framework of the Babylonian Witchcraft Ceremony Maqlû: Some Observations on the Introductory Section of the Text, Part II." In *Solving Riddles and Untying Knots: Biblical, Epigraphic, and Semitic Studies in Honor of Jonas C. Greenfield*, edited by Ziony Zevit, Seymour Gitin, and Michael Sokoloff, 467–94. Winona Lake, Ind.: Eisenbrauns, 1995.

———— "Some Reflections on Mesopotamian Witchcraft." In *Religion and Politics in the Ancient Near East*, edited by Adele Berlin, 21–33. Bethesda, Md.: University Press of Maryland, 1996.

Ackerman, Susan. "'And the Women Knead Dough': The Worship of the Queen of Heaven in Sixth-Century Judah." In *Gender and Difference in Ancient Israel*, edited by Peggy L. Day, 109–24. Minneapolis: Fortress, 1989.

———— *Under Every Green Tree: Popular Religion in Sixth-Century Judah*. HSM 46. Atlanta: Scholars Press, 1992.

Ahlström, Gösta W. "Heaven and Earth—At Hazor and Arad." In *Religious Syncretism in Antiquity*, edited by Birger A. Pearson, 67–83. Missoula, Mont.: Scholars Press, 1975.

Albani, Matthias. *Astronomie und Schöpfungsglaube: Untersuchungen zum Astronomishen Henochbuch*. WMANT 68. Neukirchen-Vluyn: Neukirchener Verlag, 1994.

Albani, Matthias, and Uwe Glessmer. "Un instrument de mesures astronomiques à Qumrân." *RB* 104 (1997): 88–115.

Albertz, Rainer. *A History of Israelite Religion in the Old Testament Period*. 2 vols. Louisville, Ky.: Westminster/John Knox, 1994.

Albright, William F. *From Stone Age to Christianity: Monotheism and the Historical Process*. Baltimore: Johns Hopkins University Press, 1940.

——— "What Were the Cherubim?" *BA* 1:1 (February 1938): 1–3.

——— *Yahweh and the Gods of Canaan: An Historical Analysis of Two Conflicting Faiths*. Garden City, N.Y.: Doubleday, 1968.

Alexander, Philip S. "The Family of Caesar and the Family of God: The Image of the Emperor in the Heikhalot Literature." In *Images of Empire*, edited by Loveday Alexander, 276–97. JSOTSup 122. Sheffield: JSOT Press, 1991.

Alfrink, Bernard. "L'expression 'šamaim or šᵉmei Haššmaim' dans l'Ancien Testament." In *Mélanges Eugène Tisserant*, edited by Eugène Tisserant, 1–7. Studie Testi 231. Vatican City: Biblioteca Apostolica Vaticana, 1964.

Alster, Bendt. "Dilmun, Bahrain, and the Alleged Paradise in Sumerian Myth and Literature." In *Dilmun: New Studies in the Archaeology and Early History of Bahrain*, edited by Daniel T. Potts, 39–74. Berliner Beiträge zum Vorderen Orient 2. Berlin: Dietrich Reimer Verlag, 1983.

Alt, Albrecht. "The God of the Fathers." In *Essays on Old Testament History and Religion*, translated by R. A. Wilson, 1–100. Garden City, N.Y.: Doubleday, 1967.

Andersen, Francis I., and David Noel Freedman. *Amos*. AB 24A. New York: Doubleday, 1989.

Annas, Julia. *An Introduction to Plato's Republic*. Oxford: Clarendon Press, 1981.

Anthes, Rudolf. "Mythology in Ancient Egypt." In *Mythologies of the Ancient World*, edited by S. N. Kramer, 15–92. New York: Doubleday, 1961.

Aristotle. *On the Heavens*. Translated by W. K. C. Guthrie. LCL. Cambridge: Harvard University Press, 1945.

Astour, Michael C. "The Nether World and Its Denizens at Ugarit." In *Death in Mesopotamia: Papers Read at the XXVIe Rencontre assyriologique internationale*, edited by Bendt Alster, 227–38. Copenhagen Studies in Assyriology 8. Copenhagen: Akademisk Forlag, 1980.

Aune, David E. "The Influence of Roman Imperial Court Ceremonial on the Revelation of John." *Bible Review* 28 (1983): 5–26.

Auscher, Dominique. "Les relations entre la Grèce et la Palestine avant la conquête d'Alexandre." *VT* 17:1 (1967): 8–30.

Baillet, Maurice. *Qumrân Grotte 4,III (4Q482–4Q520)*. DJD 7. Oxford: Clarendon Press, 1982.

Barclay, John M. G. *Jews in the Mediterranean Diaspora: From Alexander to Trajan (323 BCE–117 CE)*. Edinburgh: T&T Clark, 1996.

Barthélemy, Dominique, and J. T. Milik. *Qumran Cave 1*. DJD 1. Oxford: Oxford University Press, 1955.

Barton, Tamsyn. *Ancient Astrology*. Sciences of Antiquity. New York: Routledge Press, 1994.

Bauer, Hans, and Pontus Leander. *Historische Grammatik der hebräischen Sprache des Alten Testaments*. Hildesheim: Georg Olms Verlagsbuchhandlung, 1962.

Bauval, Robert G., and Adrian Gilbert. *The Orion Mystery: Unlocking the Secrets of the Pyramids*. London: Heinemann, 1994.

Bernstein, Alan E. *The Formation of Hell: Death and Retribution in the Ancient and Early Christian Worlds.* Ithaca, N.Y.: Cornell University Press, 1993.

Betz, Hans Dieter, ed. *The Greek Magical Papyri in Translation, Including the Demotic Spells.* Chicago: University of Chicago Press, 1985.

Bickel, Susanne. *La cosmogonie égyptienne.* OBO 134. Fribourg: Editions Universitaires, 1994.

Bickerman, Elias J. "The Historical Foundations of Postbiblical Judaism." In *The Jews: Their History, Culture, and Religion.* 3d ed. 2 vols. Edited by Louis Finkelstein, 1.70–114. New York: Jewish Publication Society of America, 1960.

Bietenhard, Hans. "Heaven, Ascend, Above—οὐρανός." In *The New International Dictionary of New Testament Theology.* 4 vols. Edited by Colin Brown, 2.191. Grand Rapids: Zondervan Publishing House, 1986.

———— *Die himmlische Welt im Urchristentum und Spätjudentum.* WUNT 2. Tübingen: Verlag J. C. B. Mohr/Paul Siebeck, 1951.

Bietenhard, Hans, and Colin Brown. "Paradise." In *The New International Dictionary of New Testament Theology.* 4 vols. Edited by Colin Brown, 2.760–64. Grand Rapids: Zondervan Publishing House, 1986.

Binger, Tilde. *Asherah: The Goddess in the Texts from Ugarit, Israel and the Old Testament.* JSOTSup 232. Sheffield: Sheffield Academic Press, 1997.

Black, Matthew, ed. *Apocalypsis Henochi graece in Pseudepigrapha Veteris Testamenti.* PVTG 3. Leiden: E. J. Brill, 1970.

Blacker, Carmen, and Michael Loewe, eds. *Ancient Cosmologies.* London: George Allen and Unwin Ltd., 1975.

Blass, Friedrich, and Albert Debrunner. *A Greek Grammar of the New Testament and Other Early Christian Literature.* Translated and revised by Robert W. Funk. Chicago: University of Chicago Press, 1961.

Bleeker, C. Jouco. "The Religion of Ancient Egypt." In *Historia Religionum: Handbook for the History of Religions.* Vol. 1, *Religions of the Past,* edited by C. Jouco Bleeker and Geo Widengren, 40–114. Leiden: E. J. Brill, 1969.

Bloch-Smith, Elizabeth. "The Cult of the Dead in Judah: Interpreting the Material Remains." *JBL* 111:2 (1992): 213–24.

———— *Judahite Burial Practices and Beliefs about the Dead.* JSOTSup 123. JSOT/ASOR Monograph Series 7. Sheffield: Sheffield Academic Press, 1992.

———— "'Who Is the King of Glory?' Solomon's Temple and Its Symbolism." In *Scripture and Other Artifacts: Essays on the Bible and Archaeology in Honor of Philip J. King,* edited by Michael D. Coogan, J. Cheryl Exum, and Lawrence E. Stager, 18–31. Louisville, Ky.: Westminster/John Knox Press, 1994.

Block, Daniel I. "Beyond the Grave: Ezekiel's Vision of Death and Afterlife." *BBR* 2 (1992): 113–41.

Boime, Albert. "Van Gogh's *Starry Night*: A History of Matter and a Matter of History." *Arts Magazine* 59:4 (December 1984): 86–103.

Bonwetsch, G. Nathanael. *Die Bücher der Geheimnisse Henochs: Das Sogenannte Slavische Henochbuch.* Texte und Untersuchungen zur Geschichte der Altchristlichen Literatur 44.2, edited by Adolf von Harnack and Carl Schmidt. Leipzig: J. C. Hinrichssche Buchhandlung, 1922.

Bordreuil, Pierre. "Le répertoire iconographique des sceaux araméens inscrits et son évolution." In *Studies in the Iconography of Northwest Semitic Seals: Proceedings of a Symposium held in Fribourg on April 17–20, 1991,* edited by Benjamin Sass and Christoph Uehlinger, 74–100. OBO 125. Göttingen: Vandenhoeck and Ruprecht, 1993.

Borger, Rykle. "Die Beschwörungsserie *bīt mēseri* und die Himmelfahrt Henochs." *JNES* 33 (1974): 183–96.

Bottéro, Jean. "Les morts et l'au-delà dans les rituels en accadien contre l'action des 'revenants'." *ZA* (1983): 153–203.

———. "La mythologie de la mort en Mésopotamie ancienne." In *Death in Mesopotamia: Papers Read at the XXVIe Rencontre assyriologique internationale*, edited by Bendt Alster, 25–52. Copenhagen Studies in Assyriology 8. Copenhagen: Akademisk Forlag, 1980.

Böttrich, Christfried. "Recent Studies in the *Slavonic Book of Enoch*." *JSP* 9 (1991): 35–42.

———. "Astrologie in der Henochtradition." *ZAW* 109:2 (1997): 222–45.

Bousset, Wilhelm. "Die Himmelsreise der Seele." *Archiv für Religionswissenschaft* 4 (1901): 136–69, 229–73.

Box, G. H. *The Apocalypse of Abraham*. London: SPCK, 1918.

Boyce, Mary. *A History of Zoroastrianism*. 3 vols. Leiden: E. J. Brill, 1975–91.

Breasted, James H. *Ancient Records of Egypt: Historical Documents from the Earliest Times to the Persian Conquest*. 5 vols. Chicago: University of Chicago Press, 1906–7.

———. *Development of Religion and Thought in Ancient Egypt*. New York: Charles Scribner's Sons, 1912.

———. *A History of Egypt: From Earliest Times to the Persian Conquest*. 2d ed. New York: Charles Scribner's Sons, 1924.

Brettler, Marc. *God is King: Understanding an Israelite Metaphor*. JSOTSup 76. Sheffield: JSOT Press, 1989.

Briant, Pierre. *Histoire de L'Empire Perse: De Cyrus à Alexandre*. Paris: Librairie Arthème Fayard, 1996.

Briquel-Chatonnet, F. *Les relations entre les cités de la côte phénicienne et les royaumes d'Israël et de Juda*. Studia Phoenicia XII. Orientalia Lovaniensia Analecta 46. Leuven: Peeters, 1992.

Broek, R. van den. *The Myth of the Phoenix*. Translated by I. Seeger. Leiden: E. J. Brill, 1972.

Brovarski, Edward. "The Doors of Heaven." *Or* 46 (1977): 107–15.

Budge, E. A. Wallis. *The Book of the Dead: An English Translation of the Chapters, Hymns, Etc., of the Theban Recension, with an Introduction, Notes, Etc.* 3 vols. in 1. 2d ed. London: Routledge & Kegan Paul Ltd., 1960.

———. *The Egyptian Heaven and Hell*. 3 vols. London: Kegan Paul, Trench, Trübner & Co., 1906.

———. *The Greenfield Papyrus in the British Museum*. London: British Museum, 1912.

Bunbury, Edward H. *A History of Ancient Geography: Among the Greeks and Romans from the Earliest Ages Till the Fall of the Roman Empire*. 2 vols. London: John Murray, 1879. Reprint. Amsterdam: J. C. Gieben, 1979.

Burchard, C. "Ein vorläufiger griechischer Text von Joseph und Asenet," *Dielheimer Blätter zum Alten Testament* 14 (1979): 2–53.

Burkert, Walter. *The Orientalizing Revolution: Near Eastern Influence on Greek Culture in the Early Archaic Age*. Revealing Antiquity 5. Cambridge: Harvard University Press, 1992.

Busse, Herbert. "Jerusalem in the Story of Muhammad's Night Journey and Ascension." *Jerusalem Studies in Arabic and Islam* 14 (1991): 1–40.

Capelle, Paul. "Elysium und die Inseln der Seligen." *Archiv für Religionswissenschaft* 25 (1927): 245–64; 26 (1928): 17–40.

Caquot, André, and Maurice Sznycer. *Ugaritic Religion*. Iconography of Religions 15:8. Leiden: E. J. Brill, 1980.

Carozzi, Claude. *Le voyage de l'âme dans l'au-delà d'après la littérature latine (Xe-XIIIe siècle)*. Collection de l'École Française de Rome 189. Rome: École Française de Rome, 1994.

Carter, Charles E. "A Social and Demographic Study of Post-Exilic Judah." Ph.D. diss., Duke University, 1991.

Casey, R. "The Apocalypse of Paul." *JTS* 34 (1933): 1–32.

Chambon, Alain, and Henri de Contenson. *Tel el-Far'ah I: L'Age du Fer*. Paris: Editions Recherche sur les civilisations, 1984.

Charles, R. H. *The Book of Enoch*. Oxford: Clarendon Press, 1912.

Charles, R. H., ed. *The Apocrypha and Pseudepigrapha of the Old Testament*. 2 vols. Oxford: Clarendon Press, 1913.

———— *The Greek Versions of the Testaments of the Twelve Patriarchs, Edited from Nine Mss. together with the Variants of the Armenian and Slavonic Versions and Some Hebrew Fragments*. Oxford: Clarendon Press, 1908. Reprint, Hildesheim: Georg Olms Verlagsbuchhandlung, 1960.

Charlesworth, James H. "The Jewish Interest in Astrology during the Hellenistic and Roman Period." *ANRW* II.20.2 (1987) 926–50.

———— *The Pseudepigrapha and Modern Research with a Supplement*. Chico, Calif.: Scholars Press, 1981.

———— *The Old Testament Pseudepigrapha and the New Testament*. Cambridge: Cambridge University Press, 1985.

Charlesworth, James H., ed. *The Old Testament Pseudepigrapha*. 2 vols. Garden City, N.Y.: Doubleday and Company, 1983–85.

Chemery, Peter C. "Sky: Myths and Symbolism." In *The Encyclopedia of Religion*. 15 vols. Edited by Mircea Eliade, 13.345–53. New York: Macmillan Publishing Company, 1987.

Chesnutt, Randall D. *From Death to Life: Conversion in Joseph and Aseneth*. JSPSup 16. Sheffield: Sheffield Academic Press, 1995.

Chiera, Edward. *Sumerian Religious Texts*. Babylonian Publications 1. Upland, Penn.: Crozer Theological Seminary, 1924.

Chittick, William C. "Eschatology." In *Islamic Spirituality: Foundations*, edited by Seyyed Hossein Nasr, 378–409. World Spirituality: An Encyclopedic History of the Religious Quest 19. New York: Crossroad, 1991.

Cicero. *De Re Publica, De Legibus*. Translated by Clinton Walker Keyes. LCL. Cambridge: Harvard University Press, 1959.

Clifford, Richard. *The Cosmic Mountain in Canaan and the Old Testament*. HSM 4. Cambridge: Harvard University Press, 1972.

Cohen, Martin Samuel. *The Shi'ur Qomah: Texts and Recensions*. Tübingen: J. C. B. Mohr/Paul Siebeck, 1985.

Collins, Adela Yarbro, "The Seven Heavens in Jewish and Christian Apocalypses." In *Death, Ecstasy, and Other Worldly Journeys*, edited by John J. Collins and Michael Fishbane, 59–93. Albany, N.Y.: SUNY Press, 1995.

Collins, John J. *The Apocalyptic Imagination*. New York: Crossroad, 1984.

———— *The Apocalyptic Vision of the Book of Daniel*. HSM 16. Missoula, Mont.: Scholars Press, 1977.

———— *Between Athens and Jerusalem: Jewish Identity in the Hellenistic Diaspora*. New York: Crossroad Publishing Co., 1983.

———— "Cosmos and Salvation: Jewish Wisdom and Apocalyptic in the Hellenistic Age." *HR* 17 (1977) 121–42.

———— *Daniel: A Commentary on the Book of Daniel*. Hermenia. Minneapolis: Fortress Press, 1993.

———— "Methodological Issues in the Study of I Enoch: Reflections on the Articles of P. D. Hanson and G. W. E. Nickelsburg." In *Society of Biblical Literature 1978 Seminar Papers*. 2 vols. Edited by Paul J. Achtemeier, 1.315–22. Missoula, Mont.: Scholars Press, 1978.

———— *The Scepter and the Star: The Messiahs of the Dead Sea Scrolls and Other Ancient Literature*. ABRL. New York: Doubleday, 1995.

———— "Testaments." In *The Jewish Writings of the Second Temple Period*, edited by Michael E. Stone, 325–55. Philadelphia: Fortress Press/Assen: Van Gorcum, 1984.

———— "A Throne in the Heavens: Apotheosis in Pre-Christian Judaism." In *Death, Ecstasy, and Other Worldly Journeys*, edited by John J. Collins and Michael Fishbane, 41–58. Albany: SUNY Press, 1995.

Collins, John J., ed. *Apocalypse: The Morphology of a Genre*. Semeia 14. Missoula, Mont.: Scholars Press, 1979.

Coogan, Michael D. *West Semitic Personal Names in the Murashu Documents*. HSM 7. Missoula, Mont.: Scholars Press, 1976.

———— *Stories from Ancient Canaan*. Philadelphia: Westminster Press, 1978.

———— "Patterns in Jewish Personal Names in the Babylonian Diaspora." *JSJ* 4:2 (1973): 183–91.

Cornelius, Izak. "Paradise Motifs in the 'Eschatology' of the Minor Prophets and the Iconography of the Ancient Near East: The Concepts of Fertility, Water, Trees, and 'Tierfrieden' and Gen. 2–3." *JNWSL* 14 (1988): 41–83.

———— "The Visual Representation of the World in the Ancient Near East and the Hebrew Bible." *JNWSL* 20:2 (1994): 193–218.

Cornwall, P. B. "On the Location of Dilmun." *BASOR* 103 (1946): 3–11.

———— "Two Letters from Dilmun." *JCS* 6 (1952): 137–45.

Cosmas Indicopleustès. *Topography Chrétienne*. 3 vols. Edited by Wanda Wolska-Conus. SC. Paris: Les Éditions du Cerf, 1968–73.

Cramer, F. H. *Astrology in Roman Law and Politics*. Philadelphia: American Philosophical Society, 1954.

Crawford, Harriet. *Sumer and the Sumerians*. Cambridge: Cambridge University Press, 1991.

Cremer, Hermann. *Biblico-Theological Lexicon of New Testament Greek*. Translated by William Urwick, 1895. Reprint, Edinburgh: T. & T. Clark, 1977.

Crenshaw, James L. *Prophetic Conflict: Its Effect Upon Israelite Religion*. BZAW 124. Berlin: de Gruyter, 1971.

Cross, Frank Moore. *Canaanite Myth and Hebrew Epic: Essays in the History of the Religion of Israel*. Cambridge, Mass.: Harvard University Press, 1973.

Crowe, Michael J. *Theories of the World from Antiquity to the Copernican Revolution*. New York: Dover Publications, Inc., 1990.

Culianu, Ioan P. "Ascension." In *The Encyclopedia of Religion*. 16 vols. Edited by Mircea Eliade, 1.439. New York: Macmillan, 1987.

———— "Astrology." In *The Encyclopedia of Religion*. 16 vols. Edited by Mircea Eliade, 1.472–75. New York: Macmillan, 1987.

———— *Psychanodia I: A Survey of the Evidence Concerning the Ascension of the Soul and its Relevance*. Leiden: E. J. Brill, 1983.

———— "Sky: The Heavens as Hierophany." In *The Encyclopedia of Religion*. 16 vols. Edited by Mircea Eliade, 13.344. New York: Macmillan, 1987.

Cumont, Franz. *Afterlife in Roman Paganism*. New Haven: Yale University Press, 1922. Reprint, New York: Dover Books, 1959.

———— *Astrology and Religion among the Greeks and Romans*. New York: Dover Publications, Inc., 1960.

———— *L'Egypte des astrologues*. Bruxelles: Fondation egyptologique, 1937.

Dahood, Mitchell. *Psalms I-III*. 3 vols. AB 16–17B. Garden City, N.Y.: Doubleday and Company, 1966–70.

Dalley, Stephanie. *Myths From Mesopotamia*. Oxford: Oxford University Press, 1989.

Davies, Philip R. *In Search of Ancient Israel*. Sheffield: JSOT Press, 1992.

Day, John. "Ashera in the Hebrew Bible and Northwest Semitic Literature." *JBL* 105 (1986): 385–408.

Day, Peggy L. *An Adversary in Heaven: Sāṭān in the Hebrew Bible*. HSM 43. Atlanta: Scholars Press, 1988.

Dean-Otting, Mary. *Heavenly Journeys: A Study of the Motif in Hellenistic Jewish Literature*. Judentum und Umwelt 8. Frankfort am Main/New York: Peter Lang, 1984.

Deist, F. E. "Genesis 1:1–2:4a: World View and World Picture." *Scriptura* 22 (1987): 1–17.

Delcor, M. "De l'origine de quelques traditions contenues dans le Testament d'Abraham." In *Proceedings of the Fifth World Congress of Jewish Studies: The Hebrew University Mount Scopus-Givat Ram, Jerusalem, 3–11 August 1969*, 192–200. Jerusalem: World Union of Jewish Studies, 1969.

Denis, Albert-Marie. *Concordance grecque des pseudepigraphes d'Ancien Testament*. Leiden: E. J. Brill, 1987.

———— *Fragmenta Pseudepigraphorum Quae Supersunt Graeca*. PVTG 13. Leiden: E. J. Brill, 1970.

———— *Introduction aux pseudepigraphes grecs d'Ancien Testament*. Leiden: E. J. Brill, 1970.

Dever, William G. "Asherah, Consort of Yahweh? New Evidence from Kuntillet 'Ajrud." *BASOR* 255 (1984): 21–37.

———— "Iron Age Epigraphic Material from the Area of Khirbet el-Kôm." *HUCA* 40–41 (1969–70): 139–204.

———— "Palace." In *The Anchor Bible Dictionary*. 6 vols. Edited by David Noel Freedman, 5.56–58. New York: Doubleday, 1992.

———— "Palaces and Temples in Canaan and Ancient Israel." In *Civilizations of the Ancient Near East*. 4 vols. Edited by J. M. Sasson, 1.605–14. New York: Charles Scribner's Sons, 1995.

———— *Recent Archaeological Discoveries and Biblical Research*. Seattle, Wash.: University of Washington Press, 1990.

———— "Religion and Cult in Ancient Israel: Social and Economic Implications." *Scienze dell'antichità: Storia Archeologia Antropologia* 3–4 (1989–90): 175–80.

———— "The Silence of the Text: An Archaeological Commentary on 2 Kings 23." In *Scripture and Other Artifacts: Essays on the Bible and Archaeology in Honor or Philip J. King*, edited by Michael D. Coogan, J. Cheryl Exum, and Lawrence E. Stager, 143–68. Louisville, Ky.: Westminster/John Knox Press, 1994.

———— "'Will the Real Israel Please Stand Up? Archaeology and Israelite Historiography: Part 1." *BASOR* 297 (1995): 61–80.

Dietrich, Manfried, and Oswald Loretz. *"Jahwe und seine Aschera": Anthropomorphes Kultbild in Mesopotamien, Ugarit und Israel: Das biblische Bilderverbot*. UBL 9. Münster: Ugarit-Verlag, 1992.

Dietrich, Manfried, Oswald Loretz, and Joaquin Sanmartin. *Die keilalphabetischen Texte aus Ugarit einschiesslich der keilalphabetischen Texte ausserhalb Ugarits 1: Transkription*. AOAT 24. Neukirchen-Vluyn: Neukirchener Verlag, 1976.

Dimant, Devorah. "1 Enoch 6–11: A Methodological Perspective." In *Society of Biblical Literature 1978 Seminar Papers*. 2 vols. Edited by Paul J. Achtemeier, 1.323–39. Missoula, Mont.: Scholars Press, 1978.

———— "Jerusalem and the Temple according to the Animal Apocalypse (1 Enoch 85–90) in the Light of the Ideology of the Dead Sea Sect." *Shnaton*/שנתון 5–6 (1981–82): 177–93.

———— "Men as Angels: The Self-Image of the Qumran Community." In *Religion and Politics in the Ancient Near East*, edited by Adele Berlin, 93–103. Bethesda, Md.: University Press of Maryland, 1996.

Dion, P. E. "YHWH as Storm-God and Sun-God: The Double Legacy of Egypt and Canaan as Reflected in Psalm 104." *ZAW* 103:1 (1991): 43–71.

Dodds, E. R. *The Greeks and the Irrational.* Berkeley: University of California Press, 1959.

Donner, Herbert, and Wolfgang Röllig. *Kanaanäische und Aramäische Inschriften.* 3 vols. Wiesbaden: Otto Harrassowitz, 1962–69.

Doumet, Claude. *Sceaux et cylindres orientaux: la collection Chiha.* OBO 9. Göttingen: Vandenhoeck and Ruprecht, 1992.

Dreyer, J. L. E. *A History of Astronomy from Thales to Kepler.* 2d ed. New York: Dover Publications Inc., 1953.

Ebeling, Erich. *Tod und Leben Nach den Vorstellungen der Babyloner.* Berlin: Walter de Gruyter and Co., 1931.

———— *Keilschrifttexte aus Assur religiösen Inhalts.* WVDOG 28. Leipzig: C. Hinrichs, 1915–23. Reprint, Osnabrück: Zeller, 1972.

Edelman, Diana Vikander, ed. *The Triumph of Elohim: From Yahwisms to Judaisms.* Kampen: Kok Pharos/Grand Rapids: Eerdmans, 1995.

Ego, Beate. "Der Diener im Palast des himmlischen Königs. Zur Interpretation einer priesterlichen Tradition im rabbinischen Judentum." In *Königsherrschaft Gottes und himmlischer Kult im Judentum, Urchristentum und in der hellenistischen Welt*, edited by Martin Hengel and Anna Maria Schwemer, 361–84. WUNT 55. Tübingen: J. C. B. Mohr/Paul Siebeck, 1991.

Eilers, Wilhelm. "Stern-Planet-Regenbogen: Zur Nomenklatur der orientalischen Himmelskunde." In *Der Orient in der Forschung: Festschrift für Otto Spies zum 5. April 1966*, edited by Wilhelm Hoenerbach, 92–146. Wiesbaden: Otto Harrassowitz, 1967.

Eisenstadt, S. N. "The Axial Age Breakthroughs—Their Characteristics and Origins." In *The Origins and Diversity of Axial Age Civilizations*, edited by S. N. Eisenstadt, 1–39. SUNY Series in Near Eastern Studies. Albany, N.Y.: SUNY Press, 1986.

Eisler, Robert. *Weltenmantel und Himmelszelt: Religionsgeschichtliche Untersuchungen zur Urgeschichte des antiken Weltbildes.* 2 vols. Munich: C. H. Beck, 1910.

Erman, Adolf. *A Handbook of Egyptian Religion.* Translated by A. S. Griffith. London: Archibald Constable & Co., 1907.

Erman, Adolf, and Herman Grapow. *Wörterbuch der ägyptischen Sprache.* 5 vols. Leipzig: J. C. Hinrichssche Buchhandlung, 1926–31.

Études Mithriaques: Actes de Congrès IV. Acta Iranica 17. Leiden: E. J. Brill, 1978.

Evers, John D. *Myth and Narrative: Structure and Meaning in Some Ancient Near Eastern Texts.* AOAT 241. Kevelaer/Neukirchen-Vluyn: Butzon and Bercker/Neukirchener Verlag, 1995.

Farnell, Lewis Richard. *Greek Hero Cults and Ideas of Immortality.* 1921. Reprint, Oxford: Clarendon Press, 1970.

Faulkner, Raymond O. *The Ancient Egyptian Coffin Texts.* 3 vols. Warminster, England: Aria & Phillips, 1973–78.

———— *The Ancient Egyptian Pyramid Texts.* 2 vols. Oxford: Oxford University Press, 1969.

———— "The King and the Star Religion in the Pyramid Texts." *JNES* 25:3 (1966): 153–61.

Festugière, André-Jean. *Personal Religion Among the Greeks*. Berkeley: University of California Press, 1954.

Fine, Steven, ed. *Sacred Realm: The Emergence of the Synagogue in the Ancient World*. New York: Yeshiva University Press/Oxford University Press, 1996.

Fischer, Ulrich. *Eschatologie und Jenseitserwartung im hellenistischen Diasporajudentum*. BZNW 44. Berlin/New York: Walter de Gruyter, 1978.

Fishbane, Michael. *Biblical Interpretation in Ancient Israel*. Oxford: Clarendon Press/New York: Oxford University Press, 1985.

———— *Text and Texture: Close Readings of Selected Biblical Texts*. New York: Schocken Books, 1979.

Fisher, Loren R., and Stan Rummel, eds. *Ras Shamra Parallels*. 3 vols. Analecta Orientalia 49–51. Rome: Pontifical Biblical Institute, 1972–81.

Fix, John D. *Astronomy: Journey to the Cosmic Frontier*. St. Louis: Mosby-Year Book, Inc., 1995.

Frankfort, Henri. *Ancient Egyptian Religion: An Interpretation*. New York: Harper & Row, 1961.

———— *The Cenotaph of Seti I at Abydos*. 2 vols. London: Egypt Exploration Society, 1933.

———— *Cylinder Seals: A Documentary Essay on the Art and Religion of the Ancient Near East*. London: Macmillan, 1939.

———— *Kingship and the Gods: A Study of Ancient Near Eastern Religion as the Integration of Society*. Chicago: University of Chicago Press, 1948.

Frankfort, Henri, H. A. Frankfort, John A. Wilson, Thorkild Jacobsen, and William A. Irwin, eds. *The Intellectual Adventure of Ancient Man: An Essay on Speculative Thought in the Ancient Near East*. Chicago: University of Chicago Press, 1946.

Freedman, David Noel. "Early Israelite Poetry and Historical Reconstructions." In *Symposia: Celebrating the Seventy-fifth Anniversary of the Founding of the American Schools of Oriental Research (1900–1975)*, edited by Frank Moore Cross, 85–96. Cambridge, Mass.: ASOR, 1979.

———— "'Who is Like Thee Among the Gods?' The Religion of Early Israel." In *Ancient Israelite Religion*, edited by Patrick D. Miller et al., 316–36. Philadelphia: Fortress Press, 1987.

Freedman, David Noel, B. E. Willoughby, H. Ringgren, and H.-J. Fabry. "*mal'ak*." In *The Theological Dictionary of the Old Testament*, edited by G. Johannes Botterweck, Helmer Ringgren, et al., 8.308–25. Grand Rapids, Mich.: William B. Eerdmans, 1986.

Freud, Sigmund. *The Interpretation of Dreams*. Translated by A. A. Brill. New York: Random House, 1950.

Frey, J. B. "La Vie de l'au-delà dans les Conceptions Juives au Temps de Jésus-Christ." *Bib* 13 (1932): 129–68.

Friedman, Richard E. *Who Wrote the Bible?* New York: Summit Books, 1987.

Fritz, Volkmar. "Temple Architecture: What Can Archaeology Tell Us about Solomon's Temple?" *BARev* 13:4 (July–August 1987): 38–49. Reprinted in *Essential Papers on Israel and the Ancient Near East*, edited by Frederick E. Greenspahn, 116–28. New York: New York University Press, 1991.

Furley, David. *The Greek Cosmologists*. 2 vols. Cambridge: Cambridge University Press, 1987.

Galling, Kurt. "Paradeisos." In *Paulys Realencyclopädie der Classischen Altertumswissenschaft*, edited by Georg Wissowa et al., 18:3.1131–34. Stuttgart: Alfred Druckenmüller, 1949.

Gardiner, Alan. *Egyptian Grammar*. 3d ed. London: Oxford University Press, 1964.

Gardiner, Eilleen, ed. *Visions of Heaven and Hell Before Dante.* New York: Italica Press, 1989.

Gibson, John C. L. "The Kingship of Yahweh against its Canaanite Background." In *Ugarit and the Bible: Proceedings of the International Symposium on Ugarit and the Bible— Manchester, September 1992,* edited by George J. Brooke, Adrian H. W. Curtis, and John F. Healey, 101–12. Münster: Ugarit-Verlag, 1994.

———— *Textbook of Syrian Semitic Inscriptions.* 3 vols. Oxford: Clarendon Press, 1971–82.

Gil, Moshe. "Enoch in the Land of Eternal Life." *Tarbiz* 38:4 (1969): 322–37 [Hebrew].

Ginzberg, Louis. *Legends of the Jews.* 7 vols. Translated by Henrieta Szold. Philadelphia: The Jewish Publication Society of America, 1909–38.

Glessmer, Uwe. "Das astronomische Henoch-Buch als Studienobjekt." *Biblische Notizen* 36 (1987): 69–129.

———— "Horizontal Measuring in the Babylonian Astronomical Compendium Mul.Apin and in the Astronomical Book of 1 En." *Henoch* 18 (1996): 259–82.

Gogh, Vincent van. *Letters of Vincent van Gogh: A Facsimile Edition.* Amsterdam: Vincent van Gogh Foundation, 1977.

Goldin, Judah, trans. *The Fathers According to Rabbi Nathan.* Yale Judaica Series 10. New Haven: Yale University Press, 1955.

Goodenough, Erwin R. *Jewish Symbols in the Greco-Roman Period.* 13 vols. New York: Bollingen Foundation, 1964.

Grabar, André. *Christian Iconography: A Study of its Origin.* Princeton: Princeton University Press, 1968.

———— "L'Iconographie du Ciel dans l'art chrétien de l'Antiquité et du haut Moyen Age." *Cahiers archeologiques* 30 (1982): 3–24.

Grabbe, Lester L. "'Canaanite': Some Methodological Observations in Relation to Biblical Study." In *Ugarit and the Bible: Proceedings of the International Symposium on Ugarit and the Bible—Manchester, September 1992,* edited by George J. Brooke, Adrian H. W. Curtis, and John F. Healey, 113–22. Münster: Ugarit-Verlag, 1994.

Grapow, Hermann. *Die Bildlichen Ausdrücke des Aegyptischen: Von Denken und Dichten Einer Altorientalsichen Sprache.* Leipzig: J. C. Hinrichssche Buchhandlung, 1924.

Grayson, A. Kirk. "Mesopotamia, History of (Assyria and Babylonia)." In *The Anchor Bible Dictionary.* 6 vols. Edited by David Noel Freedman, 4.732–77. New York: Doubleday, 1992.

Green, A. "Mischwesen, B." In *Reallexikon der Assyriologie und Vorderasiatischen Archäologie* 8:3–4 (1994): 246–64.

Greenfield, Jonas C. "Prolegomena." In Hugo Odeberg, *3 Enoch or the Hebrew Book of Enoch.* Revised Edition. New York: KTAV, 1973.

Greenfield, Jonas C., and Michael Sokoloff. "Astrological Omens in Jewish Palestinian Aramaic." *JNES* 48:3 (1989): 210–14.

———— "An Astrological Text from Qumran (4Q318): and Reflections on some Zodiacal Names." *RevQ* 16 (1995): 507–25.

Greenfield, Jonas C., and Michael E. Stone. "Appendix III: The Aramaic and Greek Fragments of a Levi Document." In *The Testaments of the Twelve Patriarchs: A Commentary,* edited by H. W. Hollander and M. De Jonge, 457–69. SVTP 8. Leiden: E. J. Brill, 1985.

———— "The Books of Enoch and the Traditions of Enoch." *Numen* 26 (1979): 89–103.

———— "The Enochic Pentateuch and the Date of the Similitudes." *HTR* 70:1–2 (1977): 51–65.

———— "Remarks on the Aramaic Testament of Levi from the Geniza." *RB* 86 (1979): 214–30.

———— "Two Notes on the Aramaic Levi Document." In *Of Scribes and Scrolls: Studies on the Hebrew Bible, Intertestamental Judaism, and Christian Origins Presented to John Strugnell on the Occasion of his Sixtieth Birthday*, edited by Harold W. Attridge, John J. Collins, and Thomas H. Tobin, 153–61. College Theology Society Resources in Religion 5. Lanham, Md.: University Press of America, 1990.

Grelot, Pierre. "La geographie mythique d'Henoch et ses sources orientales." *RB* 65 (1958): 33–69.

———— "La legend d'Henoch dans les Apocryphes et dans la Bible: origin et significa-tion." *RSR* 46 (1958): 5–26.

———— "Notes sur le Testament Araméen de Levi." *RB* 63 (1956): 391–406.

Griffiths, J. Gwyn. "The Celestial Ladder and the Gate of Heaven (Genesis xxviii. 12 and 17)." *ExpTim* 76 (1964–65): 228–30.

Gubel, Eric. "Iconography of Inscribed Phoenician Glyptic." In *Studies in the Iconogra-phy of Northwest Semitic Seals: Proceedings of a Symposium held in Fribourg on April 17–20, 1991*, edited by Benjamin Sass and Christoph Uehlinger, 101–29. OBO 125. Göttingen: Vandenhoeck and Ruprecht, 1993.

Haack, Steven C. "The Astronomical Orientation of the Egyptian Pyramids." *Archaeo-astronomy* 7 (1984): 119–25.

Haas, Volkert. "Death and the Afterlife in Hittite Thought." In *Civilizations of the Ancient Near East*. 4 vols. Edited by Jack M. Sasson, 3.2021–30. New York: Charles Scribner's Sons, 1995.

Habel, Norman C. "'He Who Stretches Out the Heavens'." *CBQ* 34 (1972): 417–30.

Hadley, Judith M. "The Khirbet el-Qôm Inscription." *VT* 37 (1987): 60–62.

———— "Some Drawings and Inscriptions on Two Pithoi from Kuntillet 'Ajrud." *VT* 37 (1987): 180–213.

Hallo, William W., and William Kelly Simpson. *The Ancient Near East: A History*. New York: Harcourt Brace Jovanovich, 1971.

———— "Disturbing the Dead." In *Minḥah lᵉNaḥum: Biblical and Other Studies Presented to Nahum M. Sarna in Honour of his 70ᵗʰ Birthday*, edited by Marc Brettler and Michael Fishbane, 183–92. JSOTSup 154. Sheffield: Sheffield Academic Press, 1993.

———— "Sumerian Religion." In *kinattūtu ša dārâti: Raphael Kutscher Memorial Volume*, edited by A. F. Rainey, 15–35. Tel Aviv: Tel Aviv University Institute of Archae-ology, 1993.

———— "Texts, Statues and the Cult of the Divine King." VTSup 40 (1988): 54–66.

Halperin, David. *The Faces of the Chariot: Early Jewish Responses to Ezekiel's Vision*. Tübingen: J. C. B. Mohr/Paul Siebeck, 1988.

———— "Heavenly Ascension in Ancient Judaism: The Nature of the Experience." In *Society of Biblical Literature 1987 Seminar Papers*, edited by Kent Harold Richards, 218–32. Atlanta: Scholars Press, 1987.

———— "Hekhalot and Mir'āj: Observations on the Heavenly Journey in Judaism and Islam." In *Death, Ecstasy, and Other Worldly Journeys*, edited by John J. Collins and Michael Fishbane, 265–88. Albany, N.Y.: SUNY Press, 1995.

———— *The Merkabah in Rabbinic Literature*. New Haven, Conn.: American Oriental Society, 1980.

Halpern, Baruch. *The Emergence of Israel in Canaan*. SBLMS 29. Chico, Calif.: Scholars Press, 1983.

Handy, Lowell K. *Among the Host of Heaven: The Syro-Palestinian Pantheon as Bureau-cracy*. Winona Lake, Ind.: Eisenbrauns, 1994.

Hanson, Paul. *The Dawn of Apocalyptic*. Philadelphia: Fortress Press, 1975.

———— "Rebellion in Heaven, Azazel, and Euhemeristic Heroes in 1 Enoch 6–11."
JBL 96:2 (1977): 195–233.

Haran, Menahem. "The Ark and the Cherubim." In *Eretz-Israel 5 (Mazar Volume)*,
ed. Michael Avi-Yonah et al., 83–90. Jerusalem: Israel Exploration Society, 1958
[Hebrew].

———— "The Ark and the Cherubim." *IEJ* 9 (1959): 30–38, 89–94 [English].

———— "The Divine Presence in the Israelite Cult and the Cultic Institutions." *Bib* 50
(1969): 251–67.

———— "Temple and Community in Ancient Israel." In *Temple in Society*, edited by
Michael V. Fox, 17–25. Winona Lake, Ind.: Eisenbrauns, 1988.

———— *Temples and Temple Service in Ancient Israel: An Inquiry into the Character of Cult
Phenomena and the Historical Setting of the Priestly School*. Oxford: Clarendon Press, 1978.

Harlow, Daniel C. *The Greek Apocalypse of Baruch (3 Baruch) in Hellenistic Judaism and
Early Christianity*. SVTP 12. Leiden: E. J. Brill, 1996.

Harrelson, Walter. "The Significance of 'Last Words' for Intertestamental Ethics." In
Essays in Old Testament Ethics, edited by James T. Crenshaw and J. T. Willis, 203–
13. New York: KTAV, 1974.

Harris, J. R., ed. *The Legacy of Egypt*. Oxford: Clarendon, 1971.

Hasel, Gerhard F. "Resurrection in the Theology of Old Testament Apocalyptic." *ZAW*
92 (1980): 267–84.

Hawking, Stephen W. *A Brief History of Time: From the Big Bang to Black Holes*. New
York: Bantam Books, 1988.

Hayes, William C. "The Middle Kingdom in Egypt." In *Cambridge Ancient History*. 3d
ed. Vol. I, Part 2: *Early History of the Middle East*, edited by I. E. S. Edwards, C. J.
Gadd, and N. G. L. Hammond, 464–531. Cambridge: Cambridge University Press,
1971.

Healey, John F. "The Immortality of the King: Ugarit and the Psalms." *Or* 53 (1984):
245–54.

Heath, Thomas L. *Aristarchus of Samos: The Ancient Copernicus*. Oxford: Clarendon
Press, 1913. Reprint, New York: Dover Publications, Inc., 1981.

———— *Greek Astronomy*. London: J. M. Dent & Sons, Ltd., 1932. Reprint, New York:
Dover Publications, 1991.

Heidel, Alexander. *The Babylonian Genesis*. 2d ed. Chicago: University of Chicago Press,
1951.

Heimpel, Wolfgang. "The Sun at Night and the Doors of Heaven in Babylonian Texts."
JCS 38:2 (1986): 127–51.

Heinrich, Ernst. *Die Tempel und Heiligtümer in Alten Mesopotamien*. Denkmäler Antiker
Architektur 14. Berlin: Walter de Gruyter, 1982.

Hengel, Martin. *The "Hellenization" of Judaea in the First Century after Christ*. Philadelphia: Trinity Press International, 1989.

———— *Jews, Greeks and Barbarians*. Philadelphia: Fortress Press, 1980.

———— *Judaism and Hellenism: Studies in Their Encounter in Palestine During the Early
Hellenistic Period*. Philadelphia: Fortress Press, 1974.

Hennecke, Edgar, Wilhelm Schneemelcher, and R. McL. Wilson, eds. *New Testament Apocrypha*. 2 vols. Rev. ed. Philadelphia: Westminster/John Knox Press, 1991–
92.

Herdner, Andrée. *Corpus des tablettes en cunéiformes alphabetiques découvertes à Ras Shamra-
Ugarit*. 2 vols. MRS 10. Paris: Imprimerie Nationale, 1963.

Herodotus. *The Persian Wars*. Translated by George Rawlinson, with an introduction
by Francis R. B. Godolphin. New York: Random House, 1942.

Hesse, Mary B. "Models in Physics." *British Journal for the Philosophy of Science* 4 (1958): 198–214.

L'Heureux, Conrad E. *Rank Among the Canaanite Gods: El, Ba'al, and the Repha'im.* Missoula, Mont.: Scholars Press, 1979.

Himmelfarb, Martha. "Apocalyptic Ascent and the Heavenly Temple." In *Society of Biblical Literature 1987 Seminar Papers*, edited by Kent Harold Richards, 210–17. Atlanta: Scholars Press, 1987.

——— *Ascent to Heaven in Jewish and Christian Apocalypses.* New York/Oxford: Oxford University Press, 1993.

——— "From Prophecy to Apocalypse: The Book of the Watchers and Tours of Heaven." In *Jewish Spirituality: From the Bible Through the Middle Ages*, edited by Arthur Green, 145–65. New York: Crossroad, 1986.

——— "The Practice of Ascent in the Ancient Mediterranean World." In *Death, Ecstasy, and Other Worldly Journeys*, edited by John J. Collins and Michael Fishbane, 123–37. Albany, N.Y.: SUNY Press, 1995.

——— "Revelation and Rapture: The Transformation of the Visionary in the Ascent Apocalypses." In *Mysteries and Revelations: Apocalyptic Studies since the Uppsala Colloquium*, edited by John J. Collins and James H. Charlesworth, 70–90. JSPSup 9. Sheffield: Sheffield Academic Press, 1991.

——— *Tours of Hell: An Apocalyptic Form in Early Jewish and Christian Literature.* Philadelphia: Fortress Press, 1988.

Hinnells, John R., ed. *Mithraic Studies: Proceedings of the International Congress of Mithraic Studies, University of Manchester 1971.* Manchester: Manchester University Press/ Totowa, N.J.: Rowman and Littlefield, 1975.

Hirth, Volkmar. *Gottes Boten im Alten Testament: die alttestamentliche Mal'ak Vorstellung unter besonderer Berucksichtigung des Mal'ak Yahweh Problem.* Theologische Arbeiten 32. Berlin: Evangelisch Verlagsanstalt, 1975.

Hoffmeier, James K. "Some Thoughts on Genesis 1 & 2 and Egyptian Cosmology." *JANES* 15 (1983): 39–49.

Hoffner, Harry A. *Hittite Myths.* SBLWAW 2. Atlanta: Scholars Press, 1990.

Hoftijzer, J., and K. Jongeling. *Dictionary of the North-West Semitic Inscriptions.* 2 vols. Handbuch der Orientalistik 21.1–2. Leiden: E. J. Brill, 1995.

Hollander, H. W., and M. de Jonge. *The Testaments of the Twelve Patriarchs: A Commentary.* SVTP 8. Leiden: E. J. Brill, 1985.

Homer. *The Odyssey.* 2 vols. Translated by A. T. Murray. Revised by George E. Dimock. LCL. Cambridge, Mass.: Harvard University Press, 1995.

Hornung, Erik. *Der Ägyptische Mythos von der Himmelskuh.* OBO 46. Göttingen: Vandenhoeck & Ruprecht, 1982.

Horowitz, Wayne. "The Babylonian Map of the World." *Iraq* 50 (1988): 147–67.

——— *Mesopotamian Cosmic Geography.* Mesopotamian Civilizations 8. Winona Lake, Ind.: Eisenbrauns, 1998.

——— "Two New Ziqpu-Star Texts and Stellar Circles." *JCS* 46 (1994): 89–98.

——— "Two Notes on Etana's Flight to Heaven." *Or* 59 (1990): 511–17.

Houtman, Cornelius. *Der Himmel im Alten Testament: Israels Weltbild und Weltanschauung.* Oudtestamentische Studiën 30. Leiden: E. J. Brill, 1993.

——— "What Did Jacob See in His Dream at Bethel?" *VT* 27:3 (1977): 337–51.

How, W. W., and J. Wells. *A Commentary on Herodotus.* Oxford: Clarendon Press, 1928.

Hoyle, Fred. *Astronomy.* Garden City, N.Y.: Doubleday & Co., 1962.

Hubaux, J., and M. Leroy. *Le mythe du phénix dans les littératures grecque et latione.* Paris: Liège, 1939.

Hunger, Hermann. *Astrological Reports to Assyrian Kings*. State Archives of Assyria 8. Helsinki: Helsinki University Press, 1992.

Hunger, Hermann, and David Pingree. *MUL.APIN: An Astronomical Compendium in Cuneiform*. AfO 24. Horn, Austria: Ferdinand Berger and Söhne Gesellschaft, 1989.

Hunkin, J. W. "The Testaments of the Twelve Patriarchs." *JTS* 16 (1915): 80–97.

Hurowitz, Victor. *I Have Built You an Exalted House: Temple Building in the Light of Mesopotamian and Northwest Semitic Writings*. JSOTSup 115. JSOT/ASOR Monograph Series 5. Sheffield: Sheffield Academic Press, 1992.

Hutter, Manfred. *Altorientalische Vorstellungen von der Unterwelt: Literar- und religionsgeschichtliche Überlegungen zu "Nergal und Ereškigal"*. OBO 63. Göttingen: Vandenhoeck and Ruprecht, 1985.

Huxley, Margaret. "The Shape of the Cosmos According to Cuneiform Sources." *JRAS* 3:7:2 (1997): 189–98.

Isaac, Ephraim. "The Oldest Ethiopic Manuscript (K-)* of the Book of Enoch and Recent Studies of the Aramaic Fragments of Qumran Cave 4." In *"Working With No Data": Semitic and Egyptian Studies Presented to Thomas O. Lambdin*, edited by David M. Golomb, 195–207. Winona Lake, Ind.: Eisenbrauns, 1987.

Jacobs, Louis. "Jewish Cosmology." In *Ancient Cosmologies*, edited by Carmen Blacker and Michael Loewe, 66–86. London: George Allen and Unwin Ltd., 1975.

Jacobsen, Thorkild. "Formative Tendencies in Sumerian Religion." In *The Bible and the Ancient Near East: Essays in Honor of William Foxwell Albright*, edited by G. Ernest Wright, 267–78. Garden City, N.Y.: Doubleday and Company, 1961.

——— *The Sumerian King List*. Assyriological Studies 11. Chicago: University of Chicago Press, 1939.

——— *The Treasures of Darkness: A History of Mesopotamian Religion*. New Haven: Yale University Press, 1976.

James, Montague Rhodes. *Apocrypha Anecdota*. Texts and Studies 2:3. Edited by J. Armitage Robinson. Cambridge: Cambridge University Press, 1893.

——— *Apocrypha Anecdota II*. Texts and Studies 5:1. Edited by J. Armitage Robinson. Cambridge: Cambridge University Press, 1897.

——— "Notes on Apocrypha." *JTS* 16 (1915): 410–13.

——— *The Testament of Abraham*. Texts and Studies 2:2. Edited by J. Armitage Robinson. Cambridge: Cambridge University Press, 1892.

James, Montague Rhodes, ed. *The Apocryphal New Testament*. Oxford: Clarendon Press, 1924.

Jansen, H. Lundin. *Die Henochgestalt: Eine Vergleichende Religionsgeschichtliche Untersuchung*. Oslo: I Kommisjon Hos Jacob Dybwad, 1939.

Janko, Richard. *Homer, Hesiod, and the Hymns*. Cambridge: Cambridge University Press, 1982.

Jastrow, Morris. *Die Religion Babyloniens und Assyriens*. 2 vols. Giessen: Alfred Töpelmann, 1912.

——— *The Religion of Babylonia and Assyria*. Handbooks on the History of Religions 2. Boston: Ginn & Company, 1898.

Jellinek, Adolph. *Bet ha-Midrasch*. 6 vols. 2d ed. Jerusalem: Wahrman Books, 1967 [Hebrew].

Jensen, P. *Die Kosmologie der Babylonier: Studien und Materialien*. Strassburg: Karl J. Trübner, 1890.

Jeremias, Alfred. *Die Babylonisch-Assyrischen Verstellungen vom Leben nach dem Tode*. Leipzig: J. C. Hinrichssche Buchhandlung, 1887.

Johimowicz, E. "Islam." In *Ancient Cosmologies*, edited by Carmen Blacker and Michael Loewe, 143–71. London: George Allen and Unwin Ltd., 1975.

Jonge, H. J. de. "Die Textüberlieferung der Testamente der zwölf Patriarchen." *ZNW* 63 (1972): 24–44; Reprinted in *Studies on the Testaments of the Twelve Patriarchs: Text and Interpretation*, edited by M. de Jonge, 45–62. SVTP 3. Leiden: E. J. Brill, 1975.

Jonge, M. de. "The Testament of Levi and 'Aramaic Levi'." *RevQ* 49–52: 13 (1988): 367–85.

———— *The Testaments of the Twelve Patriarchs: A Study of Their Text, Composition and Origin.* 2d ed. Assen: Van Gorcum, 1975.

Jonge, M. de, et al. *The Testaments of the Twelve Patriarchs: A Critical Edition of the Greek Text.* PVTG I.2. Leiden: E. J. Brill, 1978.

Joüon, Paul. *A Grammar of Biblical Hebrew.* 2 vols. Translated and revised by T. Muraoka. Subsidia Biblica 14:I–II. Rome: Pontifical Biblical Institute, 1993.

Kahana, Abraham, ed. *Hassefarim Hahitsonim.* 2 vols. Jerusalem: Makor Publishing Ltd., 1978 [Hebrew].

Kaibel, Georgius, ed. *Epigrammata graeca ex lapidibus conlecta.* Berlin: Reimer, 1878.

Kautzsch, Emil, ed. *Die Apokryphen und Pseudepigraphen des Alten Testaments.* 2 vols. Tübingen: J. C. B. Mohr, 1900.

Kee, Howard C. "Testaments of the Twelve Patriarchs." In *The Old Testament Pseudepigrapha*, edited by James H. Charlesworth, 1.775–828. Garden City, N.Y.: Doubleday and Company, Inc., 1985.

Keel, Othmar. *Jahwe-Visionen und Siegelkunst: Eine neue Deutung der Majestätsschilderungen in Jes 6, Ez 1 und Sach 4.* Stuttgarter Bibelstudien 84–85. Stuttgart: Verlag Katholisches Bibelwerk, 1977.

———— "Das sogenannte altorientalische Weltbild." *Bibel und Kirche* 40:4 (1985): 157–61.

———— *The Symbolism of the Biblical World: Ancient Near Eastern Iconography and the Book of Psalms.* Translated by Timothy J. Hallet. New York: Seabury Press, 1978.

Keel, Othmar, and Christoph Uehlinger. *Altorientalische Miniaturkunst.* Mainz am Rhein: Verlag Philipp von Zabern, 1990.

———— *Gods, Goddesses, and Images of Gods in Ancient Israel.* Translated by Allan W. Mahnke. Philadelphia: Fortress Press, 1997.

———— *Göttinnen, Götter und Gottessymbole: Neue Erkenntnisse zur Religionsgeschichte Kanaans und Israels aufgrund bislang unerschlossener ikonographischer.* Quaestiones Disputatae 134. Freiburg: Herder, 1992.

———— "Jahwe und die Sonnengottheit von Jerusalem." In *Ein Gott allein? JHVH-Verehrung und biblischer Monotheismus im Kontext der israelitischen und altorientalischen Religionsgeschichte*, edited by Walter Dietrich and Martin A. Klopfenstein, 269–306. Freiburg: Universitätsverlag Freiburg, 1994.

Kees, Hermann. *Totenglauben und Jenseitsvorstellungen der Alten Ägypter.* 2d ed. Berlin: Akademie Verlag, 1956.

———— *Der Götterglaube im altern Ägypten.* 3d ed. Berlin: Akademie Verlag, 1977.

Kempinski, Aharon. "From Death to Resurrection: The Early Evidence." *BARev* 21:5 (September/October 1995): 56–65, 82.

Kinberg, Leah. "Interaction Between this World and the Afterworld in Early Islamic Tradition." *Oriens* 29–30 (1986): 285–308.

King, Leonard W. *Babylonian Boundary-Stones and Memorial-Tablets in the British Museum.* London: British Museum, 1912.

King, Philip J. *Jeremiah: An Archaeological Companion.* Louisville, Ky.: Westminster/John Knox Press, 1993.

Kinnier-Wilson, J. V. *The Legend of Etana*. Warminster, UK: Aris & Phillips Ltd., 1985.

Kleiner, Michael. *Saul in En-Dor, Wahrsagung order Totenbeschwörung?: Eine synchrone und diachrone Untersuchung zu 1 Sam 28*. Erfurter Theologische Studien 66. Leipzig: Benno, 1995.

Knibb, Michael A. "The Date of the Parables of Enoch: A Critical Review." *NTS* 25 (1979): 345–59.

———— *The Ethiopic Book of Enoch: A New Edition in the Light of the Aramaic Dead Sea Fragments*. 2 vols. Oxford: Clarendon Press, 1978.

———— "Martyrdom and Ascension of Isaiah." In *The Old Testament Pseudepigrapha*, edited by James H. Charlesworth, 2.143–76. Garden City, N.Y.: Doubleday and Company, 1985.

Koch, Johannes. *Neue Untersuchungen zur Topographie des babylonischen Fixsternhimmels*. Wiesbaden: Otto Harrassowitz, 1989.

Koch, Klaus. "Aschera als Himmelskönigin in Jerusalem." *UF* 20 (1988) 97–120.

Koch-Westenholz, Ulla. *Mesopotamian Astrology: An Introduction to Babylonian and Assyrian Celestial Divination*. Copenhagen: Museum Tusculanum Press, 1995.

Koehler, Ludwig, and Walter Baumgartner, eds. *The Hebrew and Aramaic Lexicon of the Old Testament*. 4 vols. Revised by Walter Baumgartner and Johann J. Stamm. New York/Leiden: E. J. Brill, 1994–.

Kolbe, Dieter. *Die Reliefprogramme religiösmythologischen Charakters in den neu-assyrischen Palästen: die Figurentypen, ihre Benennung und Bedeutung*. Frankfort am Main: Peter Lang, 1981.

Kolenkow, Anitra Bingham. "The Genre Testament and the Testament of Abraham." In *Studies on the Testament of Abraham*, edited by George W. E. Nickelsburg Jr., 139–52. SBLSCS 6. Missoula, Mont.: Scholars Press, 1976.

Korpel, Marjo Christina Annette. *A Rift in the Clouds: Ugaritic and Hebrew Descriptions of the Divine*. UBL 8. Münster: Ugarit-Verlag, 1990.

Kötzsche-Breitenbruch, Lieselotte. "Zur Darstellung der Himmelfahrt Constantins des Grossen." In *Jenseitsvorstellung in Antike und Christentum*, edited by Alfred Stuiber, 215–24. Jahrbuch für Antike und Christentum 9. Münster: Aschendorff Verlag, 1982.

Kraft, Robert A. "Christian Transmission of Greek Jewish Scriptures: A Methodological Probe." In *Paganisme, Judaïsme, Christianisme: Influences et affrontements dans le monde antique, Mélanges offerts à Marcel Simon*, edited by André Benoit, Marc Philonenko, and Cyrille Vogel, 207–26. Paris: Éditions E. De Boccard, 1978.

———— "The Multiform Jewish Heritage of Early Christianity." In *Christianity, Judaism and Other Greco-Roman Cults*, edited by Jacob Neusner, 174–99. Leiden: E. J. Brill, 1975.

Kramer, Samuel Noah. "Death and Nether World According to the Sumerian Literary Texts." *Iraq* 22 (1960): 59–68.

———— "The Death of Gilgamesh." *BASOR* 94 (1944): 2–12.

———— "The Death of Ur-Nammu and his Descent to the Netherworld." *JCS* 21 (1967): 104–22.

———— "Dilmun, The Land of the Living." *BASOR* 96 (1944): 18–28.

———— "Gilgamesh and the Land of the Living." *JCS* 1 (1947): 8–9.

———— *History Begins at Sumer*. Anchor Books. Garden City, N.Y.: Doubleday and Company, 1959.

———— "Inanna's Descent to the Nether World." *RA* 34:3 (1937): 93–134.

———— "'Inanna's Descent to the Nether World' Continued and Revised." *JCS* 5 (1951): 1–17.

———— "Mythology of Sumer and Akkad." In *Mythologies of the Ancient World*, edited by Samuel Noah Kramer, 95–137. Anchor Books. Garden City, N.Y.: Doubleday and Company, 1961.

———— "New Literary Catalogue from Ur." *RA* 55 (1961): 169–76.

———— *Sumerian Mythology*. Revised ed. Westport, Conn.: Greenwood Press, 1972.

———— *The Sumerians: Their History, Culture, and Character*. Chicago: University of Chicago Press, 1963.

Kramer, S. N., and John Maier. *Myths of Enki, The Crafty God*. New York: Oxford University Press, 1989.

Kraus, Hans-Joachim. *Psalmen*. 2 vols. BKAT 15. Neukirchen: Neukirchener Verlag, 1961.

Krupp, Edwin C. "Egyptian Astronomy: A Tale of Temples, Tradition, and Tombs." In *Archaeoastronomy and the Roots of Science*, edited by E. C. Krupp, 289–320. American Association for the Advancement of Science 71. Boulder, Colo.: Westview Press, 1984.

Kugler, Robert A. *From Patriarch to Priest: The Levi-Priestly Tradition from Aramaic Levi to Testament of Levi*. Early Judaism and Its Literature 9. Atlanta: Scholars Press, 1996.

Kuhn, K. H. "A Coptic Jeremiah Apocryphon." *Le Muséon* 83:1–2 (1970): 95–135; 83:3–4 (1970): 291–350.

Kuhn, Thomas S. *The Copernican Revolution: Planetary Astronomy in the Development of Western Thought*. Cambridge: Harvard University Press, 1957.

Kuhnen, Hans-Peter. *Palästina in griechisch-römischer Zeit*. Handbuch der Archaologie, Vorderasien 2.2. München: C. H. Beck'sche Verlagsbuchhandlung, 1990.

Kümmel, W. G., et al., eds. *Jüdische Schriften aus hellenistisch-römischer Zeit*. Gutersloh: Gutersloher Verlagshaus Gerd Mohn, 1974.

Küng, Hans. *Eternal Life? Life After Death as a Medical, Philosophical, and Theological Problem*. Garden City, N.Y.: Doubleday & Co., 1984.

Kvanvig, Helge S. *Roots of Apocalyptic: The Mesopotamian Background of the Enoch Figure and of the Son of Man*. WMANT 61. Neukirchen-Vluyn: Neukirchener Verlag, 1988.

Labuschagne, C. J. *The Incomparability of Yahweh in the Old Testament*. Leiden: E. J. Brill, 1966.

Lambert, W. G. *Babylonian Wisdom Literature*. Oxford: Clarendon Press, 1960.

———— "The Cosmology of Sumer and Babylon." In *Ancient Cosmologies*, edited by Carmen Blacker and Michael Loewe, 42–65. London: George Allen and Unwin Ltd., 1975.

———— "Enmeduranki and Related Matters." *JCS* 21 (1967): 126–38.

———— "The Theology of Death." In *Death in Mesopotamia: Papers Read at the XXVIe Rencontre assyriologique internationale*, edited by Bendt Alster, 53–66. Copenhagen Studies in Assyriology 8. Copenhagen: Akademisk Forlag, 1980.

Lambert, W. G., and A. R. Millard. *Atra-hasis: The Babylonian Story of the Flood*. Oxford: Clarendon Press, 1969.

Landsberger, Benno. "Über Farben im Sumerisch-akkadischen." *JCS* 21 (1967): 139–73.

Lang, Bernhard. "Afterlife: Ancient Israel's Changing Vision of the World Beyond." *BibRev* 4:2 (1988): 12–23.

———— "Life After Death in the Prophetic Promise." In *Congress Volume: Jerusalem 1986*, edited by J. A. Emerton, 145–56. VTSup 40. Leiden: E. J. Brill, 1988.

Langdon, Stephen. *The Legend of Etana and the Eagle*. Paris: Librairie Orientaliste Paul Geuthner, 1932.

———— *Sumerian Epic of Paradise, The Flood and the Fall of Man*. University Museum Publications of the Babylonian Section 10:1. Philadelphia: University Museum, 1915.

Larson, Erik W. "The Translation of Enoch: From Aramaic into Greek." Ph.D. diss., New York University, 1995.

Laubscher, Frans du T. "Epiphany and Sun Mythology in Zechariah 14." *JNWSL* 20:1 (1994): 125–38.

Layton, Bentley. *The Gnostic Scriptures.* Garden City, N.Y.: Doubleday and Co., Inc., 1987.

Legon, John A. R. "The Orion Correlation and Air-Shaft Theories." *Discussions in Egyptology* 33 (1995): 45–56.

Lemche, Niels Peter. "The Development of the Israelite Religion in the Light of Recent Studies on the Early History of Israel." In *Congress Volume: Leiden 1989,* edited by J. A. Emerton, 97–115. VTSup 43. Leiden: E. J. Brill, 1991.

Lesko, Leonard H. "Death and the Afterlife in Ancient Egyptian Thought." In *Civilizations of the Ancient Near East.* 4 vols. Edited by Jack M. Sasson, 3.1763–74. New York: Charles Scribner's Sons, 1995.

——— "Some Observations on the Composition of the *Book of Two Ways.*" *JAOS* 91 (1971): 30–43.

Levine, Lee I. *Ancient Synagogues Revealed.* Jerusalem: Israel Exploration Society, 1981.

Lewis, Theodore J. *Cults of the Dead in Ancient Israel and Ugarit.* HSM 39. Atlanta: Scholars Press, 1989.

Lewy, H. *Chaldean Oracles and Theurgy: Mysticism Magic and Platonism in the Later Roman Empire.* New ed. Edited by Michel Tardieu. Paris: Études Augustiniennes, 1978.

Liddell, Henry George, and Robert Scott, eds. *A Greek-English Lexicon, with a Supplement.* Revised by Henry Stuart Jones. Oxford: Clarendon Press, 1968.

Lieberman, Saul. *Greek in Jewish Palestine: Studies in the Life and Manners of Jewish Palestine in the II–IV Centuries C.E.* New York: Jewish Theological Seminary of America, 1942.

——— *Hellenism in Jewish Palestine: Studies in the Literary Transmission, Beliefs and Manners of Palestine in the I Century B.C.E.–IV Century C.E.* New York: Jewish Theological Seminary of America, 1950.

——— "How Much Greek in Jewish Palestine?" In *Biblical and Other Studies,* edited by Alexander Altman, 123–41. Philip W. Lown Institute of Advanced Judaic Studies: Studies and Texts 1. Cambridge, Mass.: Harvard University Press, 1963.

Lincoln, Andrew T. *Paradise Now and Not Yet: Studies in the Role of the Heavenly Dimension in Paul's Thought with Special Reference to His Eschatology.* SNTSMS 43. Cambridge: Cambridge University Press, 1981.

Lipínski, Edward. *Dieux et déesses de l'univers phénicien et punic.* Studia Phenicia 14. Orientalia Lovaniensia Analecta 64. Leuven: Peeters, 1995.

Livingstone, Alasdair. *Mystical and Mythological Explanatory Works of Assyrian and Babylonian Scholars.* Oxford: Clarendon Press, 1986.

Loewenstamm, Samuel E. *From Babylon to Canaan: Studies in the Bible and its Oriental Background.* Jerusalem: Magnes Press/Hebrew University, 1992.

Lohfink, Gerhard. *Die Himmelfahrt Jesu: Untersuchungen zu den Himmelfahrts und Erhöhungstexten bei Lukas.* SANT 26. Kösel: Verlag München, 1971.

Luckenbill, Daniel D. *Ancient Records of Assyria and Babylonia.* 2 vols. Chicago: University of Chicago Press, 1926–27.

MacDermot, Violet. *The Cult of the Seer in the Ancient Middle East.* Berkeley, Calif.: University of California Press, 1971.

Mach, Michael. *Entwicklungsstadien des jüdischen Engelglaubens in vorrabbinischer Zeit.* Texte und Studien zum Antiken Judentum 34. Tübingen: J. C. B. Mohr, 1992.

Machinist, Peter. "On Self-Consciousness in Mesopotamia." In *The Origins and Diversity of Axial Age Civilizations*, edited by S. N. Eisenstadt, 183–202. SUNY Series in Near Eastern Studies. Albany, N.Y.: SUNY Press, 1986.

Machinist, Peter, and Hayim Tadmor. "Heavenly Wisdom." In *The Tablet and the Scroll: Near Eastern Studies in Honor of William W. Hallo*, edited by Mark E. Cohen, Daniel C. Snell, and David B. Weisberg, 146–51. Bethesda, Md.: CDL Press, 1993.

MacRae, George W., and William R. Murdock. "The Apocalypse of Paul." In *The Nag Hammadi Library in English*, 3d ed. Edited by James M. Robinson, 256–59. San Francisco: Harper and Row, 1988.

Maier, Johann. "Die Sonne im religiosen Denken des antiken Judentums." In *ANRW* II:19:1, edited by W. Haase, 346–412. Berlin: Walter de Gruyter, 1979.

Malina, Bruce J. *On the Genre and Message of Revelation: Star Visions and Sky Journeys*. Peabody, Mass.: Hendrickson, 1995.

Margalit, Baruch. "Death and Dying in the Ugaritic Epics." In *Death in Mesopotamia: Papers Read at the XXVIe Rencontre assyriologique internationale*, edited by Bendt Alster, 243–54. Copenhagen Studies in Assyriology 8. Copenhagen: Akademisk Forlag, 1980.

Matthews, Donald M. *Principles of Composition in Near Eastern Glyptic of the Later Second Millennium B.C.* OBO 8. Göttingen: Vandenhoeck and Ruprecht, 1990.

Matthews, Victor H., and Don C. Benjamin. *Old Testament Parallels: Laws and Stories from the Ancient Near East*. Mahwah, N.J.: Paulist Press, 1991.

———— *The Social World of Ancient Israel, 1250–587 BCE*. Peabody, Mass.: Hendrickson Publishers, 1993.

Maunder, E. Walter. *The Astronomy of the Bible: An Elementary Commentary on the Astronomical References of Holy Scripture*. New York: Mitchell Kennedy, 1908.

Maystre, Charles. "Le Livre de la Vache du Ciel dans les tombeaux de la Vallée des Rois." *BIFAO* 40 (1941): 53–115.

Mazar, Amihai. *Archaeology of the Land of the Bible, 10,000–563 B.C.E.: An Introduction*. ABRL. New York: Doubleday, 1990.

———— "The 'Bull Site': An Iron Age I Open Cult Place." *BASOR* 247 (1982): 27–42.

McCrindle, J. W., ed. *The Christian Topography of Cosmas, An Egyptian Monk*. New York: Burt Franklin, 1967.

McDannell, Colleen, and Bernhard Lang. *Heaven: A History*. New Haven: Yale University Press, 1988.

McGinn, Bernard. *Visions of the End: Apocalyptic Traditions in the Middle Ages*. New York: Columbia University Press, 1979.

Meissner, B. *Babylonien und Assyrien*. Heidelberg: Carl Winters Universitäts-buchhandlung, 1925.

Merkur, Daniel. "Prophetic Initiation in Israel and Judah." In *The Psychoanalytic Study of Society*, vol. 12, edited by L. Bryce Boyer and Simon A. Grolnick, 37–67. Hillsdale, N.J.: The Analytic Press, 1988.

———— "The Visionary Practices of the Jewish Apocalyptists." In *The Psychoanalytic Study of Society*, vol. 14, edited by L. Bryce Boyer and Simon A. Grolnick, 119–48. Hillsdale, N.J.: The Analytic Press, 1989.

Meshel, Ze'ev. "Did Yahweh Have a Consort?" *BARev* 5:2 (1979): 24–36.

———— "Kuntillet 'Ajrud—An Israelite Site from the Monarchical Period on the Sinai Boarder." *Qadmoniot* 9 (1976): 118–24 [Hebrew].

Mettinger, Tryggve N. D. *No Graven Image?: Israelite Aniconism in Its Ancient Near Eastern Context*. ConBOT 42. Stockholm: Almqvist & Wiksell International, 1995.

———— "YHWH SABAOTH—The Heavenly King on the Cherubim Throne." In *Studies in the Period of David and Solomon and Other Essays*, edited by Tomoo Ishida, 109–38. Tokyo: Yamakawa-Shuppansha, 1982.

Metzger, Martin. "Himmelische und irdische Wohnstatt Jahwes." *UF* 2 (1970): 139–58.

———— "Jahwe, der Kerubenthroner, die von Keruben flankierte Palmette und Sphingenthrone aus dem Libanon." In *"Wer ist wie du, Herr, unter den Göttern?" Studien zur Theologie und Religionsgeschichte Israels für Otto Kaiser zum 70. Geburtstag*, edited by Ingo Kottsieper, Jürgen van Oorschot, Diethard Römheld, and Harald Martin Wahl, 75–90. Göttingen: Vandenhoeck & Ruprecht, 1994.

———— *Königsthron und Gottesthron. Thronformen und Throndarstellungen in Ägypten und im Vorderen Orient in dritten und zweiten Jahrtausand vor Christus und deren Bedeutung für das Verständnis von Aussagen über den Thron im Alten Testament*. 2 vols. AOAT 15, 1–2. Kevelaer/ Neukirchen-Vluyn: Butzon and Bercker/Neukirchener Verlag, 1985.

Meyers, Eric M. "Second Temple Studies in the Light of Recent Archaeology: Part I: The Persian and Hellenistic Periods." *Currents in Research: Biblical Studies* 2 (1994): 25–42.

Milgrom, Jacob. *Leviticus 1–16: A New Translation with Introduction and Commentary*. AB 3. New York: Doubleday, 1991.

Milik, J. T. *The Books of Enoch: Aramaic Fragments of Qumran Cave 4*. Oxford: Clarendon Press, 1976.

———— "Henoch au pays des aromates." *RB* 65 (1958): 70–77.

———— *Ten Years of Discovery in the Wilderness of Judaea*. SBT 26. London: SCM Press Ltd., 1959.

———— "Le testament de Lévi en araméen." *RB* 62 (1955): 398–406.

Millard, Alan R. "The Celestial Ladder and the Gate of Heaven (Genesis xxviii. 12 and 17)." *ExpTim* 78 (1966–67): 86–87.

Miller, Patrick D., Jr. "El, the Creator of the Earth." *BASOR* 239 (1980): 43–46.

Moor, Johannes C. de. *Anthology of Religious Texts from Ugarit*. Nisaba: Religious Texts Translation Series 16. Leiden: E. J. Brill, 1987.

———— *The Rise of Yahwism: The Roots of Israelite Monotheism*. BETL 91. Leuven, Belgium: Leuven University Press, 1990.

———— "Ugaritic Lexicographical Notes I." *UF* 18 (1986): 255–61.

Moore, George Foot. *Judaism in the First Centuries of the Christian Era*. 2 vols. Cambridge: Harvard University Press, 1927. Reprint, New York: Schocken Books, 1971.

Moorey, P. R. S. *Ur 'Of the Chaldees': A Revised and Updated Edition of Sir Leonard Woolley's Excavations at Ur*. Ithaca, N.Y.: Cornell University Press, 1982.

Morenz, Siegfried. *Ägyptische Religion*. Die Religionen der Menschheit 8. Stuttgart: Kohlhammer Verlag, 1960.

Moscati, Sabatino. *The Face of the Ancient Orient: A Panorama of the Near Eastern Civilizations in Pre-Classical Times*. Chicago: Quadangle Books, 1960.

Mueller, Dieter. "An Early Egyptian Guide to the Hereafter." *Journal of Egyptian Archaeology* 58 (1972): 99–125.

Mugler, Charles. *Archimède*. 4 vols. Collection des universités de France. Paris: Les Belles Lettres, 1971.

Mullen, E. Theodore, Jr. *The Divine Council in Canaanite and Early Hebrew Literature*. HSM 24. Atlanta: Scholars Press, 1980.

Murphy, Frederick J. "The Book of Revelation." *Currents in Research: Biblical Studies* 2 (1994): 181–225.

Nakhai, Beth Alpert. "Religion in Canaan and Israel: An Archaeological Perspective." Ph.D. diss., University of Arizona, 1993.

———— "What's a Bamah? How Sacred Space Functioned in Ancient Israel." *BARev* 20:3 (May/June 1994): 18–29, 77–79.

Naveh, Joseph, and Shaul Shaked. *Amulets and Magic Bowls: Aramaic Incantations of Late Antiquity*. Jerusalem: Magnes Press, 1985.

———— *Magic Spells and Formulae: Aramaic Incantations of Late Antiquity*. Jerusalem: Magnes Press, 1993.

Neiman, David. "The Supercaelian Sea." *JNES* 28 (1969): 243–49.

Ness, Lester J. "Astrology and Judaism in Late Antiquity." Ph.D. diss., Miami University (Ohio), 1990.

Neugebauer, Otto. *The "Astronomical" Chapters of the Ethiopic Book of Enoch (72–82)*. Royal Danish Academy of Sciences and Letters, Mathematics-Physics Series 40/10. Copenhagen: Munksgaard, 1981.

———— *Astronomical Cuneiform Texts: Babylonian Ephemerides of the Seleucid Period for the Motion of the Sun, the Moon, and the Planets*. 3 vols. London: Lund Humphries/ Princeton: Institute for Advanced Study, 1955.

———— "The Astronomy of the Book of Enoch." *Or* 33 (1964): 58–61.

———— "Exact Science in Antiquity." In *Studies in Civilization*, edited by A. J. B. Wace, O. Neugebauer, and W. S. Ferguson, 22–31. Philadelphia: University of Pennsylvania Press, 1941.

———— *The Exact Sciences in Antiquity*. 2d ed. New York: Harper Torchbooks, 1962.

———— *A History of Ancient Mathematical Astronomy*. 3 vols. New York/Berlin: Springer-Verlag, 1975.

———— "Notes on Ethiopic Astronomy." *Or* 33 (1964): 49–71.

Neugebauer, Otto, and H. B. van Hoesen. *Greek Horoscopes*. Philadephia: American Philosophical Society, 1959.

Neugebauer, Otto, and R. A. Parker. *Egyptian Astronomical Texts*. 3 vols. Providence, R.I.: Brown University Press, 1960–69.

Neumann, Heinz. "Anmerkungen zu Johannes Koch, Neue Untersuchungen sur Topographie des babylonischen Fixsternhimmels." *AfO* 38–39 (1991–92): 110–24.

Newsome, Carol A. "Angels, Old Testament." In *The Anchor Bible Dictionary*. 6 vols. Edited by David Noel Freedman, 1.248–53. New York: Doubleday, 1992.

Nickelsburg, George W. E. "Apocalyptic and Myth in 1 Enoch 6–11." *JBL* 96:3 (1977): 383–405.

———— "The Bible Rewritten and Expanded." In *Jewish Writings of the Second Temple Period*, edited by Michael E. Stone, 110–18. Philadelphia: Fortress Press/Assen: Van Gorcum, 1984.

———— "Enoch, Levi, and Peter: Recipients of Revelation in Upper Galilee." *JBL* 100 (1981): 575–600.

———— *Jewish Literature Between the Bible and Mishnah*. Philadelphia: Fortress Press, 1981.

———— *Resurrection, Immortality, and Eternal Life in Intertestamental Judaism*. HTS 26. Cambridge: Harvard University Press, 1972.

———— "Structure and Message in the Testament of Abraham." In *Studies on the Testament of Abraham*, edited by George W. E. Nickelsburg Jr., 85–93. SBLSCS 6. Missoula, Mont.: Scholars Press, 1976.

Niditch, Susan. "The Visionary." In *Ideal Figures in Ancient Judaism*, edited by George W. E. Nickelsburg and John J. Collins, 153–79. SBLSCS 12. Chico, Calif.: Scholars Press, 1980.

Nietzsche, Friedrich. "Die frühliche Wissenschaft." In *Nietzsche Werke*, 5:2, edited by Giorgio Colli and Mazzimo Montinari, 13–335. Berlin: Walter de Gruyter, 1973.

Nielsen, Inge. "The Hellenistic Palaces of the Jewish Kings." In *In the Last Days: On Jewish and Christian Apocalyptic and its Period*, edited by Knud Jeppesen, Kirsten Nielsen and Bent Rosendal, 181–84. Esbjerg, Denmark: Aarhus University Press, 1994.

———— *Hellenistic Palaces: Tradition and Renewal*. Esbjerg, Denmark: Aarhus University Press, 1994.

Nilsson, Martin P. *A History of Greek Religion*. 2d ed. Translated by F. J. Fielden. Oxford: Clarendon Press, 1949.

North, Helen F. "Death and Afterlife in Greek Tragedy and Plato." In *Death and Afterlife: Perspectives of World Religions*, edited by Hiroshi Obayashi, 49–64. New York: Greenwood Press, 1992.

Notter, Viktor. *Biblischer Schöpfungsbericht und ägyptische Schöpfungsmythen*. Stuttgarter Bibelstudien 68. Stuttgart: Verlag Katholisches Bibelwerk, 1974.

Nougayrol, Jean, Emmanuel Laroche, Claude Virolleaud, and Claude F. A. Schaeffer, eds. *Ugaritica V*. Paris: Imprimerie Nationale, 1968.

Oates, Joan. *Babylon*. London: Thames and Hudson Ltd., 1979.

Olmstead, A. T. *History of the Persian Empire*. Chicago: University of Chicago Press, 1948.

Olyan, Saul M. *Asherah and the Cult of Yahweh in Israel*. SBLMS 34. Atlanta: Scholars Press, 1988.

———— "Some Observations Concerning the Identity of the Queen of Heaven." *UF* 19 (1987): 286–300.

———— *A Thousand Thousands Served Him: Exegesis and the Naming of Angels in Ancient Judaism*. Texte und Studien zum Antiken Judentum 36. Tübingen: J. C. B. Mohr/ Paul Siebeck, 1993.

Opelt, Ilona. "Christianisierung heidnischer Etymologien." *Jahrbuch für Antike und Christentum* 2 (1959): 70–85.

Oppenheim, A. Leo. *Ancient Mesopotamia: Portrait of a Dead Civilization*. Chicago: University of Chicago Press, 1964.

———— "A Babylonian Diviner's Manual." *JNES* 33:2 (1974): 197–220.

———— *The Interpretation of Dreams in the Ancient Near East, with a Translation of an Assyrian Dream-Book*. TAPS 46:3. Philadelphia: American Philosophical Society, 1956.

———— "The Significance of the Temple in the Ancient Near East II: The Mesopotamian Temple." *BA* 7 (1944): 58–59.

Ornan, Tallay. "The Mesopotamian Influence on West Semitic Inscribed Seals: A Preference for the Depiction of Mortals." In *Studies in the Iconography of Northwest Semitic Seals: Proceedings of a symposium held in Fribourg on April 17–20, 1991*, edited by Benjamin Sass and Christoph Uehlinger, 52–73. OBO 125. Göttingen: Vandenhoeck and Ruprecht, 1993.

Pagels, Elaine H. *The Origin of Satan*. New York: Random House, 1995.

Parker, R. A. "Ancient Egyptian Astronomy." In *The Place of Astronomy in the Ancient World*, edited by F. R. Hodson, 43–65. London: Oxford University Press, 1974.

Penglase, Charles. "Some Concepts of Afterlife in Mesopotamia and Greece." In *The Archaeology of Death in the Ancient Near East*, edited by Stuart Campbell and Anthony Green, 209–20. Oxbow Monographs 15. Oxford: Oxbow Books, 1995.

Peters, F. E. *The Harvest of Hellenism: A History of the Near East from Alexander the Great to the Triumph of Christianity*. New York: Simon and Schuster, 1970.

———— *A Reader on Classical Islam*. Princeton, N.J.: Princeton University Press, 1994.

Philo of Alexandria. *Philo.* 10 volumes. Translated by F. H. Colson and G. H. Whitaker. LCL. Cambridge: Harvard University Press, 1929–62.

Philonenko, Marc. *Joseph et Aséneth: Introduction, texts critique, traduction et notes.* Studia Postbiblica 13. Leiden: E. J. Brill, 1968.

Piankoff, Alexandre. *The Shrines of Tut-Ankh-Amon.* Bollingen Series 40:2. Egyptian Religious Texts and Representations. New York: Pantheon Books, 1955.

Picard, J.-C. "L'Apocalypse grecque de Baruch. Ie'ne Partie: traduction, primier niveau de description et questions de methode." Unpublished thesis for the licentiate in Theology. University of Strasbourg, Faculte de theologie Protestante, 1966.

——— "Observations sur l'Apocalypse grecque de Baruch I: Cadre historique fictif et efficacite symbolique." *Semitica* 20 (1970): 77–103.

Picard, J.-C., ed. *Apocalypsis Baruchi Graece.* PVTG 2, pp. 61–96. Leiden: E. J. Brill, 1967.

Pinches, T. G., J. N. Strassmaier, and A. J. Sachs. *Late Babylonian Astronomical and Related Texts.* Providence: Brown University Press, 1955.

Pindar. 2 vols. Edited and translated by William H. Race. LCL. Cambridge: Harvard University Press, 1997.

Pistis Sophia. Edited by Carl Schmidt. Translation and Notes by Violet Macdermot. Nag Hammadi Studies 9. Leiden: E. J. Brill, 1978.

Plato. *The Republic.* Translated by Paul Shorey. 2 vols. LCL. Cambridge: Harvard University Press, 1937.

Porten, Bezalel. *The Elephantine Papyri in English.* Documenta et monumenta orientalis antiqui 22. Leiden: E. J. Brill, 1996.

——— "The Religion of the Jews of Elephantine in Light of the Hermopolis Papyri." *JNES* 28 (1969) 116–21.

Postgate, J. N. *Early Mesopotamia: Society and Economy at the Dawn of History.* New York: Routledge, 1994.

Pritchard, James B., ed. *The Ancient Near East in Pictures Relating to the Old Testament.* Princeton: Princeton University Press, 1969.

——— *Ancient Near Eastern Texts Relating to the Old Testament.* Princeton: Princeton University Press, 1969.

Ptolemy, Claudius. *Claudii Ptolemaei opera quae extant omnia, Volume II: Opera astronomica minora,* ed. J. L. Heiberg. Leipzig: Teubner, 1907.

Puech, Emile. *La croyance des esseniens en la vie future—immortalite, resurrection, vie eternelle: histoire d'une croyance dans le judaisme ancien.* 2 vols. Etudes bibliques, ns 21–22. Paris: J. Gabalda, 1993.

Quinn, Esther C. *The Quest of Seth for the Oil of Life.* Chicago: The University of Chicago Press, 1962.

Radau, Hugo. *Sumerian Hymns and Prayers to God Nin-Ib from the Temple Library of Nippur.* The Babylonian Expedition of the University of Pennsylvania, Series A: Cuneiform Texts, Volume 29, Part 1, edited by H. V. Hilprecht. Philadelphia: University of Pennsylvania, 1911.

Rainey, Anson F. "Who is a Canaanite? A Review of the Textual Evidence." *BASOR* 304 (1996): 1–16.

Al-Rawi, F. N. H., and A. R. George. "Enuma Anu Enlil XIV and Other Early Astronomical Tables." *AfO* 38–39 (1991–92): 52–73.

Rees, D. A., ed. *The Republic of Plato.* 2 vols. 2d ed. Cambridge: The University Press, 1963.

Reiner, Erica. "The Etiological Myth of the Seven Sages." *Or* 30 (1961): 1–11.

——— *Shupru: A Collection of Sumerian and Akkadian Incantations.* AfO Beiheft 11. Osnabrück: Biblio Verlag, 1970.

Reiner, Erica, and David Pingree. *ENUMA ANU ENLIL Tablet 63: The Venus Tablet of Ammisaduqa.* Bibliotheca Mesopotamica 2:1. Babylonian Planetary Omens 1. Malibu, Calif.: Undena Publications, 1975.

———— *ENUMA ANU ENLIL, Tablets 50–51.* Bibliotheca Mesopotamica 2:2. Babylonian Planetary Omens 2. Malibu, Calif.: Undena Publications, 1981.

Riaud, Jean. "Apocalypse grecque de Baruch." In *La Bible: Écrits intertestamentaires,* edited by André Dupont-Summer, Marc Philonenko et al., 1141–64. Paris: Gallimard, 1987.

Riessler, Paul, ed. *Altjüdisches Schrifttum Ausserhalb der Bibel.* Heidelberg: F. H. Kerle Verlag, 1928.

Ringgren, H. "The Religion of Ancient Syria." In *Historia Religionum: Handbook for the History of Religions.* Vol. 1, *Religions of the Past,* edited by C. Jouco Bleeker and Geo Widengren, 195–222. Leiden: E. J. Brill, 1969.

Robinson, James M., ed. *The Nag Hammadi Library.* 3d rev. ed. San Francisco: Harper and Row, 1988.

Rochberg-Halton, Francesca. "Astrology in the Ancient Near East." In *The Anchor Bible Dictionary.* 6 vols. Edited by David Noel Freedman, 4.504–7. New York: Doubleday, 1992.

———— "Astronomy and Calenders in Ancient Mesopotamia." In *Civilizations of the Ancient Near East.* 4 vols. Edited by Jack M. Sasson, 3.1925–40. New York: Charles Scribner's Sons, 1995.

———— "Babylonian Horoscopes and their Sources." *Or* 58 (1989): 102–23.

———— "New Evidence for the History of Astrology." *JNES* 43:2 (1984): 115–40.

Roitman, Adolfo, ed. *A Day at Qumran: The Dead Sea Sect and Its Scrolls.* Jerusalem: Israel Museum, 1997.

Römer, W. H. Ph. "The Religion of Ancient Mesopotamia." In *Historia Religionum: Handbook for the History of Religions.* Vol. 1, *Religions of the Past,* edited by C. Jouco Bleeker and Geo Widengren, 115–94. Leiden: E. J. Brill, 1969.

Root, Margaret C. *The King and Kingship in Achaemenid Art.* Acta Iranica 19. Leiden: E. J. Brill, 1979.

Ross, J. P. "Jahweh ṣeba'ôt in Samuel and Psalms." *VT* 17:1 (1967): 76–92.

Rossiter, Evelyn. *Le Livre des Morts: Papyrus égyptiens (1420–1100 av.J.C.).* Geneve: Productions Liber SA, 1984.

Rouillard, Hedwige. "Royauté céleste et royauté terrestre en I R 22." In *Le trône de Dieu,* edited by Marc Philonenko, 100–107. WUNT 69. Tübingen: J. C. B. Mohr/Paul Siebeck, 1993.

Rubinkiewicz, Ryszard. "La vision de l'histoire dans l'Apocalypse d'Abraham." In *ANRW* II:19:1, edited by Wolfgang Haase, 137–51. Berlin/New York: Walter de Gruyter, 1979.

Rubinstein, Arie. "Hebraisms in the 'Apocalypse of Abraham,'" *JJS* 5:3 (1954): 132–35.

———— "Hebraisms in the Slavonic 'Apocalypse of Abraham,'" *JJS* 4 (1953): 108–15.

Rudolph, Kurt. *Gnosis: The Nature and History of Gnosticism.* San Francisco: Harper and Row Publishers, 1987.

Russell, Jeffrey Burton. *The Devil: Perceptions of Evil From Antiquity to Primitive Christianity.* Ithaca: Cornell University Press, 1977.

———— *Satan: The Early Christian Tradition.* Ithaca: Cornell University Press, 1981.

———— *A History of Heaven: The Singing Silence.* Princeton: Princeton University Press, 1997.

Ryan, W. F. "Astronomy in Church Slavonic: Linguistic Aspects of Cultural Transmission." In *The Formation of the Slavonic Literary Languages,* edited by Gerald Stone and Dean Worth, 53–60. UCLA Slavic Studies 11. Columbus, Ohio: Slavica Publishers, Inc., 1985.

——— "Curious Star Names in Slavonic Literature." *Russian Linguistics* 1 (1974): 139–50.

Sachs, Abraham, J. "Babylonian Horoscopes." *JCS* 6 (1952): 49–75.

——— "Babylonian Observational Astronomy." In *The Place of Astronomy in the Ancient World*, edited by F. R. Hodson, 43–50. London: Oxford University Press, 1974.

——— "A Classification of the Babylonian Astronomical Tablets of the Seleucid Period." *JCS* 2 (1950): 271–90.

——— "La naissance de l'astrologie horoscopique en Babylonie." *Archeologia* 15 (Mars-Avril 1967): 12–19.

——— "Sirius Dates in Babylonian Astronomical Texts of the Seleucid Period." *JCS* 6 (1952): 105–14.

Saggs, H. W. F. *The Encounter with the Divine in Mesopotamia and Israel.* Jordan Lectures in Comparative Religion 12. London: Athlone Press/Atlantic Highlands, N.J.: Humanities Press, 1978.

——— *The Greatness That Was Babylon.* London: Sidgwick and Jackson, 1962.

Sambursky, Shmuel. "Copernicus in the Perspective of Our Generation." In *Proceedings of the Israel Academy of Sciences and Humanities, Volume 5 (1971–1976)*, 297–312. Jerusalem: The Israel Academy of Sciences and Humanities, 1976.

Sarfatti, Gad ben-ami. "Talmudic Cosmography." *Tarbitz* 35:2 (1965): 137–48 [Hebrew].

Sarna, Nahum H. *Understanding Genesis: The Heritage of Biblical Israel.* New York: Schocken Books, 1970.

Sass, Benjamin, and Christoph Uehlinger, eds. *Studies in the Iconography of Northwest Semitic Seals: Proceedings of a symposium held in Fribourg on April 17–20, 1991.* OBO 125. Göttingen: Vandenhoeck and Ruprecht, 1993.

Sasson, J. M., ed. *Civilizations of the Ancient Near East.* 4 vols. New York: Charles Scribner's Sons, 1995.

Schaeffer, Claude F.-A. "Les Fouilles de Ras Shamra-Ugarit, Huitième campagne." *Syria* 18 (1937): 125–54.

Schäfer, Peter. *The Hidden and Manifest God: Some Major Themes in Early Jewish Mysticism.* SUNY Series in Judaica: Hermeneutics, Mysticism, and Religion. Albany, N.Y.: SUNY Press, 1992.

——— *Rivalität zwischen Engeln und Menschen.* Studia Judaica. Berlin: Walter de Gruyter, 1975.

Schiffman, Lawrence. "4QMysteries[a]: A Preliminary Edition and Translation." In *Solving Riddles and Untying Knots: Biblical, Epigraphic, and Semitic Studies in Honor of Jonas C. Greenfield*, edited by Ziony Zevit, Seymour Gitin, and Michael Sokoloff, 207–60. Winona Lake, Ind.: Eisenbrauns, 1995.

——— *Reclaiming the Dead Sea Scrolls: The History of Judaism, the Background of Christianity, the Lost Library of Qumran.* Philadelphia: Jewish Publication Society, 1994.

Schirmann, Jefim. "The Battle Between Behemoth and Leviathan According to an Ancient Hebrew *Piyyut*." In *Proceedings of the Israel Academy of Sciences and Humanities* 6 (1969–70), 327–69. Jerusalem: The Israel Academy of Sciences and Humanities, 1971.

Schmidt, Brian B. *Israel's Beneficent Dead: Ancestor Cult and Necromancy in Ancient Israelite Religion and Tradition.* Forschungen zum Alten Testament 11. Tübingen: J. C. B. Mohr/Paul Siebeck, 1994.

Schmidt, Francis. *Le Testament grec d'Abraham.* Tübingen: J. C. B. Mohr/Paul Siebeck, 1986.

Schmidt, Nathaniel. "The Two Recensions of Slavonic Enoch." *JAOS* 41 (1921): 307–12.

Schneider, Gerhard. "'Im Himmel—auf Erden,' eine Perspektive matthäischer Theologie." In *Studien zum Matthäusevangelium: Festschrift für Wilhelm Pesch*, edited by Ludger Schenke, 283–97. Stuttgart: Verlag Katholisches Bibelwerk, 1988.

Schniedewind, William. *Society and the Promise to David*. New York/Oxford: Oxford University Press, 1999.

Scholem, Gershom G. *Jewish Gnosticism, Merkabah Mysticism, and Talmudic Tradition*. 2d ed. New York: Jewish Theological Seminary of America, 1965.

——— *Major Trends in Jewish Mysticism*. 3rd rev. ed. New York: Schocken Books, 1954. Reprint, New York: Schocken Books, 1961.

——— *Ursprung und Anfänge der Kabbala*. Studia Judaica: Forschungen zur Wissenschaft des Judentums 3. Berlin: Walter de Gruyter, 1962.

Schroer, Silvia. *In Israel Gab Es Bilder: Nachrichten von darstellender Kunst im alten Testament*. OBO 74. Göttingen/Freiburg: Vandenhoeck and Ruprecht/Universitätsverlag Freiburg, 1987.

Schultz, Joseph P. "Angelic Opposition to the Ascension of Moses and the Revelation of the Law." *JQR* 61 (1970–71): 282–307.

Schwegler, T. *Probleme der biblischen Urgeschichte*. Munich: 1960.

Schwemer, Anna Maria. "Irdischer und himmlischer König. Beobachtungen zur sogenannten David-Apokalypse in Hekhalot Rabbati §§122–126." In *Königsherrschaft Gottes und himmlischer Kult im Judentum, Urchristentum und in der hellenistischen Welt*, edited by Martin Hengel and Anna Maria Schwemer, 309–59. WUNT 55. Tübingen: J. C. B. Mohr/Paul Siebeck, 1991.

Scurlock, Jo Ann. "Death and the Afterlife in Ancient Mesopotamian Thought." In *Civilizations of the Ancient Near East*. 4 vols. Edited by Jack M. Sasson, 3.1883–94. New York: Charles Scribner's Sons, 1995.

Segal, Alan F. "Heavenly Ascent in Hellenistic Judaism, Early Christianity and their Environment." In *ANRW* II:23:2, edited by Wolfgang Haase, 1333–94. Berlin/New York: Walter de Gruyter, 1980.

Seow, C. L. "Linguistic Evidence and the Dating of Qohelet." *JBL* 115:4 (1996) 643–66.

——— *Myth, Drama, and the Politics of David's Dance*. HSM 44. Atlanta: Scholars Press, 1989.

Sepher Ha-Razim: The Book of the Mysteries. Translated by Michael A. Morgan. Chico, Calif.: Scholars Press, 1983.

Sethe, Kurt. *Übersetzung und Kommentar zu den Altägyptischen Pyramidentexten*. 6 vols. Glückstadt: J. J. Augustin, 1935–62.

Shanks, Hershel, ed. *Understanding the Dead Sea Scrolls*. New York: Random House, 1992.

Silverman, Michael H. *Religious Values in the Proper Names at Elephantine*. AOAT 217. Kevelaer/Neukirchen-Vluyn: Verlag Butzon and Bercker/Neukirchener Verlag, 1985.

Silverstein, Theodore. *Visio Sancti Pauli: The History of the Apocalypse in Latin Together with Nine Texts*. London: Christophers, 1935.

Sisson, Paige. "Intercession and the Denial of Peace in 1 Enoch 12–16." In *Hebrew Annual Review* 11, edited by Reuben Ahroni, 371–86. Columbus: Ohio State University, 1987.

Sjöberg, Åke W., and E. Bergmann. *The Collection of the Sumerian Temple Hymns*. Texts from Cuneiform Sources 3. Locust Valley, N.Y.: J. J. Augustin Publisher, 1969.

Sjöberg, E. *Der Menschensohn im Äthoipischen Henochbuch.* Lund: C. W. K. Gleerup, 1946.

Smith, Jane I., and Yvonne Y. Haddad. *The Islamic Understanding of Death and Resurrection.* Albany, N.Y.: SUNY Press, 1981.

Smith, Mark S. *The Early History of God: Yahweh and the Other Deities in Ancient Israel.* San Francisco: Harper and Row, 1990.

———— "The Near Eastern Background of Solar Language for Yahweh." *JBL* 109:1 (1990): 29–39.

Smith, Mark S., and Elizabeth M. Bloch-Smith. "Death and Afterlife in Ugarit and Israel." *JAOS* 108:2 (1988): 277–84.

Smith, Morton. "Ascent to the Heavens and Deification in 4QMª." In *Archaeology and the History in the Dead Sea Scrolls:The New York University Conference in Memory of Yigael Yadin,* edited by Lawrence H. Schiffman, 181–88. JSPSup 8. JSOT/ASOR Monographs 2. Sheffield: Sheffield Academic Press, 1990.

———— *Palestinian Parties and Politics That Shaped the Old Testament.* New York: Columbia University Press, 1971.

———— "Two Ascended to Heaven—Jesus and the Author of 4Q491." In *Jesus and the Dead Sea Scrolls,* edited by James H. Charlesworth, 290–301. ABRL. New York: Doubleday, 1992.

Soden, Wolfram von. *Akkadisches Handwörterbuch.* Wiesbaden: Harrassowitz, 1965–81.

———— *The Ancient Orient: An Introduction to the Study of the Ancient Near East.* Translated by Donald G. Schley. Grand Rapids: William B. Eerdmans, 1994.

———— *Grundriss der Akkadischen Grammatik.* Analecta Orientalia 33/47. Rome: Pontificium Institutum Biblicum, 1969.

Soldt, Wilfred H. van. *Solar Omens of Enuma Anu Enlil: Tablets 23 (24):–29 (30).* Istanbul: Nederlands Historisch-Archaeologisch Instituut, 1995.

Spencer, A. J. *Death in Ancient Egypt.* New York: Penguin Books, 1982.

Spronk, Klaas. *Beatific Afterlife in Ancient Israel and in the Ancient Near East.* Neukirchen-Vluyn: Neukirchener Verlag/Kevelaer: Butzon and Bercker, 1986.

Stadelmann, Luis I. J. *The Hebrew Conception of the World: A Philological and Literary Study.* AnBib 39. Rome: Pontifical Biblical Institute, 1970.

Stähli, Hans-Peter. *Solare Elemente im Jahweglauben des Alten Testaments.* OBO 66. Göttingen: Vandenhoeck und Ruprecht, 1985.

Steindorf, Georg. *Die Apokalypse des Elias: Eine unbekannte Apokalypse und Bruchstücke der Sophonias-Apokalypse.* TU 17.3. Leipzig: J. C. Hinrichssche Buchhandlung, 1899.

Steindorff, George, and Keith C. Seele. *When Egypt Ruled the East.* Chicago: University of Chicago Press, 1942.

Stern, Ephraim. *Material Culture of the Land of the Bible in the Persian Period 538–332 BC.* Warminster: Aris and Phillips, 1982.

Stern, Menahem. *Greek and Latin Authors on Jews and Judaism: Edited with Introductions, Translations and Commentary.* 3 vols. Jerusalem: Israel Academy of Sciences and Humanities, 1974–84.

Stieglitz, Robert R. "The Hebrew Names of the Seven Planets." *JNES* 40:2 (1981): 135–37.

Stone, Michael E. "Abel-Meholah." In *Encyclopedia Judaica.* 16 vols., 2.62. Jerusalem: Keter Publishing House Ltd., 1971.

———— "Apocalyptic Literature." In *Jewish Writings of the Second Temple Period,* edited by Michael E. Stone, 383–441. CRIANT II:2. Philadelphia: Fortress Press/Assen: Van Gorcum, 1984.

———— "Apocalyptic—Vision or Hallucination." *Milla wa-Milla* 14 (1974): 47–56.

———— "An Armenian Tradition Relating to the Death of the Three Companions of Daniel." *Muséon* 86 (1973): 111–23.

———— "The Book of Enoch and Judaism in the Third Century BCE." *CBQ* 40 (1978): 479–92.

———— "The Concept of the Messiah in IV Ezra." In *Religions in Antiquity: Essays in Memory of Erwin Ramsdell Goodenough*, edited by Jacob Neusner, 295–312. Leiden: E. J. Brill, 1968.

———— "Enoch, Aramaic Levi and Sectarian Origins." *JSJ* 19:2 (1988): 159–70.

———— "Eschatology, Remythologization, and Cosmic Aporia." In *The Origins and Diversity of Axial Age Civilizations*, edited by S. N. Eisenstadt, 241–51. SUNY Series in Near Eastern Studies. Albany, N.Y.: SUNY Press, 1986.

———— *Fourth Ezra: A Commentary on the Book of Fourth Ezra*. Hermenia. Minneapolis: Augsburg Fortress, 1990.

———— "Lists of Revealed Things in Apocalyptic Literature." In *Magnalia Dei: The Mighty Acts of God*, edited by F. M. Cross, W. E. Lemke, and P. D. Miller Jr., 414–52. Garden City, N.Y.: Doubleday, 1976.

———— "Methodological Issues in the Study of the Text of the Apocrypha and Pseudepigrapha." In *Proceedings of the Fifth World Congress of Jewish Studies, The Hebrew University, Mount Scopus—Givat Ram, Jerusalem, 3–11 August 1969*, 211–17. Jerusalem: World Union of Jewish Studies, 1969.

———— "A New Edition and Translation of the *Questions of Ezra*." In *Solving Riddles and Untying Knots: Biblical, Epigraphic, and Semitic Studies in Honor of Jonas C. Greenfield*, edited by Ziony Zevit, Seymour Gitin, and Michael Sokoloff, 293–16. Winona Lake, Ind.: Eisenbrauns, 1995.

———— *Scriptures, Sects and Visions*. New York: Collins, 1980.

———— *The Testament of Abraham: The Greek Recensions*. SBLTT 2. Pseudepigrapha Series 2. Missoula, Mont.: Society of Biblical Literature, 1972.

Stone, Michael E., ed. *Jewish Writings of the Second Temple Period*. CRIANT II:2. Philadelphia: Fortress Press/Assen: Van Gorcum, 1984.

Stone, Michael E., and Jonas C. Greenfield. "Aramaic Levi Documents." In *Qumran Cave 4. XVII: Parabiblical Texts, Part 3*, edited by G. Brooks et al., 1–72. DJD XXII. Oxford: Clarendon Press, 1996.

Stone, Michael E., and David Satran, eds. *Emerging Judaism: Studies on the Fourth & Third Centuries B.C.E.* Minneapolis: Fortress Press, 1989.

Strange, John. "Hellenism in Archaeology." In *In the Last Days: On Jewish and Christian Apocalyptic and its Period*, edited by Knud Jeppesen, Kirsten Nielsen, and Bent Rosendal, 175–80. Esbjerg, Denmark: Aarhus University Press, 1994.

Strugnell, John. "The Angelic Liturgy at Qumran—4QSerek Šîrôt 'Olat Haššabbat." VTSup 7 (1960): 318–45.

Suter, David W. *Tradition and Composition in the Parables of Enoch*. SBLDS 47. Missoula, Mont.: Scholars Press, 1979.

Swartz, Michael D. "Book and Tradition in Hekhalot and Magical Literatures." *Journal of Jewish Thought and Philosophy* 3:2 (1994): 189–229.

———— "'Like Ministering Angels': Ritual and Purity in Early Jewish Mysticism and Magic." *AJSRev* 19:2 (1994): 135–67.

Syreeni, Kari. "Between Heaven and Earth: On the Structure of Matthew's Symbolic Universe." *JSNT* 40 (1990): 3–13.

Tabor, James D. "'Returning to the Divinity': Josephus's Portrayal of the Disappearances of Enoch, Elijah, and Moses." *JBL* 108:2 (1989): 225–38.

———— *Things Unutterable: Paul's Ascent to Paradise in its Greco-Roman, Judaic, and Early Christian Contexts.* Lanham, Md.: University Press of America, 1986.

Talmon, Shemaryahu. "The Calendar Reckoning of the Sect from the Judaean Desert." In *Aspects of the Dead Sea Scrolls*, edited by Chaim Rabin and Yigael Yadin, 162–99. Scripta Hierosolymitana 4. Jerusalem: Magnes Press/Hebrew University, 1965.

———— "The 'Dead Sea Scrolls' or 'The Community of the Renewed Covenant'?" In *Echoes of Many Texts: Reflections on Jewish and Christian Traditions—Essays in Honor of Lou H. Silberman*, edited by William G. Dever and J. Edward Wright, 115–45. BJS 313. Atlanta: Scholars Press, 1997.

———— "The Presentation of Synchroneity and Simultaneity in Biblical Narrative." In *Studies in Hebrew Narrative Art Through the Ages*, edited by Joseph Heinemann and S. Werses, 9–26. Scripta Hierosolymitana 27. Jerusalem: Magnes Press/Hebrew University, 1978.

———— *The World of Qumran from Within.* Jerusalem: Magnes Press, 1989.

Tappy, Ron. "Did the Dead Ever Die in Biblical Judah?" *BASOR* 298 (1995): 59–68.

Taylor, J. Glen. *Yahweh and the Sun: Biblical and Archaeological Evidence for Sun Worship in Ancient Israel.* JSOTSup 111. Sheffield: Academic Press, 1993.

Thompson, R. Campbell. *The Reports of the Magicians and Astrologers of Nineveh and Babylon in the British Museum.* 2 vols. London: Luzac and Co., 1900.

Tigay, Jeffrey. *The Evolution of the Gilgamesh Epic.* Philadelphia: University of Pennsylvania Press, 1982.

Toomer, G. J. "Mathematics and Astronomy." In *The Legacy of Egypt*, edited by J. R. Harris, 27–45. Oxford: Clarendon, 1971.

Toorn, Karel van der, "Anat-Yahu, Some Other Deities, and the Jews of Elephantine." *Numen* 39 (1992): 80–101.

———— "Funerary Rituals and Beatific Afterlife in Ugaritic Texts and the Bible." *Bibliotheca Orientalis* 48 (1991): 40–66.

Ben-Tor, Amnon. "Hazor." In *The New Encyclopedia of Archaeological Excavations in the Holy Land.* 4 vols. Edited by Ephraim Stern, Ayelet Levinzon-Gilboa, and Joseph Aviram, 2.594–606. Jerusalem: Israel Exploration Society & Carta/New York: Simon & Schuster, 1993.

Tov, Emanuel, Stephen J. Pfann, Stephen A. Reed, and Marilyn J. Lundberg. *The Dead Sea Scrolls on Microfiche: A Comprehensive Facsimile Edition of the Texts from the Judean Desert.* Leiden: E. J. Brill, 1993.

Traub, Helmut. "Septuagint and Judaism." *Theological Dictionary of the New Testament*, ed. Gerhard Kittel et al., 5.509–11. Grand Rapids, Mich.: W. B. Eerdmans, 1964–76.

Trigger, B. G., B. J. Kemp, D. O'Connor, and A. B. Lloyd. *Ancient Egypt: A Social History.* Cambridge: Cambridge University Press, 1983.

Tsevat, M. "God and the Gods in Assembly." *HUCA* 40 (1969): 123–37.

Turdeanu, Emile. "L'Apocalypse d'Abraham en slav." *JSJ* 3 (1972): 153–80.

Uehlinger, Christoph. "Audienz in der Götterwelt: Anthropomorphismus und Soziomorphismus in der Ikonographie eines altsyrischen Zylindersiegels." *UF* 24 (1992): 339–59.

Ulansey, David. *Origins of Mythraic Mysteries: Cosmology and Salvation in the Ancient World.* New York/Oxford: Oxford University Press, 1989.

Ullendorf, Edward. *Ethiopia and the Bible.* The Schweich Lectures, 1967. London: Oxford for the British Academy, 1968.

Ussishkin, David. "King Solomon's Palaces." *BA* 36:3 (1973): 78–105.

Vaillant, A. *Le livre des secrets d'Hénoch: texte slave et traduction française.* Paris: Institut d'etudes slaves, 1952.

VanderKam, James C. "Calendrical Texts and the Origins of the Dead Sea Scroll Community." In *Methods of Investigation of the Dead Sea Scrolls and the Khirbet Qumran Site,* edited by Michael O. Wise et al., 371–88. Annals of the New York Academy of Sciences 722. New York: New York Academy of Sciences, 1994.

———— *The Dead Sea Scrolls Today.* Grand Rapids, Mich.: Eerdmans, 1994.

———— *Enoch: A Man for All Generations.* Studies on Personalities of the Old Testament. Columbia, S.C.: University of South Carolina Press, 1995.

———— *Enoch and the Growth of an Apocalyptic Tradition.* CBQMS 16. Washington: The Catholic Biblical Association of America, 1984.

———— "The Scrolls, the Apocrypha, and the Pseudepigrapha." *Hebrew Studies* 34 (1993): 35–47.

Vaux, Roland de. "Les chérubins et l'arche d'alliance, les sphinx gardiens et les trônes divins dans l'ancien Orient." In *Bible et Orient,* 231–59. Paris: Éditions du Cerf, 1967.

Velde, H. te. "Some Remarks on the Mysterious Language of the Baboons." In *Funerary Symbols and Religion: Essays Dedicated to Professor M. S. H. G. Heerma van Voss,* edited by J. H. Kamstra, H. Milde, and K. Wagtendonk, 129–37. Kampen, The Netherlands: J. H. Kok, 1988.

———— "The Theme of Separation of Heaven and Earth in Egyptian Mythology." *Studia Aegyptica* 3 (1977): 161–70.

Vermes, Geza. *The Dead Sea Scrolls in English.* Revised and extended fourth edition. New York, N.Y.: Penguin Books, 1995.

Vermes, Geza and Martin D. Goodman, eds. *The Essenes According to the Classical Sources.* Oxford Centre Textbooks 1. Sheffield: Sheffield Academic Press, 1989.

Vincent, Albert. *La religion des judéo-araméens d'Éléphantine.* Paris: Librairie Orientaliste Paul Geuthner, 1937.

Volz, Paul. *Die Biblischen Altertümer.* Calw and Stuttgart: Verlag der Vereinsbuchhandlung, 1914.

Vuippens, P. Ildefonse de. *La paradis terrestre au troisième ciel: Exposé historique d'une conception chrétienne des premiers siècles.* Fribourg: Librairie de l'oeuvre de S.-Paul, 1925.

Waerden, Bartel L. van der. "Babylonian Astronomy, II: The Thirty-Six Stars." *JNES* 8 (1949): 6–26.

———— "Babylonian Astronomy, III: The Earliest Astronomical Computations." *JNES* 10 (1951): 20–34.

———— "History of the Zodiac." *AfO* 16 (1952–53): 216–30.

———— *Science Awakening II: The Birth of Astronomy.* Leiden: Noordhoff International Publishing/New York: Oxford University Press, 1974.

Wahl, Otto, ed. *Apocalypsis Esdrae, Apocalypsis Sedrach, Visio Beati Esdrae.* PVTG 4. Leiden: E. J. Brill, 1977.

Weicker, Georg. *Der Seelenvogel in der alten Literatur und Kunst: Eine mythologische-archaelogische Untersuchung.* Leipzig: Teuber, 1902.

Weidner, Ernst F. "Die astrologische Serie Enûma Anu Enlil." *AfO* 14 (1941–44): 172–95, 308–18; 17 (1954–56): 71–89; 22 (1968–69): 65–75.

———— "Ein babylonisches Kompendium der Himmelskunde." *American Journal of Semitic Languages and Literatures* 40 (1924): 186–208.

———— *Handbuch der babylonischen Astronomie.* Assyriologische Bibliothek 23. Leipzig: J. C. Hinrichssche, 1915.

Weinfeld, Moshe. *Deuteronomy and the Deuteronomic School.* Oxford: Clarendon Press, 1972.

Weiss, Hans-Friedrich. *Untersuchungen zur Kosmologie des Hellenistischen und Palastinischen Judentums.* Texte und Untersuchungen zur Geschichte der Altchristlichen Literatur 97. Berlin: Akademie Verlag, 1966.

Wertheimer, Abraham Joseph. *Batei Midrashot.* 2 vols. Jerusalem: haRav Kook, 1950–53. Reprint, Jerusalem: Katav-yad ve-Sepher, 1989 [Hebrew].

Westendorf, Wolfhart. *Altägyptische Darstellungen des Sonnenlaufes auf der abschüssigen Himmelsbahn.* Münchner Ägyptologische Studien 10. Berlin: Bruno Hessling, 1966.

Whitney, Charles A. "The Skies of Vincent van Gogh." *Art History* 9 (1986): 351–62.

Wilkinson, Richard H. "The Horus Names and the Form and Significance of the Serekh in the Royal Egyptians Inscriptions." *Journal of the Society for the Study of Egyptian Antiquities* XV:3 (1987): 98–104.

——— *Symbol and Magic in Egyptian Art.* New York: Thames and Hudson, 1994.

Willett, Elizabeth Ann Remington, "Women and Household Shrines in Ancient Israel." Ph.D. diss., University of Arizona, 1999.

Williams, Michael A. *Rethinking "Gnosticism": An Argument for Dismantling a Dubious Category.* Princeton: Princeton University Press, 1996.

Wilson, John A. "Egypt." In *The Intellectual Adventure of Ancient Man: An Essay on Speculative Thought in the Ancient Near East,* edited by Henri Frankfort, H. A. Frankfort, John A. Wilson, Thorkild Jacobsen, and William A. Irwin, 31–121. Chicago: University of Chicago Press, 1946.

Winter, Urs. *Frau und Göttin: Exegetische und ikonographische Studien zum weiblichen Gottesbild im alten Testament und dessen Umwelt.* OBO 53. Göttingen: Vandenhoeck & Ruprecht/Freiburg: Universitätsverlag Freiburg, 1983.

Wise, Michael, Martin Abegg Jr., and Edward Cook. *The Dead Sea Scrolls: A New Translation.* New York: HarperCollins, 1996.

Wright, J. Edward. "Baruch: His Evolution from Scribe to Apocalyptic Seer." In *Biblical Figures Outside the Bible,* edited by Michael E. Stone and Theodore Bergren, 264–89. Philadelphia: Trinity Press International, 1998.

——— *From Scribe to Seer: Baruch ben Neriah in History and Tradition.* Studies on Personalities of the Old Testament. Columbia, S.C.: Univeristy of South Carolina Press, forthcoming.

——— "The Social Setting of the Syriac Apocalypse of Baruch." *JSP,* 16 (1997): 83–98.

Wyatt, Nicolas. "The Stela of the Seated God from Ugarit." *UF* 15 (1983) 271–77.

Xella, Paolo. "Death and the Afterlife in Canaanite and Hebrew Thought." In *Civilizations of the Ancient Near East.* 4 vols. Edited by Jack M. Sasson, 3.2059–70. New York: Charles Scribner's Sons, 1995.

Yadin, Yigael. *Hazor I.* Jerusalem: Magnes Press/Hebrew University, 1958.

Yamauchi, Edwin M. *Persia and the Bible.* Grand Rapids, Mich.: Baker Book House, 1990.

Zadok, Ran. *The Jews in Babylonia During the Chaldean and Achaemenian Periods According to the Babylonian Sources.* Haifa, Israel: University of Haifa, 1979.

Zaleski, Carol. *The Life of the World to Come: Near-Death Experience and Christian Hope.* New York/Oxford: Oxford University Press, 1996.

——— *Otherworldly Journeys: Accounts of Near-Death Experiences in Medieval and Modern Times.* New York/Oxford: Oxford University Press, 1987.

Zandee, J. *Death as an Enemy.* Studies in the History of Religions. Leiden: E. J. Brill, 1960.

Zettler, Richard. *The Ur III Temple of Inanna at Nippur: The Operation and Organization of Urban Religious Institutions in Mesopotamia in the Late Third Millen-

nium BC. Berliner Beiträge zum Vorderen Orient 11. Berlin: Dietrich Reimer Verlag, 1992.

Zevit, Ziony. "The Khirbet el-Qôm Inscription Mentioning a Goddess." *BASOR* 255 (1984): 39–47.

———— "Proclamations to the Fruitful Tree and the Spiritualization of Androgyny." In *Echoes of Many Texts: Reflections on Jewish and Christian Traditions—Essays in Honor of Lou H. Silberman*, edited by William G. Dever and J. Edward Wright, 43–50. BJS 313. Atlanta: Scholars Press, 1997.

———— "Three Ways to Look at the Ten Plagues." *BibRev* 6:3 (June 1990): 16–23, 42.

INDEX

INDEX TO BIBLICAL AND
ANCIENT SOURCES